Saichō

Saichō

The Establishment of the Japanese Tendai School

with a new preface

Paul Groner

University of Hawai'i Press

HONOLULU

Library of Congress Cataloging-in-Publication Data

Groner, Paul.
  Saichō : the establishment of the Japanese Tendai
School / Paul Groner
    p. cm.
  Originally published: Berkeley : Center for South
and Southeast Asian Studies, University of California,
Institute of Buddhist Studies, 1984, in series: Berkeley
Buddhist studies series ; 7. With new pref.
  Includes bibliographical references and index.
  ISBN 0–8248–2371–0 (pbk. : alk. paper)
    1. Saichō, 767–822. 2. Tendai (Sect)—History.
3. Priests, Tendai—Japan—Biography. I. Title.

BQ9149.S357 G76 2000
294.3′92—dc21
                                        00–059937

Cover designed by Santos Barbasa

Printed by Edwards Brothers Inc.

TABLE OF CONTENTS

LIST OF CHARTS

ABBREVIATIONS

BD	*Mochizuki Bukkyō daijiten*
BKD	*Bussho kaisetsu daijiten*
BZ	*Dainihon Bukkyō zensho*
DDK	*Dengyō Daishi kenkyū*
DZ	*Dengyō Daishi zenshū*
GR	*Gunsho ruijū*
IBK	*Indogaku Bukkyōgaku kenkyū*
JAS	*Journal of Asian Studies*
JZ	*Jōdoshū zensho*
KT	*Shintei zōhō Kokushi taikei*
T	*Taishō shinshū daizōkyō*
TG	*Tendai gakuhō*
TZ	*Chūge gōhen Tendai Daishi zenshū*
Z	*Dainihon zokuzōkyō*
ZGR	*Zoku gunsho ruijū*

PREFACE TO THE PAPERBACK EDITION

Sixteen years have passed since my book *Saichō: The Establishment of the Japanese Tendai School* was published. The research was based on my doctoral dissertation, "Saichō and the Bodhisattva Precepts," presented to Yale in 1979. As the title indicates, the book focuses on the changes that Saichō proposed for the ordination system used by the Tendai School and the institutional changes that followed his proposals. Since *Saichō* was published, significant new research on Saichō has appeared. The twelve-hundredth anniversary of the founding of Enryakuji on Mount Hiei occurred in 1987 and was marked by the publication of a detailed index of Saichō's works.[1] In 1988, Tamura Kōyū published a biographical study of Saichō; it was followed by several biographical studies by Saeki Arikiyo.[2] Tamura was also the author of several detailed studies of Saichō's doctrinal position that focused on his debates with Tokuitsu.[3] Takagi Shingen published important new studies of Saichō's relationship with Kūkai.[4] The development of the Tendai School after Saichō was investigated by Sueki Fumihiko and Ōkubo Ryōshun.[5] These studies have provided me with important insights into how Saichō's thought was interpreted by his successors. In addition, numerous journal articles and several other books have appeared in recent years.

Since 1984, my research has focused on later developments in Tendai history and doctrine. At some point, I would like to rewrite my study of Saichō and bring it up to date by taking these recent studies into account. However, I have chosen to republish this book without changes because rewriting it would have taken me away from other projects. Most of the changes would have been expanding topics such as Saichō's doctrinal innovations; however, the focus of the book on Saichō's use of the ordi-

---

[1] Tendai shūten hensanjo, *Dengyō Daishi zenshū sakuin* (Tokyo: Sekai seiten kankō kyōkai, 1988).

[2] Tamura Kōyū, *Saichō* Jinbutsu sōsho (Tokyo: Yoshikawa kōbunkan, 1988); Saeki Arikiyo, *Dengyō Daishi no kenkyū* (Tokyo: Yoshikawa kōbunkan, 1992); Saeki Arikiyo, *Saichō to sono monryū* (Tokyo: Yoshikawa kōbunkan, 1993); and Saeki Arikiyo, *Wakaki hi no Saichō to sono jidai* (Tokyo: Yoshikawa kōbunkan, 1994).

[3] Tamura Kōyū, *Saichō kyōgaku no kenkyū* (Tokyo: Shunjūsha, 1992); Tamura Kōyū (ed.), *Tokuitsu ronsō* (Tokyo: Kokusho kankōkai, 1986).

[4] Takagi Shingen, *Kūkai: Shōgai to sono shūhen* (Tokyo: Yoshikawa kōbunkan, 1997); and Takagi Shingen, *Kūkai to Saichō no tegami* (Kyoto: Hōzōkan, 1999). Also see Saeki Arikiyo, *Saichō to Kūkai* (Tokyo: Yoshikawa kōbunkan, 1998).

[5] Sueki Fumihiko, *Heian shoki Bukkyō shisō no kenkyū* (Tokyo: Shunjūsha, 1995); and Ōkubo Ryōshun, *Tendai kyōgaku to hongaku shisō* (Kyoto: Hōzōkan, 1998).

nation system in establishing the autonomy of the Tendai School requires little change. When the University of Hawai'i Press asked me if I would contribute a new preface, I was excited by the chance to reflect on Saichō's significance in Tendai history and include some of the changes in scholarship on Saichō and Tendai that have appeared in recent years. In the following pages, three topics are considered: Saichō and Esoteric Buddhism, Saichō's doctrinal innovations, and Saichō's role in the history of the Tendai School. The following comments reflect my views on Saichō as my own perspective has broadened to include a variety of other topics. Because the comments are intended as supplements to the book, not as corrections or replacements, I have inserted references to the relevant pages of this book.

Saichō and Esoteric Buddhism

Saichō's receipt of Esoteric Buddhist initiations in China has often been portrayed as a chance event that occurred while he was waiting for the ship that would carry him back to Japan. Evidence that Saichō was already interested in Esoteric Buddhism before leaving for China is mentioned here (pp. 51–52). However, additional evidence has appeared in recent years. I-hsing (673–727), the co-author along with Śubhakarasiṃha (637–735) of the *Ta-jih ching i-shih,* the commentary on the *Mahāvairocana-sūtra* that was one of the most influential texts in East Asian Esoteric Buddhism, had been influenced by a syncretistic tradition of T'ien-t'ai located at Yü-ch'üan ssu that had combined T'ien-t'ai with Esoteric Buddhism, Ch'an, and vinaya. Early influences on Saichō, such as his teacher Gyōhyō (724–797), may have been affected by this tradition through his teacher Tao-hsüan (702–760). Moreover, Chien-chen (688–763) and his students had belonged to this tradition. In particular, Chien-chen's disciple Dōchū had been a major supporter of Saichō and had sent him a number of students including Enchō (771–836). Enchō probably received Esoteric initiations while he was still studying under Dōchū.[6] Saichō had made a copy of I-hsing's commentary that had been brought to Japan by Te-ching, a monk who may have been one of Chien-chen's Chinese students.[7] Thus, Saichō might well have read this seminal Esoteric text before going to China. After he had returned from China and set up his educational system, Saichō specified texts for the Esoteric

    [6] Tamura Kōyū, "Saichō kenkyū no shomondai," *Bukkyōgaku* 36 (1994): 61–63.
    [7] Ono Katsutoshi, *Nittō guhō gyōreki no kenkyū: Chishō Daishi hen* (Kyoto: Hōzōkan, 1986) 2: 469; Ishida, *Ganjin: Sono kairitsu shisō* (Tokyo: Daizō shuppansha, 1974), p. 49.

course that he had not carried back from China. These texts had probably been brought to Japan by Genbō (d. 746) and may well have been read by Saichō before traveling to China.[8] Such evidence does not suggest that Saichō was aware of an Esoteric Buddhist tradition that was distinct from exoteric Buddhism; as Ryūichi Abé has argued, that sectarian self-awareness developed at a later date.[9]

The Esoteric transmissions that Saichō received in China have also been subjected to renewed scrutiny. Saichō described the transmission from Shun-hsiao as having Diamond-realm contents but a Womb-realm lineage (pp. 52–61). As a result, modern scholars have disagreed about how this transmission should be interpreted. In fact, Tendai monks during the century after Saichō's death were not sure about the contents of the transmission. Recent scholarship by Jinhua Chen suggests a chronology for many of the sources concerning Saichō's transmission from Shun-hsiao.[10] Chen suggests that the account found in the *Esshūroku,* the bibliography of the texts that Saichō brought back from Yüeh-chou, is trustworthy, but that a transmission document included in the *Kenkairon engi,* an official document cited in the *Denjutsu isshinkaimon,* and Saichō's descriptions of the lineages of the teachings he had received in the *Kechimyakufu* were composed later, possibly by Saichō's disciples in an effort to bolster Tendai claims to an Esoteric tradition equal to or surpassing that of the Shingon School. However, the canonical basis of Saichō's Esoteric transmission continued to elude Tendai monks. Both Enchin (814–891) and Henjō (816–890) commented on this difficulty. Annen (841?–915?) eventually claimed to have found the canonical source for the transmission (*T* 907). Chen argues that Annen may well have compiled one of these texts (*T* 907) while claiming that it was actually a translation by Śubhakarasiṃha. Chen then claims that two other texts (*T* 905–906) were subsequently written by Japanese during the following century and also said to be translations by Śubhakarasiṃha. Later Tendai monks argued that these three texts were the basis of Saichō's transmission from Shun-hsiao. Much of Chen's overall argument is convincing, although at times his claims that certain documents have been forged are not com-

---

[8] Tamura, "Saichō kenkyū no shomondai," pp. 63–71.

[9] Ryūichi Abé, *The Weaving of Mantra: Kūkai and the Construction of Esoteric Buddhist Discourse* (New York: Columbia University Press, 1999), pp. 151–184.

[10] Jinhua Chen, "The Construction of Early Tendai Buddhism: The Japanese Provenance of Saichō's Transmission Documents and Three Esoteric Buddhist Apocrypha Attributed to Śubhakarasiṃha," *Journal of the International Association of Buddhist Studies* 21.1 (1998): 21–76. Chen's article is based on his 1997 doctoral dissertation from McMaster University, "The Formation of Tendai Esoteric Buddhism in Japan: A Study of Three Japanese Esoteric Apocrypha."

pletely persuasive. Even though the leading Japanese scholars who work in Tendai Esoteric Buddhism have not been completely convinced by his arguments, they have also not replied to them in any detail. At the very least, Chen has suggested a new narrative for the development of certain aspects of Tendai Esoteric Buddhism that should stimulate further research.

Saichō's relationship with Kūkai is one of the more dramatic events in early Heian religious history (pp. 77–87). The primary source for Saichō's relations with Kūkai is a series of letters that Saichō and Kūkai exchanged. The vast majority of the letters that have survived were sent by Saichō to Kūkai. Saichō's letters later were edited into a collection by the Shingon monk Ningai (951–1046), probably the most important scholar of his day in the Shingon School. At that time, Shingon scholarship had been eclipsed by the vitality of the Tendai Esoteric tradition and the various transmissions brought back from China by Ennin (794–864) and Enchin. In addition, Ningai compiled Saichō's letters into a collection at a time when the Tendai monks from Onjōji were trying to obtain the court's permission to set up an ordination platform separate from that on Mount Hiei; the Shingon and other schools had been asked for their opinions on Onjōji's ordination platform. Thus Ningai edited Saichō's letters to Kūkai and Taihan into a collection against the background of considerable sectarian rivalry.[11] The result gives the impression that Saichō was constantly borrowing the texts that Kūkai had brought back from China. Although the contents of Ningai's compilation have not been seriously questioned, their possible bias must be taken into account. Only four or five letters from Kūkai to Saichō have survived. As a result, the difference in numbers and the editing of the collection written by Saichō by a partisan Shingon scholar suggest that Saichō was constantly pressing Kūkai for more texts while attempting to incorporate Kūkai's teachings into Tendai. Although this view may very well be accurate, the relationship may not have been as one-sided as has usually been thought.

New insights are gained when events in Kūkai's biography are considered. For example, after his return from China, Kūkai sent out letters urging a number of monks to help him propagate Esoteric Buddhism by copying thirty-five fascicles of texts. In a "Letter of Propagation" *(Kan'en no sho)* dated 815, he lamented the lack of progress in his efforts.[12] Saichō

---

[11] Takagi Shingen, *Kūkai to Saichō no tegami* (Kyoto: Hōzōkan, 1999), pp. 11–14, 128.

[12] Katsumata Shunkyō, ed., *Kōbō Daishi chosaku zenshū* (Tokyo: Sankibō Busshorin, 1970) 3: 386–392. Takagi, *Kūkai to Saichō no tegami*, p. 244. For excerpts of the letter, see Abé, *The Weaving of Mantra*, pp. 190–191.

had played a vital role in supporting Kūkai during this period by helping Kūkai establish himself at the Wake clan temple Takaosanji. Thus, Saichō helped Kūkai build an institutional basis for the propagation of Esoteric Buddhism. In 812, Kūkai seems to have feared that he did not have long to live. When Saichō went to visit him at Otokunji (also known as Otokunidera), Kūkai said that he felt he would not live much longer and that he hoped to spend his remaining time at Takaosanji and would give Saichō the texts that he had brought back from China. Saichō describes the situation in letters to his student Taihan (b. 778) and to Fujiwara no Fuyutsugu (775–826). In one letter, Saichō urges Taihan to come and receive the Esoteric initiations that Kūkai would confer at Takaosanji. At the end of his letter, Saichō asks Taihan to bring food with him if he comes.[13] The plea is repeated in several other letters, revealing the poverty of Saichō and his disciples at this time. Thus, Kūkai's vain efforts around this time to propagate the teachings he had brought back from China by having some of them copied and his fear that he might not live long serve as the background for Saichō's letters asking to borrow and copy the texts.

What eventually led to the break between the two men? Several factors besides those discussed in Chapter 6 must be noted. Saichō's approach to the propagation of Buddhism had been the careful copying of texts. This pattern began shortly after he climbed Mount Hiei as he strove to assemble a canon and continued during his short stay in China as he traveled and collected a large number of texts in a short period. Finally, after returning to Japan he borrowed and copied many of the texts that Kūkai had brought to Japan. This approach eventually led to tensions with Kūkai, who stressed the importance of the personal transmission of Esoteric rituals and teachings. In addition, Saichō seems to have felt that he might receive Kūkai's teachings with little time spent training under Kūkai. After all, Saichō had received Esoteric initiations in China with little preparation. When Saichō read Kūkai's report of his stay in China (*Goshōrai mokuroku*), he learned that Hui-kuo had readily initiated Kūkai into Esoteric teachings and probably felt that Kūkai would quickly confer the techniques of Esoteric ritual. When Kūkai informed Saichō that he would have to study under Kūkai for three years, it proved to be an insur-

---

[13] Takagi, *Kūkai to Saichō no tegami*, pp. 179–181, 257–259; Takagi, *Kūkai*, pp. 146–147. Takagi compares Kūkai's statement with the following passage in the *Lotus Sūtra:* "Who can broadly preach the Scripture of the Fine Dharma in this Sahā Land? Now is the very time! Not long hence, the Buddha shall enter *nirvāṇa*. The Buddha hopes for someone to whom this Scripture of the Blossom of the Fine Dharma may be assigned" (Hurvitz, *Lotus Blossom,* p. 11; *T* 9: 33c).

mountable obstacle.[14] If Kūkai had readily initiated Saichō and his disciples into Esoteric Buddhism with little preparation, Kūkai would have been disregarding the considerable time that his own students had devoted to study and practice.

Finally, Saichō and Kūkai had irreconcilable positions towards other Buddhist traditions. Saichō believed that Tendai and Esoteric teachings had the same purport and that their Perfect teachings were so far superior to Nara Buddhism that they rendered most of the Nara traditions obsolete. Kūkai argued that Esoteric Buddhism was superior to Tendai and other forms of exoteric Buddhism (p. 287); however, Kūkai pursued a policy of reconciliation and cooperation with the Buddhists of Nara that was markedly different from that of Saichō. As these differences became more evident, cooperation between the two men became impossible.

Saichō's doctrinal innovations

More than half of Saichō's works were written during the course of his debates with the Hossō monk Tokuitsu. The defense of Tendai and the *Lotus Sūtra* against Hossō interpretations remained important issues for Tendai monks for a century but gradually faded after the time of Genshin (942–1017). A key reason for their decline was that the Tendai School had surpassed Hossō in institutional importance by the end of the tenth century.[15] The polemical quality and hasty composition of Saichō's works meant that they were not systematic. Saichō seemed to be searching for a set of terms that would express his views. As a result, the origins of his terminology are sometimes obscure, and the meaning of even important terms might change from text to text. In addition, Saichō depended on much more than T'ien-t'ai teachings when he wrote. His early training had included both Hua-yen and Consciousness-only teachings; in fact, he used Consciousness-only teachings in many of his arguments. Saichō respected Hsüan-tsang and believed that Consciousness-only teachings had been perverted by Hsüan-tsang's disciple and the de facto founder of the Hossō School, Tz'u-en (632–682).[16] These factors all contribute to the complexity of analyzing Saichō's thought. Moreover, the meanings of his terminology sometimes changed as he deepened his familiarity with T'ien-t'ai and Esoteric Buddhist doctrine.

For example, the terms "direct path" *(jikidō)* and "great direct path" *(daijikidō)* are sometimes used interchangeably; at other times, they are

---

[14] Takagi, *Kūkai to Saichō no tegami,* pp. 266–267.

[15] This issue is discussed in my forthcoming monograph *Ryōgen: The Transformation of the Tendai School* (Honolulu: University of Hawai'i Press).

[16] Tamura Kōyū, "Saichō kenkyū no shomondai," pp. 72–73.

differentiated with "direct path" referring to the Perfect Teaching *(engyō)* before the *Lotus Sūtra* was revealed and "great direct path" referring to the Perfect Teaching after the revelation of the *Lotus Sūtra*. However, the origins and nuances of terms such as this can be even more difficult (pp. 183–190). For example, the terms "great path" and "realization of Buddhahood with this very body" are found in I-hsing's commentary on the *Mahāvairocana-sūtra,* a text that must have influenced his Esoteric Buddhist thought but that he referred to only infrequently.[17]

Certain passages and terms in Saichō's writings came to play roles in Tendai discourse that far surpassed their original significance. The concept of *sokushin jōbutsu* (realization of Buddhahood with this very body) serves as an example of the way in which a term took on a life of its own. Saichō wrote a short passage about the term near the end of his life as part of a series of arguments about how the *Lotus Sūtra* was superior to other scriptures. However, the term was also used within the Shingon School.[18] As a result, the interpretation of the term was an important issue for Tendai monks. Saichō's use of the term had been sufficiently vague that his followers had written to Chinese T'ien-t'ai monks about the term. The term was virtually unknown in Chinese T'ien-t'ai; as a result, Chinese T'ien-t'ai monks frequently did not reply with answers that would help the Japanese compete with the Shingon School. The meaning of the term was developed further in a series of debate manuals in the tenth century. Eventually, the term came to be used in ways that went far beyond Saichō's original intention. At the same time, Saichō's original interpretation of the term through the story of the Nāga girl in the *Lotus Sūtra* continued to provide an important basis for Tendai discussions of the "realization of Buddhahood with this very body." Research into Saichō's doctrinal stance must take into account both the earlier history of terms and concepts as well as their subsequent development within Japanese Buddhism.[19]

[17] Tendai shūten hensanjo, ed., *Zoku Tendaishū zensho* (Tokyo: Shunjūsha, 1993), Mikkyō 1:81b and 508b. I am indebted to Prof. Ōkubo Ryōshun of Waseda University for calling my attention to these references.

[18] The most important source for the term *sokushin jōbutsu* in the Shingon School is the *Sokushin jōbutsugi,* attributed to Kūkai. However, Ōkubo Ryōshun has pointed out a number of problems in the attribution of the text without coming to a definitive conclusion ("Nihon Bukkyō no kyōgaku kenkyū to bunken," *Nihon no Bukkyō* 5 [1996]: 5–10).

[19] Paul Groner, "The *Lotus Sūtra* and Saichō's Interpretation of the Realization of Buddhahood with This Very Body *(sokushin jōbutsu),*" in *The Lotus Sūtra in Japanese Culture,* eds. George and Willa Tanabe (Honolulu: University of Hawai'i Press, 1989), pp. 53–74; Paul Groner, "Shortening the Path: Early Tendai Interpretations of the realization of Buddhahood with this Very Body *(Sokushin Jōbutsu),* (Honolulu: University of Hawai'i Press, 1992), pp. 439–473; Paul Groner, "Tendai Interpretations of the Realization of Buddhahood with This Very Body After the Death of Saichō: A Survey of Selected Sources," in *T'ien-t'ai Thought and Asian Culture: Festschrift for Young-ja Lee's Sixtieth Birthday* (Seoul, 1997) pp. 131–155.

As is indicated by the discussion of terms such as "direct path" and "realization of Buddhahood with this very body," Saichō was particularly interested in defining the goal of Buddhism. However, the classification of doctrines and the scope of those who could realize enlightenment also concerned him (pp. 96–106).

Saichō's role in Tendai history

As the founder of the Tendai School, Saichō receives more attention than any other figure in Tendai history. One need only look at the bibliographies of scholarly journal articles published by Ryūkoku University to see that the quantity of scholarship on Saichō dwarfs that on any other Tendai figure.[20] Young Tendai monks in training at Taishō University or the Eizan Gakuin seminary frequently write papers on Saichō. However, Saichō's major works were rarely the object of commentaries, and the extent to which they were actually studied during the centuries after Saicho's death is often not clear. Two factors contributed to these tendencies. First, because Saichō's works were mostly polemical, written during a few years shortly before his death to respond to particular challenges or problems, they were not systematic texts that a monk might use to master Tendai doctrine. Once an issue such as the ordination system or the doctrinal debates with Hossō had been resolved, little need remained for the systematic study of his writings. As a result, few commentaries on Saichō's writings were written; when they were composed, they were written with a specific objective in mind, such as the revivals of certain of Saicho's views on monastic discipline that occurred during the efforts to tighten monastic discipline at Kurodani on Mount Hiei during the Kamakura period and later during the Tokugawa period among a group of monks at the Anrakuin on Mount Hiei.

As a result, Saichō's works are cited in a sporadic, rather than a systematic, fashion in later Tendai writing. For example, his view of a doctrinal issue might be mentioned along with those of other Chinese and Japanese Tendai thinkers but not necessarily given special attention. Much of the respect for Saichō arose from his status as founder of the school. However, even for this, Saichō was less honored as an institutional figure than was Ryōgen (912–985), the Tendai monk who restored the school's fortunes 150 years later. Second, Saichō died at the comparatively young age of fifty-four or fifty-five before he could develop the institutional and

---

[20] Ryūkoku daigaku Bukkyōgaku kenkyūshitsu, ed. *Bukkyōgaku kankei zasshi ronbun bunrui mokuroku* Vol. 4. (Kyoto: Nagata bunshōdō, 1986).

doctrinal frameworks that might have allowed his disciples to put his views into effect in a systematic manner. In fact, Saichō was still working out the terminology appropriate for his ideas at the time of his death. As a result, his successors were left to interpret his views on the basis of new transmissions from China and their own studies.

Nevertheless, Saichō played a crucial role in setting many of the later institutional and doctrinal parameters of the Tendai School. Tendai monks continued to be ordained with *Fan-wang* (Brahmā's Net) precepts. The headquarters of the school remained on Mount Hiei, the site to which Saichō had retreated early in his life. In keeping with the award of two yearly ordinands, one to study Esoteric Buddhism and one to study Tendai meditation, the role of Esoteric Buddhism played a major role in subsequent Tendai development.

However, later Tendai interpretations of many issues were decidedly different than those proposed by Saichō. For example, Saichō had clearly favored a strict interpretation of monastic discipline. However, later figures, particularly Annen, interpreted the precepts in such a manner that strict adherence to any precepts seemed to be optional.[21] This was due in part to a very selective reading of Saichō's works. For example, a provision that monks remain on Mount Hiei for twelve years following their ordination was largely ignored. Saichō had suggested that the "Hīnayāna precepts" be received by monks as an expedient after they had completed their twelve years of training, but this had been largely ignored by later monks (pp. 195–205). If this provision had been followed, practice within the Tendai School and Tendai's relationship with the Nara schools would have changed in important ways.

In terms of doctrine, Saichō's focus on Tendai teachings and practices advanced by Chih-i (538–597) and Chan-jan (711–782) has continued to influence Japanese Tendai thought to the present day. Pointing out the importance of the thought of these two men may seem obvious, but Japanese Tendai received many influences; its constant return to the teachings of Chih-i and Chan-jan is one of its hallmarks. One need only look at the contents of modern journals on Tendai such as *Tendai gakuhō* to see articles on their thought. The first two volumes of a set of texts for Tendai monks in modern Japanese translation begin with works by Chih-i, and the first CD-ROM for the study of Tendai doctrine was composed of the major texts of Chih-i and Chan-jan.[22] The traditional Tendai education system

---

[21] Paul Groner, "The *Fan-wang ching* and Monastic Discipline in Japanese Tendai: A Study of Annen's *Futsū jubosatsukai kōshaku*," in *Chinese Buddhist Apocrypha,* ed. Robert Buswell (Honolulu: University of Hawai'i Press, 1990), 251–290.

[22] Muranaka Yūshō (ed.), *Tendai shūkyō seiten* (Tokyo: Sankibō Busshorin, 1997–current); *Tendai denshi Butten CD 1* (Sakamoto: Tendai shūten hensanjo, 1997).

frequently focused on the interpretation of problematic issues from Chih-i's works.[23] At the same time, medieval Tendai monks often interpreted these teachings in dramatically new ways. T'ien-t'ai teachings were taken out of the context of Chih-i's works and used in innovative manners.[24]

Saichō's commitment to the identity of the purport of Tendai and Esoteric Buddhism continued to influence the school's position, even while Tendai monks remained uncertain about the contents of Saichō's Esoteric Buddhism. In fact, more of the content of the Tendai Esoteric Buddhist tradition can be traced back to Ennin and Enchin than to Saichō.

The unfinished and unsystematic quality of Saichō's teachings would work to Tendai's historical advantage. The school developed in new and often unforeseen ways during the centuries following Saichō's death as Tendai was stimulated by competition with the Shingon and Hossō schools. In addition, new movements from within Tendai such as Pure Land and *hongaku* thought came to play increasingly important roles.

In the years since publishing *Saichō,* I have continued to work on a variety of aspects of Tendai history and thought. The friendships that this study has brought me have remained a highpoint of my academic life. Although I cannot single out all of the people who have encouraged me over the years, I would like to mention a few of them. In Japan, Yoshizu Yoshihide, Sueki Fumihihiko, Ikeda Rosan, Ōkubo Ryōshun, Misaki Ryōshū, Tamura Kōyū, Saitō Enshin, Ichishima Shōshin, Tonegawa Hiroyuki, Nomoto Kakujō, and others have offered their support in a variety of ways. I look forward to continuing our friendship in the coming years. In the west, Jackie Stone, Ruben Habito, Robert Rhodes, and Jean-Nöel Robert have helped through their interest in Japanese Tendai. The research of Daniel Stevenson and Daniel Getz on Chinese T'ien-t'ai has helped me to look at Japanese Tendai in new ways. Nishimura Keishō and Joan Piggott contributed to the list of corrections in the original text. I cannot imagine a better editor than Patricia Crosby at the University of Hawai'i Press; I thank her for her help over the years. Finally, the friendship and advice of my mentor Stanley Weinstein at Yale University has been an unfailing inspiration.

When *Saichō* was published, I dedicated it to my wife Cindy. I am delighted to have the opportunity to thank her again for her help and support in so many ways. Raising a family with her has been one of the joys of my life.

---

[23] See the chapter on the examination system in Groner, *Ryōgen.*

[24] Groner, "A Medieval Japanese Reading of the *Mo-ho chih-kuan:* Placing the *Kankō ruijū* in Historical Context," *Japanese Journal of Religious Studies* 22.1–2 (1995): 50–81; Jacqueline Stone, *Original Enlightenment and the Transformation of Medieval Japanese Buddhism* (Honolulu: University of Hawai'i Press, 1999).

PREFACE

The subject of this study is the life and thought of the founder of the Japanese Tendai School, Saichō 最澄 (767–822), also known by the posthumous title, Dengyō Daishi 傳教大師. The book focuses on the reforms in the ordination system and monastic discipline advocated by Saichō during the last years of his life. These reforms played a crucial role in the establishment of the Tendai School and its eventual rise to eminence in the middle and late Heian period.

The book opens with an introductory chapter containing background information necessary for understanding Saichō's role in Japanese Buddhism. The study is then divided into three major parts. The first part is a detailed biography of Saichō, consisting of seven chapters which include annotated translations of Saichō's petitions concerning administrative reforms. The biography focuses on the development of the controversy over the *Fan wang* precepts, but also extensively examines Saichō's attempts to master Esoteric Buddhism and considers his dispute with Tokuitsu over the Buddha-nature.

The second part is an analysis of Saichō's thought concerning the Hīnayāna and Mahāyāna precepts. It consists of five chapters. Chapter Nine is a discussion of the position of the precepts in Saichō's thought. In Chapter Ten, the more specialized problem of Saichō's attitude towards the Hīnayāna precepts is considered. Chapters Eleven and Twelve are investigations of the texts and traditions which contributed to Saichō's unprecedented proposals for monastic discipline. In Chapter Thirteen, the integration of the various traditions propagated by Saichō is discussed.

Part Three is an examination of the effects of Saichō's proposals on the development of the Tendai School during the two or three decades following Saichō's death. The importance of Saichō's administrative reforms is clearly demonstrated during this period, although the potential for future problems in the interpretation of the precepts can also be discerned.

This book is a substantially revised version of my doctoral dissertation for Yale University. Among the many people who offered advice and encouragement were Stanley Weinstein of Yale University, Hirakawa Akira of Waseda University, Tamura Yoshirō of Risshō University, Sonoda Kōyū of Kansai University and Tada Kōryū, Shioiri Ryōdō,

Taira Ryōshō and Ōkubo Ryōjun, all of Taishō University. Special mention must also be made of several scholars whom I did not meet, but whose work was particularly helpful: Misaki Ryōshū, Ishida Mizumaro and Tsuchihashi Shūkō. My research was supported by grants from The Japan Foundation, Daizō Shuppansha, Rotary Yoneyama Memorial Foundation and a Yale-Sumitomo Fellowship. After the book had been accepted for the Berkeley Buddhist Series, a generous grant from the Sange gakkai helped to accelerate the publication schedule. I take this opportunity to express my heartfelt gratitude to all of these people and organizations.

I dedicate this book to my wife Cindy and thank her for her many hours of work on it.

CHAPTER ONE
BACKGROUND: BUDDHISM DURING THE LATE NARA PERIOD

The first part of the ninth century has long been considered one of the most critical periods in Japanese Buddhist history. Japanese scholars have traditionally distinguished the forms of Buddhism established in the ninth century by calling them 'Heian Bukkyō' (Buddhism of the Heian period, from 794 to 1180). The Buddhism of the preceding period is called 'Nara Bukkyō' (Buddhism of the Nara period, from 710 to 784).

Two new schools of Buddhism, Tendai and Shingon, were established in Japan during the early ninth century. These two new schools are substantially different from the schools of Nara Buddhism in several ways. Nara Buddhism had been under state control for the most part and centered in Nara, the capital. The Tendai School, in contrast, asserted a substantial degree of autonomy from court influence. Both the Tendai and Shingon schools established major monastic centers in the mountains away from the capital and were more aggressive in their attempts to spread Buddhism to the provinces than the Nara schools.[1] During the Nara period the efforts of most of the prominent monks had been devoted to mastering the academic Buddhist systems imported from China or to fostering and maintaining court patronage. While the Tendai and Shingon monks were certainly concerned with academics and patronage, they placed new emphasis on religious practice and argued that enlightenment was possible in the near future, perhaps even in this very existence. Nara Buddhism, in contrast, did not show much doctrinal innovation.

Monks with academic interests generally devoted themselves to mastering the intricacies of the Hossō and Sanron doctrinal systems. While Tendai and Shingon monks were vitally interested in the Indian and Chinese origins of their schools, they were self-confident enough to develop their own innovative ideas about Buddhist practice and doctrine.

---

[1] Some temples were located in the mountains during the Nara period, but often these were small temples used by a few monks for intensive religious practice, not major monastic centers. See Furue Ryōnin, "Nara jidai ni okeru sanji kenkyū," *Taishō daigaku kenkyū kiyō* 39 (1954): 1–47; Sonoda Kōyū, "Kodai Bukkyō ni okeru sanrin shugyō to sono igi," *Nanto Bukkyō* 4 (1957): 45–60.

Buddhist history in the early ninth century is dominated by two figures: Saichō (767–822), founder of the Japanese Tendai School, and Kūkai (774–835), founder of the Shingon School. Kūkai has been discussed in Hakeda Yoshito's book *Kūkai: Major Works*.[2] Saichō, however, has not been discussed at length in any western language. The purpose of this book is to describe and analyze Saichō's career and thought against the background of China and Japan in the late eighth and early ninth centuries.

Both Saichō and Kūkai journeyed to China to study a particular Buddhist tradition and then claimed that they were transmitting that tradition to Japan. However, the Tendai and Shingon schools cannot be viewed merely as transplanted Chinese schools. Saichō spent a short period of time in China and could not speak Chinese. Many of his teachings, particularly those concerning Esoteric Buddhism and the Hīnayāna and Mahāyāna precepts, were influenced more by circumstances in Japan than by Chinese teachers. In addition, both Tendai and Esoteric texts had been imported to Japan during the Nara period. Saichō was not the first Japanese monk to encounter Tendai texts. Saichō was able to successfully establish the Tendai School in Japan because of certain historical circumstances. In order to provide some of the background necessary to evaluate Saichō's activities, certain trends in Japanese Buddhism during the last half of the eighth century must be considered. Although a thorough investigation of this period would require a monograph, it will be useful to consider several themes which are crucial to this study.

State Buddhism and the Ordination of Monks
One of the distinguishing characteristics of Buddhism during the Nara period (710–784) was the lavish expenditure of money by the state for temples, Buddhist images, and the copying of Buddhist texts. The merit from such activities was often devoted to the protection of the state and its ruler from various catastrophes. Records of Buddhist activities during the Nara period reveal that the ceremonies performed and the *sūtras* chanted were often directly related to state Buddhism. The establishment of a nationwide system of provincial temples (*kokubunji* 國分寺) with the Tōdaiji temple at Nara as its center is one of the crowning achievements of state Buddhism at this time. Buddhism was thus used to integrate the provinces and the capital.

---

[2] Yoshito Hakeda, *Kūkai: Major Works* (New York: Columbia University Press, 1972

Qualified monks were required to keep the system functioning. The monks had to be able to chant the *sūtras* which would protect the state. They also were expected to have led a chaste life so that they could accumulate the powers for the ceremonies to be effective. In order to insure that the men who joined the Buddhist order were able to perform these ceremonies, the court established requirements which candidates for initiation as novices or ordination as monks had to meet. According to an edict issued in 734, a candidate for initiation was required to be able to chant the *Lotus Sūtra* (*Fa hua ching,* Skt. *Saddharmapuṇḍarī-kasūtra*) or the *Sūtra of Golden Light* (*Chin kuang ming ching,* Skt. *Suvarṇaprabhāsasūtra*), to know how to perform ceremonies worshipping the Buddha, and to have led a chaste life for at least three years.[3] The requirements were designed to insure that the candidate would be able to effectively perform religious ceremonies. Little attention was paid to the candidate's ability to explain Buddhist doctrine. If a candidate met the requirements, he would be initiated at the court at the beginning of the year, with the merit resulting form his initiation devoted to the welfare of the state. Successful candidates were called 'yearly ordinands' (*nenbundosha* 年分度者).[4]

Because ordination freed people from their tax and corvée labor obligations and gave them the opportunity to live a life of relative ease devoted to religion, large numbers of people wished to be ordained. Although the court wished to promote Buddhism for the purposes of state ceremonies and religion, it was not willing to suffer a large loss of revenue from its treasury because of large numbers of ordinations.

---

[3] *Shoku Nihongi,* Tenpyō six, eleventh month, twenty–first day (*KT* 2:135).

[4] *Nenbundosha* 年分度者 (or *reidosha* 例度者) first appear in 696. Ten men were to be initiated into the Buddhist order and read the *Chin kuang ming ching* (T no. 665, *Suvarṇa prabhāsasūtra*) on the last day of the year. Because this was to be done every year, and because they were to pray for the well–being of the state for the coming year, they were known as *nenbundosha* or yearly ordinands. The system was closely related to the *Konkōmyō–e* 金光明經會 assembly, which was based on the *sūtra* and held annually during the first month of the year. In 738 the ordinands were also instructed to recite the *Lotus Sūtra*. Around this time the system greatly expanded with the building of temples and carving of Buddhas, until several hundred men were initiated at once. Near the end of the Nara period, the court tried to improve the quality of the Buddhist order by putting additional restrictions on who could become a *nenbundosha*. In 793 the Sino–Japanese reading of *sūtras* was required. In 798 an age limit of at least thirty–five was imposed, though this requirement was soon dropped. Also a test consisting of ten sections was introduced, of which the candidate had to pass five. In 801 a distinction between Sanron and Hossō monks was made; and two years later, each school was allotted five yearly ordinands. Finally it should be noted that not all ordinands were *nenbundosha*. See Sonoda, *Saichō,* pp. 425–26; Futaba Kenkō, "Nenbundosha no gengi to sono henka" in *Nihonshi no kenkyū: Kimura Takeo Sensei no kanreki kinen,* (Kyoto: Mineruva Shobō, 1970), pp. 83–100.

The court attempted to impose numerical limits on the numbers of monks by allowing only certain numbers of men to pass the examinations for the yearly ordinands, although on certain special occasions additional men might be ordained even if they had not passed the examinations. Many men simply ignored the court's restrictions on numbers and initiated and ordained themselves as monks (shidosō 私度僧).

The court was also wary of unrestricted activities of monks among the populace. If monks and nuns travelled and preached among the common people without restriction, they might foment unrest and rebellion. To control the numbers and activities of monks and nuns, the court instituted the "Regulations for Monks and Nuns" (Sōniryō 僧尼令) early in the eighth century.[5] Even earlier, in 624, several senior monks were appointed by Empress Suiko to oversee the other monks.[5] These appointments mark the first appearance in Japan of the Office of Monastic Affairs (Sōgō 僧綱), a government department staffed with court–appointed monks.[6] One of its major functions was the supervision of the examination, ordination and behavior of monks and nuns. Perhaps one of the most interesting efforts by the government to control the Buddhist order was its support for Japanese Buddhist plans to bring Chinese vinaya masters to Japan to supervise ordinations and monastic education.

Chien-chen 鑑眞

In the early part of the eighth century, Japanese monks such as Ryūson 隆尊 (702–760) were concerned about whether they had received orthodox ordinations. Orthodox ordinations were to be performed by ten monks (five in outlying areas) who had, in turn, been correctly ordained. Since the required number of properly ordained monks had never assembled in Japan to conduct ordinations, the ordinations of Japanese monks were invalid according to Buddhist monastic law.

In the year 733 the court dispatched two monks, Fushō 普照 and Eiei 榮叡, to China to invite Chinese Ssu fen lü[7] 四分律 masters to Japan,

---

[5] See the translation of the Sōniryō by George Sansom, "Early Japanese Law and Administration," Transactions of the Asiatic Society of Japan, second series 9 (1932): 66–109; and 11 (1934): 117–149.

[6] For a short description in English of the Sōgō and Sōniryō, see Nakamura Kyoko, Miraculous Stories from the Japanese Buddhist Tradition (Cambridge, Massachusetts: Harvard University Press, 1973) pp. 18–29.

[7] The Ssu fen lü (Dharmaguptakavinaya), Taishō shinshū daizōkyō (hereafter abbreviated T) no. 1428, was the vinaya generally followed throughout East Asia by the time of Saichō.

to perform orthodox ordinations. In sponsoring their voyage, the court hoped to raise the educational standards of Japanese monks and to impose stricter controls over the ordinations of monks and nuns. At the invitation of Eiei and Fushō, Chinese monks such as Tao–hsüan[8] 道璿 (702–760), the teacher of Saichō's preceptor Gyōhyō 行表 (722–797) and the renowned *vinaya* master Chien–chen 鑑眞 (J. Ganjin, 688–763) travelled to Japan.

When Chien–chen arrived in Nara from China in 754 after five unsuccessful attempts to travel to Japan, he brought both the T'ien–t'ai and Lü–tsung (*Vinaya* School) traditions with him to Japan.[9] Because the T'ien–t'ai School in China had been eclipsed in the early seventh century by the Fa–hsiang, Hua–yen and Ch'an schools, its works had not been brought to Japan by earlier travellers. Chien–chen was thus the first person to bring T'ien–t'ai texts to Japan even though over one–hundred fifty years had passed since Chih–i's death. Because Chien–chen's primary purpose in Japan was to teach the correct practice of the *Ssu fen lü* precepts, he entrusted the task of propagating T'ien–t'ai teachings to two of his disciples who accompanied him to Japan, Fa–chin 法進 (709–778) and Ssu–t'o 思託 (d. 805?). Fa–chin wrote a commentary on the *Fan wang ching* which relied heavily on T'ien–t'ai doctrines[10] and lectured four times on the works of Chih–i 智顗 (538–597), the *de facto* founder of the T'ien–t'ai school. Ssu–t'o called himself a Tendai monk, and lectured on the *Lotus Sūtra* in 770, relying on T'ien–t'ai works. After the deaths of these two monks, the T'ien–t'ai tradition seems to have disappeared in Japan until Saichō rediscovered the T'ien–t'ai works which Chien–chen had brought to Japan.[11]

---

[8] Tao–hsüan 道璿 should be distinguished from the famous Buddhist historian and *vinaya*–master Tao–hsüan 道宣 (596–667) who was the author of the most commonly accepted commentaries of the *Ssu fen lü* in East Asia. To avoid any confusion between the two, the latter's name is romanized as Daoxuan hereafter.

[9] *Tōdaiwajō tōseiden*, in Ishida Mizumaro, *Ganjin: sono kairitsu shisō* (Tokyo: Daizō shuppansha, 1973), p. 314.

[10] Fa–chin's commentary on the *Fan wang ching* is said to have been based on T'ien–t'ai teachings. Saichō read it before he went to China (*Ehyo Tendaigishū, DZ* 3:344; and *Denjutsu isshinkaimon, DZ* 1:565), and was probably influenced by it. The commentary does not survive, however, making it impossible to determine to what degree it influenced Saichō. Although Fa–chin's commentary is quoted almost one hundred times in Gyōnen's *Bonmōkai honsho nichijushō* (T no. 2247), none of the quotations suggest that the commentary played a role in Saichō's later proposals [Taira Ryōshō, "Enkai seiritsu kō," *Fuyō hakushi koki kinen: Mikkyō bunka ronshū*, special issue of *Chizan gakuhō* 19 (1970): 189].

[11] Tokuda Myōhon (*Risshū gairon* [Kyoto: Hyakkaen, 1969], pp. 568, 575) claims that the Tendai texts which Chien–chen brought to Japan continued to be studied until Saichō's time. In contrast, Sekiguchi Shindai (*Tendai shikan no kenkyū* [Tokyo: Iwanami shoten,

Shortly after arriving in Japan, Chien–chen built a precepts platform in front of the hall housing the great image (*Daibutsu*) of Rushana,
and granted the bodhisattva precepts (*bosatsukai*) to the retired Emperor
Shōmu, Emperor Kōken and over four hundred other people.[12] He
then granted the *Ssu fen lü* precepts to more than eighty monks who
had renounced the precepts they had taken earlier.[13] All evidence
indicates that the bodhisattva precepts conferred by Chien–chen were
the *Fan wang* 梵網 precepts.[14] Chien–chen brought commentaries on
the *Fan wang ching* by Chih–chou 智周 (678–733) and Fa–hsien 法銑
(718–778) with him to Japan.[15] Shortly after the ordination, one-
hundred copies of the *Fan wang ching* were distributed by court order.[16]

1969], pp. 285–95) argues that shortly after Chien–chen's death, Tendai works were no longer
studied. Little evidence can be found which supports Tokuda's view.

[12] In the *Tōdaiwajō tōseiden* (annotated text included in Ishida, *Ganjin*, p. 317), Ōmi
no Mifune did not clearly state what type of precepts were received by the four hundred
people ordained after the imperial family's ordination. The most natural reading would be
that they, too, received the bodhisattva precepts (Mochizuki Shinkō, ed., *Bukkyō Daijiten*
[hereafter abbreviated *BD*], Second ed., 10 vols. [Tokyo: Sekai seiten kankō kyōkai, 1958–63],
1:470a); however, Tokiwa Daijō (*Nihon Bukkyō no kenkyū* [Tokyo: Meiji shoin, 1944;
reprint ed., Tokyo: Kokusho kankōkai, 1972], p. 370) believed they received the *upasampadā*,
and were thus ordained as monks with the *Ssu fen lü*. The passage is vague on a number of
other points. For a discussion of it, see Ishida, *Ganjin*, pp. 82–84.

[13] Most of the monks had probably been previously ordained by figures such as Tao-
hsüan. However, these ceremonies were declared invalid in view of Chien–chen's orthodox
ceremony. Other Japanese monks had administered the precepts to themselves (*jisei jukai*
自誓受戒) in front of a Buddha image following instructions found in the *Chan ch'a ching*
(*T* no. 839) and the *Yü ch'ieh lun* (*T* no. 1579, *Yogācārabhūmiśāstra*). These monks asserted
that their ordinations were valid since they were based on scriptural references and received
in front of an image of the Buddha. Only after Chien–chen had argued that such ordinations
would leave the order without commonly accepted standards of conduct, did the monks
agree to renounce their old precepts and be ordained by Chien–chen (from a biography of
Fushō compiled by Chien–chen's disciple Ssu–t'o, quoted in the *Nihon kōsōden yōmonshō, BZ*
62: 52c). Self–ordinations based on the *Chan ch'a ching* were also performed in Korea during
the eighth century (Chae In–hwan, "Shiragi ni okeru *Senzatsu* sange kaihō no jissen,"
Bukkyō no jissen genri, pp. 379–99, edited by Sekiguchi Shindai [Tokyo: Sankibō Busshorin,
1977]).

[14] Many Mahāyāna *sūtras* contained lists of precepts or guidelines for conduct. These
were often called bodhisattva precepts (*bosatsukai* 菩薩戒) or Mahāyāna precepts (*daijōkai*
大乗戒). In East Asia one of the most popular sets of bodhisattva precepts was found in the
Fan wang ching 梵網經 (*T* no. 1484).

[15] *Tōdaiwajō tōseiden* in Ishida, *Ganjin*, p. 219. Part of the first fascicle of Fa–hsien's
four–fascicle commentary, the *Fan wang ching p'u sa chieh su*, is preserved in Z 1.60.3. It was
influenced by Hua–yen doctrines. The second and fourth fascicles of Chih–chou's five fascicle
commentary, the *Fan wang ching p'u sa chieh pen su* is preserved in Nakano Tatsue et al.,
eds., *Dainihon zokuzōkyō* (hereafter cited as Z), 750 books (Tokyo: Zōkyō shoin, 1905–12),
1. 60. 2. Although Chih–chou was a Fa–hsiang monk, his commentary included a number
of T'ien–t'ai doctrines such as Chih–i's classification of Buddhist teachings into four types.

[16] Ienaga Saburō, "Tōdaiji Daibutsu no Busshin wo meguru shomondai," *Jodai Bukkyō
shisōshi kenkyū*, revised ed. (Kyoto: Hōzōkan, 1966), p. 119. The *Fan wang ching* had not

Later, Chien–chen's disciple Fa–chin wrote a commentary on the *Fan wang ching.*

The second tradition which Chien–chen brought to Japan was Daoxuan's 道宣 (596–667) Nan–shan 南山 School of interpretation of the *Ssu fen lü.*[17] Chien–chen had been specifically invited to Japan by Eiei and Fushō to perform orthodox ordinations as part of the court's program to control and improve the educational system for candidates for the Buddhist order. Thus Chien–chen and his disciples were to supervise all ordinations performed in Japan as officials of the Sōgō (Office of Monastic Affairs). Officials of the Sōgō continued to administer all monastic ordinations in Japan until Saichō's time although the Sōgō gradually came to be dominated by monks of the Hossō School.

Chien–chen and other monks in Nara followed both the *Ssu fen lü* and *Fan wang* precepts. Almost every East Asian monk of the eighth century believed that the conferral of the full *Ssu fen lü* ordination qualified a person as a monk. Although the *Ssu fen lü* had been compiled as the *vinaya* of the Hīnayāna Dharmaguptaka School, Daoxuan and his followers had argued that the *Ssu fen lü* was at least partially Mahāyāna in import (*buntsū daijō* 分通大乘). Thus a monk who considered himself to be a Mahāyānist could follow the *Ssu fen lü* precepts without any qualms.

The *Fan wang* precepts were a set of Mahāyāna rules compiled in China in the fifth century. They were very popular in East Asia and often conferred on laymen in order to strengthen their Buddhist ties. Chien–chen used them in this manner when he performed *Fan wang* ordinations shortly after his arrival in Japan, In addition, the *Fan wang* precepts were also conferred on monks and nuns, not to give them the status of monk and nuns, but to reinforce the Mahāyāna quality of their attitudes and practices. Most monks saw no conflict between receiving the *Ssu fen lü* full ordination (*upasampadā*) first and the *Fan wang* ordination second.

---

been widely circulated in Japan prior to Chien–chen's arrival. It quickly gained in popularity once Chien–chen had used it in ordinations. Its quick acceptance by the nobility may have been partly due to the identification of the central figure in the *sūtra,* Rushana Butsu, with the Great Buddha (Daibutsu) which had just been built at Tōdaiji. Ienaga argued in the above article that the court's view of the Daibutsu was based on the *Hua yen ching* (*Avataṃsakasūtra*) before Chien–chen's arrival, but influenced by the *Fan wang ching* after his arrival.

[17] Chien–chen also brought works from the two other Chinese *Ssu fen lü* traditions, the Hsiang–pu 相部 School and the Tung–t'a 東塔 School, both of which he had studied in China. However, by the time he arrived in Japan, Chien–chen had already decided to focus his teachings on the Nan–shan School.

Chien–chen considered himself to be Mahāyānist and believed that the Risshū 律宗 (*Vinaya* School) was essentially a Mahāyāna School. This view was maintained by Risshū monks in Saichō's time. A contemporary of Saichō, the Risshū monk Buan 豊安 wrote in 829:

Question: Should the Risshū be classified as a Hīnayāna or Mahāyāna teaching?

Answer: This school takes all of the precepts and gathers them into one school. There are only bodhisattva *vinaya* masters in Japan. From the beginning there have been none who one–sidedly clung to Hīnayāna teachings. Moreover, the import of the *Ssu fen lü* is Mahāyāna....[18]

Dōkyō 道鏡

State involvement in Buddhism eventually resulted in the participation of monks in government and, at times, in their exercise of undue influence at court. The dangers of monastic involvement at the court were made evident by the spectacular career of the monk Dōkyō 道鏡 (d. 772).[19] Dōkyō was born into a clan of low–ranking provincial aristocracy. Little is known about his early life, except that he had a Confucian teacher and studied under the Hossō monk Gien 義淵. Dōkyō also studied Sanskrit, a skill rarely found in Japanese monks at this time, which may indicate that Dōkyō was much more learned than most monks. He had studied some Esoteric Buddhist texts and also spent some time meditating in retreat on Mount Katsuragi, an area which had connections with the "shamanistic monk," En no Gyōja 角行者. Dōkyō was said to be able to cure illnesses with the powers he had gained through his religious practices. In 761 he was called upon to minister to the ailing retired empress Kōken (718–770, r. 749–58, later reascended the throne as Shōtoku from 764 to 770). Although such sources as the *Nihon ryōiki* compiled around 822 state that Dōkyō became the lover of the retired empress, other sources such as the *Shoku Nihongi* state only that Dōkyō received the favor of the retired empress.

In 762, Kōken began to reassert her influence and eventually reascended the throne in 764. By this time she had been ordained as a

[18] Quoted in Gyōnen, *Sankoku Buppō dentsū engi*, in *Dainihon Bukkyō zensho* (hereafter cited as *BZ*), edited by Suzuki gakujutsu zaidan, second edition, 100 volumes (Tokyo: Suzuki gakujutsu zaidan, 1972–75), 62:19.

[19] For a thorough treatment of Dōkyō, see Yokota Ken'ichi, *Dōkyō*, Jinbutsu sōsho no. 18 (Tokyo: Yoshikawa kōbunkan: 1959). A good treatment of Dōkyō in English is found in Ross Bender, "The Hachiman Cult and the Dōkyō Incident," *Monumenta Nipponica* 34 (1979): 125–153.

nun. Dōkyō began a rise to power that was unprecedented in Japanese history. He was first appointed to high monastic posts. In 764 an edict was issued that an empress who had been ordained a nun should have a monk as her grand minister and Dōkyō was given the title 'chief minister and meditation master' (*daijin zenji* 大臣禪師). The following year he was made prime minister (*daijō daijin zenji* 大政大臣禪師). Dōkyō devoted himself to insuring his own position by appointing officials friendly to him and by trying to stop Fujiwara power. He also issued a number of edicts which were favorable to Buddhism and to the establishment of more temples. Finally, in 766 he was given the title of Dharma king (*hō-ō* 法皇), which was similar to that accorded retired emperors who had been ordained. According to the *Shoku Nihongi,* Dōkyō's food, clothing and palanquin were like those of an emperor. Finally, in 769 an oracle from the *kami* Hachiman arrived in Nara which stated that Dōkyō should be made emperor. Dōkyō's designs on the throne were thwarted only when another oracle from Hachiman was obtained which stated that a subject (namely Dōkyō) could not be made emperor. The following year the empress died and Dōkyō was exiled to be the steward of Yakushiji in Shimotsuke. He died in 772.

The Reform of Buddhism

After Dōkyō's death, the next two emperors, Kōnin (709–781; r. 770–781) and Kanmu (737–806, r.781-806), attempted to reform the Buddhist church and bring it back under control.[20]

During Emperor Kōnin's reign efforts were made on two fronts to rectify relations between the court and the clergy. First, under Dōkyō, governmental controls over the numbers of monks ordained and donations to temples had become very lax. The growth of the Buddhist establishment had an adverse effect on the treasury since monks were excused from tax obligations. Consequently, edicts were issued in 779 directing that registers of monks be checked in order to control privately ordained monks. In addition, the practice of ordaining new monks with the name of a deceased monk was forbidden. This practice had contributed to the increase in the numbers of monks.

Second, the court attempted to improve the quality of the monks in the order. Monks known for the purity of their practice and the correctness of their demeanor had been dismissed from office during

---

[20] For an analysis of the edicts, see Katsuno Ryūshin "Kanmuchō ni okeru shūkyō seisaku," in *Kanmuchō no shomondai,* ed. Kodaigaku kyōkai, pp. 216–28.

Dōkyō's reign. Many of them had fled to the mountains. In 770, soon after Dōkyō's exile, one of these monks, Jikun 慈訓 (d. 777), was restored to his former office of lesser supervisor (shōsōzu) in the Office of Monastic Affairs and a ban on practice in the mountains was lifted as a gesture of good will to those monks who had sequestered themselves in the mountains to protest Dōkyō's rule. In 771 six monks were appointed as Masters of Decorum (igishi 威儀師); they were to insure that monks and nuns behaved correctly and that monastic ceremonies were orthodox. In 772, ten Meditation Masters (zenji 禪師) were appointed to insure that religious practice was properly conducted.

Most of the edicts issued during Kōnin's reign can be viewed as an attempt to revive the Sōniryō, the regulations for monks and nuns which had served as guidelines for monastic behavior during much of the Nara period. However, changes in religious life had made it obvious that many parts of the Sōniryō were obsolete and that additional reforms would be needed. These reforms were instituted during the reign of Emperor Kanmu.

Kanmu was one of Japan's more able and active emperors. He had an interest in the reform of Buddhism and issued many edicts regulating the order during his reign. At first, his attitude towards Buddhism was similar to that of Kōnin. In 783 the provincial temples were prohibited from filling their vacancies without government approval. In 785, monks and nuns were prohibited from entering market places and telling stories about miracles connected with Buddhism, because such tales misled the people. Later, Kanmu began to develop his own policies towards Buddhism.

One of the most notable of Kanmu's reforms was the redefinition of the requirements for candidates to become yearly ordinands. Earlier, as we noted above, little or no emphasis was placed on their ability to explain Buddhist doctrine. In 798, an edict dramatically redefined these requirements. The edict began, "yearly ordinands generally have been youths. Although they know how to chant two sūtras, they still do not understand the purport of the three vehicles.... Although they are monks in dress, their actions are the same as laymen."[21] The edict specified that in the future only people who were at least thirty-five years old would be chosen as yearly ordinands. Middle-aged men were desirable because, "their conduct would already be set, their knowledge and actions would be admirable." For the first time a test of the

---

[21] *Ruijū kokushi*, fascicle 187, *Butsudō* 14, *dosha* (KT6:313).

candidate's ability to explain doctrine was instituted. In order to be initiated as a novice, the candidate had to answer five of ten questions; to be ordained as a monk, he had to answer eight out of ten questions. Rather than emphasizing the memorization and recitation of *sutras,* the importance of textual exegesis was stressed.

In 784, Emperor Kanmu decided to move the capital to Nagaoka for a variety of reasons. Later, in 793, he abandoned his plans to establish the capital at Nagaoka and decided to establish it at Heiankyō (modern Kyoto) where the court would remain until 1868. Earlier, when the capital had been moved to Nara from Asuka, several of the major temples had moved with it. However, under Kanmu, the great temples of Nara were not relocated in the new capital. The Buddhist establishment in Nara, as well as some elements of the nobility, had opposed the move. Moreover, Emperor Kanmu undoubtedly hoped that by physically separating the court and the Buddhist establishment, he could put an end to monastic involvement in court affairs. As a result, only two new temples were to be built in the new capital. They were located to the left and right of the south gate to the city, and were called Tōji (eastern temple) and Saiji (western temple). These were official temples established to protect the new capital, not centers for the Nara schools. In fact, they were probably built to be used by the Bureau of Buddhists and Foreigners (*genbaryō* 玄蕃寮 or *kōroji* 鴻臚寺) as centers for entertaining foreign guests.[22] Only later were they used in more traditional ways as Buddhist monastic centers. In 823 Tōji was given to Kūkai as a center for the Shingon School.

Under Kanmu the court issued edicts to purge the Nara schools of those monks who were not serious Buddhists. Monks with sons were ordered laicized and monks who broke the precepts were denied permission to live in temples in 798. Fujiwara no Sonondo 藤原園人 (d. 812), the governor of Yamato and one of the most prominent officals, was instructed to investigate the Buddhist monks of Nara. Laicizations of monks who had broken the precepts occurred in 800. The investigation of monks and nuns was extended to provincial temples in 801.

The court's activities under Kanmu might at first glance seem to be directed against Nara Buddhism. However, Kanmu was clearly trying to reform Nara Buddhism, not destroy it. He patronized and supported serious monks from Nara. The Sanron monk Gonsō 勤操 (758–827)

---

[22] Murao Jirō, *Kanmu Tennō,* Jinbutsu sōsho no. 112, Tokyo: Yoshikawa kōbunkan, 1963, pp. 222f.

and Hossō monk Shūen 修圓 (d. 835) were honored by Kanmu. In addition, under the reforms instituted by the court, studies of the complex doctrinal system of the Hossō School flourished even as the school's secular influence was curtailed. Among the eminent Hossō scholars of this period were Zenju 善珠 (723–797), Gyōga 行賀 (729–803) and Gomyō 護命 (750–834). Indeed the Hossō School became so influential that it threatened to completely overwhelm its chief rival, the Sanron School, during the late Nara period. The court hoped to foster a more even balance between the Hossō and Sanron schools. An edict dated 798 laments the decline of the Sanron School. In 801, the court ordered that separate examinations be held for yearly ordinand candidates of the Sanron and Hossō schools, thus attempting to insure that the two schools would eventually be equal in strength. The court's support of Tendai was at least partially motivated by the need to establish a school which would balance the powerful Hossō School and to encourage a doctrinal system which might bridge some of the differences between the Sanron and Hossō schools.

Saichō

Saichō was born while Dōkyō's power was at its peak. He grew to be a young man and was ordained a monk while the courts of Kōnin and Kanmu were actively attempting to reform Buddhism. Saichō was thus fortunate to live at a time when government policies were often favorable to the establishment of new forms of Buddhism. Yet he often encountered obstacles in his quest to establish the Tendai School. The story of Saichō's quest is our subject.

PART I

BIOGRAPHY OF SAICHŌ

CHAPTER TWO
EARLY YEARS

Sources

Many biographies of Saichō have been written. Almost all of them, however, are based on two early works. The first of these primary sources is the *Eizan Daishiden* 叡山大師傳 (Biography of the Great Teacher of Mount Hiei) in one fascicle.[1] This work was almost certainly written only a few years after Saichō's death in 822 by his disciple Ichijō Chū 一乗忠. Despite its detailed documentation of many events in Saichō's life, the *Eizan Daishiden* has a number of major omissions in it. Neither Saichō's relations with Kūkai, nor his defense of Tendai doctrine against the Hossō monk Tokuitsu 德一, are mentioned in it. In addition the general condition of the extant manuscripts is poor, with many copyist errors. Despite these problems, the biography, when used critically, has proven to be an invaluable source for Saichō's life.

The second major source is the *Denjutsu isshinkaimon* 傳述一心戒文 (Concerning the Essay on the One-mind Precepts) in three fascicles by Saichō's disciple Kōjō 光定 (779–858).[2] Kōjō was initiated in 810 as one of the Tendai School's first yearly ordinands. During the controversy over the bodhisattva precepts, he served as Saichō's liason to the court, carrying numerous messages between Mount Hiei and Kyoto. More than any other person, he was responsible for obtaining court approval for Saichō's proposals. He thus was in an excellent position to know Saichō's thoughts concerning the precepts during the last few years of his life and to record the events surrounding the controversy over the bodhisattva precepts.

Kōjō probably wrote the *Denjutsu isshinkaimon* around 833–34 during a bitter fight over who would succeed Gishin 義眞 (781–833) as the second head (*zasu* 座主) of the Tendai School. After the dispute had been resolved, Kōjō apparently lost interest in the text and never finished working on it. The result is a poorly edited and sometimes confusing

---

[1] A number of different manuscripts of the *Eizan Daishiden* exist. These have been collated and annotated in Nakao Shunpaku, *Sange gakushōshiki josetsu* (Kyoto: Nagata Bunshōdō, 1980), pp. 315–525.

[2] Found in Hieizan senshuin–nai Eizan gakuin, ed., *Dengyō Daishi zenshū* (hereafter cited as *DZ*), five vols., second edition (Hieizan: Tosho kankōkai, 1926–27); reprint edition (Tokyo: Nihon Bussho kankōkai, 1975), 1:523–648.

source which contains very valuable first person accounts of the events surrounding the struggle to secure the right for the Tendai School to ordain its own monks.

As has happened so many times in religious history, Saichō's biography was written and rewritten by later authors in ways which responded to the needs of their times. In this process, a number of legends were mixed in with the facts. One of the most famous stories concerns young Saichō's discovery of a relic of the Buddha in his fire on Mount Hiei. After wondering what he should use to enshrine it, he found a reliquary in the ashes of the fire.

Those aspects of Saichō's biography which gave him a heroic or miraculous cast were also emphasized. These tendencies first appeared in writings by Saichō and his disciples, but became most pronounced in later works. For example, Saichō signed his name on most of his petitions to court as the "Monk Saichō who went to China in search of the Dharma." In the *Sange gakushōshiki* and other petitions he often called the reader's attention to past patronage by the Emperor Kanmu. In these ways, Saichō himself, as well as his later biographers, emphasized those aspects of his life which would give him more prestige. In works compiled several hundred years after Saichō's death such as the *Konjaku monogatari, Sanbō ekotoba,* and *Uji shūi monogatari,* legends were increasingly mixed with facts[3].

Based on these various sources, a large number of modern biographies, both pious and scholarly, were written before World War II. Of these, the two most scholarly are by Shioiri Ryōchū and Miura Shūkō.[4] During the twenty-five years after World War II, many scholarly articles concerning Saichō's life and thought were written. Perhaps because many aspects of traditional scholarship on Saichō were being questioned, only one lengthy critical biography of Saichō was written during this period.[5] The re-evaluation of Saichō was capped by the publication in 1973 of *Dengyō Daishi kenkyū* (Studies on Dengyō Daishi),[6] a massive volume of essays issued to commemorate the eleven-hundred fiftieth anniversary of Saichō's death. The publication of this work was

[3] For a bibliography and discussion of such works, see Watanabe Shujun, "Setsuwa bungaku no Dengyō Daishi," in *Dengyō Daishi kenkyū,* ed. Tendai gakkai (Tokyo: Waseda daigaku shuppanbu, 1973), p. 1516. Hereafter this work is cited as *DDK.*

[4] Shioiri Ryōchū, *Dengyō Daishi* (Tokyo: Nihon hyōronsha, 1937); Miura Shūkō, *Dengyō Daishiden* (Hieizan: Tendaishūmuchō, 1921).

[5] Katsuno Ryūshin, *Hieizan to Kōyasan* (Tokyo: Shibundō, 1963).

[6] See note 3. A second volume (*Bekkan*) was published in 1980.

followed by lengthy critical biographies of Saichō by Sonoda Kōyū, Kiuchi Hiroshi, and Watanabe Shujun.[7]

Birth

In recent years a major controversy has revolved around the date of Saichō's birth. Several traditions exist concerning the day, with the eighteenth day of the eighth month being the most commonly accepted one. This tradition is a late one, however, dating from the Tokugawa Period.[8]

Two theories exist concerning the year of Saichō's birth. Saichō's initiation and ordination certificates[9] and Saichō's work, the *Kechimyakufu*,[10] place it in 766. On the other hand, according to the the *Eizan Daishiden*,[11] the *Denjutsu isshinkaimon* and most later biographies, Saichō died in 822 at age 56. Counting backwards would indicate that the year of his birth was 767.

During the Edo Period the monk Jihon (1794–1866) proposed the theory which until recently has been used to explain this discrepancy.[12] According to this explanation, Saichō was to take the place of a yearly ordinand (*nenbundosha*) named Saishaku 最寂[13] who had recently died at Saichō's temple, the Kokubunji in Ōmi. To do so, he had to be at least fifteen years old and have had three years of training. Saichō, however, was only fourteen. Since this opportunity was not to be missed, his teacher listed him as being one year older than he actually was. Because taxes, ownership of land, and corvée labor, as well as ordinations were regulated in accordance with age, it was not uncommon to falsify birthdates during the Nara and Heian periods.

This theory has been criticized in recent years by Fukui Kōjun,[14]

---

[7] Sonoda Kōyū and Andō Toshio, *Saichō* (Tokyo: Iwanami shoten, 1974); Kiuchi Hiroshi, *Dengyō Daishi no shōgai to shisō* (Tokyo: Daisan bunmeisha, 1976), and *Saichō to Tendai kyōdan* (Tokyo: Kyōikusha, 1978); Watanabe Shujun, *Dengyō Daishi Saichō no kokoro to shōgai* (Tokyo: Yūzankaku, 1977).

[8] Fukui Kōjun, "Dengyō Daishi seinenkō shingi," *DDK*, p. 1200; Katsuno, *Hieizan*, p. 41.

[9] Hieizan senshuin, ed., *Dengyō Daishi zenshū* (hereafter cited as *DZ*), 5 vols., 2nd ed. (Hieizan: Tosho kankōkai, 1926–27; reprint ed., Tokyo: Nihon Bussho kankōkai, 1975), 5 (*Bekkan*): 101–3.

[10] *DZ* 1:214.

[11] *DZ* 5 (*Bekkan*):41.

[12] *Tendai kahyō*, fasc. 2A, in *Dainihon Bukkyō zensho* (hereafter cited as *BZ*), ed. Suzuki gakujutsu zaidan, 2nd ed., 100 vols. (Tokyo: Suzuki gakujutsu zaidan, 1972–75) 41:244.

[13] No biography exists, but note that the first character from his name was used in Saichō's name.

[14] A number of articles on the problem have been written, but the most easily available

who considered the 766 date found in the initiation and ordination certificates to be correct. The original certificates are preserved in the Raikōin on Mount Hiei. Thus the 766 date cannot be due to a copyist's error Fukui angued that if Saichō had falsified his age, he would have been breaking the very precepts he was taking. His sponsor, Gyōhyō, would have been risking discovery at a time when government supervision of such documents was strict, due to the reforms in the system instituted during Emperor Kanmu's reign (781–806). The document requesting permission to initiate Saichō required twenty-four official seals and the initiation certificate required twenty-three, indicating that the documents were carefully scrutinized.[15] The *Engishiki* specified that officials from both the Jibushō (Ministry of Civil Administration) and the Genbaryō (Bureau of Buddhism and Aliens) attend ordination ceremonies to verify the accuracy of the candidate's documents. Proponents of the the 766 date attribute the 767 date in the *Eizan Daishiden* to an error by either the author or a copyist. This mistake was then picked up by the author of the *Denjutsu isshinkaimon* and later works.

Scholars favoring the traditional date of 767 have noted that official documents of the time are often not trustworthy, and feel that more weight should be given to the sources written by two of Saichō's close disciples. The problem, then, revolves around how to explain the discrepancies between the sources in a way which is more feasible than the traditional one of considering it to be a fabrication by Saichō and his teachers. Sonoda Kōyū[16] has recently suggested that the difference in the documents originated from the time Saichō's parents registered him as a child. Sonoda argued that Saichō's parents claimed that their son was born in 766, one year earlier than his actual birthdate, in order to hasten the day when he would be entitled to a share of land.

At this time the law required that a newly ordained monk's name be moved from lay to monastic registers, thus freeing him from the obligations of corvée labor and taxation. This process involved cross-checking the registers three times.[17] Thus Saichō and his teachers probably could not have changed his records at the time Saichō became a yearly ordinand (*nenbundosha*). Moreover, the format of the initiation and

---

of those arguing that the date is 766 are: (1) Fukui Kōjun, "Dengyō Daishi seinenkō shingi," *DDK*, pp. 1171–1200; (2) Tsugunaga Yoshiteru, "Dengyō Daishi no seinen ni tsuite," *DDK*, pp. 877–97.

[15] *DZ* 1: frontispiece.

[16] Sonoda Kōyū, *Saichō*, pp. 448–51. Also see Katsuno Ryūshin, "Dengyō Daishi tanjō nengi no mondai," *Bukkyōshi kenkyū* 12 (1969): 4–36.

[17] Sonoda, *Saichō*, pp. 449–50.

ordination documents indicates that the wording was taken directly from Saichō's lay register. If Sonoda's explanation is correct, it would imply that Saichō was born into a relatively poor family. The dispute is still far from being settled. Since the traditional date of 767 has not yet been decisively discredited, it will be used in this study.

Saichō's birthplace is traditionally claimed to be Sakamoto at the foot of Mount Hiei. This tradition too has been questioned, but authorities agree that he was born in this general area.[18]

Family

Saichō's father was named Mitsu no Bitomomoe 三津首百枝. The family boasted a lineage that went back to Emperor Hsiao-hsien 孝獻 (r. 189–220) of the Later Han Dynasty. No positive evidence exists proving this lineage authentic; however, according to the *Shinsen seishiroku* 新撰姓氏録 compiled in 815, other families in the same area were of Chinese ancestry. In addition, migrations of Chinese to Japan, such as that of Achi no Omi 阿智使主 in 289, could correspond to that of Saichō's ancestors. Saichō's family was thus probably a branch of one of the more prominent clans in the area, but only an average farming family.[19] Little is known about Saichō's direct ancestors, except that one of them was engaged as a copyist or proof-reader of *sūtras* at Tōdaiji during the Nara period.

Saichō's father was a devout Buddhist, even to the point of turning his own house into a temple; but it is not known whether he also became a monk. According to the *Eizan Daishiden,* when Saichō's father was still childless, he climbed Mount Hiei to perform religious practices and pray for a son. While there, he pledged to the *kami* (deity) on Mount Hiei that he would perform religious austerities if his prayers were answered. Later he received a sign that Saichō (called Hirono 廣野 during his youth) would be born.[20] In order to give thanks, Saichō's father built a thatched hut called the Jingū zen'in 神宮禪院 at the foot of Mount Hiei and dedicated it to the *kami*. Saichō's father may not have been completely able to fulfill his pledge. Thus Saichō may have intended to fulfill his father's promise when he climbed Mount Hiei shortly after his ordination.[21]

---

[18] Ibid., p. 451.

[19] Ibid., p. 452; also see Katsuno, *Hieizan,* pp. 40–1. Kiuchi (*Dengyō Daishi no shōgai to shisō* pp. 25–27) suggests he may have been a low official.

[20] *DZ* 5 (*Bekkan*): 1.

[21] Sonoda Kōyū, "Heian Bukkyō no seiritsu," in *Ajia Bukkyōshi,* ed., Nakamura Hajime

Education

At the age of seven Saichō is said to have gone to a village school.[22] This school was probably designed to educate children of Chinese descent in reading, writing, the *yin-yang* school of thought, medicine, and building. These were the skills which might allow a man to be employed as a low-level official or secretary in the capital or provinces. Alternatively such a man might choose to copy *sūtras*, hold an official position on one of the government missions to China, or even travel as a monk accompanying a mission. Men from the same area and background as Saichō had, in fact, held such positions.

During this time Saichō seems to have decided to become a monk. At the age of twelve, he went to the Kokubunji in Ōmi to study under Gyōhyō 行表.[23] Perhaps he was inspired to do so by his devout father. Economic factors might also have played a role in Saichō's decision: if Saichō were at a monastery, his family would have one less mouth to feed. In addition, since monasteries sometimes advanced funds or lent tools for clearing or reclaiming land, having a son at a monastery might help a family gain access to a monastery's resources.[24] No clear evidence exists indicating any economic motives behind Saichō's decision, but such factors certainly affected other would-be monks.

Saichō's Teacher Gyōhyō

Many of Saicho's later doctrinal predilections were determined during the few years he spent studying with Gyōhyō. An investigation of the biographies of Gyōhyō and Tao-hsüan 道璿 (702–766), Gyōhyō's teacher, reveals that Saichō's interests in religious practice at mountain retreats, the *Ssu fen lü* and *Fan wang* precepts, meditation, and Hua-yen doctrine all date from his study with Gyōhyō.[25]

Tao-hsüan was born in Hunan in 702.[26] He was initiated as a novice

et al., 20 vols. (Tokyo: Kōsei shuppansha, 1974), *Nihon-hen* 2: 105.

[22] *Eizan Daishiden*, DZ 5 (*Bekkan*): 2. This is the only mention of such a school in Nara and early Heian documents.

[23] Late sources claim that Saichō and Gyōhyō were distant relatives, but these are not reliable (Katsuno, *Hieizan*, p. 56). Saichō probably entered Kokubunji because it was near his home.

[24] George Sansom, *A History of Japan to 1334* (Stanford, CA: Stanford U. Press, 1958), p. 88.

[25] Gyōhyō's teacher Tao-hsüan should not be confused with the great Chinese *vinaya* master and historian Tao-hsüan 道宣 (596–667), who is mentioned later in this study. To avoid such confusion, the latter's name will be romanized Daoxuan.

[26] Tao-hsüan's biography is based primarily on an account by Kibi no Makibi 吉備眞備 (693–775) which is quoted in the *Kechimyakufu* (DZ 1:211–213) and in the *Denjutsu isshin-*

while a youth, and was ordained a monk at the Ta-fu 大福 Temple in Lo-yang by Ting-pin 定賓 of the Hsiang-pu 相部 sect of the Lü-tsung 律宗 (*Vinaya* School). After studying the *Ssu fen lü* with Ting-pin, Tao-hsüan decided to travel and study with different teachers. Subsequently he practiced meditation under the Northern School Ch'an master P'u-chi 普寂 (651–739). He also studied the doctrines of the Nan-shan sect of the Lü-tsung, as well as those of the Hua-yen and T'ien-t'ai Schools under other teachers. Tao-hsüan later returned to the Ta-fu Temple in Lo-yang to lecture.

In 733 the two Japanese monks Eiei 榮叡 (d. 748) and Fushō 普照 (d. 758?) traveled to China in search of a *vinaya* master who would agree to come to Japan in order to conduct orthodox ordinations there. Soon after arriving in China, they received orthodox *Ssu fen lü* ordinations from Tao-hsüan's teacher, Ting-pin.[27] At the invitation of the two Japanese monks, Tao-hsüan journeyed to Japan in 736. Since Tao-hsüan was not accompanied by the ten monks required to perform orthodox ordinations, Eiei and Fushō remained in China to seek out the remaining monks. It was not until Chien-chen (Jap. Ganjin) and his disciples arrived in Japan in 754 that a sufficient number of monks qualified to perform orthodox ordinations could gather in Japan. However, Tao-hsüan must have performed some type of ordination previous to this since he served as Gyōhyō's preceptor at an *upasampadā* ordination in 743. Unfortunately, little information of the type of ordination Tao-hsüan performed has survived.

After he arrived in Japan, Tao-hsüan stayed at the Saitōin at Daianji 大安寺 in Nara where he lectured on the *Fan wang ching* and Daoxuan's *Ssu fen lü hsing shih ch'ao* (*T* no. 1804). Tao-hsüan also chanted *dhāraṇī* at the dedication ceremony of the great Buddha at Tōdaiji. In 751 he was appointed as *risshi* (vinaya master) in the Sōgō (Office of Monastic Affairs). When Chien-chen arrived in Japan in 754, Tao-hsüan went to greet him. Sometime later, Tao-hsüan suddenly became ill and withdrew to the mountain temple Hisodera in Yoshino where he died in 760. Saichō's retreat to Mount Hiei may have been influenced by Tao-hsüan's withdrawal to Hisodera. Tao-hsüan is reported to have adhered strictly to the *Ssu fen lü* precepts. In addition, he recited the *Fan wang ching* everyday[28] and wrote a three-fascicle commentary on the *sūtra*.

---

kaimon (*DZ* 1:617–18). Other relevant information can be found in *BD* 4:3883.

[27] Tokuda Myōhon, *Risshū gairon* (Kyoto: Hyakkaen, 1969), p. 503.

[28] Because Tao-hsüan's chanting voice was clear and resonant, he is traditionally said to have played an important role in the early development of Buddhist chanting (*shōmyō*

Unfortunately, the commentary has not survived; however, it is quoted twice in the *Denjutsu isshinkaimon* and over forty times in Gyōnen's 凝然 (1240–1321) *Bonmōkai honsho nichijushō*.[29] These quoted passages indicate that the work was based on T'ien-t'ai doctrines and relied heavily on Chih-chou's *Fan wang ching* commentary.[30]

For almost twenty years Tao-hsüan was accompanied by one of his closest disciples, Gyōhyō (720–797).[31] Gyōhyō had studied Kegon, Zen, Ritsu and Hossō doctrines, but was primarily known as a meditation teacher. After Tao-hsüan's death in 760, Gyōhyō went to the province of Ōmi where he held various positions. He became *daikokushi* (greater provincial teacher) of Ōmi in 778, and was young Saichō's teacher for six years at the Kokubunji in Ōmi.

According to the *Eizan Daishiden*, Saichō mainly studied *yuishiki* 唯識 ('ideation-only') doctrines while he was with Gyōhyō. This training proved to be very useful to him in later life when he debated Hossō monks. Saichō probably did not study orthodox Hossō doctrine at this time, however.

The *yuishiki* texts Saichō studied under Gyōhyō probably belonged to the group of texts translated before Hsüan-tsang. Many of them concerned the doctrine of universal salvation, the position which Saichō later defended in his debates with Hossō monks. In addition, Tao-hsüan is credited with introducing the Kegon school to Japan; and the temple Daianji where he and his disciple Gyōhyō spent much of their time was also known as a center of Sanron 三論 thought.

Saichō's interest in meditation certainly dates from this period. In the *Kechimyakufu,* the Zen teaching he received from Gyōhyō was the only teaching which Saichō traced back to his training in Japan; the Tendai tradition, the *Fan wang* precepts, and the Esoteric traditions were all said to have come from China. While studying under Gyōhyō, Saichō also became well-acquainted with the *Lotus Sūtra*[32]

声明) in Japan (*BD* 3: 2780a).

[29] *T* no. 2247.

[30] *Z* 1. 60. 2. Chih-chou 智周 (556–622) was the third patriarch of the Fa-hsiang School.

[31] Many traditional biographies stated that Gyōhyō lived to be 140 years old, but these dates are clearly wrong. For a discussion of Gyōhyō's dates and life, see Tsugunaga Yoshiteru, "Daianji Gyōhyō den no kenkyū," *Bukkyō shigaku* 12, no. 3 (1966): 16–32.

[32] The *Lotus Sūtra* (*T* no. 262) in its translation by Kumārajīva done in 406 was the most popular single *sūtra* during the Nara period. It was required that all yearly ordinands be able to read it. It is the most commonly mentioned *sūtra* in documents recommending laymen for ordination as monks (*Kōshin ubasoku* 貢進優婆塞). A statistical analysis of *sūtras* mentioned in the *Kōshin ubasoku* is given in Takagi Yutaka's *Heian jidai Hokke Bukkyōshi kenkyū* (Kyoto: Heirakuji shoten, 1973), pp. 194–96. The *Lotus Sūtra* was

and the *Chin kuang ming ching*,[33] two *sūtras* which would play an important role in his teaching later. A number of other works mastered by Saichō during this period are mentioned in the official document concerning his initiation.[34] Among them are the *Chin kang pan jo ching* (*Vajracchedikā prajñāpāramitāsūtra*) and the *Yao shih ching*, a *sūtra* devoted to Bhaiṣajyaguru Buddha. All of the above-mentioned works were used frequently in the training of young monks during the Nara period. Saichō also studied a commentary on the *Fang kuang ching* 方廣經, a text which may have been used in ceremonies to expiate sins and has been tentatively identified as *T* no. 2871.[35] He also studied several other works which have not yet been identified, as well as some secular works. Although it is not mentioned in the documents concerning his initiation, Saichō might have read Tao-hsüan's commentary on the *Fan wang ching* at this time. According to the *Denjutsu isshinkaimon*, he read it before going to China.[36] Thus, when the nineteen-year old Saichō left Gyōhyō to go to Nara for his ordination, his doctrinal predilections had been set for life.

Ordination

Although Saichō became a novice at fourteen, replacing the deceased Saishaku, he did not receive the government certificate (*dochō*) recognizing his status until three years later.[37] This arrangement may have

also frequently recited at the request of the court in order to protect the state. It does not have any specific passage which guarantees protection of the state, as did most of the other *sūtras* used for this purpose. Rather, this use of the *sūtra* stems from its claim that it is the most authoritative of all *sūtras* and from stories that those with faith in the *sūtra* were protected from harm. In addition, it was a very popular *sūtra* among the common people, being the *sūtra* most often mentioned in the *Nihon ryōiki*. [See the English translation by Kyoko Nakamura, *Miraculous Stories from the Japanese Buddhist Tradition*, Harvard–Yenching Institute Monograph Series, vol. 20 (Cambridge, Mass.: Harvard University Press, 1973).]

[33] The *Chin kuang ming tsui sheng wang ching* 金光明最勝王經 (*T* no. 665, *Suvarṇaprabhōsa* [*uttamarāja*] *sūtra*) was translated by I-ching in 703. This was a newer translation of a *sūtra* translated earlier by such figures as Dharmarakṣa (385–433) and Paramārtha (499–569). It was very popular during the Nara period and was distributed by imperial order throughout the provincial temples (*kokubunji*) of Japan. See Inoue Kaoru, *Naracho Bukkyō no kenkyū* (Tokyo: Yoshikawa kōbunkan, 1966), pp. 61–77 for an analysis of the use of the *sūtra*. Like the *Lotus Sūtra*, it was used especially to guard the nation and to expiate sins, and is mentioned often in *Kōshin ubasoku*. It did not enjoy the same popularity as the *Lotus Sūtra* among the common people, however.

[34] *Kokufuchō, DZ* 5 (*Bekkan*): 101.

[35] Kiuchi, *Dengyō Daishi no shōgai to shisō*, pp. 33–35.

[36] *DZ* 1: 565.

[37] Four years later, Emperor Kanmu severely restricted the practice of replacing a monk who had died or left the order with a new candidate for ordination. His order indicates the

been adopted to enable Saichō's family to use his allotment of land for three more years. At age eighteen Saichō would have been subjected to taxes and corvée labor. Consequently, he had to apply for the certificate giving him immunity from these burdens before he was eighteen years old[38]

When he was nineteen Saichō went to Tōdaiji in Nara to be ordained as a monk. Ever since Chien-chen's arrival in Nara in 754, the court had sought to control the numbers of monks by permitting full ordinations to be performed only on officially recognized precepts platforms (*kaidan* 戒壇). At first, ordinations were permitted only at Tōdaiji; but in 761, the court also allowed ordinations at Yakushiji 薬師寺 in Shimotsuke and at Kanzeonji 観世音寺 in Chikuzen to make it easier for people in the provinces to be ordained. After being ordained, most monks were expected to undergo a period of training in the 250 precepts of the *Ssu fen lü* which lasted for several months.[39] After Saichō had completed his training period, he left Nara and climbed Mount Hiei.

---

practice of substitution was often abused.

[38] See Tsugunaga Yoshiteru, "Dengyō Daishi den ni kansuru ichi ni no kōsatsu," *Rekishi kyōiku* 13, no. 5 (1965): 71, for an analysis of the laws concerning this problem.

[39] Saichō's disciple Kōjō underwent a three-month period of training in the full precepts of the *Ssu fen lü* following his ordination. The training occurred in Nara and included an ordination in the bodhisattva precepts (*Denjutsu isshinkaimon, DZ* 1: 518–519).

CHAPTER THREE
THE YEARS ON MOUNT HIEI

Retreat at Mount Hiei

Up to this point Saichō's life is not at all unusual. But leaving the capital, the center of Buddhist activity, and retreating to Mount Hiei was an almost unprecedented step for a young monk. A number of explanations have been proposed for it.

One of the most famous early examples of a Japanese monk retreating to the mountains for a prolonged stay is that of Saichō's teacher Gyōhyō, who retreated to a mountain temple with Tao–hsüan. Saichō's decision was influenced by his teacher's example. In addition, Saichō's temple, the Kokubunji in the province of Ōmi, burned down the same year that Saichō climbed Mount Hiei probably making it impossible for him to return to it. It is not known, however, whether the temple burned before or after Saichō climbed Mount Hiei.[1] Saichō also may have climbed Mount Hiei to fulfill the vow which his father made to the *kami* on Hiei but had not been able to keep.[2]

The *Eizan Daishiden* states only that Saichō retreated to Mount Hiei because he was moved by the transiency of life.[3] The Kokubunji in Ōmi was located on one of the main roads to the Eastern Provinces (Tōgoku). Here Saichō probably observed many of the people on their way to fulfill their corvée obligations and their suffering from heavy taxes. Men sometimes died by the road from sickness or starvation on their way home from such duties. The woman and children who had been left behind had to maintain the farming operations without adequate help. Such difficulties led some families to leave their land. Saichō probably saw the human suffering brought about by such problems and the breakdown of the *ritsuryō* system. He undoubtedly heard about the rebellions of the Ezo to the north and about the men who had been drafted to fight and control the Ezo. He must have known

---

[1] *Nihon kiryaku: zenpen*, fasc. 14, in *Shintei zōhō Kōkushi taikei* (hereafter cited as *KT*), ed., Kuroita Katsumi, 66 vols., (Tokyo: Yoshikawa kōbunkan: 1929–66) 10:311. The *Nihon kiryaku* was compiled in the late Heian period. The burning of the Kokubunji in Ōmi has led to some doubt about its location. For a discussion of two possible sites, see Kiuchi, *Dengyō Daishi no shōgai to shisō*, p. 27.

[2] *Eizan Daishiden, DZ* 5 (*Bekkan*): 1–2, Sonoda, *Ajia Bukkyōshi,* Nihon-hen 2:105.

[3] *DZ* 5 (*Bekkan*): 3.

about Emperor Kanmu's plan to move the capital to Nagaoka and heard about the labor required, and the dislocations caused by the attempted move.

Furthermore, Saichō must also have been aware of a major political incident which involved Fujiwara no Tanetsugu 藤原種継 (737–785) and Ōtomo no Tsugihito 大伴継人 (d. 785), two of the men who signed his *dochō* (initiation certificate). The emperor had appointed Tanetsugu to help supervise construction at the new capital at Nagaoka. He was assassinated, however, and later on the court discovered that Tsugihito and Crown Prince Sawara 早良 (d. 785) were among the perpetrators of the crime. Tsugihito was executed and Sawara died on his way to exile at Awaji. These events occured two months after Saichō had climbed Mount Hiei and must have reinforced his decision to stay.

Shortly after he climbed Mount Hiei, Saichō composed a short work, the *Ganmon* 願文 (*Vows*[4]) which tells of his decision to retreat to the mountains. It is an impressive work for so young a man, showing a deep sense of the transiency of life. The heart of the work lies in the five vows Saichō made at the end of the work:

(1) So long as I have not attained the stage where my six faculties are pure, I will not venture out into the world.[5]

---

[4] *DZ* 1:1–3. The *Ganmon* was probably not circulated as an independent work until after Saichō's death. It is first found in the *Eizan Daishiden* by Ninchū and later in the biography of Saichō by Enchin (*DZ* 5 [*Bekkan*]: 3–5, 49–50). One of the vows found in the *Ganmon* is identical to a pledge found in one of Saichō's letters (Sekiguchi Shindai, "Dengyō Daishi Ganmon ni tsuite," *DDK*, p. 603). Thus most traditional and modern scholars consider the work to be authentic.

In recent years, however, a number of arguments against it have been advanced. First of all, it is not found in Gishin's bibliography of Saichō's works, one of the most important authorities for evaluating the authenticity of Saichō's works. The *Ganmon* exhibits a mastery of Chinese which is difficult to imagine in Saichō at such a young age. Moreover, it is stylistically different from his other works. Since the *Ganmon* is stylistically similar to the *Eizan Daishiden*, Ushiba Shingen has suggested that it might have been written by the author of the *Eizan Daishiden* to dramatize Saichō's retreat to Mount Hiei (*"Eizan Daishiden* no seirisu ni tsuite," *DDK*, pp. 87–88).

Some of the criticisms concerning the authenticity of the *Ganmon* have been discredited. Its elegant style is probably due to the influence of such works as the *Lotus Sūtra, Fan wang ching,* Chih–i's *T'ien t'ai hsiao chih kuan* and the *Tōdaiji kenmotsuchō* 東大寺献物帳 by Empress Kōmyō, composed in 756 (Sonoda, *Saichō,* p. 464, and Tamura Kōyū, *Saichō jiten* [Tokyo: Tokyōdō shuppan, 1979], p. 38). Critics attempting to prove that the *Ganmon* is a later dramatization of Saichō's retreat have also not considered the inclusion of the *Ganmon* in Enchin's biography of Saichō, compiled fifty–nine years after Saichō's death. The quotation of the entire text of the *Ganmon* in this work indicates that it was considered to be authentic several decades after Saichō's death. Consequently, the work must be considered to be authentic until stronger criticisms are presented.

[5] The six faculties are the five senses and the mind. The stage referred to here is the fourth in a Tendai scheme of six stages called the *roku soku* 六即:

(2) So long as I have not realized the absolute, I will not acquire any special skills or arts (such as medicine, divination, and calligraphy).

(3) So long as I have not kept all of the precepts purely,[6] I will not participate in any lay donor's Buddhist meeting.[7]

(4) So long as I have not attained wisdom (*hannya*), I will not participate in worldly affairs unless it be to benefit others.

(5) May any merit from my practice in the past, present, and future be given not to me, but to all sentient beings so that they may attain supreme   enlightenment.[8]

(a) *Ri soku* 理即. The common man who has not yet even heard the names of the doctrines of the perfect teaching.

(b) *Myōji soku* 名字即. He hears of the Buddha's teaching from a friend or reads about it in the   scriptures.

(c) *Kangyō soku* 觀行即. He begins practicing on the basis of his understanding of the teaching.

(d) *Sōji soku* 相似即. He cuts off all delusions. His six faculties are pure (*rokukon shōjō* 六根清淨). He resembles (*sōji*) the Buddha. In this stage, he is free from the danger of backsliding; thus he may go out and preach to others.

(e) *Bunshin soku* 分眞即 or *bunshō soku* 分證即. He cuts off ignorance and partially apprehends the absolute.

(f) *Kukyōsoku* 究竟即. He has completely cut off ignorance and realized the true nature (*jissō* 實相) of things. This is the stage of ultimate enlightenment.

The term *soku* is used to characterize the stages because they are all only apparent differences. For example, in the first stage, the Buddha and the man who has not yet even heard of Buddhism are different in terms of phenomena (*ji* 事). However, in terms of the absolute (*ri* 理), they are the same. Thus the ordinary non–believer is potentially a Buddha.

According to the *Eizan Daishiden*, the *Ganmon* was composed after Saichō had climbed Mount Hiei, but before he had studied Tendai doctrines. His use of the Tendai term *rokukon sōji* 六根相似 and the contents of the five vows have led some scholars to hold that Saichō must have studied Tendai doctrines before he climbed Mount Hiei, possibly in Nara. For example, see Shioiri Ryōchū, *Shin jidai no Dengyō Daishi no kyōgaku* (Tokyo: Daitō shuppansha, 1939), pp. 12–17, 43–52. Some scholars have postulated that Saichō might have had a limited knowledge of Tendai doctrine through Gyōhyō, who in turn might have studied it under Tao–hsüan. Another possibility is that some Tendai doctrines may have been included in the syncretistic and liberal Buddhism at Daianji. However, if this theory is accepted, Saichō's choice of Tendai terms to express himself even before he had seriously studied them is remarkable. A good discussion of this problem can be found in Sekiguchi Shindai, "Dengyō Daishi no *Ganmon* ni tsuite," *DDK*, pp. 603–23.

6 The precepts referred to (literally the pure precepts or *jōkai*) are probably the *Ssu fen lü* which Saichō studied after his Tōdaiji ordination, but they have also been interpreted as the *Fan wang* precepts or the three collections of pure precepts (*sanju jōkai* 三聚淨戒) by later Tendai scholars.

7 This vow may have been influenced by the first seven vows in the thirty–sixth minor precept of the *Fan wang ching*, which are found in *T* 24: 1007c–8a. The follower of these vows promises that so long as he is not pure in keeping the precepts, he will not accept anything from a lay donor.

8 *DZ* 1:2. This type of vow, called the *ekō* 回向, is very common in Mahāyāna writings and services.

The *Ganmon* reveals that young Saichō was a very serious monk, interested in following the precepts he had just taken and in assiduously pursuing his religious practices. To do so, Saichō felt he had to leave the capital and go to the mountains where there were few distractions which might hinder his meditation. Saichō's concern with maintaining the precepts and thus purifying himself presaged his later concern with monastic reform. The *Ganmon* is also noteworthy for showing a degree of self–examination and reflection unusual in such a young person.

Activities on Mount Hiei

On Mount Hiei Saichō read and chanted the *Lotus Sūtra,* the *Chin kuang ming ching (Suvarṇaprabhāsasūtra)*, the *Pan jo ching (Perfection of Wisdom sūtras)* and other Mahāyāna *sūtras* every day and sat in meditation.[9] During his first years on the mountain, he also read the Hua–yen (Jap. Kegon) master Fa–tsang's (653–712) *Ch'i hsin lun shu* and *Hua yen ching wu chiao chang*. Saichō first learned about T'ien–t'ai through Fa–tsang's works, probably from several passages which praised the meditation practices followed by the two Tien–t'ai patriarchs, Hui–Ssu and Chih–i.[10] Saichō's ability to read these difficult Chinese texts was due to the training he had received at the school in his village and at the Kokubunji in Ōmi. According to the *Eizan Daishiden,* Saichō was able to meet an unidentified person who knew the whereabouts, probably at Tōdaiji, of the T'ien–t'ai works which Chien–chen had brought to Japan in 754. Saichō managed to obtain copies of the most important works by Chih–i, the *de facto* founder of T'ien–t'ai.

In 788 Saichō carved a statue of Yakushi Nyorai 藥師如來 (Bhaiṣajyaguru Tathāgata) and installed it in a small hall, which he called Hieizanji 比叡山寺 (Mount Hiei Temple). His choice of Yakushi Nyorai for the central image of the temple probably reflects his earlier study of the *Yao shih ching* 藥師經, a *sūtra* concerning that Buddha. In 793 he renamed this building the One–Vehicle Meditation Hall (Ichijō shikan'in 一乘止觀院), an indication of his growing interest in Tendai. According to later accounts, he also built a library (*kyōzō* 經藏), a hall dedicated to Mañjuśrī (Monjudō 文殊堂), and other buildings at this time.[11]

---

[9] *Eizan Daishiden, DZ* 5 (*Bekkan*): 3.

[10] Ibid., pp. 5–6. For the passages which probably influenced Saichō, see *T* 44: 283c and 45:480c.

[11] *Eigaku yōki,* in *Gunsho ruijū* (hereafter cited as *GR*), ed. Hanawa Hokinoichi, 19 vols. (Tokyo: Keizai zasshisha, 1893–1902) 15: 523, 527–28, 556.

Early Relations With the Court

Mount Hiei proved to be a very fortunate choice for Saichō because it was to the northeast of what would several years later become Kyoto, the new capital of Japan. According to the Chinese geomantic views popular at the Japanese court in the early Heian period, Kyoto was thought to be particularly vulnerable to untoward influences from the northeast. Saichō later came to the attention of Emperor Kanmu partly because of the geomantic significance of Mt. Hiei's location.

In the ninth month of 794 Emperor Kanmu is said to have visited the mountain temple for the dedication of the Main Hall (Konpon chūdō 根本中堂). A number of prominent officials and monks, including Gomyō 護命, Shūen 修圓, and Gonsō 勤操 are said to have been present. The earliest accounts of this, however, are found in the *Eigaku yōki* 叡岳要記 and the *Kuin bukkakushō* 九院佛閣抄,[12] both works probably dating from the fourteenth century. No account can be found in the official histories; however, since part of the *Nihon kōki* has not survived, it could have been included in a lost section of that work. Because Kanmu was preoccupied with the move to Kyoto at this time and because the story does not appear in any earlier accounts, it must be considered doubtful.

A more likely explanation of how Saichō came to the Emperor's attention is found in the *Eizan Daishiden*. One of the ten monks who served at court (*naigubu* 內供奉),[13] Jukō 壽興, read Saichō's *Ganmon* and made a similar pledge.[14] Saichō's appointment in 797 to one of the monks' posts at court was probably due to Jukō's recommendation. Saichō's appointment probably marked the end of his stay on Mount

---

[12] Ibid., p. 534; *Kuin Bukkakushō, GR* 15:594. Also see Katsuno (*Hieizan,* p. 57) for comments on the early temple complex on Mount Hiei.

[13] *Naigubu* were monks who served at the court chapel (*naidōjō* 內道場); however, there are also examples of monks who held the rank but probably did not go to the court (see note 15 below). The office originated in China and was first instituted in Japan in 772. Monks who strictly kept the precepts and were particularly learned were appointed to the office. They were to serve as a model for other monks. Because originally ten monks were appointed, they were also called the ten meditation teachers (*jūzenji* 十禪師). Scholars differ as to whether the number of appointees was limited to ten or not. The appointment carried financial remuneration and two servant boys. Beginning in 795 with the Bonshakuji 梵釋寺, the official temple founded by Emperor Kanmu, separate groups of ten were installed at various temples. Saichō's appointment is an indication that he was respected for his purity in keeping the precepts by the time he was thirty. For the early history of the office, and some of the scholarly debates surrounding it, see Futaba Kenkō, "Bukkyō ni taisuru kokka tōsei seido no seiritsu to sono seikaku–jūji to jūdaitoku," *Ryūkoku daigaku ronshū,* no. 396 (June 1971), pp. 1–29.

[14] *Eizan Daishiden, DZ* 5 (*Bekkan*): 5. No biography for Jukō has survived, but he may have been a Hossō monk (*BD* 6 [*Furoku*]: 31).

Hiei since his designation as *naigubu* presumably entailed an appearance at court. If he had not come down from Mount Hiei since he climbed there in 785, he would have remained on it continuously for a total of twelve years, the same period of time he later asked his students to spend on it. However, Katsuno Ryūshin argues that Saichō did not come down until 802, the date of the Takaosanji lectures.[15] No conclusive evidence for either theory exists since early sources remain silent on how long Saichō initially was on Mount Hiei.

Copying the Canon

With his appointment as *naigubu,* Saichō also received a stipend from the taxes of Ōmi.[16] He soon proclaimed his intention of remedying one of the major obstacles to practicing on Mount Hiei, the lack of religious texts. Announcing a plan to copy the Buddhist canon (*issaikyō* 一切經), he asked for help from the Nara temples and received some texts. His biggest benefactor, however, was Chien–chen's disciple Dōchū 道忠 who sent 2,000 volumes along with one of his most talented disciples, Enchō 圓澄.

Saichō's relationship with Dōchū at this time is noteworthy. Dōchū's dates are unknown. He was ordained by Chien–chen, who stated that Dōchū observed the precepts more faithfully than any of his other disciples. Later Dōchū travelled through the country preaching, finally settling in Musashino and founding Jikōji 慈光寺. The local people respected him greatly and called him 'bosatsu' (bodhisattva). Although there is no evidence that Saichō and Dōchū ever met, Dōchū must have respected him greatly to send him 2,000 fascicles of texts and Enchō, a prized disciple who would later become the second head (*zasu* 座主) of the Tendai sect. Dōchū's esteem for Saichō was probably due to Saichō's strict adherence to the precepts and his Tendai affiliations. Dōchū's teacher, Chien-chen, had also been a Tendai monk. Some scholars also hypothesize that Dōchū may have been important in helping young Saichō obtain copies of Chih-i's works.[17]

Copying *sūtras* was, and still is, considered to be a form of Buddhist practice and a way of making merit. Copying the Buddhist canon was an enormous task. The cost of paper, ink and brushes, not to mention paying for copyists and proofreaders, must have been too great

---

[15] Katsuno, *Hieizan*, p. 62.

[16] *Eizan Daishiden, DZ* 5 (*Bekkan*): 6.

[17] Sonoda, "Saichō no Tōgoku dendō ni tsuite," *Bukkyō shigaku* 3 (1952): 149.

for a relatively unknown monk like Saichō to raise. The difficulties involved have led some scholars to term the account a fabrication or exaggeration.[18] Others have theorized that he received help from rich relatives and friends, especially from the Hata 秦 family, who were of Chinese descent and influential in government.[19] Temple libraries in Nara at this time ranged from 1,500 to 10,000 volumes.[20] With the contribution from Dōchū, the Hieizanji collection would have fallen near the smaller end of the scale.

Lectures on the Lotus Sūtra

Saichō's days on Mount Hiei were not all spent meditating and copying *sūtras*. In the eleventh month of 798, Saichō began what would become an annual series of ten lectures on the *Lotus Sūtra* and its opening (*kaikyō* 開經) and closing *sūtras* (*kekkyō* 結經).[21] The *Lotus Sūtra* is composed of eight fascicles, and its opening *sūtra,* the *Wu liang i ching* 無量義經, and closing *sūtra,* the *Kuan p'u hsien ching* 觀普賢經, of one fascicle each.[22] Each lecture covered one fascicle. The entire series would take five days with two lectures being given each day. The occasion for the lectures seems to have been the anniversary of Chih-i's death.[23] The lectures may have been modeled on similar ones held by the Chinese T'ien-t'ai school. Also, two years earlier the Sanron monk Gonsō[24] had decided to begin an annual series of eight lectures on the

---

[18] Ushiba Shingen, *"Eizan Daishiden* ni okeru ni san no mondai," *Nanto Bukkyō* 26 (1971): 59–62.

[19] Katsuno, *Hieizan,* pp. 54–55.

[20] Akamatsu, "Saichō to Kūkai," *Ōtani gakuhō* 53, no. 2 (1973): 2–3.

[21] This lecture series was later called the Shimotsuki-e 霜月會.

[22] *T* nos. 276 and 277.

[23] Shioiri Ryōtatsu, "Dengyō Daishi," in *Dengyō Daishi Kōbō Daishi shū,* ed. Shioiri Ryōtatsu and Nakano Yoshiteru, vol. 3 of Bukkyō kyōiku hōten (Tokyo: Tamagawa daigaku shuppanbu, 1972), p. 14.

[24] Gonsō (758?–827) was a member of the Hata family from Yamato. When he was twelve, he studied under Shinrai 信禮 at Daianji, and later studied Sanron under Zengi 善議 (729–812). He was famous for his wide learning. In 813 he was appointed *risshi* (*vinaya* master). Later, he concurrently held positions as *shōsozu* (lesser supervisor) and *bettō* (chief administrator) of Tōdaiji. His final positions were as *daisōzu* (greater supervisor) and *bettō* of Saidaiji.

Though he was primarily a Sanron scholar, defending Sanron in debates at court in 813, Gonsō also was interested in Esoteric Buddhism. He was probably one of Kūkai's early teachers, initiating him into Kokūzō 虚空藏 practice, an Esoteric ritual designed to improve the memory. In addition, he also maintained close relations with Saichō and studied Tendai teachings. For a biography of Gonsō, see Ikeda Genta, "Iwabuchidera Gonsō to Heian Bukkyō," *Nanto Bukkyō* 5 (1958): 26–40; for Gonsō's lectures, see Takagi, *Heian jidai Hokke Bukkyō,* pp. 209–11.

Lotus Sūtra at his temple, Iwabuchidera 石淵寺. In this series one monk was responsible for each fascicle of the *Lotus Sūtra,* the whole series lasting eight days. Lectures on the *Wu liang i ching* and *Kuan p'u hsien ching* were not included in the eight-lecture series.

From the beginning the Tendai lectures were attended by monks from Nara; but the lectures given in 801 proved to be especially important. Saichō invited ten monks[25] from the seven great temples of Nara to give the lectures, each monk being responsible for one lecture. This meeting enabled Saichō to listen to what the monks in Nara were preaching. Among the gifts he later carried to China was a record of these lectures.[26] This assembly also must have given Saichō the opportunity to expound upon Tendai doctrines and interpretations of the *Lotus Sūtra.*

The Takaosanji 高雄山寺 Lectures

One year later, in 802, Saichō was to receive some help from one of the most politically important families in Japan, the Wake. The Wake family were pious Buddhists with a strong interest in reforming Buddhism and keeping it separated from politics. Wake no Kiyomaro 和氣清麻呂 (733–799) led the opposition to Dōkyō 道鏡 (d. 772), who was discussed above Kiyomaro. later became a trusted adviser to Emperor Kanmu and played a major role in the decision to move the capital to Kyoto. The court and the Wake were particularly interested in encouraging new types of Buddhism which would not be a threat to government. Consequently, in 802 two of Kiyomaro's sons, Hiroyo[27] 廣世 and Matsuna[28] 眞綱, invited fourteen important monks to

---

[25] *Eizan Daishiden, DZ* 5 (*Bekkan*): 7. Though the names of the ten monks are listed, very little is known about them. See Sonoda, *Saichō,* p. 477, and Katsuno, *Hieizan,* pp. 60–61, for discussions of the ten men.

[26] *Kenkairon engi, DZ* 1:268. The work was called the *Kutsujūdaitokusho* 屈十大德疏; it has not survived.

[27] The *Eizan Daishiden* (*DZ* 5 [*Bekkan*]: 8) states that the Wake brothers issued the invitation. According to the the *Denjutsu isshinkaimon* (*DZ* 1: 626–27), they were following Emperor Kanmu's orders.

Wake no Hiroyo (d. 809) was Wake no Kiyomaro's eldest son. He held a number of posts, finally rising to become head of the university and governor of Awa. In 793 he gave 100 *chō* of new fields in Bizen to help the poor. He also gave 20 *chō* to be used for scholarships to the university. To the south of the university, he established the Kōbun'in 弘文院, the Wake clan's school with a library of several thousand volumes. Hiroyo held ranks of Assistant Vice-Minister (*shōyu*) and Vice-Minister (*tayu*) in the Bureau of Ceremonies (*Shikibushō*). He was one of Saichō's most important supporters.

[28] Wake no Matsuna (783–846) was Kiyomaro's fifth child and Hiroyo's younger brother. Along with Hiroyo, he was an important lay supporter of Saichō. In 834 be became

Takaosanji[29] to participate in a retreat and study Tendai works. Besides nine of the ten monks who participated in Saichō's Mount Hiei meeting, five other monks attended: Zengi 善議,[30] Gonsō, Shūen 修圓,[31] Saikō 歲光[32] and Dōshō 道證.[33] The retreat is thought to have started the nineteenth of the first month and to have continued until autumn or winter of that year. The plans were to begin with lectures on the *Fa hua hsüan i,* continue on to study the *Fa hua wen chü,* and conclude with the *Mo ho chih kuan.*[34] These three texts, all by Chih-i, are the most important Tendai works (Tendai *sandaibu*). The *Hsüan i* lectures, however, were not finished until the early part of the ninth month, throwing the

lay administrator (*zoku bettō*) of the Tendai monastery complex on Mount Hiei. For accounts of Matsuna's activities as *zoku betto,* see *DZ* 1: 647–48; and Shibuya Jikai, ed., *Kōtei sōbu Tendai zasuki* (Tokyo: Daiichi shobō, 1973) p. 8.

[29] Takaosanji is located in Sakyō-ku, Kyoto. The temple was probably founded by Wake no Kiyomaro (733–99) as part of a vow to save the country from the machinations of Dōkyō. Its original location is unclear. Later, during Kanmu's reign, it was moved to Takaosan and designated an official temple (*jōgakuji* 定額寺). At this time its name was changed from the original Jinganji 神願寺 to Jingoji 神護寺. It also served as the Wake clan temple. Besides the 802 Tendai meeting, it was the site of the Esoteric initiation Saichō performed after returning from China. In 812 it became the headquarters for Kūkai, and in 829 was formally given to him. It thus played a key role in the Wake family's patronage of the Tendai and Shingon Schools.

[30] Zengi (729–812) is said to have studied Sanron under Dōji 道慈 (d. 744). He later went to China. After his return he lived at Daianji, propagating Sanron teachings. He was in charge of the Takaosanji meeting.

[31] Shūen (d. 835) was from the Otani 小谷 family of Yamato. He studied Hossō under Senkyō 宣教 and Kenkei 賢憬. In 810 he was appointed *risshi* (*vinaya* master); in 812 he became *bettō* (administrator) of Kōfukuji, and in 827, was appointed *shōsōzu* (lesser supervisor) in the Office of Monastic Affairs (Sōgō 僧綱). He participated in the Takaosanji meeting, and later in Saichō's Esoteric initiations. In addition, he appears in the *Gakushō meichō* (*DZ* 1: 251) as the teacher of one of Saichō's *shanagō* (Esoteric Course) students, in fact, of the only *shanagō* monk who was still on Hiei in 817. Thus, relations between Shūen and Saichō appear to have been close for a long time.

Shūen also is said to have been on good terms with Kūkai. This claim is based on a passage in a letter written by Kūkai to Saichō in which Kūkai refers to a monk at Murōzan. While Andō Toshio claimed that the reference was to Shūen, noting that Shūen eventually died at a temple there, (Sonoda, *Saichō,* p. 403), Katsumata Shunkyō claimed it referred to Kenne 堅慧. See *Kōbō Daishi chōsaku zenshū,* ed. Katsumata Shunkyō, 3 vols. (Tokyo: Sankibō Busshorin, 1968–73) 3: 579. The issue is still unresolved, but Shūen does appear to have been deeply interested in the new developments in Buddhism typified by the Tendai and Shingon Schools.

The *Tōiki dentō mokuroku* (*BZ* no. 837) lists Shūen as the author of fourteen works on Hossō doctrine, indicating that he was one of the more prolific and important scholars of his time.

[32] No information on Saikō survives.

[33] Dōshō (756–816) was a well–known Hossō scholar.

[34] The *Fa hua hsüan i* or *The Inner Meaning of the Lotus Sūtra* (*T* no.1716) is an exposition of the overall meaning of the *sūtra.* The *Fa hua wen chü* (*T* no. 1718) is a textual commentary on the *Lotus Sūtra.* The *Mo ho chih kuan* (*T* no. 1911) concerns meditation and religious practice.

proposed schedule into disarray.

Saichō does not seem to have been invited to the lectures at first.[35] Probably he still was not known well enough to have been included. Wake no Hiroyo undoubtedly heard about Saichō from the monks who had attended the lectures on Mount Hiei the previous year,[36] and finally invited him the fourteenth day of the fourth month, almost three months after the retreat had begun. The many years which Saichō had devoted to the study of Tendai texts must have enabled him to make a strong and lasting impression at the lectures.

The interest of the Wake brothers and other members of the court in the Takaosanji lectures arose in part out of hopes that Tendai teachings might provide a bridge between the two preeminent schools of Japanese Buddhism at that time, the Hossō and the Sanron. These two schools had long been rivals in Nara. The competition between them had intensified when the court had designated Kyoto as the new capital, but had required the Buddhist establishment to remain in the old capital, Nara. The Hossō School had emerged as the dominant force on the

---

[35] The above account of the Takaosanji lectures differs from most traditional accounts in several ways. The first problem is determining when the retreat began. The date of the nineteenth of the first month for the invitation to the lecturers is considered by some to be the date the invitation was issued. However, I have followed Akamatsu Toshihide and Sonoda Kōyū here in taking it as the opening day of the lectures [DZ 5 (Bekkan): 7; Sonoda, Saichō, p. 478]. Many traditional accounts place the opening date for the lectures sometime in the seventh month, and thus maintain the position that Saichō was not invited after the other monks. Moreover, Saichō plays a central role in the lectures from the beginning in most traditional accounts. This interpretation is based on the passage in Saichō's invitation which states that Saichō will be the main figure in the retreat; this, however, is probably just a polite overstatement (Sonoda, Saichō, p. 479). The traditional account also implies that Saichō was the chief authority on Tendai. While Saichō was probably the best informed monk on Tendai in Japan, he was not the only monk who was acquainted with Tendai doctrine. In fact, there were probably a number of prominent monks in Japan who were interested in Tendai teachings at the time. Zengi and the other monks at the meeting, all of whom were Hossō and Sanron monks, effusively expressed their admiration of Tendai doctrines in memorials to Emperor Kanmu and the future Emperor Heizei [DZ 5 (Bekkan): 9–11, 105–7].

One of the best defenses of the traditional theory which gives Saichō a more central role in the retreat is bySuehiro Shōkei in Ninchū, Yakuchū Eizan Daishiden, trans. and annot. Honda Kōyū, with an appendix by Suehiro Shōkei (Hieizan: Goonki jimukyoku, 1917), appendix, pp. 11–16. In defending the traditional theory, Suehiro discusses in detail the problematic parts of the Eizan Daishiden, finally concluding that the author of the biography must have been mistaken. Sonoda's interpretation is based on a more literal reading of the text. Also see Nakao Shunpaku, Sange gakushōshiki josetsu, pp. 81–92, 381–391.

[36] Some scholars believe that the Wake brothers' patronage of Saichō was due to a connection between Saichō and their father, Kiyomaro; however, their claim is based on tenuous evidence. For example, see Yokota Ken'ichi, "Wakeshi to Saichō to Daianji to Hachimanjin" in Nihon kobunka ronkō, ed. Kashihara kōko kenkyūjo (Tokyo: Yoshikawa kōbunkan, 1970), pp. 415–16.

monastic scene. However, in 802 the court attempted to restore the balance of power between the various schools in Nara by requiring that they appear in equal strength at the Saishō-e (the annual lectures on the *Chin kuang ming ching* [*Suvarṇaprabhāsasūtra*]) and the Yuima-e (the annual lectures on the *Wei mo ching* [*Vimalakīrtinirdeśasūtra*]). Although the lectures may have been intended to bridge or ameliorate the differences between the various schools, in fact their major impact was to provide the spring board for Saichō's rise to eminence.[37]

---

[37] For a discussion of the rivalry between the Hossō and Sanron Schools in the early Heian period, see Hirai Shun'ei, "Heian Shoki ni okeru Sanron Hossō kakuchiku wo meguru shomondai," *Komazawa daigaku Bukkyō gakubu kenkyū kiyō* 37 (1979), 72–91.

CHAPTER FOUR
VOYAGE TO CHINA

Permission to Travel to China

The Takaosanji lectures were Saichō's first lectures away from Mount Hiei. Through them Saichō established relations with Wake no Hiroyo, his most important early supporter. With Hiroyo's support, he soon came to the attention of Emperor Kanmu. On the seventh day of the ninth month of 802, Hiroyo and Saichō discussed plans for propagating the Tendai School. The result was a petition to the court in which Saichō asked that two students be sent to study T'ien–t'ai in China. One would return to Japan after a short period of study and the other would stay in China longer. The request was immediately granted.

Two monks, Enki 圓基 and Myōchō 妙澄, were chosen to go. However, on the twelfth the Emperor let it be known that he actually wanted Saichō himself to go and study for a short period of time. Enki and Myōchō would both be long–term students. Exactly what became of these two monks is unclear. Enki did in fact travel to China, but because of an eye ailment he had to return to Japan early. Myōchō probably never went at all, but is mentioned in several of Saichō's letters to Kūkai.[1]

In his petition asking that students be sent to China,[2] Saichō claimed that the Tendai texts transmitted to Japan contained many copyist errors. In addition, a direct transmission from Chinese teachers to Japanese students was needed to insure the orthodoxy of the Tendai School in Japan. Saichō criticized both the Hossō and Sanron schools for being based on *śāstra* (commentaries), not on *sūtras* (the Buddha's words). Hossō and Sanron monks considered only the branches 末 of the Buddha's doctrines and neglected the roots 本. Tendai teachings, because they valued the *Lotus sūtra* above all other authorities, were not subject to this criticism. Thus even before he went to China, Saichō declared his intention to establish the Tendai School in Japan.

His criticism found a receptive ear at court. In late 803 an edict had been issued chiding Hossō and Sanron scholars for arguing. It

---

[1] *Eizan Daishden, DZ* 5 (*Bekkan*): 12; Enchin, *Gyōryakushō, BZ* 72:572a; *Dengyō Daishi shōsoku, DZ* 5: 452, 457.

[2] The petition is quoted in *Eizan Daishiden, DZ* 5 (*Bekkan*): 11–12.

ended with the warning that prospective monks must read the *sūtras,* especially the *Lo tusSūtra, Chin kuang ming ching(Suvarṇaprabhāsasūtra),* *Hua yen ching* (*Avatamsakasūtra*) and the *Nieh p'an ching* (*Mahāpari-nirvāṇasūtra*), as well as the *śāstras.* Anyone who read only the *śāstras,* to the detriment of the *sūtras,* was not to be initiated.[3]

Later Saichō also petitioned for, and was granted, permission to take along a novice named Gishin 義眞 as interpreter. Although Saichō could read Chinese, he could not speak it. Gishin had studied spoken Chinese under Jiken 慈賢 of Tōdaiji.[4] Unfortunately, no biography for Jiken exists; but even if Jiken were Chinese and Gishin were an able language student, oral communication still must have been a major problem for them in China.

Prince Ate 安殿, who would later rule as Emperor Heizei 平城 (r. 806–809), presented Saichō with two sets of the *Lotus* group of three *sūtras* 法華三部: the *Lotus sūtra, Wu liang i ching* and the *Kuan p'u hsien ching*) with the titles written in gold letters, and several hundred *ryō* of gold and silver to be used for expenses during his stay in China. These funds, supplemented by the aid he received from Chinese monk and government officials, were sufficient to meet his needs in China. One copy of the *sūtras* was taken to China and deposited in the Hsiu–ch'an–ssu 修禪寺 on Mount T'ien–t'ai. The other set was given to the library on Mount Hiei.[5] The court also allowed Saichō to take along an attendant.

Journey to China

Saichō first attempted to go to China in the third month of 803 with the offical mission to China. The ships were damaged by strong winds, however, and forced to return to Kyushu. Saichō spent the next year at Sōmonji 竈門寺 in Dazaifu, where he carved statues of Yakushi Nyorai (Bhaiṣajyaguru Buddha) for each of the four ships and read *sūtras* to pray for a safe journey. During this time he probably also met the monk Kūkai 空海 who was to go to China with the same mission. Kūkai was being sent with the expectation that he would remain in China for a prolonged period of time to study Esoteric Buddhism (Mikkyō). Saichō, on the other hand, was expected to return after a short period of study.

---

[3] *Ruijū kokushi,* fasc. 179, *KT* 6: 238).
[4] *Kenkairon engi, DZ* 1 :267, 289.
[5] Ibid., p. 268; *Eizan Daishiden, DZ* 5 (*Bekkan*): 15.

In the seventh month of the following year, the mission set sail from Kyushu. Kūkai was on the first ship with the chief envoy, Fujiwara no Kadonomaro 藤原葛野麻呂 (d. 818), and Saichō was on the second under Sugawara no Kiyogimi 菅原清公 (d. 832). Again strong winds arose and the ships were separated; two of them were lost. Saichō's ship finally arrived in Ming–chou 明州 (in northern Chekiang) on the first day of the ninth month. The official party departed immediately for the capital, Ch'ang–an. Saichō intended to travel directly to Mount T'ien–t'ai, headquarters of the T'ien–t'ai School. However, because he was too sick to travel, Saichō did not leave for ten lays. Meanwhile, Kūkai's boat had landed in Fu–chou 福州 (modern Fukien) and Kūkai had started on his way to Ch'ang–an. The two Japanese monks were not to meet in China.

Studies in China

On the twelfth, Saichō received a pass from the governor of Ming–chou, Ch'eng Shen–ts'e 鄭審則, permitting him to travel to Mount T'ien–t'ai. The governor also supplied him with a boat and porters.[6] He finally left on the fifteenth and arrived in T'ai–chou 台州 (in modern Chekiang) on the twenty–sixth.

In T'ai–chou Saichō met the governor, Lu Shun 陸淳.[7] The governor was very sympathetic to Saichō's mission and aided Saichō in a number of ways. Especially important was the introduction to the T'ien–t'ai monk Tao–sui 道邃 which the governor provided. About the same time, Lu shun had invited Tao–sui to lecture on the *Mo ho chih kuan* at the Lung–hsing–ssu 龍興寺[8] in T'ai–chou. It is unclear, however, when

---

[6] This document is included in *Kenkairon engi*, *DZ* 1:268. Little is known about Ch'eng Shen–ts'e.

[7] Lu Shun (d. 805) was a native of Wu–chün (in modern Kiangsu). His personal name was changed from Shin to Chih 質 to avoid conflict with the tabooed personal name of Emperor Hsien–tsung. His pen name was Yüan–chung 元沖. He studied the *Spring and Autumn Annals* under Chao–k'uang 趙匡 and tried to unify the three main commentaries on the *Spring and Autumn Annals* (*Tso chuan, Kung yang chuan,* and *Ku liang chuan*). He held various posts and was at one time tutor to the crown prince. Later, however, he was demoted to the post of governor of Hsin–chou and T'ai–chou, the position he held when Saichō arrived. The year Saichō returned to Japan, the crown prince succeeded to the throne as Emperor Hsien–tsung (r. 805–820) and recalled Lu Shun, his former tutor. But Lu Shun died before he could assume the new post. Lu Shun was the author of a number of books (Sonoda, *Saichō,* p. 401.).

[8] A Chung–hsing–ssu 中興寺 (Mid–dynasty Restoration Temple) was established in each province in 705 after the usurper. Empress Wu, was forced to abdicate. Because the name of the temples implied that the T'ang fortunes had been cut off during Empress Wu's reign, objections were made. As a result, in 707, the third year of the Shen–lung (Divine Dragon) era, the name was changed to Lung–hsing–ssu (Dragon Restoration Temple).

exactly Saichō met Tao–sui. Scholars have traditionally claimed that Saichō was introduced to Tao–sui the day he arrived in T'ai–chou and remained with him until the seventh day of the next month, a total of ten days, before leaving for Mount T'ien–t'ai. This account is based on the *Tendai hokkeshū denbōge* 天台法華宗傳法偈 (Verses on the Transmission of the Dharma in the Tendai Lotus School), a work which was almost certainly compiled much later.[9] Saichō may actually have journeyed directly to Mount T'ien–t'ai and met Tao–sui only after he had returned from the mountain and gone to the Lung–hsing–ssu.[10]

On Mount T'ien–t'ai[11] Saichō presented the various gifts he had brought from Japan to the temples. Besides the *sūtras* from Prince Ate, Saichō was also carrying quartz rosaries, a cedar statue of Suiten Bosatsu 水天菩薩 (Nāgavajra? Bodhisattva), a work on doctrinal disputes in Japan, and a record of the lectures given on Mount Hiei by monks from Nara in 802.[12] He probably discussed the contents of these last two works while in China. The instruction he received while discussing these works contributed to his defense of the Tendai position after his return to Japan.

Saichō's T'ien–t'ai Teacher: Tao–sui

Tao–sui is counted as the seventh patriarch of the T'ien–t'ai School; however, very little is known about him, not even the dates of his birth

---

As recipients of imperial patronage, the Lung–hsing Temples, were usually among the larger temples in a province. They were the model for Japan's Kokubunji system.

[9] *DZ* 5: 28. The *Denbōge* contains the most detailed chronology available of Saichō's stay in China. Ōkubo Ryōjun ("*Tendai hokkeshū denbōge* ni tsuite," *DDK*, pp. 115–130) has argued convincingly that the *Denbōge* was written sometime between the tenth and thirteenth centuries. Important discrepancies exist between the chronologies in the *Denbōge* and early authentic sources such as the *Eizan Daishiden*. Moreover, the *Denbōge* lineage of T'ien–t'ai masters differed from the lineage found in Saichō's *Kechimyakufu*. The roles of Tao–sui and Saichō are emphasized at the expense of Hsing–man and Gishin, and the honorifics used to refer to Saichō's teachers differ from those found in Saichō's authentic works. Finally, the *Denbōge* is not mentioned in early Tendai works such as Annen's 安然 (841?–889?) *Kyōji sōron* 教時諍論 (*T* no. 2395) and Renkō's 蓮鋼 (815?–880?) *Jōshūron* 定宗論 (*T* no. 2369). Among modern Japanese scholars, Ushiba Shingen has suggested that Eisai may have written both the *Denbōge* and *Kechimyakufu;* his argument, however, is weak ["Dengyō Daishi Saichō no zenbō sōjō ni tsuite," *IBK* 17 (1968) 250–53]. Shimaji Daitō (*Tendai kyōgakushi*, p. 341) also considered the *Denbōge* to be a later production. No scholar has considered the possibility that the work may be based on a text originally written by Saichō.

[10] Sonoda, *Saichō*, p. 481.

[11] Saichō's movements on Mount T'ien–t'ai are difficult to trace. Kasuga Reichi ("Dengyō Daishi no nittō ni tsuite," in *DDK*, pp. 317–20) attempted to located the temples which Saichō is said to have visited using old records of the T'ien–t'ai area. His research was only moderately successful.

[12] *Kenkairon engi, DZ* 1: 268.

and his death. The most detailed extant biography of him is only one page long, written by his disciple Kan–shu 乾淑 and included in Saichō's *Kenkairon engi*.[13] Later Chinese biographical works, such as the Sung dynasty Buddhist history, *Fo tsu t'ung chi* 佛祖統記, based their biographies of Tao–sui on Kan–shu's biography. The *Fo tsu t'ung chi* entry indicates that by the thirteenth century, Tao–sui's place in Chinese Buddhist history rested almost solely on his meeting with Saichō and Saichō's subsequent transmission of the T'ien–t'ai School from China to Japan.[14]

According to Kan–shu's biography, Tao–sui was born in Ch'ang–an. He served as an official when he was young, but soon abandoned his career as a bureaucrat to become a monk. He was ordained a monk when he was twenty–four and then thoroughly studied the *Ssu fen lü* precepts. Later he decided to study Mahāyāna doctrines. Consequently, he commenced copying Tz'u–en's *Fa hua hsüan tsan* 法華玄贊 (*T* no. 1723), a commentary on the *Lotus Sūtra* based on Fa–hsiang doctrines. However, he soon had a dream in which a monk advised him to study T'ien–t'ai teachings. Eventually he decided to abandon his copying project in order to travel in search of the T'ien–t'ai master Chan–jan 湛然 (711–782). While staying at the Fa–yün Temple 法雲寺 in Yang–chou for several weeks, he had another dream in which the same monk told him to hurry to Miao–le Temple 妙樂寺 in Ch'ang–chou because Chan–jan was already lecturing on the chapter on "Expedient Devices" of the *Lotus Sūtra*. Since this was one of the most important sections of the *sūtra,* Tao–sui resumed his journey and upon arriving at the Miao–le Temple, found that his dream had been correct. After studying with Chan–jan for five years, Tao–sui left to travel and lecture on Chih–i's three major works. He later settled on Mount T'ien–t'ai and became head monk of Hsiu–ch'an–ssu. He is said to have recited the Hīnayāna and Mahāyāna *prātimokṣa* (lists of precepts) and the *Lotus Sūtra* daily.

Tao–sui seems to have held orthodox Chinese T'ien–t'ai positions on monastic discipline and on doctrinal issues. However, his teachings on meditation may have varied from standard T'ien–t'ai practices. Chih–li 智禮 (960–1028), a Sung dynasty monk who tried to reform the T'ien–t'ai School, noted that Tao–sui's teaching on T'ien–t'ai meditation practices deviated from the orthodox position.[15] Chih–li's charge

---

[13] *DZ* 1: 273–75.
[14] *T* 49: 190a.
[15] Andō Toshio, *Tendaigaku ronshū* (Kyoto: Heirakuji shoten, 1975) p. 454.

is especially interesting when it is juxtaposed with Saichō's statement that Tao–sui taught him how to realize the three views in an instant (*isshin sankan* 一心三觀) through a single word.[16] This passage suggests that Tao–sui may have utilized Ch'an practices.

Saichō mentions Tao–sui in his writings primarily to prove that he had received a personal transmission of T'ien–t'ai teachings, but never quotes directly from Tao–sui's writings. Only one work which is unquestionably by Tao–sui survives, the *Mo ho chih kuan chi chung i i* 摩訶止觀記中異義.[17] Saichō brought this work, as well as commentaries on the *Wei mo ching* (*Vimalalakīrtinirdeśasūtra*) and the *Nieh–p'an ching* (*Mahāparinirvāṇasūtra*) back to Japan.[18] In addition, subcommentaries attributed to Tao–sui on Chan–jan's commentaries on Chih–i's three major works survive. Scholars disagree about whether the commentaries are by the Chinese T'ien–t'ai monk or a Japanese monk whose name was written with the same characters, Dōzui (d. 1157). Tokiwa Daijō and Ōkubo Ryōjun have offered convincing arguments for the thesis that the works are of Chinese origin, but the issue has still not been satisfactorily resolved.[19]

Further Studies

On the thirteenth day of the tenth month of 804, Saichō is said to have received a transmission in the Niu–t'ou 牛頭 (Ox Head) School of Ch'an from Hsiu–jan 脩然 of the Ch'an–lin–ssu (Meditation Grove Temple) on Mount T'ien–t'ai.[20] Nothing is known about Hsiu–jan, although there was a monk by this name who was a disciple of Ma–tsu Tao–i 馬祖道一 (709–788) of the Southern School of Ch'an. Whether the two men are the same is unclear.[21] The account of this transmission

---

[16] *Kenkairon, DZ* 1: 35 A similar statement is made by governor Lu shun (*BZ* 95: 231a). This passage later assumed great importance for Tendai advocates of oral transmissions (*kuden* 口傳). See Ōkubo Ryōjun, "Edan ryōryū homonchū no Dengyō Daishi," *DDK* (*Bekkan*), pp. 74–82.

[17] *Z* 2. 4. 2.

[18] *BZ* 95: 228–34.

[19] Tokiwa, *Zoku Shina Bukkyō no kenkyū* (Tokyo: Shunjūsha, 1941), pp. 131–202 and Ōkubo, *BZ* 97: 42–44, 277–79. The subcommentaries are contained in *BZ*, vols. 3, 4, and 37.

[20] *Kechimyakufu, DZ* 1:214–15. Chih–i stayed at the Ch'an–lin–ssu while on T'ien–t'ai. As its name suggests, it was long noted as a center for meditation. Ennin reported in an entry dated the 19th day of the intercalary month of 839, that 40 monks permanently lived there, and 70 lived there during summer retreats. See Ono Katsutoshi, *Nittō guhō junrei kōki no kenkyū,* 4 vols. (Tokyo: Suzuki gakujutsu zaidan, 1964–69) 1: 381–83.

[21] Ui Hakuju, *Nihon Bukkyō gaishi* (Tokyo: Iwanami shoten, 1951), p. 27.

in the *Kechimyakufu* is appended to a much longer passage concerning Gyōhyō's transmission of Northern School Ch'an to Saichō. The brevity of Saichō's account suggests that he did not attach much value to the Niu-t'ou transmission.

Saichō also received an Esoteric transmission from Wei-hsiang 惟象 at the Kuo-ch'ing-ssu 國淸寺 (Monastery for the Purification of the Empire) on Mount T'ien-t'ai during that same month.[22] The initiation, called the Daibutsuchōhō 大佛頂法, had long been practiced by at least some T'ien-t'ai monks. Chien-chen's disciple Ssu-t'o 思託 had performed a similar ceremony at the Japanese court.[23] The practice was a 'Mixed Esoteric' (*zōmitsu* 雜密) one and was usually performed to prevent calamities from occurring.[24] It also may have been connected with meditation practice.[25] Saichō brought back a *maṇḍala* and several works written in both Chinese and Sanskrit concerning the ceremony.[26]

This ceremony is representative of a type of Esoteric Buddhist ritual which flourished during the latter part of the T'ang dynasty. Over fifty works concerning varieties of *butsuchō* 佛頂 rituals were translated into Chinese. It was used for both worldly and spiritual objectives. The term *butsuchō* (*tathāgata-uṣṇiṣa*) refers to the protuberance on top of the Buddha's head, one of the thirty-two special

---

[22] No biography for Wei-hsiang survives. The Kuo-ch'ing-ssu was the central temple for the T'ien-t'ai School in China. Though planned by Chih-i, it was not built until after his death. In his travel diary, Ennin reported in the entry for the 19th day of the intercalary month in 839 that there were 150 monks permanently at the temple and that more than 300 monks participated in the summer retreats. After Saichō, many Japanese Tendai monks went to Kuo-ch'ing-ssu (Ono, *Kōki no kenkyū* 1: 381).

[23] *Nihon kōsōden yōbunshō*, fasc. 3, *BZ* 62: 52a.

[24] Japanese Esoteric Buddhism is often divided into the categories of *zōmitsu* and *junmitsu* 純密. *Junmitsu* or Pure Esoteric Buddhism refers to the Taizōkai 胎藏界 (Womb-realm) and Kongōkai 金剛界 (Diamond-realm) traditions and has connotations of being a more philosophic, less worldly type of Buddhism, more concerned with attaining enlightenment. The term is usually used in contrast with *zōmitsu* (Mixed Esoteric Buddhism), which refers to a less organized, less philosophic type of Esoteric Buddhism, more concerned with gaining benefits in this world. However, the meanings and the area defined by the terms may vary according to author. The terms themselves probably first appeared in the late Muromachi or early Edo period; but since both Saichō and Kūkai used similar terms, their use in regards to early Heian period Esoteric Buddhism seems appropriate. See Misaki Ryōshū, "Junmitsu to zōmitsu ni tsuite," *Indogaku Bukkyōgaku kenkyū* (hereafter cited as *IBK*) 15 (1966): 525–40.

[25] Shimizutani Kyōjun, *Tendai Mikkyō no seiritsu ni kansuru kenkyū* (Tokyo: Bun' ichi shuppansha, 1972), pp. 42–43; Mochizuki Shinkō, ed., *Bukkyō daijiten* (hereafter cited as *BD*), 2nd ed., 10 vols. (Tokyo: Sekai seiten kankō kyōkai, 1958–63), 4:3390; and Ono Genmyō, *Bussho kaisetsu daijiten* (hereafter cited as *BKD*), 2nd ed., 14 vols. (Tokyo: Daitō shuppansha, 1964–1978), 8: 456.

[26] *Taishūroku*, *BZ* 95: 230.

marks which distinguished a Buddha's body, This mark was idealized as representing the essence of the Buddha. Many of the works on *butsuchō* ceremonies describe light or various beings emanating from this mark.[27]

Saichō was still at Kuo–ch'ing–ssu on Mount T'ien–t'ai during the eleventh nonth. According to the *Denbōge,* after studying with Hsing–man for about a month, Saichō returned with Hsing–man to the Lung–hsing–ssu at T'ai–chou on the fifteenth. There he studied for about one–hundred thirty days under Tao–sui.[28] The *Denbōge* account must be questioned, however, due to an entry in the *Kenkairon engi* which notes that Gishin was ordained as a monk at the Kuo–ch'ing–ssu on the seventh day of the twelfth month.[29] Many scholars thus believe that Gishin and Saichō returned to Mount T'ien–t'ai. Since no corroborating evidence supporting the *Denbōge* account of Saichō's return to the Lung–hsing–ssu exists, Saichō and Gishin might have stayed on Mount T'ien–t'ai until the twelfth month. They thus probably spent much more time with Hsing–man than the thirty days which most traditioñal biographies claim.

Saichō's Forgotten Teacher Hsing–man

The tendency to downplay Hsing–man's role as a teacher has its origins in Saichō's lack of biographical information about Hsing–man. In the *Kechimyakufu* both teachers are given an equal place, but the entry for Tao–sui is much longer than that for Hsing–man, giving the impression that Tao–sui was the more influential of the two. The difference in treatment is probably due only to the difference in the amount of information Saichō brought back about each man. However, by Ennin's time, Tendai monks had already begun to ignore Hsing–man's role. This tendency continued until only Tao–sui was listed as Saichō's teacher. In the Kamakura period a new movement emerged in the Tendai School. Adherents of this movement held that man is already enlightened (*hongaku* 本覺 or 'original enlightenment') just as he is. In their efforts to demonstrate that the origins of their teaching could be traced back to China, they attributed them to Tao–sui. At the same time they resurrected Hsing–man and claimed that he had taught Saichō the inferior teachings which the *hongaku* group opposed. The *Denbōge*

---

[27] Misaki Ryōshū, "Butsuchōkei no mikkyō," in Yoshioka kanreki kinenkai, ed., *Dōkyō kenkyū ronshū* (Tokyo: Kokusho kankōkai, 1977) pp. 477–499.

[28] *Denbōge DZ* 5: 28–29.

[29] *Kenkairon engi, DZ* 1: 286–88.

was probably composed during this time, and thus included claims that Saichō spent much more time with Tao–sui than with Hsing–man.[30]

The small amount of reliable information that survives about Hsing–man is found in Saichō's *Kechimyakufu*.[31] Hsing–man, a native of Su–chou (in modern Kiangsu), was initiated when he was twenty and ordained as a monk when he was twenty–five. He studied the *Ssu fen lü* precepts for five years. In 768 he met Chan–jan and attended a number of his lectures on Chih–i's major works (*Tendai sandaibu*). At the time of Saichō's arrival in China, he was the head of the Fo–lung temple 佛隴寺 on Mount T'ien–t'ai. Hsing–man encouraged Saichō in his studies, giving him eighty–two fascicles of T'ien–t'ai works. He also told Saichō that Chih–i had predicted that a foreign monk would come to China in order to propagate T'ien–t'ai teachings in a country to the east of China.[32] Predictions such as this one probably helped foreign monks such as Saichō and Kūkai gain ready acceptance by Chinese monks. Hsing–man assiduously practiced religious austerities and authored a number of works.[33] He died around the year 823 when he was over eighty years old.[34]

Saichō referred to Hsing–man in order to stress the direct nature of the T'ien–t'ai transmission he had received. He did not quote any of Hsing–man's works.

Collecting and Copying Texts

Saichō apparently spent the next several months at Lung–hsing–ssu, participating in the copying of works, and studying under Tao–sui. Saichō's primary purpose in travelling to China had been to obtain accurate copies of T'ien–t'ai works. In this he was assisted by Governor Lu Shun who asked Tao–sui to assemble copyists to help with the work.[35] Hsing–man also aided Saichō by presenting him with eighty–two fascicles of important T'ien–t'ai works.[36] By the second month

---

[30] Ōkubo Ryōjun, "*Tendai Hokkeshū denbōge* ni tsuite," *DDK*, pp. 121–27; Sonoda, *Saichō*, pp. 481–82.

[31] *Kechimyakufu*, *DZ* 1: 229.

[32] *Eizan Daishiden*, *DZ* 5 (*Bekkan*): 17–18.

[33] At least three of Hsing–man's works survive: *Nieh p'an su ssu chi* 涅槃疏私記 (*Z* 1. 57. 5), *Liu chi i* 六卽義 (*Z* 2. 5. 4), and *T'ien t'ai ta i* 天台大意 (*BZ* 41: 186).

[34] Ono Katsutoshi, "Nittōsō Enshū Kenne to sono *Kechimyaku zuki*," *Ishihama Sensei koki kinen: Tōyōgaku ronsō*, pp. 106–7, note 1.

[35] *Kenkairon engi*, *DZ* 1: 270. According to the *Tendai Hokkeshū denbōge* (*DZ* 5: 28), Lu Shun contributed twenty copyists and four–thousand sheets of paper, abou one–half the amount required.

[36] *Eizan Daishiden*, *DZ* 5 (*Bekkan*): 17–18.

of 805, the copying project was completed. On the nineteenth Saichō compiled a bibliography of the works copied,[37] and Lu Shun certified it the following day.[38] In all Saichō brought back about 120 works in 345 fascicles from T'ai–chou.[39] Included were many works by T'ien–t'ai masters such as Chih–i 智顗 (538–597), Kuan–ting 灌頂 (561–632), Chan–jan 湛然 (711–782), Tao–sui and Ming–kuang 明曠. Twelve texts concerning Esoteric Buddhism were also copied. The most important of these texts was the *Su hsi ti chieh lo ching* 蘇悉地羯羅經 (*Susiddhikaramahātantrasādhanopāyikapaṭala*), a work which later was used as the basis of one of the three main traditions (*sanbu* 三部) of Tendai Esoteric Buddhism. Saichō listed the *Su hsi ti chieh lo ching* with several works on the precepts rather than with the works on Esoteric Buddhism, suggesting that he may not have valued it very highly as an Esoteric work.[40]

Five works concerning the precepts were listed in the *Taishūroku*. They were:

1. The *P'u sa chieh ching i chi* in two fascicles is a commentary on the second fascicle of the *Fan wang ching*. Although traditionally it has been attributed to Chih–i, in recent years its authorship has been questioned.[41]

2. The *Shou p'u sa chieh wen* is a one–fascicle ordination manual

---

[37] *Taishūroku, BZ* 95: 230.

[38] Ibid., p. 231.

[39] Sources differ on the number of works which Saichō brought back from T'ai–chou. According to a document in the *Kenkairon engi* (*DZ* 1: 276), Saichō brought back 102 works in 345 fascicles from T'ai–chou. The *Taishūroku* (*BZ* 95:230) includes a figure of 120 works in 345 fascicles in an almost identical passage. Finally, an actual count of the works in the bibliography yields 157 works in 406 fascicles. Ushiba Shingen has suggested that the *Taishūroku* may have been tampered with in order to make it compare more favorably with Kūkai's *Shōrai mokuroku* (*BZ* no. 877), but his theory has not met with widespread acceptance. See his article "Jōdoinhan *Dengyō Daishi shōrai mokuroku* ni tsuite," *Tendai gakuhō* (hereafter cited as *TG*), vols. 12 (1970) and 14 (1972). Misaki Ryōshū (*BZ* 99 [*Kaidai* 3]: 279–80) suggests that certain categories of works should not be counted in the total, and thus substantially reduces the discrepancies, bringing the total number of works closer to 120. He also points out errors in the attribution of certain texts.

[40] The *Su hsi ti chieh lo ching* corresponds to *T* no. 893. Kūkai also included it among works concerning the precepts. The reasons for considering it to be a text on the precepts are not clear. See Misaki Ryōshū, "Dengyō Daishi ni okeru mikkyō shisō no shomondai," *DDK* (*Bekkan*), pp. 482–83.

[41] *T* no. 1811. Satō Tetsuei [*Tendai Daishi no kenkyū* (Kyoto: Hyakkaen, 1960), pp. 412–15] noted that the work differed in a number of ways from works by Chih–i and that it was not mentioned in Chinese sources for a century after Chih–i's death, but arrived at no conclusion concerning the authorship of the text. Modern Tendai scholars have usually argued that the work is by Chih–i; see Takeda Chōten, "Shōmusakeshiki no kaitairon," *TG* 4 (1962): 12–16. It is still not clear whether the work is by Chih–i.

traditionally attributed to Hui–ssu 慧思 (515–577). Recent scholarship has shown that it is by Hui–wei 慧威 (fl. 7*th* century).[42]

3. The *Shou p'u sa chieh wen* is a one–fascicle ordination manual authored by Chan–jan. The *Wakokubon* ordination manual, attributed to Saichō, was based on it.[43]

4. The *P'u sa chieh ching* in one fascicle has not been identified due to the paucity of information concerning it contained in Saichō's bibliography.

5. The *Ssu fen lü ch'ao chi* in nineteen fascicles is a commentary on Daoxuan's *Ssu fen lü hsing shih ch'ao*. The work has tentatively been identified with Lang–jan's 朗然 (724–777) commentary which is quoted in the *Kenkairon*.[44] Lang–jan's commentary has not survived and the number of fascicles in it is unknown,[45] making the identification of it with the work listed in Saichō's bibliography questionable.

None of the works listed in the *Taishūroku* advocated abandoning or reducing the importance of the Hīnayāna precepts. The inclusion of a major text on the *Ssu fen lü* indicates that Saichō was still interested in the Hīnayāna precepts.

Investigation of the works Saichō wrote after his return to Japan has led some scholars to theorize that Saichō also brought back a number of works on the precepts which he did not include in his bibliographies. The most important of these is Ming–kuang's commentary on the *Fan wang ching* written in 777.[46] If Saichō did not bring it back with him, it is difficult to imagine how he could have obtained it after returning to Japan.[47]

While studying under Tao–sui, Saichō compiled a list of ten questions, the *Tendaishū miketsu* 天台宗末決 (Problems of the Tendai School).[48]

---

[42] *Z* 2.10.1. Taira Ryōshō ["Den–Eshi–hon *Jubosatsukaigi* ni tsuite," *Taishō daigaku kenkyū kiyō* 40 (1955): 1–36] has convincingly demonstrated that this manual is by Hui–wei.

[43] *JZ* 15: 872–78. The *Jubosatsukaigi* 授菩薩戒儀 or *Wakokubon* 和國本, attributed to Saichō, is found in *DZ* 1: 303–334.

[44] *DZ* 1:80; and Sonoda, *Saichō*, p. 48. Daoxuan's work corresponds to *T* no. 1804.

[45] Tokuda Myōhon, *Risshū bunken mokuroku* (Kyoto: Hyakkaen, 1974), p. 21.

[46] *T* no. 1812. This work is discussed in Chapter 12.

[47] Taira Ryōshō, "Myōkōsen *Tendai bosatsukaisho* ni tsuite," *TG* 10 (1968): 108.

[48] *DZ* 5: 41–47. This document is considered to be authentic by most authorities. It should not be confused with such works as the *Zaitō mondō* 在唐問答 (*DZ* 5: 158) which have a similar format, but clearly date from the Kamakura or Muromachi periods. The *Tendaishū miketsu* has not yet received the study it warrants, but useful comments can be found in: Tajima Tokuon, s. v. *Tōketsu*, *BKD* 8: 221; Nakao Shunpaku, *Nihon Shoki Tendai no kenkyū* (Kyoto: Nagata bunshōdō, 1973), pp. 295–96; and Asai Endō, *Jōko Nihon Tendai hōmon shisōshi* (Kyoto: Heirakuji shoten, 1973), pp. 61, 70–72, 133–35, 159.

The questions focussed mainly on Saichō's study of Chih-i's *Mo ho chih kuan,* but questions were also raised concerning Chih-i's *Fa hua hsüan i, Fa hua wen chü,* and *Ching ming hsüan su* 淨名玄疏, as well as the *Chan ch'a ching* 占察經.[49] They indicated that Saichō was especially interested in the classification and comparison of the various teachings in Buddhism (*kyōhan*). Saichō's questions concerned such issues as how the practitioner progresses through the stages of the path to enlightenment, the distinctions between those with sharper and duller faculties, and the differences between the three vehicles. Saichō was also concerned with the differences between the Tendai and Kegon positions on the four-vehicle classification, and with comparisons of the concepts of ideation-only (*yuishiki* 唯識), mind-only (*yuishin* 唯心), and one-mind (*isshin* 一心). These problems were typical of those debated by Japanese monks at this time, and foreshadow some of the issues Saichō would later write about in his debates with Tokuitsu.[50] Tao-sui's answers represented the orthodox Tendai position.

The Fan Wang Ching Ordination

On the second day of the third month, Saichō and Gishin, together with twenty-seven Chinese monks, received the Perfect Teaching (*engyō*) bodhisattva precepts (*bosatsukai*) from Tao-sui at the Lung-hsing-ssu.[51] The *Fan wang* ordination which Saichō received from Tao-sui was typical of bodhisattva ordinations performed in both China and Japan during the eighth century.[52] These ordination ceremonies were conferred on monks, nuns, and lay believers in order to encourage them to live their lives in accordance with Mahāyāna ideals. Bodhisattva ordinations were never used to confer the status of being a novice, monk or nun on a person; those statuses could be conferred only by initiations or full ordinations (*upasaṃpadā*) using the *Ssu fen lü* precepts. The bodhisattva precepts were viewed by monks and nuns as the culmination of a series of *Ssu fen lü* initiations and ordinations.

---

[49] The last two works correspond to *T* nos. 1777 and 839. The *Chan ch'a ching* is probably a Chinese work (Tajima Tokuon, s. v. *Senzatsu zennaku gōhōkyō, BKD* 6: 329).

[50] See Chapter 8 for a discussion of the debates.

[51] *Kechimyakufu, DZ* 1: 236.

[52] The development of the bodhisattva precepts in China is a complex topic which I plan to discuss in a subsequent study. For a description of how Chinese monks used the *Fan wang* precepts in ordinations earlier in this century, see Holmes Welch, *The Practice of Chinese Buddhism* (MA: Harvard University Press, 1967) pp. 285–96.

The *Fan wang* ordination which Saichō and Gishin received from Tao–sui was obviously very different from the purely Mahāyāna ordinations which Saichō proposed near the end of his life.[53] In a purely Mahāyāna ordination, a monk would be ordained with the *Fan wang* precepts rather than the *Ssu fen lü* precepts. Gishin had received the Hīnayāna ordination only three months earlier at one of the most important T'ien–t'ai temples in China. At least one of the monks participating in Gishin's ordination, Wen–chü 文舉 (760–842), was a scholar of the *Ssu fen lü,* as well as of the *Lotus Sūtra.*[54] Tao–sui himself had taken the Hīnayāna precepts, and no record exists of him objecting to Gishin's *Ssu fen lü* ordination though he was not present at it. Thus nothing indicates that Saichō's later advocacy of using solely the bodhisattva precepts to ordain monks was based on the ordination from Tao–sui. The monks on T'ien–t'ai probably held a position close to that of T'ien–t'ai masters such as Chan–jan and Chien–chen (Jap. Ganjin).[55] They probably had no problem reconciling the differences between the *Ssu fen lü* and *Fan wang* precepts. The *Ssu fen lü* precepts were to be followed with a Mahāyāna mind. Moreover, Saichō did not claim that his concept of the bodhisattva precepts came from Tao–sui. He included the documents pertaining to Gishin's Hīnayāna ordination in the *Kenkairon engi.*[56] When Saichō mentioned the *Fan wang* ordination which he had received from Tao–sui in the *Kechimyakufu,* it was to prove that he was qualified to ordain others. At the same time, Saichō conveniently overlooked the radical differences between the ordination he had received from Tao–sui and his own interpretation of the bodhisattva precepts.

Having accomplished his primary purpose of obtaining accurate copies of T'ien–t'ai works, Saichō returned to Ming–chou 明州. The Japanese mission's main ship had landed in Fu–chou 福州, however, and was not brought to Ming–chou until the first day of the fourth month. About one and one–half months remained before the ships would be ready to return to Japan. Saichō was to devote this time mainly to obtaining Esoteric texts and initiations. His permit to continue his travels, issued by the Chinese authorities on the sixth day of the fourth month, states that he was going to the Lung–hsing–ssu and Fa–

---

[53] See Chapter 8.
[54] Sonoda, *Saichō,* p. 425.
[55] Tsuchihashi Shūkō, *Kairitsu no kenkyū* (Kyoto: Nagata bunshōdō, 1980), pp. 968–990.
[56] *Kenkairon engi, DZ* 1: 286–89.

hua–ssu 法華寺 in Yüeh–chou to search for works he had not yet been able to copy.[57] The journey was about ninety kilometers each way.

Esoteric Buddhism in the Tien-t'ai School Before Saichō

Before discussing Saichō's Esoteric initiations in Yüeh-chou 越州, the relations between T'ien-t'ai and Esoteric Buddhism in China at this time must be considered. Saichō's earlier Esoteric initiation by Wei-hsiang indicates that at this time T'ien-t'ai monks were performing Esoteric ceremonies even in the Kuo-ch'ing-ssu, the headquarters of the T'ien-t'ai sect. Indeed, even earlier, Chih-i had utilized a number of zōmitsu Esoteric elements in his four types of meditation 四種三昧. He advocated the use of dhāraṇī in ceremonies to cure disease, extend the lifespan, and expiate sins. By Chan-jan's time, the rise of Pure Esoteric Buddhism (junmitsu) had begun to influence the T'ien-t'ai School. Chan-jan is known to have met one of Amoghavajra's students, Han-kuang 含光, and to have discussed Esoteric practices at times. Esoteric Buddhism did not occupy a central place in the interests of either Chih-i or Chan-jan. However both T'ien-t'ai and junmitsu Esoteric Buddhism were major interests of I-hsing 一行 (683–727).[58]

I-hsing had been trained in T'ien-t'ai at the Yü-ch'üan-ssu 玉泉寺 in Ching-chou (modern Hopei, Tang-yang-hsien). This temple had been established by Chih-i, and was the site of the lectures which were later edited into the *Mo ho chih kuan* and *Fa hua hsüan i*. While the temples on Mount T'ien-t'ai languished after Chih-i's death, Yü-ch'üan-ssu became the center of much activity. Its Buddhism was especially famous for its syncretism. T'ien-t'ai monks studied Esoteric Buddhism, the *Ssu fen lü*, Ch'an and other traditions.[59] Later when the Mount T'ien-t'ai temples rose to prominence, they were surely influenced by the syncre-tism of Yü-ch'üan-ssu scholarship. Saichō, consequently, was able to

---

[57] Ibid., pp. 277–78. No information is available on the Fa–hua–ssu.

[58] I–hsing is often cited as a forerunner to Saichō because he studied Tendai, Esoteric Buddhism, Zen and Ritsu, the same traditions in which Saichō was interested during his stay in China. Saichō certainly gave I–hsing an important place in the *Kechimyakufu* (*DZ* 2: 238–242). However, I–hsing's position on the precepts was quite different from Saichō's position on the *Fan wang* precepts. The most thorough research on I–hsing is Osabe Kazuo's *Ichigyō zenji no kenkyū* (Kobe: Kobe shōka daigaku gakujutsu kenkyūkai, 1963). Osabe argues that I–hsing was not as interested in combining Tendai and Esoteric doctrines as Saichō and others believed (pp. 50–65, 181–196).

[59] Other monks who had connections with Yü–ch'üan–ssu include Heng–ching 恒景 (634–712) who served as preceptor at Chien–chen's ordination, and Shen–hsiu 神秀 (d. 706), patriarch of Northern School Ch'an. The most thorough research on Yü–ch'üan–ssu is by Sekiguchi Shindai, *Tendai shikan no kenkyū* (Tokyo: Iwanami shoten, 1969), pp. 185–205.

obtain initiations into Esoteric Buddhism, Ch'an and the *Fan wang* precepts, as well as in T'ien-t'ai during his stay on Mount T'ien-t'ai. After Saichō's death, his Japanese successors carried on a dialogue with Chinese T'ien-t'ai monks concerning the proper classification of the Esoteric Buddhist *sūtra*, the *Ta jih ching* 大日經.[60]

Saichō's interest in Esoteric Buddhism was not accidental. Before he went to China, he had studied I-hsing's commentary on the *Ta jih ching*.[61] Probably on the basis of these studies, he asked Enchō to perform an Esoteric ritual, the *Gobutsuchōhō* 五佛頂法.[62] Although the date of the service is not known, it was performed in Japan prior to Saichō's return from China. According to a court document issued in 805 attesting to Saichō's studies, before Saichō travelled to China, he "sought out Esoteric practices, and yearned for the ways of the Tendai patriarchs."[63] Finally, in a letter to Kūkai, Saichō mentioned that before going to China he had carved images of the Eleven-faced Kannon and the Thousand-armed Kannon, both Esoteric deities.[64] Saichō's interest in Esoteric Buddhism was well established by the time he went to China. Thus it is not surprising to find him actively seeking out Esoteric initiations in China.

The Esoteric Initiations from Shun-hsiao

On the eighteenth of the fourth month, Saichō and Gishin received

---

[60] *T* no. 848, *Mahāvairocana* (*abhisambodhivikurvitādhiṣṭhānavaipulyasūtra*).

[61] Enchin, *Dainichikyō gishaku mokuroku* (dated 884), *BZ*, 1st ed., 26: 701. Ōyama Kōjun ("Dengyō Daishi no Mikkyo ni tsuite," *DDK*, p. 160) believes that Saichō began his study of the text in 797.

[62] *Denjutsu isshinkaimon*, *DZ* 1: 638. According to the *Ruijū kokushi* (*KT* 6: 228), Saichō ordered Enchō to perform the *Gobutsuchō* ceremony for Emperor Kanmu during the period that Saichō was in China. However, Misaki Ryōshū has questioned the accuracy of the *Ruijū kokushi* passage ["Dengyō Daishi Saichō no mikkyō shisō," *Firosofia* 56 (1969): 62–63]. Mizukami Bungi has examined several descriptions of the ceremony and indicated a number of discrepancies among them, but finally concluded that the ceremony did occur ["Dengyō Daishi Saichō no mikkyō shuhō shiryō ni kansuru ichi ni no kōsatsu," *TG* 18 (1975): 151–53; and "Shoki taimitsu ni okeru gobutsuchōhō," *IBK* 53 (1978): 136–37].

The content of this ceremony is difficult to determine, but it was probably similar to the *daibutsuchō* ceremony Saichō learned from Wei–hsiang on Mount T'ien–t'ai. The *gobutsuchō* ceremony involved a *maṇḍala* with Buddhas in the four directions and center. This ceremony was particularly appropriate for this occasion because the central figure was probably *ichiji butsuchō rinnō* 一字佛頂輪王, a universal ruler (*cakravartin*) figure who could easily be identified with Emperor Kanmu (Mizukami, ibid., and Misaki Ryōshū, "Butsuchōkei no mikkyō," in *Dokyō kenkyū ronshū*, p. 484).

[63] *Eizan Daishiden*, *DZ* 5 (*Bekkan*): 23. The translation of the passage quoted here is by Stanley Weinstein, "The Beginnings of Esoteric Buddhism in Japan: The Neglected Tendai Tradition," *Journal of Asian Studies* 34 (1974): 182.

[64] *DZ* 5: 451–52.

Esoteric initiations from Shun-hsiao 順曉 at a mountain temple east of Ching-hu 鏡湖 in Yüeh-chou.[65] In the Esoteric Buddhist tradition, special initiation ceremonies were performed before a person could receive certain teachings. The ceremony would vary in accordance with the teaching and the degree of mastery of the student. The contents of the initiations which Saichō received from Shun-hsiao have long been the subject of much controversy. Since Kūkai had based his Shingon philosophy on the Pure Esoteric (*junmitsu*) Kongōkai and Taizōkai *maṇḍalas*,[66] Tendai scholars have long wanted to claim that Saichō had received these two transmissions (*ryōbu* 兩部) while in China, so that the Tendai School could compete effectively with Kūkai's Shingon School. In the *Kenkairon*[67] and the *Kechimyakufu*,[68] both submitted in 820, Saichō made exactly such an assertion. His claim, however, has been criticized by both Shingon monks and modern scholars. The Diamond and Womb Realm *maṇḍalas* were probably not combined into a single system until the time of Amoghavajra (705–774).[69] Amoghavajra and his followers practiced mainly in the capital, Ch'ang-an, where

---

[65] *Kenkairon engi DZ* 5: 277–78. Ushiba ["Jōdoin *Dengyō Daishi shōrai mokuroku* ni tsuite," *TG* 14 (1972): 88] has made an unsuccessful attempt to identify the temple. No biography of Shun-hsiao survives.

[66] The Kongōkai 金剛界 and Taizōkai 胎藏界 *maṇḍalas* are the two major graphic representations in East Asian Esoteric Buddhism. The Kongōkai *maṇḍala* is based on the *Chin kang ting ching* 金剛頂經 (*T* no. 865–866, *Vajraśekharasūtra*). The name Kongōkai (Skt. Vajradhātu) means 'Diamond Realm' and refers to the wisdom of Mahāvairocana, which is indestructible like a diamond and can cut through all delusions to lead sentient beings to enlightenment.

The Taizōkai 胎藏界 *maṇḍala* is based on the *Ta jih ching* (*T* no. 848, *Mahāvairocanābhisambodhivikurvitādhiṣṭhānavaipulyasūtra*). The name Taizōkai (Skt. Garbhadhātu) means 'Womb Realm' and refers to the potential within all sentient beings to realize Buddhahood. The compassion of Mahāvairocana protects and nurtures this potential just as a mother nurtures a child in her womb or a lotus blossom nourishes and protects its seeds.

[67] *Kenkairon, DZ* 1:35.

[68] *Kechimyakufu, DZ* 1:237–44.

[69] Monks have long disagreed about the date at which the *ryōbu* tradition emerged. Some have argued that Śubhakarsiṃha (637–735), translator of the *Ta jih ching*, and Vajrabodhi (671–741), translator of the *Chin kang ting ching*, initiated each other (*konzengoju* 金善互授) into their respective traditions. This theory does not appear until the middle of the ninth century, a century after the two men had died, however, and thus seems questionable. Today many scholars would agree that the *ryōbu* tradition appeared at the time of Amoghavajra, thirty years after Vajrabodhi's death. Matsunaga Yūkei [*Mikkyō no rekishi*, Sāra sōsho no. 19 (Kyoto: Heirakuji shoten, 1969), pp. 146–47] has suggested that Amoghavajra valued *Chin kang ting ching* teachings above *Ta jih ching* teachings. The integration of the two traditions into a harmonious system in which neither was considered to be superior to the other (*ryōbu funi* 兩部不二) may not have occurred until the time of Kūkai's teacher Hui-kuo (746–805). Hui-kuo conferred only Diamond or Womb Realm initiations on most of his disciples. Kūkai and a few other prized disciples were the only monks privileged to receive both initiations.

Kūkai went to study. At the time of Saichō's arrival in China, Amoghavajra's teachings probably had only begun to spread to the provinces where Saichō studied.[70]

Saichō's claim that he received the Diamond and Womb Realm initiations from Shun-hsiao can be examined by referring to several documents dating from Saichō's study in China. These documents, written while Saichō was still in China, antedate by fifteen years the claims in the *Kenkairon* and *Kechimyakufu* that Saichō received the dual (*ryōbu*) initiations from Shun-hsiao. The earlier documents thus reflect Saicho's understanding of the initiations he received from Shun-hsiao before he was influenced by Kūkai's teachings. The following investigation of these documents indicates that at first Saichō did not consider the initiations from Shun-hsiao to be a dual initiation. In fact, Saichō probably only became aware of the importance of the *ryōbu* tradition after he had returned to Japan and had begun his association with Kukai.

Saichō's bibliography of the works he brought back from Yüeh-chou, the *Esshūroku,* describes the initiation ceremony as being based on a five-part *maṇḍala* and consecration (*gobu kanjō mandara* 五部灌頂曼陀羅).[71] A document describing the initiation included in the *Kenkairon engi* portrays it as involving a *maṇḍala* with thirty-seven honored ones (*sanjūshichi son* 三十七尊).[72] Both of these descriptions indicate that the initiation was of the Diamond Realm (Kongōkai) variety. In addition, the only Esoteric works listed in the *Esshūroku* which are not mixed Esoteric (*zōmitsu*) texts are several with the terms *sanjūshichi son* (thirty-seven honored ones) or *juhachie* 十八會 (eighteen assemblies) in their titles. These titles also suggest that Saichō received a Diamond Realm initiation from Shun-hsiao.

Saichō did not bring back a copy of Amoghavajra's translation of the *Chin kang ting ching* 金剛頂經,[73] the most important *sūtra* of the Diamond Realm group. Although an older translation of this *sūtra* by Vajrabodhi[74] existed in Nara, Saichō still would probably have brought back the newer translation if he had been able to see and copy it. Later, in 812, Saichō had to ask Kūkai to loan him Amoghavajra's translation

---

[70] Saichō's bibliographies indicate that at most he only brought back three one–fascicle works translated by Amoghavajra. See Misaki Ryōshū, "Dengyō Daishi no Mikkyō shisō," *Firosofia* 56: 64.

[71] *BZ* 95: 233b–c.

[72] *DZ* 1: 279, 290.

[73] *T* no. 866, *Vajraśekharasūtra.*

[74] *T* no. 865.

of the *sūtra*.[75] Thus the Diamond Realm initiation conferred by Shun-hsiao was probably of an earlier type than that transmitted by Amoghavajra.

A short description of the initiation received from Shun-hsiao which appears in the *Kenkairon engi* document complicates attempts to identify it as a Diamond Realm transmission.[76] The initiation consisted of three levels of *shitsuji* 悉地 (attainments or powers), higher, middle and lower. A five-syllable *dhāraṇī* was given for each level. This formula has been identified as one found in the *San chung hsi ti p'o ti yü i kuei* 三種悉地破地獄儀軌 (Manual on the Ceremony for Escaping [the Torments of] Hell Through the Three Attainments).[77] This work, in turn, alludes to the *Su hsi ti ching* 蘇悉地經, a *sūtra* which is of the same family as the *Ta jih ching*.[78] By 834 the *Su hsi ti ching* was sufficiently popular in China to be ranked equal to the *Ta jih ching* and the *Chin kang ting ching,* thus forming a system of three interrelated works (*sanbu* 三部).[79] Tendai Esoteric Buddhism (Taimitsu 台密) adopted this system while Kūkai's Shingon School retained its adherence to the dual (*ryōbu*) form of Esoteric Buddhism based on the *Ta jih ching* and *Chin kang ting ching*. Thus if Saichō's initiation from Shun-hsiao consisted in part of a *Su hsi ti ching* initiation, it would indicate that the Taimitsu triple (*sanbu*) system had its origins in the initiations which Saichō received from Shun-hsiao.

The *San chung hsi ti p'o ti yü i kuei* on which Shun-shiao's initiation may have been based has been identified with four different works; three of them are said to have been translated by Śubhakarasiṃha.[80] In fact, they were probably written by Chinese monks sometime during the period after Amoghavajra (d. 774).[81] These works are collectively called

---

[75] *DZ* 5: 454–55. The letter is dated, but the timing of the letter is strange, as Saichō is said to have visited Kūkai the very next day.

[76] Misaki ("Dengyō Daishi Saichō no Mikkyō shisō," *Firosofia* 56: 52) notes that the *maṇḍala* used in the ceremony differs from that used in the Tendai School after Ennin and from that used by Hui-kuo and Kūkai.

[77] *T* no. 893, *Susiddhikaramāhatantrasādhanopāyikapaṭala*.

[78] *T* no. 848.

[79] Matsunaga, *Mikkyō no rekishi*, pp. 147–48. The 834 date is based on a passage in Hai-yün's 海雲 *Liang pu ta fa hsiang ch'eng shih tzu fu fa chi* 兩部大法相承師資付法記, *T* 51: 786a.

[80] *T* nos. 905–7 are attributed to Śubhakarasiṃha. The name of the supposed translator of *T* no. 899 is unknown. The attribution of these works to Śubhakarasiṃha may help explain some of the problems with Shun-hsiao's lineage.

[81] Osabe Kazuo, *Tōdai Mikkyōshi zatsukō* (Kobe: Kobe shōka daigaku gakujutsu kenkyūkai, 1971), p. 200. Scholars have not reached a consensus concerning which of these works Shun-hsiao might have used. Tajima Tokuon (s. v. *Birushana betsugyōkyōshō, BKD*

called *P'o ti yü i kuei* 破地獄儀軌 (Manuals on Escaping [the Torments] of Hell). The works borrow from a number of sources. They are set in a world in which Birushana Butsu[82] manifests myriads of Shakamuni (Śākyamuni) Butsu, a description which shows the influence of the *Hua yen ching* and *Fan wang ching*. Furthermore, the *P'o ti yü i kuei* manuals consist of elements from the Womb Realm, Diamond Realm and mixed Esoteric works, as well as from Taoist works. Some scholars have maintained that the manuals represent an attempt to further develop *ryōbu* thought.[83] If those scholars are correct, Saichō's claim to have received a dual initiation would have some basis. However, the type of *ryōbu* initiation described in the *P'o ti yü i kuei* is still very different from that used by Kūkai.

Later events in the Tendai School indicate that either Saichō or his disciples did not completely understand the initiation from Shun-hsiao. Although the *san chung hsi ti* (three attainments) initiation was transmitted to other Japanese Tendai monks by Saichō, both Enchin 圓珍 (814–891) and Henjō 遍照 (817–890) expressed doubts about the text upon which the initiation was based. The *san chung hsi ti* were not clearly identified as being of *Su hsi ti ching* origins until Annen 安然 (841–889?) noted their similarity to formulas found in the *P'o ti yu i kuei*.[84] Since none of the works concerning the *P'o ti yü i kuei* ritual are found in the bibliographies of works which Saichō brought back from China, the identification of the Shun-hsiao initiation with that found in the *P'o ti yü i kuei* is questionable.

The difficulty of identifying the three types of attainments which made up the Shun-hsiao initiation can be further illustrated by investigating a similar term. In the previously mentioned *Kenkairon engi* documents,[85] Shun-hsiao is called the transmitter of the *sanbu sanmaya* 三部三昧耶 (three vows or symbols). This term probably refers to the three parts of the initiation: the higher, middle and lower attainments

---

9: 148) argues that *T* no. 899 was used. In contrast, Nasu Seiryū ("Dengyō Daishi shoden no Mikkyō," *DDK*, pp. 1009–17) extensively analyzes the ceremony using a number of sources including *T* no. 905, but not *T* no. 899.

[82] The manner in which Vairocana's (or Mahāvairocana's) name is transliterated into Chinese plays an important role in Tendai thought. Consequently, his name has been left in its Japanese form, Birushana or Rushana, in this study.

[83] Nasu, "Dengyō Daishi shoden no Mikkyō," p. 1016. However, Osabe (*Tōdai Mikkyōshi*, p. 201) discounts the importance of *ryōbu* influence on the work.

[84] Annen, *Taizōkai daihō taijuki*, fasc. 5, quoted in Misaki, "Dengyō Daishi Saichō no Mikkyō shisō," *Firosofia* 56: 63. Enchin is discussed on p. 48 of the same article.

[85] *DZ* 1: 279, 291.

(*san chung hsi ti*). The *Su hsi ti ching* has three main divisions: *Butsubu* (Buddha), *Rengebu* (Lotus), and *Kongōbu* (Diamond). The Diamond division would explain the performance of the initiation on a Diamond Realm type of platform. Another interpretation regards the phrase as a reference to the *sanbu* (three traditions) of Taimitsu, consisting of the Diamond Realm (Kongōkai) based on the *Chin kang ting ching*, the Womb Realm (Taizōkai) based on the *Ta jih ching*, and the Soshitsuji based on the *Su hsi ti ching*.[86] However, these traditions were probably not organized into a group of three by this time. A third interpretation identifies the term as referring to the three divisions (*sanbu*) of the Womb Realm (Taizōkai) transmission.[87] This interpretation is probably based on the lineage given in the document, which is in fact a Womb Realm lineage.

The arguments that Saichō may have received a Womb Realm initiation deserve further consideration. The *Esshūroku* bibliography contains no works belonging to the Womb Realm (Taizōkai) tradition.[88] This lack can perhaps be explained by the hurried character of Saichō's trip. He surely did not have time to copy all the works he would have liked. The initiation itself was performed in haste, with the required implements only being assembled on the morning of the initiations. Saichō bought them at considerable trouble and expense.[89] In addition, Saichō was aware of the Taizōkai works available in Nara and thus might not have felt as much need to copy them as to copy Diamond Realm (Kongōkai) works.

As is shown above, the phrase *sanbu sanmaya* (three vows or symbols) found in the *Kenkairon engi* document is too vague to indicate that Saichō received a Womb Realm initiation. However, the lineage given in that document does provide some evidence. Beginning with Śubhakarasiṃha, one of the translators of the *Ta jih ching*, the transmission continues on to I-lin 義林 and then on to Shun-hsiao.[90] (See Chart 1.) The two figures, I-lin and Shun-hsiao, diminish the credibility of the

---

[86] Shimizutani Kyōjun ("Dengyō Daishi no sōjō ni kanren shite," *DDK*, pp. 592–93) attributes this opinion to Ono Katsutoshi. Also see Suehiro, *Yakuchū Eizan Daishiden*, p. 43.

[87] Shimizutani, "Dengyō Daishi no sōjō," pp. 592–93; and Sonoda, *Saichō*, p. 422.

[88] Annen attempted to compensate for the absence of the *Ta jih ching* and other works in Saichō's bibliographies by claiming that Saichō, in fact, had brought them back from China. See Annen, *Shoajari Shingon Mikkyō burui sōroku*, *BZ* 95: 139–58; and Nasu, "Dengyō Daishi shoden no Mikkyō," *DDK*, pp. 1026–29.

[89] A letter describing the hurried efforts to assemble the needed materials is included in the *Kenkairon engi*. *DZ* 1: 278–79.

[90] Ibid., pp. 279–280, 291.

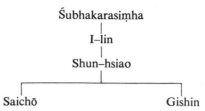

Chart 1. Lineage for the initation from Shun–hsiao based on the *Kenkairon engi*.

lineage. Nothing is known about either man. Their names do not appear in any T'ang Dynasty documents. Nor does Saichō give any details concerning their doctrinal positions or the transmission of their teachings. The lineage is thus too vague to serve as conclusive proof that Saichō received a Womb Realm initiation from Shun-hsiao.[91] In fact, the lineage as it stands could also refer to an early form of Diamond Realm (Kongōkai) ceremony, since Śubhakarasiṃha is known to have translated an early Kongōkai work which mentioned a *maṇḍala* with thirty-seven honored figures.[92]

Fifteen years later, in the *Kechimyakufu,* Saichō augmented the lineage by claiming that Śubhakarasiṃha received the teaching directly from Birushana and then granted the teaching to both I-lin and I-ṃ hsing. [93] (See Chart 2.) I-hsing aided Śubhakarasiṃha in the translation of the *Ta jih ching* and in writing a commentary on the *sūtra,* the *Ta jih ching i shih*[94] 大日經義釋. This lineage clearly presents a Womb Realm (Taizōkai) transmission. The addition of the famous monk I-hsing also helped compensate for the obscurity of I-lin and Shun-hsiao. The change in the lineage indicates that Saichō's view of the initiation from Shun-hsiao was evolving. The *Kechimyakufu* lineage was used to support his claim that he had received the dual (*ryōbu*) initiation in China.

The foregoing discussion has examined claims that Saichō received Womb Realm, Diamond Realm, and *Su hsi ti* initiations from Shun–

---

[91] Matsunaga Yūkei, *Mikkyō no sōjōsha* (Kyoto: Hyōronsha, 1973), Tōyōjin no kōdō to shisō, no. 3, p. 246. The lineage has long been criticized by Shingon monks. See Sasaki Kentoku, "Kōbō Daishi no *Goyuigō* wo utagaute Jungyō Ajari no koto ni oyobu," *Nihon Bukkyōgaku kyōkai nenpō* 12 (1940): 129.

[92] Matsunaga, *Mikkyō no rekishi,* p. 70.

[93] *DZ* 1: 237–244.

[94] Two versions of this work exist. One is a twenty–fascicle work, the *Ta p'i lu che na ch'eng fo ching su* 大毘盧遮那成佛經疏(*T* no. 1796). This text was later reworked into a fourteen–fascicle version, the *Ta jih ching i shih* (*Z* 1. 36. 3–5) by Chih–yen 智儼 and Wen–ku 溫古. The first version is used by the Shingon School and the second by the Tendai School. In general, the two texts are not very different.

Chart 2. The Taizōkai lineage based on the *Kechimyakufu*.

hsiao. All three types of initiations were later used in Taimitsu. Consequently, Tendai monks were concerned with tracing all of them back to Saichō. However, only the claim that Saichō received a Diamond Realm (Kongōkai) initiation is supported by the lists of works in the *Esshūroku* (the bibliography of works which Saichō brought back from Yüeh-chou in China). Thus the *Kenkairon engi* documents dating from Saichō's stay in China do not support Saichō's later claim that he received both the Diamond and Womb Realm initiations in China. One modern Tendai scholar has tried to explain these discrepancies by suggesting that Saichō may have lost the documents concerning the Diamond and Womb Realm initiations and only included the document concerning his *Su hsi ti* initiation in the *Kenkairon engi*.[95] If this is so, then Saichō should have referred to the *Su hsi ti* initiation in the *Kechimyakufu* and *Kenkairon.* Yet he did not do so, even though he included a number of mixed Esoteric initiations in the *Kechimyakufu*.

A more convincing explanation of the discrepancies between Saichō's earlier and later descriptions of the initiations which he received from Shun-hsiao focusses on the development of Saichō's thought. Saichō probably changed his view of the ceremony as a result of his association with Kūkai.[96] The initiation from Shun-hsiao was a very hurried affair which was conducted in Chinese and included secret teachings. Some of the teachings were sufficiently vague that Enchin and Henjō were uncertain of their contents. Given this situation, Saichō might well have reinterpreted the initiation during the fifteen years which elapsed between his meeting with Shun-hsiao and his authorship of the *Kenkairon*. During those fifteen years Saichō had received the Diamond

95 Shimizutani, "Dengyō Daishi no sōjō," *DDK,* p. 591.
96 Kiuchi Hiroshi, "Dengyō Daishi no taikon ryōbu ni tsuite," *IBK* 13 (1964): 164–65.

and Womb Realm initiations from Kūkai, but he did not mention these initiations in either the *Kenkairon* or the *Kechimyakufu*. By reinterpreting the initiation from Shun-hsiao, Saichō had obviated any need to mention the teachings he had received from Kūkai.

Additional evidence for this interpretation of events is found in a *Kenkairon engi* document issued by the Japanese court which instructed Saichō to perform an Esoteric consecration ceremony.[97] According to the *Kenkairon engi* document Shun-hsiao was in Amoghavajra's lineage. A comparison of the wording of the *Kenkairon engi* document with a passage from the *Denjutsu isshinkaimon* reveals that the characters "Wu-wei" 無畏 (Śubhakarasiṃha) in the *Denjutsu isshinkaimon* have been changed to "Pu-k'ung" 不空 (Amoghavajra) in the *Kenkairon engi*.[98] In the *Kechimyakufu*, Shun-hsiao was portrayed both as being in the same lineage as Śubhakarasiṃha and as a direct disciple of Amoghavajra.[99] (See Chart 3.) The description of Amoghavajra's lineage in the *Kechimyakufu* is very short and contains little detail about the individuals named in it or the circumstances surrounding the transmission of the teaching. The conciseness of the description of Amoghavajra's lineage, especially when compared to the fuller descriptions of Śubhakarasiṃha's lineage, adversely affect the credibility of the claim that Shun-hsiao studied under Amoghavajra. The discrepancies found in the *Kenkairon engi* and the *Kechimyakufu* may be the result of an attempt by Saichō or a later Tendai monk to upgrade Shun-hsiao's lineage by claiming that Shun-hsiao had studied under Amoghavajra, probably the earliest exponent of the dual (*ryōbu*) teaching. This lineage would have placed Shun-hsiao on the same level as Kūkai's teacher Hui-kuo, who was one of Amoghavajra's most promising disciples.[100] It thus would have allowed Tendai School monks to argue that Saichō's Esoteric lineage included figures as illustrious as those in Kūkai's lineage.

Saichō was deeply influenced by the *Pu k'ung piao chi,* a collection of documents concerning Amoghavajra which he had borrowed from

---

[97] *DZ* 1: 285.

[98] *Denjutsu isshinkaimon, DZ* 1: 573.

[99] *DZ* 1: 243.

[100] Two passages in the *Goyuigō* 御遺告 (*T* no. 2431) attributed to Kūkai refer to Shun-hsiao as a disciple of Amoghavajra. Sasaki Kentoku ("Kōbō Daishi no *Goyuigō,*" pp. 127–139) has effectively argued that the *Goyuigō* was probably written after Kūkai's death. Sasaki has claimed that the references to Shun–hsiao were included as part of an attempt to ease tensions with the Tendai School and to blunt Tendai criticisms of the use of alcoholic beverages by Shingon monks by recording that both Hui–kuo and Shun–hsiao stated that drinking for medicinal purposes was acceptable.

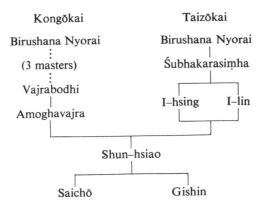

Chart 3. The Kongōkai and Taizōkai lineages based on the *Kechimyakufu.*

Kūkai. In fact, he based many of his administrative reforms on petitions submitted to the Chinese court by Amoghavajra. He was also obviously impressed by the position of Amoghavajra in Kūkai's interpretation of dual (*ryōbu*) Esoteric Buddhism. Later, Saichō's disciples were so eager to connect Saichō with Amoghavajra in some way that they even claimed that the obscure monk Wei-hsiang 惟象, who had conferred the Daibutsuchōhō initiation on Saichō, in fact, was identical to a disciple of Amoghavajra named Wei-shang 惟上. This claim was not maintained seriously by later Tendai monks.[101]

Zōmitsu Teachings and Initiations

On the fifth day of the fifth month, Saichō received a series of mixed Esoteric (*zōmitsu*) teachings and initiations.[102] These consisted of:

(1) the Gobutsuchōhō 五佛頂法 and Myōdō mushasai 冥道無遮齋 from the monk T'ai-su 太素

(2) the Fushūedan 普集會壇 and Nyoirindan 如意輪壇 from the layman Chiang-pi 江秘

(3) the Gundarihō 軍荼利法 from the monk Ling-kuang 靈光

---

[101] This lineage is found in the *Sōjō kechimyakufu* attributed to Kōjō (*Tendai kahyō, BZ* 41: 258b) and in Enchin's *Taikon kechimyakuzu* (*BZ* 65: 207). Also see Mizukami Bungi, "Dengyō Daishi Saichō no mikkyō shuhō shiryo ni kansuru ichi ni no kōsatsu," *TG* 18 (1975): 153–55.

[102] *Kechimyakufu, DZ* 1: 245. Misaki ("Dengyō Daishi Saichō no Mikkyō shisō," p. 43) has suggested that Saichō may have recorded all the *zōmitsu* transmissions as occurring on the same date in the *Kechimyakufu* simply because he had not recorded the correct dates fifteen years earlier in China. The *Kechimyakufu* date may have been taken from the colophon of a text or *maṇḍala* which Saichō brought back.

The *Esshūroku* bibliography lists a number of works concerning the *zōmitsu* transmissions. Partly because of the precedent set by these initiations, *zōmitsu* traditions have always played a more important part in Taimitsu 台密 (Tendai Esoteric Buddhism) than in Tōmitsu 東密 (Shingon Esoteric Buddhism).

The teachings from the layman Chiang-pi probably concerned the construction and layout of two types of initiation platforms, the Fushū-edan and Nyoirindan, and may not have involved the actual performance of a ceremony. The texts upon which the platforms were based were well-known in Japan at the time of Saichō's voyage, and Saichō may already have been aware of their contents. Knowledge of Esoteric texts, in this case the *T'o lo ni chi ching* 陀羅尼集經 and the *Ju i lun t'o lo ni ching*[103] 加意輪陀羅尼經, did not necessarily enable a reader to construct a platform or perform a ceremony. An Esoteric teacher who could explain and amplify the text was usually required. Since Chinese Esoteric masters did not travel to Japan and Japanese monks did not travel to China specifically to study Esoteric Buddhism during the Nara period, Saichō was probably acquiring a skill unknown in Japan.[104]

The Gundarihō initiation from Ling-kuang, as well as the Daibutsuchōhō initiation which Saichō had received from Wei-hsiang, were probably based on Atikūṭa's (Chin. O-ti-chü-to 阿地瞿多) translation of the *T'o lo ni chi ching*. Gundari refers to Kuṇḍalin, the king (*vidyārāja*) who protects the south from calamities. The inclusion of Atikūṭa's name in the *Kechimyakufu* supports this hypothesis.[105]

T'ai-su differed from other Esoteric Buddhist masters in a number of ways. He had a style name, Hai-ching 海鏡; adopting a style name was a practice more typical of laymen than of monks. His temple's name, the Ts'ao-t'ang-ssu 草堂寺 or Grass-hall Temple, suggests a rustic hut rather than the larger temples from which Esoteric masters usually came.[106] Finally the Myōdō mushasai mentioned in the *Kechimyakufu* was a ceremony open to both laymen and monks, possibly with the purpose of freeing the deceased from hell. The ceremony was probably a mixture of Buddhist and Taoist elements, typical of many ceremonies in Chinese folk religion. Aside from being mentioned in the *Kechimyakufu* and *Esshūroku,* the Myōdō mushasai is only referred to in the title of a work

---

[103] *T* nos. 901 and 1080: *Dhāraṇīsamuccaya* (?) and *Padmacintāmaṇidhāraṇīsūtra* (?)

[104] Misaki Ryōshū, "Nara jidai no Mikkyō ni okeru shomondai," *Nanto Bukkyō* 22 (1968): 70.

[105] *DZ* 1: 245–46. The *T'o lo ni chi ching* is *T* no. 901, *Dhāraṇīsamuccaya* (?).

[106] The large temple built for Kumārajīva in Ch'ang–an, however, did have this name.

brought to Japan from China by Enchin.[107] It never played a significant role in Japanese Buddhism. T'ai-su was undoubtedly a monk with strong connections with Chinese folk religion.

T'ai-su also conferred the Gobutsuchōhō initiation on Saichō. This ceremony was probably related to the Daibutsuchōhō initiation which Saichō received from Wei-hsiang. Saichō was familiar with this type of initiation even before he left Japan. The authenticity of a related text, the *Ta fo ting shou leng yen ching* 大佛頂首楞嚴經 had been the subject of a bitter debate in Japan during the Nara period, and had thus attracted much interest.[108] Monks such as Chien-chen's disciple Ssu-t'o 思託 and Saichō's disciple Enchō are said to have performed similar ceremonies before Saichō left for China; and Eichū 永忠 (fl. late 8th c.) wrote two works concerning it.[109] The term 'Butsuchōshū' (Butsuchō School) appears in Saichō's *Ehyō Tendaishū* indicating that some monks extensively practiced this type of initiation.[110] The Butsuchō ceremonies are performed in order to prevent disasters from occurring. The Gobutsuchōhō eventually became an important ceremony in Tendai Esoteric Buddhism. It is not performed, however, in the Shingon School.

In addition to works on T'ien-t'ai and Esoteric Buddhism, the *Esshūroku* also lists two one-fascicle works concerning Daoxuan's *Ssu fen lü hsing shih ch'ao* 四分律行事鈔 and a single one-fascicle work on the bodhisattva precepts, the *P'u sa chieh wen chü* 菩薩戒文句, which has not been identified. Another work, the *Erh ting erh chieh t'i* 二定二戒體 also concerns the precepts, but has not been identified. Nothing in the *Essūhroku* indicates that Saichō was considering rejecting the Hīnayāna precepts.

Saichō left Yüeh-chou about the tenth day of the fifth month of 805, and was back in Ming-chou by the thirteenth, the day he compiled the *Esshūroku,* the bibliography of works he had obtained and copied in Yüeh-chou. On the nineteenth, the Japanese mission set sail for Japan. Saichō was on the first ship. On the fifth day of the sixth month, the boat stopped at the island of Tsushima, and later went on to land in Nagato in the northern part of present day Yamaguchi-ken, Honshu.

---

[107] Annen, *Shoajari Shingon Mikkyō burui sōroku, BZ* 95: 154a; and Misaki, "Dengyō Daishi Saichō no Mikkyō," p. 44.

[108] *T* no. 345. The debate over the *sūtra's* authenticity is mentioned in Kaimyō's 戒明 biography in the *Nihon kosōden yōmonshō,* fasc. 3, *BZ* 62: 57a.

[109] Annen, *Shoajari Shingon Mikkyō burui sōroku, BZ* 95: 143b–c; and Misaki, "Nara jidai no jidai no Mikkyō," pp. 69–70.

[110] *DZ* 3: 360.

Saichō spent only eight and one-half months in China. The short duration of Saichō's sojourn in China, his inability to speak Chinese, and the many initiations which he received led to debates among Japanese monks about Saichō's mastery of the subjects he studied in China. However, Saicho's studies in China gave a legitimacy to his teachings that could only come through receiving direct transmissions from Chinese teachers. The *Naishō Buppō kechimyakufu,* which includes the lineages for Saichō's teachings, lists all but one transmission, that of Northern School Ch'an, as dating from his stay in China. Still, despite the importance which Saichō placed on his transmissions from China, the content of most of Saichō's teachings came from his studies in Japan before and after his stay in China.

Saichō looked upon himself as the first in a series of Japanese monks who were to go to China to study. He hoped to send other Japanese monks later and to be able to maintain one long-term and one short-term student in China at all times. He even had a hall built at the Ch'an-lin-ssu monastery which was to serve as living quarters for Japanese students. The building was destroyed in the Hui-ch'ang persecutions in 845, but was later rebuilt by Enchin with funds supplied by the *udaijin* (Minister of the Right), Fujiwara no Yoshisuke 藤原良相. The new quarters were moved to Kuo-ch'ing-ssu, where they continued to exist until well into the Northern Sung Dynasty.[111]

---

[111] Ono, *Kōki no kenkyū* 4: 364, 374.

CHAPTER FIVE
RETURN TO JAPAN

Even while Saichō was in China, the court in Kyoto had exhibited considerable interest in Tendai. In the second month of 804, the court requested that Chih-i's *Fa hua hsüan i* and *Fa hua wen chü* be brought to it from Tōdaiji.[1] Thus an interested audience awaited Saichō's return.

The ships probably arrived in Japan late in the sixth month of 805. The official mission to China (*kentōshi*) reported to the court in Kyoto on the first day of the seventh month of 805, and Saichō probably submitted his report to the court soon after. On the fifteen he submitted bibliographies of the works he had brought back, as well as copies of the *Lotus Sūtra* and its related *sūtras* written in gold letters. The court ordered the Tendai works which Saichō had brought from China copied and distributed to the seven great temples 七大寺 of Nara. The copying of the Tendai works was not actually completed until ten years later, in the third month of 815, when Emperor Saga calligraphed the title for the *Mo ho chih kuan*. The copies were then deposited in the seven great Nara temples.[2] In the meantime a copy had been placed in the Tendaiin 天台院 at Nodera 野寺.[3] Dōshō 道證, Shūen, Gonsō, Shuson 守魯, Jiun 慈蘊, and Jikan 慈完 were ordered to study it.[4]

Saichō rapidly rose to prominence. On the ninth day of the eighth month, after an earthquake, Saichō was asked to appear at court to read *sūtras* and conduct confession services (*sange* 懺悔) in order to forestall a recurrence of the earthquake.[5]

Upon his return Saichō found that Emperor Kanmu was more interested in Esoteric Buddhism than in the Tendai teachings that Saichō had originally been sent to study. Kanmu had been ill since the end of 804 and had gone to great lengths to mollify the vengeful spirit of Prince Sawara, posthumously awarded the title of Emperor Sudō 崇道. Monks

---

[1] Tsuji Zennosuke, *Nihon Bukkyōshi*, 10 vols., (Tokyo: Iwanami shoten, 1944–55) 1: 258.

[2] *Eizan Daishiden, DZ* 5 (*Bekkan*): 30.

[3] Ibid., p. 21. Nodera was located in Sakyō–ku, Kyoto.

[4] Jiun had taught Hossō doctrine to Gishin; no biographies of Shuson, Jiun, and Jikan have survived.

[5] *Nihon kiryaku*, fasc. 13, *KT* 10: 283. Confession services, often mixed with Esoteric elements, were popular during the Nara period. See Misaki ("Nara jidai no Mikkyō," pp. 62–64) for an analysis of the services.

were ordained, temples built, special services performed, and pardons issued, all in an attempt to hasten the ailing emperor's recovery.[6] Saichō's Esoteric Buddhism provided new and impressive rites which also could be used for this purpose. Furthermore, Esoteric Buddhism attracted Kanmu as being the newest type of Buddhism from China. Nothing could be more fitting than to use the most recently imported form of Buddhism with its colorful rituals in the new capital of Kyoto.

Saichō did not have long to wait before Kanmu commanded Wake no Hiroyo to make the arrangements for the first Japanese performance of the *kanjō* 灌頂 (Skt. *abhiṣeka,* an Esoteric ritual involving the symbolic sprinkling of water on the heads of those initiated).[7] On the twenty-seventh day of the eighth month, Emperor Kanmu told Shūen 修圓 and Gonsō 勤操 that they were to receive the *kanjō* initiation from Saichō.[8] They were to act as stand-ins for the ill Emperor. Kanmu also told them that they were not to worry about any criticism. Apparently, opposition to Saichō and his new type of Buddhism had already appeared. The presence of Gonsō and Shūen at the various assemblies which Saichō conducted during this period is noteworthy. Although Gonsō was a Sanron monk and Shūen a Hossō monk, they both were part of the more progressive wing of Nara Buddhism and were interested in Tendai and Esoteric Buddhism. Along with Saichō, they enjoyed Kanmu's favor.

---

[6] A detailed list of the measures taken appears in Nakao, *Nihon shoki Tendai,* p. 193.

[7] *Eizan Daishiden, DZ* 5 (*Bekkan*): 21; *Kenkairon engi, DZ* 1: 283–84; and *Ruijū kokushi,* fasc. 178, *KT* 6: 228. These sources specifically state that Saichō performed the first *kanjō* (Skt. *abhiṣeka*) ceremony in Japan. The term *kanjō,* however, appears in Nara period sources. Misaki ("Nara jidai no Mikkyō," pp. 67–68) suggests that in such cases such cases the term *kanjō* refers to banners (*kanjōban*) used in *kanjō* and other ceremonies. Such banners were probably used for ceremonies other than *kanjō* during the Nara period. Saichō was able to perform the *kanjō* only because he had been instructed in it while he was in China.

[8] *Kenkairon engi, DZ* 1: 283–84. Instead of using the monastic names of the two monks, the text refers to them by their family names or places of residence. This method of referring to the monks is vague and has led to disagreements about which monks are indicated in the text. Two theories have been advanced.

(a) Suehiro (*Yakuchū Eizan Daishiden,* p. 51) and Tsuji (*Nihon Bukkyōshi* 1: 263) claim that Ishikawa 石川 refers to the monk Kōi 光意 and that Nibu 樫生 refers to Enchō. Nibu was Enchō's family name.

(b) Sonoda (*Saichō,* pp. 402–3) and Ono Katsutoshi ["Saichō Kūkai kōyūkō," *Ryūkoku daigaku ronshū,* no. 394 (1970), pp. 10, 12] argue that Ishikawa refers to the monk Gonsō. They claim that the characters which Suehiro and Tsuji read as Nibu should be read as Murō and refer to Shūen. Shūen had close connections with the temple Murōji and eventually died there. This theory is commonly accepted today. Nakao Shunpaku (*Sange gakushōshiki josetsu,* p. 415) also follows this reading.

The actual ceremony was held the first day of the ninth month at Takaosanji, the Wake clan temple which had been the site of the 802 meeting on Tendai doctrine. The platform was elaborately constructed. Ono no Takamori 小野岑守 supervised more than twenty men who installed a statue of Birushana as the main figure and erected a *daimandara* 大曼荼羅 (great *maṇḍala*), a canopy, over fifty pennants, and numerous Buddhist images. The Esoteric implements which Saichō had brought from Yüeh-chou were probably employed. The ceremony may also have been the first in Japan to use a *maṇḍala*, and one of the first to use *dhāraṇī* written in an Indian script.[9] Emperor Kanmu instructed Wake no Hiroyo that cost was of no consequence and that he should carefully follow Saichō's instructions.

The ceremony itself is difficult to identify. Since the terms 'Butsu-chō' and 'Gobutsuchō' are mentioned in documents describing the ceremony, it was probably based on the mixed Esoteric (*zōmitsu*) initiations which Saichō had received in China. It may also have utilized the Fushū-edan, the platform which Saichō had learned to construct in Yüeh-chou.[10] Some scholars, however, believe that the initiation was closer to the Diamond Realm (Kongōkai) initiation which Saichō had received from Shun-hsiao.[11] In addition, a set of precepts, the *sanmayakai* 三昧耶戒, were conferred.[12] Eight monks received the initiation: Dōshō 道證, Shūen, Gonsō, Shōnō 正能, Shōshū 正秀, Kōen 廣圓, Enchō, and Kōi 光意.[13]

---

[9] For the use of *maṇḍalas* and Indian script during the Nara period, see Misaki, "Nara jidai no Mikkyō," pp. 66, 72 (note 31).

[10] Sakai Keijun, "Dengyō Daishi to Taimitsu," *DDK*, pp. 480–82; and Misaki, "Dengyō Daishi Saichō no Mikkyō shisō," pp. 45–47.

[11] Ono, "Saichō Kūkai kōyūkō," pp. 7, 22–23.

[12] *Eizan Daishiden, DZ* 5 (*Bekkan*): 22. This source states that the *kongōhōkai* 金剛寶戒 (diamond precepts) were granted. This term is often used to refer to the *Fan wang* precepts, but other sources indicate that it refers to the *sanmayakai*. The *sanmayakai* were given to a candidate for initiation before he entered the platform where the ceremony was to be performed. The precepts included such provisions as vowing to attain enlightenment. Although it is not possible to determine the contents of the *sanmayakai* which Saichō used, they probably were not very different from those which Kūkai used. Saichō does not seem to have been very interested in the *sanmayakai* after this time. For an English translation of the *sanmayakai* used by Kūkai, see Hakeda Yoshito, *Kūkai: Major Works* (New York: Columbia University Press, 1972), pp. 95–96. Katsumata Shunkyō traces the history of the *sanmayakai* and discusses Kūkai's conception of them in *Mikkyō no Nihonteki tenkai* (Tokyo: Shunjūsha, 1972), pp. 65–104. Misaki ("Dengyō Daishi Saichō no Mikkyō shisō," *Firosofia* 56 (1969). 62–63, note 10) disagrees with the above interpretation, and notes that the *sanmayakai* were not used in Tendai Esoteric ceremonies until after the time of Ennin.

[13] No biographies are available and for Shōnō, Shōshū and Kōen. Kōi (737–814) was

Early in the ninth month Kanmu asked that the ceremony be repeated at Nodera in Nishino, Kyoto. This time Buan 豊安, Ryōfuku 靈福, and Taimyō 泰命, as well as the eight monks who had been initiated at Takaosan, were to take part in the ceremony.[14] All were to receive certificates from the government attesting to their participation. In addition, Saichō and Gishin were to receive official certificates concerning their studies in China.[15]

On the seventeenth day of the ninth month of 805, Saichō was summoned to court to perform ceremonies which focussed on Birushana (Vairocana) Buddha.[16] On the third day of the tenth month, Saichō is said to have performed the *Chinshō yasha* 鎮將夜叉 ceremony, conferring it on Prince Katsurabara 葛原 (786–853); however, this claim is probably a later fabrication.[17]

The health of Saichō's chief patron, Emperor Kanmu, was rapidly failing. If Saichō were to insure his future and establish the Tendai School in Japan, he would have to act soon. A key aspect of Emperor Kanmu's policy toward Buddhism had been to reduce the dominance of the Hossō School over the other schools. To this end, an edict had been issued in 802 stating that monks from all six Nara schools were to be represented at the government sponsored assemblies held each year. The following year another edict was issued stating that the Hossō and Sanron schools were to be granted five men each as yearly ordinands (*nenbundosha*). In 804 the court further ordered that candidates for ordination from the Hossō and Sanron schools should be examined in separate groups.[18] Until this time yearly ordinands had not been allotted

---

a native of Kawauchi–koku, Ishikawa–gun. He was famous as a lecturer.

[14] No biographies exist for Ryōfuku and Taimyō. Buan (764?–840) studied Ritsu under Chien–chen's Chinese disciple Ju–pao 如寶 (d. 815) and later succeeded his teacher, becoming the fifth abbot of Tōshōdaiji. Buan was interested in Tendai teachings, probably because he was in the same lineage as Chien–chen (*Denjustsu isshinkaimon, DZ* 1: 548). He conferred the bodhisattva precepts on Emperor Heizei and many nobles. In 834 at the request of the court, he wrote the *Kairitsu denraiki* 戒律傳來記 in three fascicles (*T* no. 2347). Only one fascicle survives. The following year he was appointed *daisōzu* (greater supervisor). Buan was one of the monastic officials who later signed the petition opposing Saichō's stand on the bodhisattva precepts.

[15] The certificate awarded to Saichō is found in the *Kenkairon engi, DZ* 1: 284–85.

[16] *Nihon kiryaku:* zenpen, fasc. 13, *KT* 10: 283.

[17] The ceremony was one of the more important ones in Taimitsu. It had Bishamon 毘沙門 (Skt. Vaiśravana) as its central figure and was used to protect the state. Three works on the ritual attributed to Saichō are found in *DZ* 4: 567–94, but are not authentic. See Misaki Ryōshū, "*Chinshō yashahō* ni tsuite," *DDK*, pp. 1383–1404. Prince Katsurabara was the son of Emperor Kanmu and an important supporter of Saichō.

[18] *Ruijū kokushi,* fasc. 179, *KT* 6: 237.

according to schools.

On the third day of the first month of Enryaku 25 (late 805), Saichō proposed a revision of the ordination system in accordance with these policies.[19] The proposal suggested that the Kegon, Tendai, and Ritsu Schools each be allotted two yearly ordinands annually. The Sanron School was to be allotted three, one of whom was to study the *Ch'eng shih lun* 成實論 (*Tattvasiddhiśāstra?*); and the Hossō was to be allotted three, one of whom was to study the *A p'i ta mo chü she lun* 阿毘達磨 俱舍論 (*Abhidharmakośaśāstra*).[20] The proposal probably enjoyed support from the Ritsu and Kegon schools, neither of which had much influence at the time. However, it drastically reduced the number of monks received by the two most powerful schools, the Hossō and Sanron, each of which had previously received five yearly ordinands. Yet despite this, two days later a group of influential Nara monks submitted a statement supporting Saichō's proposal.[21] It was signed by most of the leading monastic officials in Nara:[22] Shōgo[23] 勝虞, Jōtō[24] 常騰, Ju-pao[25] 如寶, Shūtetsu[26] 修哲, and Eichū 永忠.[27] Since the proposal benefited the Ritsu School and Ju-pao was a Ritsu monk, as well as a disciple of the T'ien-t'ai monk Chien-chen, his approval was to be

---

[19] *Kenkairon engi, DZ* 1: 292–93.

[20] *T* nos. 1646 and 1558.

[21] *Kenkairon engi, DZ* 1: 293–94.

[22] Two *vinaya* masters (*risshi*), Kinchō 均竉 and Eun 慧雲 did not sign the petition. For a list of monastic officials of this time, see the *Sōgō bunin* 僧綱補任 fasc. 1, *BZ* 65: 7. The information in this work is sometimes questionable, as in the case of Eichū.

[23] Shōgo (732–811) was a Hossō monk from Daianji. In 797 he was appointed *vinaya* master (*risshi*), in 805 lesser supervisor (*shōsōzu*), and in 806, greater supervisor (*daisōzu*).

[24] Jōtō (740–815) first studied Hossō with Eigon 永嚴 at Kōfukuji 興福. Due to an argument with Chūbun 忠芬, he later moved to Saidaiji 西大寺. He was one of the most prolific writers on Hossō of his time. In 805 he was appointed *vinaya* master and then lesser supervisor.

[25] Ju-pao (723–814) came to Japan with his teacher Chien-chen and helped found Tō-shōdaiji 唐招提寺. He was famous for his adherence to the precepts. Along with Saichō's benefactor Dōchū 道忠, he went to Tōgoku to preach. After returning to the capital, he gained Kanmu's favor and administered the precepts to the Emperor in 804. He was named *vinaya* master in 797 and lesser supervisor in 806.

[26] Shūtetsu (d. 831) was a Tōdaiji monk who held various posts at the temple. The *Sōgō bunin* (*BZ* 65: 8a) states that he was appointed *vinaya* master in 810, but in the 806 petition found in the *Kenkairon engi,* he is already called *risshi*.

[27] Eichū went to China to study in 777 and returned to Japan at the same time as Saichō in 805. He was famous for his wide learning, adherence to the precepts, and knowledge of music. Unfortunately, his sectarian affiliation is not known. The court awarded him two novices and Saichō three novices in 806. The court's similar treatment of the two monks may indicate a close relationship between them. Some biographies, however, claim that Eichū returned to Japan in the 780's and rapidly rose to prominence. He is said to have compiled the *Bonshakuji mokuroku* 梵釋寺目録.

expected. Eichū, after studying in China for over twenty-five years, probably returned to Japan from China on the same ship as Saichō; the two men may have been friends. The approval of the petition by the two eminent Hossō monks, Shōgo and Jōtō, is difficult to explain. Possibly they believed that the proposal had Emperor Kanmu's support and that resistance to it would be futile. In fact, the very same day that the Nara monks submitted their statements, Emperor Kanmu granted Saichō three novices (*dosha*); Eichū also received one, and Prince Katsurabara received two.[28]

On the twenty-sixth, the court issued an edict which adopted most of Saichō's suggestions.[29] The edict differed from Saichō's proposal in one very significant way, however. The Tendai monks were to be divided into two categories in accordance with the course of study they followed. One course of study, called the Shanagō (Esoteric Course), focussed on the *Ta p'i lu che na ching* 大毘盧遮那經, (*Mahāvairocanasūtra*), the text on which the Womb Realm (Taizōkai) *maṇḍala* was based. The title of the course, Shanagō, was taken from the Japanese title of this *sūtra, Daibirushanakyō.* Other *sūtras* were added in Saichō's later works, the *Kenkairon* and *Sange gakushōshiki.* However, the absence of the *Chin kang ting ching* 金剛頂經 (*Vajraśekharasūtra*) and the *Su hsi ti ching* 蘇悉地經 (*Susiddhikaramahātantrasādhanopāyikapaṭalasūtra*), two of the three most important works in the three traditions (*sanbu*) of later Tendai Esoteric Buddhism, is notable. Not until Ennin's time were yearly ordinands who specialized in these two texts added to Tendai rolls.[30]

Saichō's decision to base the Esoteric Course on the *Ta p'i lu che na ching,* the basic text for Womb Realm (Taizōkai) initiations reveals much about the depth of his studies of Esoteric Buddhism in China. During his stay in China, Saichō probably did not receive a Taizōkai initiation. Moreover, he brought back no text concerning the Taizōkai initiation. His training in the Mixed (*zōmitsu*) and Diamond Realm (Kongōkai) forms of Esoteric Buddhism while in China enabled Saichō to perform some Esoteric ceremonies, such as the consecration (*kanjō*) on Takaosan in 805. However, this training was not sufficient to enable Saichō to establish a long-term program of study in Esoteric Buddhism.

---

[28] *Ruijū kokushi,* fasc. 187, *KT* 6: 315.

[29] *Kenkairon engi, DZ* 1: 294–96.

[30] A list of yearly ordinands granted to the Tendai School is found in the *Ruijū sandaikyaku,* fasc. 2. Takagi has systematized this material, and gives an account of the increase of Tendai School yearly ordinands after Saichō's death in *Heian jidai Hokke Bukkyōshi kenkyū,* pp. 17–22.

Saichō, therefore, turned to a text which he had studied before his journey in China, the *Ta p'i lu che na ching*. The commentary on the *sūtra* by I-hsing and Śubhakarasiṃha which Saichō studied undoubtedly suggested ways in which Esoteric Buddhism could be harmoniously combined with Tendai doctrines. Saichō's statements about Esoteric Buddhism during the rest of his life continued to reflect his interest in Taizōkai teachings and ceremonies. Kongōkai texts and ceremonies were rarely mentioned, indicating that Saichō's study of Esoteric Buddhism in China did not significantly affect the content of the Tendai School course in Esoteric Buddhism.[31]

The other course, the Shikangō (Meditation Course) was based on Chih-i's masterful treatise on meditation techniques, the *Mo ho chih kuan* and took its name from that work (Jap. *Makashikan*). The monks in this course were to study exoteric doctrines, especially those of the Tendai School. Whether monks from one course could study in the other is unclear; however, the *Gakushō meichō* (Register of students) does indicate that the Shanagō was the less developed of the two courses, as might be expected in view of Saichō's own scholarly strengths and weaknesses. This indicates that it probably was not easy to switch courses, since if it had been, more Shanagō students would have remained on Mount Hiei to study Tendai. On the other hand, Ennin, Kōjō, and Toku-en, all of whom were Shikangō students, are known to have studied Esoteric Buddhism along with Tendai. The Shikangō and Shanagō categories continued to be used in granting yearly ordinands at least until 890.

It is significant that the Esoteric Course (Shanagō) was mentioned first in the court's edict and continued to be placed first in all documents until 818, when Saichō wrote the *Rokujōshiki*. The order in which the two courses were mentioned probably reflected Kanmu's interest in Esoteric Buddhism. Because of the difference between Saichō's initial petition which did not mention Esoteric Buddhism and the resulting edict, some scholars have argued that Esoteric Buddhism was added to Tendai largely at Emperor Kanmu's insistence.[32] Saichō, however, certainly could not have been adverse to this change.

On the seventeenth day of the third month of 806, Emperor Kanmu

---

[31] Information on Saichō's study of Esoteric Buddhism before his voyage to China is found in the preceding chapter. Misaki ("Dengyō Daishi Saichō no Mikkyō shisō," pp. 49–54) lists and analyzes Saichō's statements concerning Esoteric Buddhism.

[32] Nakao, *Nihon Shoki Tendai*, pp. 163–80.

died, and Saichō lost his most important supporter. A few years later Wake no Hiroyo also died. Since his return from China, Saichō had been highly visible, often appearing at court, as is obvious from the frequent mention of his name in court records. After Kanmu's death, Saichō's name almost completely disappears from historical records for several years. The new emperor, Heizei 平城 (774–824; r. 806–809), had previously supported Saichō, encouraging him during the assembly at Takaosanji in 802 and financing much of his 804 voyage to China. Yet, from the time Heizei ascended the throne in 806, he did nothing to help Saichō. Heizei's change in attitude was probably due to his adoption of the financially conservative policies initiated by Kanmu shortly before his death. Kanmu had stopped construction in the new capital and had abandoned plans for a new military campaign in the north in order to reduce expenses. Emperor Kanmu's adoption of these policies was also influenced by the commonly held belief that he could gain merits, which would help him recover his health, by reducing the financial burden on the people. Emperor Heizei's adoption of financially conservative policies similar to those of Kanmu resulted in the cancellation of building projects at many temples and government appropriation of some of the lands controlled by temples. These policies stifled any new developments in both Tendai and Nara Buddhism.[33]

At the same time, the Fujiwara family began making a comeback after a period of decline. Kōfukuji, a Hossō temple and one of the seven great temples of Nara, was the Fujiwara clan temple (*ujidera*), and the family thus tended to favor Nara Buddhism, especially the Hossō School. Gomyō[34] 護命, a Hossō monk who later became one of Saichō's chief

---

[33] Sonoda, *Ajia Bukkyōshi: Nihon–hen* 2: 116; and *Ruijū kokushi*, KT 6: 258, 316.

[34] Gomyō (750–834) was from the Hata 秦 family of Mino. He entered the Konkōmyōji in Mino at the age of ten. When he was fifteen, he went to Gankōji in Nara and studied under Shōgo. He passed the government exams for monastic candidates, and was ordained by Fa-chin 法進 at age twenty. He studied with Fa–chin for a number of years, later leaving to go into retreat at Yoshino, where he meditated and performed the *kokūzōhō* 虚空藏法 ceremony, an Esoteric Buddhist ritual which improved the memory. Gomyō spent one–half of each month of Gankōji in Nara and one–half in retreat at Yoshino. According to the *Sōgō bunin* (*BZ* 65: 7c), he travelled abroad to study sometime during the Enryaku era (782–805), but since this event is not mentioned in most other biographies, the historicity of it must be doubted. He was called to Kyoto in 791 and set up a hermitage at Yamada. In 805 he lectured on the *Chin kuang ming ching* at court. Six months later Gomyō was granted the rank of grand Dharma master (*daishosshi*). Shortly thereafter he was appointed *vinaya* master. He was named lesser supervisor in 815 and greater supervisor in 816. Gomyō led the opposition to Saichō's proposals for the *Fan wang* precepts. After his side had lost, he tried to resign from the Sōgō on the pretext of age but was not permitted to do so. Still, he retired to Bonshakuji and Yamadaderor. He rose to prominence again during the Tenchō era (824–

antagonists, was appointed to the Sōgō[35] 僧綱 (Office of Monastic Affairs) the month after Emperon Kanmu died,[36]

Saichō's activities for the next few years are almost impossible to trace. Most records place him on Mount Hiei. However, all of these records were compiled long after Saichō's death. Here only the highlights of his reported activities will be mentioned. On the twenty-third day of the twelfth month of 807, Saichō is said to have conferred the bodhisattva precepts on Enchō and over one-hundred other people. The earliest sources for this ceremony are the *Ruijū kokushi*,[37] compiled in 892, and the *Jikaku Daishiden*,[38] a biography of Ennin which was edited into its present-day form over one-hundred years after this ceremony was supposed to have taken place. No reference is made of the event in such early sources as the *Eizan Daishiden* or the *Denjutsu isshinkaimon*. The latter is a work very much concerned with establishing Enchō's qualifications to lead the Tendai order. Although at least one-hundred other people are said to have been ordained, no mention of the ordination occurs in any other biographies.

According to Enchō's biography in the *Genkō shakusho*,[39] Enchō

---

33) and was appointed chief executive (*sōjō*) in 827. He died in 834 (*Honchō kōsōden*, fasc. 5, *BZ* 63: 46–47).

Along with the Hossō monk Zenju 善珠, Gomyō was one of the most renowned scholars of his time. A large number of works on logic and *yuishiki* (ideation–only) are attributed to him, including three works totalling nineteen fascicles on the *Lotus Sūtra*. He certainly must have known of Saichō's debates with Tokuitsu on the *Lotus Sūtra* and this must have contributed to his disagreements with Saichō on the *Fan wang* precepts. Unfortunately, only one of his works survives, the *Daijō hosso kenjinshō* 乗法相研神章 (*T* no. 2309) in five fascicles, written in 822, and submitted to Emperor Junna in 830 at imperial request. This work demonstrates that Gomyō was a master of Hossō doctrine and familiar with the doctrines of other schools, including Tendai. It is also important as one of the only surviving works from the Nanji 南寺 branch of the Hossō School dating from the early Heian period.

35 The Sōgō was the government office which supervised monks and nuns in the capital. Monks and nuns in the provinces were supervised by lecturers (*kōji*) and readers (*dokushi*). Worthy monks were appointed to posts in the Sōgō. During the early Heian period, a monk appointed to the Sōgō would hold one of four ranks. Beginning with the highest, the four ranks were *sōjō* (chief executive), *daisōzu* (greater supervisor), *shōsōzu* (lesser supervisor), and *risshi* (*vinaya* master). The lesser ranks were held by several monks at one time.

36 *Sōgō bunin*, fasc. 1, *BZ* 65: 7.

37 *Ruijū kokushi*, fasc. 179, *KT* 6: 239.

38 *Zokugunsho ruijū* (hereafter cited as *ZGR*), 70 vols. (Tokyo: Zokugunsho ruijū kankōkai, 1923–30), 8: 686. Both the *Ruijū kokushi* and *Jikaku Daishiden* note that this ordination was the first transmission of the *endon bosatsu daikai* (Perfect, Sudden and full bodhisattva precepts) in Japan. However, this entry is not found in the Sanzen'in version of the *Jikaku Daishiden*, ed. by Ono Katsutoshi (Kobe: Goten shoin, 1967).

39 *Genkō shakusho*, fasc. 2, *BZ* 62: 80. This account also states that Enchō was ordained twice with the full Hīnayāna percepts, once by Dōchū, and again in 804 by a Chinese monk, T'ai–hsin 泰信. No explanation for the two ordinations is given. However, Enchō's biography

received the bodhisattva precepts from Dōchū. Since ordinations with the bodhisattva precepts are said to last forever, it seems unusual that Enchō received a second ordination with the bodhisattva precepts. If, as all accounts claim, the second ordination was an *endonkai* 圓頓戒 (Perfect-sudden Precepts) ceremony, then it might have been substantially different from the first. However, no evidence exists which indicates that Saichō had developed his own unique interpretation of the bodhisattva precepts by this time. The account may have its origin in the dispute between Enchō and Enshū over the leadership of the Tendai order, and thus be a later fabrication attempting to show that Enchō had received the precepts directly from Saichō. When later medieval Tendai scholars used lineages to prove that certain new doctrines were orthodox, they often traced them through Enchō to Saichō and then back to China. For example, according to the *Genkō shakusho,* when Saichō was on his death bed, he transmitted a teaching on meditation to Enchō.[40] On the other hand, a certain amount of evidence for the authenticity of the 806 ordination does exist. Gishin was chosen over Enchō as first *zasu* (Head of the Tendai Order) because Gishin was the senior monk, though probably younger than Enchō. However, all of Enchō's ordinations are earlier than the equivalent ones for Gishin with the exception of Enchō's 806 ordination. Thus the ordination may provisionally be accepted as authentic. Enchō's bodhisattva ordination was not intended to replace the *Ssu fen lü* ordination. Saichō would not make his unprecedented proposals for monastic reform for another twelve or thirteen years.

In the fourth month of 809, Emperor Heizei abdicated and was succeeded by Emperor Saga 嵯峨 (786–842; r. 809–823). The new emperor's attitude toward Buddhism was more positive than that of Emperor Heizei. While he did not favor Saichō and the Tendai School over the Nara schools, he did try to be scrupulously fair in mediating the disputes that arose between them.

Although Kanmu had granted the Tendai School yearly ordinands to be awarded annually, the combination of Kanmu's death and Heizei's lack of interest had meant that the edict was not actually put into effect until Saga's reign began. Finally on the fourteenth day of the first month of Daidō 5 (late 809), Saichō was granted eight yearly ordinands at the Konkōmyōe (annual assembly on the *Chin kuang ming*

---

is also puzzling on a number of other points, including the date of his death.
[40] *BZ* 62: 81a.

ching [*Suvarṇaprabhāsasūtra*]) at court.[41] The eight men represented the number Saichō should have received from 806 to 809. Thereafter, the Tendai School would receive two yearly ordinands each year.

The award of the yearly ordinands signified renewed court interest in the Tendai School. The influx of monks to Mount Hiei and the financial support from the court which accompanied them gave Saichō new impetus to advance his plans for the Tendai School. Mount Hiei soon began to bustle with activity. The next year,[42] Saichō instituted lectures on the *Lotus Sūtra,* the *Chin kuang ming ching,* and the *Jen wang ching* 仁王經 (*Sūtra of the Benevolent King*).[43] In doing so, Saichō developed the basic course of study for the students of the Tendai School's Meditation Course. Although all three texts had been popular during the Nara period as *sūtras* protecting the nation, Saichō was probably the first to combine the three into a unified course of study. They later became known as the three *sūtras* protecting the state (*gokoku sanbukyō* 護國三部經).[44]

In the seventh month of 812, Saichō also built a 'Lotus blossom of the Dharma' Meditation Hall (Hokke zanmaidō 法華三昧堂). Five or six practitioners were selected to perform the confession ceremonies

---

[41] *Eizan Daishiden, DZ* 5 (*Bekkan*): 27.

[42] A number of dates for the beginning of the lecture system on Hieizan can be found ranging from 807 to 810. For the sources, see Shibuya Jikai, ed., *Teisei Nihon Tendaishū nenpyō* (Tokyō: Daiichi Shobō, 1973) pp. 7–8. The date found in the earliest source, the *Eizan Daishiden* (*DZ* 5 [*Bekkan*]: 27), is followed in this account. Three works by Saichō concerning the lectures survive:

(a) *Chōkō Konkōmyōkyō eshiki* 長講金光明經會式 in one fascicle (*DZ* 4: 277–93);
(b) *Chōkō Ninnō hannyagyō eshiki* 長講仁王般若經會式 in one fascicle (*DZ* 4: 295–313);
(c) *Chōkō Hokekyō eshiki* 長講法華經會式 in two fascicles (*DZ* 4: 241–76). The authenticity of the second fascicle of this work has been questioned. See Shibuya Ryōtai, "Shūsosen *Chōkō Hokekyō ganmon* ryūdenshi no nenpyō to shiron," *DDK*, pp. 573–84; and Fukui Kōjun, "*Chōkō Hokekyō ganmon* no kenkyū," *Tōyō shisō no kenkyū* (Tokyō: Risōsha, 1955), pp. 240–277.

[43] The *Jen wang ching* is thought by many scholars to be a Chinese production. Two versions exist: one said to be translated by Kumārajīva (*T* no. 245), and one by Amoghavajra (*T* no. 246). The *sūtra* was frequently lectured on during the Nara period. A government–sponsored annual assembly (*Ninnōe*) in which the *sūtra* was used to ward off calamities was established in 657 [Umeda Yoshihiko, *Kaitei sōbu Nihon shūkyō seidoshi,* 4 vols., (Tokyō: Tokyo shuppansha, 1971), 1: 51, 202].

[44] The *Lotus sūtra, Chin kuang ming ching* and the *Jen wang ching,* traditionally grouped together as 'the three *sūtras* which protect the nation' (*gokoku sanbukyō*), were certainly popular in the Nara period. They do not appear, however, to have been strongly linked together in this way until 877, when an order from the Chancellor's office stated that all lecturers (*kōji*) at the summer retreats must speak on all three *sūtras* (*Ruijū sandaikyaku, KT* 25: 51). Saichō's establishment of lectures on these three *sūtras* was instrumental in linking them together as a set group.

which this meditation involved and chant the *Lotus Sūtra* without cease. The Hokke zanmai is one form of the half-walking half-sitting *samādhi* 半行半座三昧 described in Chih-i's *Mo ho chih kuan*. After Saichō's death, halls were built for all four types of meditation 四種三昧 described in the *Mo ho chih kuan*.[45]

---

[45] *Eizan Daishiden, DZ* 5 (*Bekkan*): 27. For a description of the *Hokke zanmai* in English, see Leon Hurvitz, *Chih-i, Mélanges Chinois et Bouddhiques,* no. 12 (1960–62), pp. 323–25. Halls for all four types of meditation were probably planned by Saichō (*Kenkairon, DZ* 1: 73–74). For the later development of the meditation halls on Mount Hiei, see Shigematsu Akihisa, "Eizan ni okeru shishu sanmaiin no hatten," *DDK* (*Bekkan*), pp. 205–223.

CHAPTER SIX
RELATIONS WITH KŪKAI

Saichō had established a course of study for his disciples who were to be trained in Tendai; however, the more difficult task remained of formulating a course of study for those who were to be trained in Esoteric Buddhism. Saichō's knowledge of Esoteric Buddhism, though probably advanced for his time, was not so detailed that he could readily establish a program study in it. Yet in accordance with Emperor Kanmu's wishes and the court's interest in Esoteric Buddhism, Saichō had already committed half of his disciples to the study of it. Saichō's limited understanding of Esoteric Buddhism was revealed by a completely unexpected event, the sudden return of Kūkai from China.[1] Kūkai had been sent with the instructions and financial support to study Esoteric Buddhism in China for twenty years. However, after he had been there for about two and one-half years, his teacher Hui-kuo 惠果 (d. 805) died, and Kūkai decided to return to Japan. While in China, Kūkai had studied in Ch'ang-an, the capital of China and the center of Esoteric Buddhism. He returned to Japan with a substantially deeper understanding of Esoteric Buddhism than Saichō. Moreover, Kūkai had studied with a disciple of Amoghavajra, the Esoteric Buddhist master who had received considerable patronage at the T'ang court. In contrast, Saichō's Esoteric Buddhist teachers seemed obscure. Moreover, Saichō's studies of Esoteric Buddhism in China had been brief

---

[1] Kūkai waited in Kyushu for at least a year before he went to Kyoto to submit his report to the court. Scholars have speculated that Kūkai was delayed in Kyushu because Emperor Heizei favored Saichō (although no evidence of favoritism can be found during Heizei's reign). It has also been suggested that the court was unsure about how it ought to treat Kūkai since Saichō had already been recognized as a master of Esoteric Buddhism (Hakeda, *Kūkai,* p. 35; Katsumata, *Mikkyō,* p. 238). Little positive evidence exists for these views. Recently, two new theories have been advanced.

(a) Inoue Mitsusada [*Nihon kodai kokka to Bukkyō* (Tokyo: Iwanami shoten, 1971) pp. 109, 127] theorizes that Kūkai was not permitted to come to the capital because his uncle had taught Prince Iyo 仁予, who had been involved in a plot with Fujiwara no Nakanari 藤原仲成. As a result Iyo was forced to commit suicide in 807. These events occurred after Kūkai's return from China, however, and do not explain why Kūkai had remained in Kyushu from 806–7.

(b) Akamatsu Toshihide ["Saichō to Kūkai, " *Ōzaki gakuhō* 53, no. 2 (1973): 9–11] argues that the decision to stay in Kyushu was made by Kūkai himself, because he was hesitant to have the Esoteric works which he had brought back copied and distributed to other temples.

since most of his effort had been devoted to the study of T'ien-t'ai. Kūkai had carried back many Esoteric ritual implements, some of them from India, and many Esoteric *sūtras* and treatises, including a number translated by Amoghavajra. Saichō had brought a smaller number of implements and Esoteric texts.[2] The difference between the training of the two men in Esoteric Buddhism would have been evident to any informed person who had read the reports made to the court after their arrivals in Japan. Since the court had been particularly interested in Saichō's knowledge of Esoteric Buddhism, Kūkai's sudden arrival in Japan clearly presented Saichō with a potential problem.

Saichō and Kūkai probably met for the first time in Kyushu, while waiting to go to China.[3] The next meeting occurred about 809, shortly after Kūkai had arrived in the capital from Kyushu to report on his studies in China. Some scholars believe the two men renewed their acquaintance in the second month of 809 when Kūkai went to Mount Hiei to call on Saichō and ask for instruction in Tendai doctrine.[4] Later, in the eighth month of 809, Saichō dispatched his disciple Kyōchin 經珍 with instructions to borrow twelve works from Kūkai.[5] This letter is the earliest extant piece of correspondence between the two men, but its brevity and style suggest that contact between the two men had, in fact, already occurred.

The Correspondence Between Saichō and Kūkai

The primary source material concerning the relationship between

---

[2] Kūkai's report, the *Goshōrai mokuroku*, is partly translated in Hakeda, *Kūkai: Major works*, pp. 140–150.

[3] No record of such a meeting exists, but such an encounter can reasonably be assumed to have taken place. For a different view, see Hakeda, *Kūkai*, p. 43.

[4] The theory that Kūkai asked Saichō for instruction in Tendai is based on Kūkai's calling card, the type of language Kūkai used in his letters, and the thesis that it was this request by Kūkai that enabled Saichō, in turn, to become Kūkai's disciple (Akamatsu, "Saichō to Kūkai," p. 11).

A long debate has developed concerning the calling card. Shingon scholars have maintained that it is a Tendai forgery, designed to restore some of Saichō's prestige in his relationship with Kūkai. Other scholars have defended it. The *locus classicus* for the card is usually said to be the *Tendai kahyō* (fasc. 2A, *BZ* 41 : 246), a late work compiled in 1771 and expanded in 1867. The editor of the work comments that the card is found in the *Eizan gokoku engi* in which there is a comment that the card is in Kūkai's handwriting. The work referred to is found in the *Gunsho ruijū* (27, no. 2: 472) under the title *Enryakuji gokoku engi*. It was probably compiled in the thirteenth century. It is a very polemical work, the card being included as part of an attempt to prove that Kūkai was Saichō's disciple. The earliest known use of such cards among monks is from the first half of the twelfth century on Mount Kōya. The card thus seems to be of dubious authenticity. However, Akamatsu Toshihide argues that the calling card is authentic in *Kyōto jishikō* (Kyoto: Hōzōkan, 1972), pp. 44–45.

[5] *DZ* 5: 453.

Saichō and Kūkai consists mainly of Saichō's letters to Kūkai. About forty of Saichō's letters were copied and edited into a single volume in 1381 by a Shingon monk from Tōji 東寺 named Dōkai 道快.[6] About half of these letters were addressed to Kūkai. A few were written to Saichō's disciple Taihan 泰範 and to several other people. Since the letters were edited by a Shingon monk at a time when there was a strong rivalry between the Shingon and Tendai schools, the whole collection was probably edited in a way unfavorable to Saichō. The letters illustrate Saichō's dependence on Kūkai for Esoteric texts and initiations and a deep emotional dependence on his disciple Taihan.

Since one of the letters still exists in Saichō's handwriting, the authenticity of the whole collection has gone unchallenged.[7] However, recently Ono Katsutoshi has called for a critical investigation of the letters on stylistic grounds. He believes that the letters must be reexamined considering such criteria as the use of honorific language. He also has noted that although some of the letters include a preface inquiring about matters such as the addressee's health, other letters simply request the loan of texts without making any prefatory remarks. The paucity of other primary source materials on the relationship between the two monks makes a critical evaluation of their correspondence difficult. Moreover, as is discussed below, the authenticity of several letters concerning a break in the relations between Saichō and Kūkai has been questioned. An additional difficulty is posed by the absence of a date including the year on about half of Saichō's letters to Kūkai.[8]

Early Relations with Kūkai
In his earliest extant letter to Kūkai, Saichō asked to borrow twelve

---

[6] *Dengyō Daishi shōsoku, DZ* 5: 441–74. Dōkai of Tōji is said to have copied the letters in 1381. In 1809 they were recopied and checked for errors by Sonkan 尊観 of Ishiyama-dera. In 1819, they were again copied, this time by Jōshō 淨聖 of Mount Hiei (*DZ* 5: 472). This last version is the work included in the *Dengyō Daishi zenshū.*

[7] For example, see Shioiri Ryōchū, *BKD* 8: 161–62; and Watanabe, *Saicho Kūkai shū,* pp. 55–56.

[8] A number of scholars have studied and arranged at least some of the letters in a chronological sequence. The most important studies are: Miura Shūkō, *Dengyō Daishiden*; Takeuchi Rizō, *Heian ibun,* vol. 8; Kawasaki Kōshi, *"Dengyō Daishi shōsoku* ni tsuite," in *Tayama Hōnan sensei kakō kinen ronbunshū* (Tokyo: Tayama Hōnan sensei kakō kinenkai, 1963), pp. 36–46; Akamatsu Toshihide, *Kyōto jishikō* pp. 41–63; and Akamatsu, "Saichō to Kūkai," *Ōzaki gakuhō* 53, no. 2 (1973): 1–13; Ono Katsutoshi, "Saichō Kūkai kōyūkō," *Ryūkoku daigaku ronbunshū* 394 (1970): 1–29; Nakao Shunpaku, *Sange gakushōshiki josetsu,* pp. 152–164; and Watanabe Shōko, *Saichō Kūkai shū,* pp. 55–108 (includes a modern Japanese translation of the letters).

works which Kūkai had brought from China.[9] Four texts concerned Tai-zokāi (Womb realm) Esoteric teachings and practices, three were on the *shittan* 悉曇 (Skt. *siddham*) or Sanskritic styles of writing, two on Kegon teachings and one each on Kongōkai (Diamond-realm) Esoteric Buddhism, *zōmitsu* and Amoghavajra. The works on Taizōkai practices and teachings were probably intended for use in teaching the students in the Esoteric Course. The precise reasons for requesting the other works, however, are not known. In general, modern scholars have not been able to pinpoint Saichō's scholarly aims or interests by analyzing the contents of the works which he borrowed from Kūkai. Especially in his later letters, Saichō's requests do not shed much light on his position on Esoteric Buddhism. Rather, Saichō seems to have wanted to borrow and copy all of the works which Kūkai had brought back from China.[10] Saichō had obtained a copy of the list of works which Kūkai had brought back to Japan and probably based many of his requests for texts on that list.[11]

In late 809, when Saichō appeared in court to receive the first eight yearly ordinands, he probably met Kūkai again.[12] Shortly after returning to Mount Hiei from the court, Saichō asked that he not be disturbed, and appointed Taihan 泰範 and Kyochin 經珍 to oversee the everyday affairs of the order.[13] While Saichō claimed that he was exhausted, he probably also withdrew from administering Hieizanji in order to devote more time to studying and copying the Esoteric Buddhist texts which he had borrowed from Kūkai. Meanwhile Kūkai was becoming more active. On the first day of the eleventh month of 810, he performed an Esoteric initiation at Takaosanji. By the second month of the next year, Saichō had decided to go to Takaosanji and had asked Kūkai for the Henjō isson 遍照一尊 consecration.[14] In doing so, Saichō acknowledged Kūkai's superiority to him in matters concerning Esoteric Buddhism.

---

[9] *DZ* 5: 453.

[10] Misaki, "Dengyō Daishi Saichō no Mikkyō," pp. 56–57.

[11] A copy of Kūkai's *Goshōrai mokuroku* exists in Saichō's handwriting. See Tsuji Zen-nosuke, *Nihon Bukkyōshi* 1: 284.

[12] Akamatsu, *Kyōto jishikō*, p. 46. Akamatsu cites no positive evidence for the meeting.

[13] Jichin 治珍 should be read as Kyōchin 經珍 in this letter [Takeuchi Rizō, ed. *Heian ibun*, 13 vols. (Tokyo: Tōkyōdō, 1963–70), rev. ed., vol. 10, document no. 4899].

[14] *DZ* 5: 456. Whether Saichō actually went to Takaosanji at this time is unclear. Watanabe Shōkō [*Saichō Kūkaishū*, Nihon no shisō, vol. 1 (Tokyo: Chikuma shobō, 1969) pp. 60, 82] claims that he did not go. However, *Heian ibun* (vol. 8, document no. 4382) dates the letter upon which Watanabe bases his argument two years later. The disagreement occurs because many of Saichō's letters to Kūkai were not dated with the year.

The contents of the Henjō isson kanjō (consecration from the honored one whose light pervades everywhere [Vairocana]) are unclear. Perhaps Saichō was unsure of the exact nature of the teachings which Kūkai had studied. Kiuchi Hiroshi considers this letter to be a request for the Taizōkai and Kongōkai initiations which Saichō received in 812 from Kūkai.[15]

In the fifth month of 812, Saichō was in ill health and wrote a will indicating that Taihan was to become general administrator (*sōbettō* 總別當) and thus be in charge of monastic affairs on Mount Hiei. Enchō was to be head monk (*zasu*) and other monks were put in charge of the library.[16] Taihan, however, seems to have had difficulties in managing affairs on Mount Hiei and tried to refuse the assignment, citing an unspecified problem with the precepts as an excuse.[17] Saichō immediately sent Taihan a letter encouraging him to accept the position.[18] Nevertheless, Taihan left Mount Hiei a short time later. Meanwhile, the friendship between Kūkai and Saichō was developing. Saichō's letter dated the nineteenth day of the eighth month is very optimistic. He proposed that he and Kūkai propagate their two schools together since there was no essential difference between the two One-Vehicle teachings.[19] In effect, Saichō was virtually asking Kūkai to train the Mount Hiei students in Esoteric Buddhism.

On the twenty-seventh day of the tenth month, while returning from a pilgrimage to Sumiyoshi Jinja 住吉神社 and the Yuimae (annual assembly on the *Vimalakīrtinirdeśasūtra*) at Kōfukuji, Saichō and Kōjō went to visit Kūkai at Otokunji 乙順寺.[20] As a result of their talks, Kūkai moved to Takaosanji 高雄山寺 and the two monks agreed that Kūkai would grant Saichō and his disciples Esoteric initiations in the twelfth month. Saichō wrote to Taihan inviting him to go to Takaosanji to study Esoteric Buddhism.[21]

---

[15] *Dengyō Daishi no shōgai to shisō*, p. 148.

[16] DZ 5: 425. Also found in *Heian ibun*, vol. 8, no. 4351. The authenticity of the will has been questioned by some scholars. However, their arguments have been analyzed and refuted.

[17] Ibid., no. 4354.

[18] Some confusion exists as to which letter was sent to comfort Taihan. Some scholars claim that it was *Heian ibun*, nos. 4355–56, and others argue that it was no. 4413. See Akamatsu, *Kyōto jishikō*, p. 48.

[19] DZ 5: 446–47.

[20] *Denjutsu isshinkaimon*, DZ 1: 529. Kūkai had been named administrator (*bettō*) of Otokunji in 811. A temple in the same area is mentioned in the *Wakokubon* ordination manual (*DZ* 1: 322–23) as the site of a bodhisattva precepts ordination at which the disciples of Saichō were present. Unfortunately the information in the *Wakokubon* is insufficient to identify the event.

[21] DZ 5: 463.

A few days later, on the fifteenth day of the eleventh month, Saichō and the Wake brothers were given the Kongōkai initiation by Kūkai.[22] The ceremony was small, with only four people receiving the initiation. One month later Saichō, Kōjō, Enchō, Taihan and 141 other people, including many laymen, received the Taizōkai initiation from Kūkai.[23] Saichō had received initiations into the two (ryōbu) most important traditions in East Asian Esoteric Buddhism. Later he would interpret the initiations he had received in China from Shun-hsiao as ryōbu intiations, as was noted above.

Esoteric initiations were usually thought of as being exclusively for monks. When laymen participated, the ceremonies were less serious. Thus some scholars argue that the ordinations Saichō received were elementary ones (kechien kanjō 結縁灌頂).[24] Later, in the Kechimyakufu, when Saichō described the lineages upon which his teachings were based, he did not mention the Esoteric initiations he had received from Kūkai. Perhaps Saichō felt that the initiations were only elementary ones and thus did not merit inclusion. However, since Saichō included a number of seemingly insignificant teachings which he had received while in China, the omission of Kūkai's name in the Kechimyakufu lineages obviously reflects the later break in relations between Saichō and Kūkai.

Some scholars, on the basis of a letter from Enchō to Kūkai dated 831,[25] have maintained that the initiation was an intermediate one. (jimyō kanjō 持明灌頂). However, the term jimyō kanjō (literally, initiation into mudrās and dhāraṇīs) might also refer to an introductory initiation into Esoteric ritual.[26] Yet even if the ordination were an intermediate one, it is clear that Saichō spent only a few months with Kūkai. Because he

---

[22] Kūkai, Takao kanjōki (Record of the Initiations on Takao), Kōbō Daishi chōsaku zenshū 3: 555. A manuscript of the work in Kūkai's handwriting exists.

[23] Ibid., p. 556.

[24] Ono, "Saichō Kūkai," p. 26.

[25] Rankeiionshū, Kōbō Daishi zenshū, ed. Sofu son'yoe, 15 vols. (Tokyo: Yoshikawa kōbunkan, 1910), 15: 337–39. The Tendaishū shanagō haja benshōki 天台宗遮那業破雅辨正記 (Records of the Esoteric course of the Tendai School Criticizing the Heterodox and Defending the Orthodox), compiled in 1109 by Yakushun 藥雋 (Tendaishū zenshō, ed., Tendai shūten kankōkai, 26 vols. [Hieizan: Tendai shūten kankōkai, 1935–37; reprinted Tokyo: Daiichi shobō, 1973–74] 7: 229–34) lists thirty reasons why the letter is not authentic; however, Yakushun's work was composed during a period of intense rivalry between the Tendai and Shingon Schools. Many modern scholars accept the letter as authentic. But Saichō's mastery of Esoteric Buddhism is criticized in the letter, and it is questionable whether Saichō's disciples would have couched their request in such terms. However since the letter does correspond to an event in Enchō's life (see Denjutsu isshinkaimon, DV 1: 639), it is probably authentic.

[26] Kiuchi, Dengyō Daishi no shōgai to shisō, p. 150.

had to return to Mount Hiei to attend to affairs in the Tendai School, he was unable to study further with Kūkai and obtain higher initiations. Thus at the same place where only eight years earlier Saichō had performed Japan's first Esoteric consecration (*kanjō*), Saichō now received an initiation from Kūkai. Saichō's willingness to recognize Kūkai's superior knowledge of Esoteric Buddhism testifies to his earnestness in pursuing the study of Esoteric Buddhism.

Close relations continued between Saichō and Kūkai for at least a year, with Saichō sending his most trustworthy disciples, Taihan,[27] Kōjō,[28] and Enchō,[29] to study further under Kūkai early in 813. Since the three monks had not been present when Saichō received his Kongō-kai initiation the year before, Kūkai granted them this initiation in the third month of 813.[30] Enchō and Kōjō, for unknown reasons, did not stay with Kūkai for very long, and thus did not complete their Esoteric studies. Taihan, however, did remain with Kūkai and served as liaison between Saichō and Kūkai for the next several years.

The Deterioration of Relations Between Saichō and Kūkai

Yet cooperation between the two monastic leaders could not continue for long. Saichō's view that Lotus Exoteric teachings and Shingon Esoteric teachings were fundamentally the same differed from Kūkai's view that Shingon teachings were superior to all Exoteric teachings. Saichō certainly could not have been ignorant of this difference. Kūkai had stated his position in the *Goshōrai mokuroku* 御請來目錄, his report to the court and bibliography of the works he brought back to Japan with him,[31] and Saichō had made a copy of this work.[32]

In addition, Saichō and Kūkai held conflicting attitudes concerning the study and transmission of Esoteric doctrine. Since Saichō was busy with affairs on Mount Hiei, he could not spare long periods of time to study under Kūkai. Instead, he tried to study Esoteric teachings by borrowing and copying books. Surviving correspondence indicates that Saichō borrowed at least thirty works from Kūkai. While most of these were Esoteric texts, some Kegon and Tendai works were also included. Saichō may have used the Kegon and Tendai works to collate texts in

---

[27] *DZ* 5: 460.
[28] *DZ* 1: 529.
[29] *DZ* 5: 448–49.
[30] *Takao kanjōki, Kōbō Daishi chōsaku zenshū* 3: 561.
[31] *Goshōrai, mokuroku, Kōbō Daishi chōsaku zenshū* 2: 14.
[32] Tsuji, *Nihon Bukkyōshi* 1: 284.

his own library. In Esoteric Buddhism, however, the importance of the transmission of the teaching from teacher to disciple has traditionally been stressed. Copying and studying texts without a teacher does not lead to an accurate understanding of Esoteric teachings.

With such differences, it was not long before a break came in the relations between the two men. On the twenty-third day of the eleventh month, Saichō is said to have dispatched his disciple Jōsō 貞聰 to Kūkai with a letter requesting the loan of the *Li ch'u shih ching* 理趣釋經.[33] This work was translated or perhaps composed by Amoghavajra. It is a two-fascicle commentary on the *Adhyārdhaśatikāprajñājpāramitā,* a work interpreting perfection of wisdom teachings in Esoteric terms. Saichō had brought a copy of the *sūtra* back from China and was naturally interested in the commentary which Kūkai had carried back.[34] The commentary contained some sexual imagery which required instruction from a teacher to be interpreted correctly. In an undated reply addressed to the Dharma-master Chō (Chō Hosshi 澄法師), Kūkai refused to lend the text in no uncertain terms:

> If you seek the truth, you should follow the teachings of the Buddha. If you follow the teachings of the Buddha, you should respect the *sanmaya* (vows). If these vows are violated, then neither the person conferring the initiation nor the recipient benefits. The fate of Esoteric teachings rests with you and me. If you receive (an initiation) incorrectly or I grant it incorrectly, how will people seeking the truth later know what to follow? Incorrect initiations are called stealing the Dharma because they constitute an attempt to deceive the Buddha. The profundities of the secret doctrines are not to be found in words, but in a transmission from mind to mind. Words are rubble. If you take only dregs or rubble, you lose the essence. It is a fool's way to throw away the real for the false. You should not seek the way of a fool.[35]

If the letter was intended for Saichō, as most scholars assert,[36] the terms in which the letter was written must have hurt him. The letter

[33]*DZ* 5: 449. The *Li ch'u shih ching* is *T* no. 1003.

[34]*Esshūroku BZ* 95: 232a.

[35]*Shōryōshū, Kōbō Daishi chōsaku zenshū* 3: 434–35.

[36]A recent example of this view is found in Katsumata, *Mikkyō,* p. 242–46.

[37]For examples see the *Fūshinchō, Kōbō Daishi chōsaku zenshū* 3: 577–79. The original manuscripts of these letters in Kūkai's handwriting survive.

[38]Akamatsu, *Kyōto jishikō,* pp. 59–61. This theory dates back to Jihon in the *Tendai kahyō,* fasc. 7D, *BZ* 42: 156.

is completely devoid of the politeness found in the few other surviving letters from Kūkai to Saichō.[37] Because of this, a number of scholars[38] have suggested that the letter was not addressed to Saichō but to his disciple Enchō. On the other hand, Tsuji Zennosuke[39] 辻善之助 considers the letter to be a forgery, noting that the last three volumes of the *Shōryōshū* 性靈集 in which the letter was included were not compiled until 1739 and contain many forgeries. Ono Katsutoshi[40] 小野勝年 also feels the letter as it stands cannot be considered authentic.

One other problem concerning the letter is its dating. Scholars who consider it authentic and addressed to Saichō usually date it soon after Saichō's 813 letter requesting the *Li ch'u shih ching*. Although the frequency of correspondence between the two monks decreases after 813, two letters dated 814 and 816 survive, proving that relations between the two men did not completely cease.[41] Akamatsu Toshihide 赤松俊秀 has suggested that Kūkai's letter refusing the loan of the *Li ch'u shih ching* was written around 816, two years later than most scholars date it. Although none of these theories has been satisfactorily proven, an examination of Saichō's extant letters indicates that by early 814 contacts between the two men were probably decreasing and that Saichō was concerned about whether Kūkai would continue to loan him works.[42]

The cooperation between the two monks probably ended over a dispute concerning Saichō's disciple Taihan. After Taihan had gone to study with Kūkai in 813, he probably did not return to Mount Hiei even though Saichō wrote several letters inviting him back. After a lapse of several years, Saichō decided to try one last time and on the first day of the fifth month of 816 wrote Taihan a heart-felt letter. In it he described Mount Hiei as still in a state of turmoil because of internecine struggles. He continued:

> I wander alone in the world bearing the Lotus One-Vehicle teaching. I only regret that Taihan Ācārya is somewhere else. In years past, we vowed to devote ourselves to supporting the Buddha's teaching. (Tendai's right to) yearly ordinands has been recognized, and extensive lectures on the *Lotus Sūtra* have begun. I have never forgotten your help even for an instant. Together we were initiated on Takao (by Kūkai in 812) and sought the Way with

---

[39] Tsuji, *Nihon Bukkyōshi* 1: 304.
[40] Ono questions the whole episode. See "Saichō Kūkai kōyūkō," pp. 17, 20.
[41] *DZ* 5: 450, 454.
[42] Akamatsu, *Kyōto jishikō,* pp. 61–62.

the same determination. But you have long been away.

It is the way of the world to reject the inferior and choose the superior. But what difference can there be between the Lotus One-Vehicle and the Shingon One-Vehicle. They follow the same teaching, and are truly like good friends. You and I are tied together by karma in this world and (in the future) will probably meet (again in front of) Maitreya.

Saichō concluded the letter to Taihan with an invitation to accompany him to Tōgoku the following spring.[43]

Three versions of Taihan's reply in which he refuses to return are extant.[44] The first version of the letter appears to be written by Taihan. The second version is by Kūkai. In the third version, characters meaning "so-and-so" 厶甲 replace the name of the sender. These discrepancies are usually explained by claiming that Kūkai wrote the letter for Taihan. Recently, however, Akamatsu Toshihide has advanced the theory that both Saichō's letter to Taihan and the letter in reply have been tampered with.[45] His argument is unfortunately too brief to properly evaluate. Even if parts of the letters are forged, Taihan's name does not appear in any literature related to Saichō after 816, while it does appear in later Shingon School records. Taihan later played an important role in helping Kūkai establish the Shingon monastery on Mount Kōya.[46] He was also included in a list of Kūkai's ten leading disciples compiled by Shinga 眞雅 (801–879) in 878.[47] Thus Taihan must have broken his ties with Saichō by 816 at the latest.

The defection of one of his most beloved and promising disciples must have been a very grave emotional blow to Saichō. In addition, it must have severely hurt Saichō's hope for establishing an effective training program in Esoteric Buddhism. Of all Saichō's disciples, Taihan had spent the most time with Kūkai and had the most advanced understanding of Esoteric Buddhism. If he had returned to Mount Hiei it would have greatly aided the Tendai program in Esoteric Buddhism.

Relations between Saichō and Kūkai probably did not end as abruptly and as bitterly as most traditional accounts have maintained. About

---

[43]*DZ* 5: 468–70.

[44]*Shōryōshū, Kōbō Daishi chōshaku zenshū* 3: 427. Two other versions are found in *Sangō shiki: Shōryōshū,* ed. Watanabe Shōkō and Miyasaka Yūshō, Nihon koten bungaku taikei, vol. 71 (Tokyo: Iwanami shoten, 1965), p. 440.

[45]"Saichō to Kūkai," p. 12.

[46]*Kōya zappitsushū,* in Katsumata, ed., *Kōbō Daishi chōsaku zenshū,* 3: 488.

[47]Matsunaga, *Mikkyō no rekishi,* p. 197.

[48]See Kiuchi Hiroshi, "Dengyō Daishi no montei to Mikkyō," *Tendai gakuhō* (hereafter

ten years after Saichō's death, Kōjō and Enchō probably went to study under Kūkai.[48] Furthermore, a letter survives from Kūkai's disciple Shintai 眞泰 to the head monk (*zasu*) of the Tendai School, Gishin, which was written sometime after Saichō's death. In the letter a pledge between Gishin and Shintai is mentioned.[49] In light of such evidence, a more gradual and less acrimonious break between Saichō and Kūkai must be postulated. During Saichō's last years, Kūkai was writing works clarifying his stand that Esoteric Buddhism was superior to all other types of Buddhism. Shortly after Saichō's death, he asked that the monastery Tōji 東寺 in Kyoto be designated as an exclusively Shingon temple. Such sectarian tendencies undoubtedly made it increasingly difficult for Saichō and Kūkai to work together. Moreover, Saichō was increasingly busy with the Tendai School on Mount Hiei. Thus the split was probably a natural and gradual one, punctuated by Taihan's defection and the end of the exchange of texts.

Saichō never did develop an Esoteric Buddhist philosophy that could compete with Kūkai and the Shingon School. A list of Saichō's disciples shows that virtually no one in the Esoteric Course stayed on Mount Hiei. Out of the ten yearly ordinands in the Esoteric Course from 810 to 816, only one remained on Mount Hiei in 819.[50] The majority of the rest had by this time defected from Mount Hiei to study Hossō in Nara. Even Ennin 圓仁 (794–864), one of the great figures in Tendai Esoteric Buddhism, was not a product of the Esoteric Course; he was the yearly ordinand for the Tendai course in 814.

As his prospects for integrating Esoteric Buddhism with Tendai doctrine looked increasingly bleak, Saichō began to turn his attention to defending the Tendai interpretations of the *Lotus Sūtra* against Hossō criticisms and to administering the Tendai order. Later, after Saichō's death his successors would develop a Tendai form of Esoteric Buddhism.

cited as *TG*) 8: 60–61.
[49]See Sonoda, "Sōsōki Murōji wo meguru sōryo no dōkō," *Kokushi ronbun*, pp. 411–12. The letter is found in *Kōya zappitsushū* fasc. 2, *Kōbō Daishi chōsaku zenshū* 3: 540.
[50]*Gakushō meichō*, *DZ* 1: 252.

CHAPTER SEVEN

THE PROPAGATION AND DEFENSE OF THE TENDAI SCHOOL

Several years earlier when his relationship with Kūkai was deteriorating, Saichō had begun a campaign to define and defend the Tendai position against that of the Nara schools. In doing so, he was continuing a tradition of debating doctrinal issues which can be traced from the Nara period in Japan back to China and India. Saichō was aware of these antecedents and discussed them at length in the *Hokke shūku* 法華秀句 (Elegant Words Concerning the *Lotus Sūtra*).[1]

In the ninth month of 813, Saichō compiled the main body and postface of the *Ehyō Tendaigishū* 依憑天台義集 (also called the *Ehyōshū*, full title: The Dependence on Tendai Doctrine by the Scholars from the Other Schools of China and Korea).[2] In this work, he demonstrated how often and extensively other schools had borrowed from Tendai texts and praised its teachings. At this time, however, he was not very critical of the other schools. The *Ehyōshū* may have been the result of Saichō's participation in a debate at Kōfukuji chaired by Fujiwara no Fuyutsugu several months earlier. Saichō and Kōjō argued against Gige 義解 and Gien 義延 of Kōfukuji that Tendai doctrines were superior to Hossō doctrines.[3] On the fourteenth day of the first month of the next year (late 813), the last day of a *Saishōe* assembly (for lectures on the *Chin kuang ming ching*) at court, Saichō debated with monks from other temples. Two months later on the anniversary of Kanmu's death, Kōjō defended the Tendai position against the attacks of Shin'en 眞苑, the head of the Bureau of Buddhism and Aliens (*Genbaryō*) who had previously been a monk at Kōfukuji.[4] Two months afterwards, Saichō appeared at a debate at Daianji, having been invited by Wake no Matsuna.[5]

---

[1]Saichō's discussion is found in the *chū* 中 fascicles of the *Hokke shūku* (*DZ* 3: 111–240). Many scholars believe that these fascicles were added to the *Hokke shūku* by a later scholar. Shioiri Ryōchū argues that the *chū* fascicles were originally part of another work by Saichō (*BKD* 10: 70–71).

[2]*DZ* 3: 365. Some scholars claim that the whole work was compiled in 816 and that the 813 date was a later fabrication; this seems unlikely. See Tamura Kōyū, "Saichō *Ehyōshū* ni tsuite," *IBK* 21, no. 2 (1973): 60–65; and Yoshizawa, "*Ehyō Tendaishū* ni tsuite," *TG* 14 (1971): 197.

[3]*Denjutsu isshinkaimon DZ* 1: 530. No biographies exist for Gige and Gien.

[4]Ibid., p. 530.

This exchange seems to have been a bitter one. During these years, Saichō's attitudes toward the Nara schools gradually hardened. Although he had criticized the Hossō and Sanron schools in his 802 petition requesting permission to go to China, Saichō had maintained friendly relations with many Hossō and Sanron scholars, such as Shūen and Gonsō, since returning to Japan. In his 806 petition asking for Tendai yearly ordinands, he had not criticized the other schools.

However, by 816 when he wrote the short introduction to the *Ehyō Tendaigishū,* his tone had changed. In the text, he made pointed criticisms of the Shingon, Kegon, Sanron and Hossō schools.[6] Moreover, it was in this same work that he first announced the radical concept that the faculties of all Japanese people were suitable for the Perfect (Tendai) teachings,[7] the implication being that there was no longer any need for the less perfect, expedient teachings of the other schools. Later, Saichō argued that since all Japanese had Perfect faculties 圓機, they no longer needed to follow the Hīnayāna precepts.

During this period, Saichō began to travel and propagate Tendai doctrines in new areas. In 814 he went to Kyushu to fulfill vows he had previously made at several shrines to insure a safe voyage to China. While in Kyushu, he carved a cedar statue of a one-thousand armed Kannon (Skt. Avalokiteśvara) and made two copies of the *Ta pan jo ching (Mahāprajñāpāramitāsūtra)* in 600 fascicles, as well as 1000 copies of the *Lotus Sūtra.* He also is said to have lectured on the *Lotus Sūtra* before the *kami* Hachiman Daijin 八幡大神 at Usa Jingū 宇佐神宮 and before the *kami* Kawara Myōjin 香春明神 at Kawara Jingū.[8]

In the spring of 816, Saichō submitted three works to the court, which related the history of the Tendai School and supported its stand on the universality of the Buddha-nature.[9]

---

[5]*Eizan Daishiden, DZ* 5 (*Bekkan*): 36. Yokota Ken'ichi ("Wakeshi to Saichō," pp. 416–18) has suggested that the Wake family were important lay donors at Daianji, and may have requested that debates at Daianji be held in order to give Saichō an opportunity to spread Tendai doctrines.

[6]*DZ* 3: 344.

[7]Ibid., p. 343. Saichō's concept of Perfect faculties is discussed in Chapter 9.

[8]*Eizan Daishiden, DZ* 5 (*Bekkan*): 28–29. The account seems exaggerated, both in the vast numbers of *sūtras* Saichō is said to have copied, and in an account of how Kawara Myōjin appeared to him in a dream and promised to protect him. However, these descriptions are probably based on an actual trip to Kyushu by Saichō. His belief in *kami* is noteworthy and can be seen as a forerunner to later Tendai Sannō Shintō. Usa Jingū, located in Usa-shi, Oita-ken, is the center of Hachiman worship in Japan. Kawara (or Kawaru) is located in Tagawa-gun, Fukuoka-ken.

[9]*Nihon kiryaku: zenpen, KT* 10: 303. The three works were: the *Tendai ryōōzuhondenshū*

This period was a crucial one for Saichō. His plans for studying Esoteric Buddhism had not succeeded. During the remaining years of his life, Saichō spent little time studying Esoteric Buddhism. In addition, he still had not successfully defended and defined the Tendai position against Hossō attacks. His disciples were fighting amongst themselves and gradually leaving Mount Hiei. Furthermore, the many arduous years of practicing on Mount Hiei had adversely affected his health. In China in 804, in his will of 812, and in letters written late in his life, there are indications that Saichō was not well. By 816 he had already turned fifty. If he were to build a strong foundation for the Japanese Tendai School, he would have to act soon. Far from being discouraged by these difficulties, Saichō was stimulated by them. The result was Saichō's most creative period. During the next six years, Saichō wrote almost all of his major works and developed the ideas that have made him a major figure in Japanese Buddhist history.

Preaching in Tōgoku

The turning point in Saichō's career began with a trip to Tōgoku 東國 (Eastern provinces) in 817.[10] There he is said to have lectured to

---

天台靈應圖本傳集 in ten fascicles (two fascicles survive, see *DZ* 4: 165–226), the *Shinshū shōgyōjo* 新宗聖教序 in three fascicles by Saichō (not extant), and the *Shih tzu hou* 獅子吼 (Lion's Roar) chapter of the *Nieh p'an ching* 涅槃經 (*Mahāparinirvāṇasūtra*). The last work is concerned with the universality of the Buddha-nature and the first two are compilations of works relating to Tendai history.

[10] Most accounts of Saichō's life follow the *Eizan Daishiden* [*DZ* 5 (*Bekkan*): 30–31] in claiming that after Saichō went to Daianji in Nara to take part in debates with monks from other schools, he immediately left for Tōgoku. Thus his trip would have started in the autumn of 815 and ended by the spring of 816, when Saichō presented three works to the throne (see preceeding note).

On the other hand, a number of other documents suggest that Saichō went to Tōgoku after he had submitted the three works:

(a) According to Enchō's *Sōjō kechimyaku* 相承血脈, dated 837 (*Tendai kahyō,* fasc. 2A, *BZ* 41: 258), Saichō received the *ryōbu* Esoteric initiations in China and then conferred them on Enchō and Kōchi 廣智 in front of the Lotus Pagoda (Hokketō) at Mitonodera on the fifteenth day of the fifth month of 817. It also includes a statement that Enchō had previously received the *ryōbu* initiations from Kūkai; but the numbers of men who participated in the initiations is greatly exaggerated. Because of the intensity of the controversy surrounding the claims that Saichō had received the *ryōbu* initiations in China, this document must be viewed with suspicion.

(b) Ennin also accompanied Saichō to Tōgoku. According to the *Jikaku Daishiden* (*ZGR* 8: 686), Ennin received the *endon bosatsukai* (Sudden–Perfect bodhisattva precepts) ordination on the sixth day of the third month of 817. Ennin's participation in the first bodhisattva precepts ordination on Mount Hiei in 823 as teacher would seem to indicate that this report is accurate. However, another biography of Ennin, the *Hieizan Enryakuji Shingon Hokkeshū daisan hosshu Jikaku Daishiden,* does not mention the ordination (Kiuchi, *Dengyō Daishi no shōgai to shisō,* p. 161). Since all other evidence indicates that Saichō did not publicly

thousands on the *Lotus Sūtra, Jen wang ching* and the *Chin kuang ming ching*. He set up *Hokketō* 法華塔 (pagodas containing one-thousand copies of the *Lotus Sūtra*) at Mitonodera 緣野寺 in Kōzuke (in present day Gunma-ken) and at Onodera 小野寺 in Shimotsuke (in present day Tochigi-ken). He also is said to have performed Esoteric initiations and to have conferred the bodhisattva precepts in Tōgoku. During this time, Saichō received assistance from the disciples of the late Dōchū. Dōchū's earlier gift of texts for the library on Mount Hiei and the production of so many copies of the *Lotus Sūtra* indicate the presence of a long tradition of copying texts among Dōchū and his disciples. Dōchū's former disciple Enchō, as well as Ennin, a native of Shimotsuke, accompanied Saichō. Later, on the basis of this trip and Saichō's close relationship with Dōchū's disciples, the Kantō region would prove to be a Tendai stronghold. In fact, many of the early leaders of the Tendai School came from Kantō.

The Debates with Tokuitsu 德一[11]

During his travels in Tōkoku, Saichō probably heard about the Hossō monk Tokuitsu, who was staying at Enichiji 慧日寺 in Aizu (in Fukushima-ken).[12] Tokuitsu was said to be the ninth son of Emi no Oshikatsu 惠美押勝 (also known as Fujiwara no Nakamaro 藤原仲麻呂, 706–64). However, like many elements of Tokuitsu's life, his parentage has been questioned. For reasons that are not clear, he left the capital shortly after his twentieth birthday. According to traditional accounts, he studied Hossō under Shūen of Kōfukuji; however, this seems doubtful. Despite his own contacts with Shūen, Saichō does not seem to have

---

advocate replacing the *Ssu fen lü* precepts with the precepts of the *Fan wang ching* until two years later, this report must be viewed with caution.

(c) The *Tokuen Ajari injin* 德圓阿闍梨印信 (*Tendai kahyō*, fasc. 2B, *BZ* 41: 265) states that also on the sixth day of the third month of 817, Saichō granted Tokuen 德圓 a Kongōkai ordination at Daijisanji in Shimozuke.

(d) In Saichō's last letter to Taihan (*DZ* 5: 469) dated the first day of the fifth month of 816, he invited Taihan to travel with him the following spring.

(e) A letter from Ōtomo Kunimichi 大伴國道 to Gishin and Enchin dated 825 mentions Saichō's activities in Tōgoku and places them in 817 (*Tendai kahyō*, fasc. 2B, *BZ* 41: 256). The weight of the evidence, thus indicates that Saichō was in Tōgoku in 817.

[11]The reading Tokuitsu rather than the more usual Tokuichi is used here because it reflects some of the alternate ways in which Tokuitsu's name was written: 德益 and 德逸, See Tamura, *Saichō jiten*, pp. 185–88.

[12]The temple was founded by Tokuitsu and later became a major monastery. The name of the temple may have been chosen by Tokuitsu to reflect his devotion to the Fa–hsiang patriarch Hui–chao 慧沼 (650–714), the author of the *Hui jih lun* 慧日論 (*T* no. 1863). See Tamura, *Saichō jiten*, pp. 15–18.

known who Tokuitsu's teachers were.[13] The birth dates of Shūen (770–834) and Tokuitsu (780?–842?) indicate that they were more likely contemporaries than teacher and student. Regardless of who his teacher was, Tokuitsu was a competent scholar. He is credited with the authorship of approximately seventeen works in seventy fascicles.[14] Unfortunately, only two of his works survive: an attack on the Shingon School entitled the *Shingonshū miketsu* 眞言宗末決,[15] and a short work entitled the *Shikanron* 止觀論[16] which is quoted in its entirety in Saichō's *Shugo kokkaishō*. Many of his other works are quoted extensively by Saichō, as well as by Genshin (in the *Ichijō yōketsu* 一乘要決), Teikyō 貞慶 (in the *Hokke kaijishō* 法華開持抄) and others. Among his works was a fourteen-fascicle commentary on the *Lotus Sūtra* entitled the *Hokke shinsho* 法華新疏 (New Commentary on the *Lotus Sūtra*).

Tokuitsu was highly respected by the local populace. His biographies report that the people called him a 'bodhisattva' and that he had many disciples. He is said to have scorned luxuries, preferring to eat rough foods and wear poor clothing. According to the *Genkō shakusho*, when he died his body did not decay, a sign of his virtue.[17] Tokuitsu is credited with founding and aiding over thirty temples during his lifetime.[18] Since Saichō's late benefactor Dōchū[19] had also preached in Tōgoku and had been a highly respected figure in the area, a fierce rivalry between Dōchū's disciples and Tokuitsu probably existed before Saichō's visit to Tōgoku. Because Dōchū's teacher Chien-chen had Tendai affiliations, Dōchū's disciples were undoubtedly very receptive to Saichō's Tendai teachings. The dispute between Tokuitsu and Saichō probably

---

[13]*Hokke shūku, DZ* 3: 76. Sonoda (*Saichō*, p. 492) questions the claim that Tokuitsu was the son of Fujiwara no Nakamaro.

[14]Tamura Kōyū, "Tokuitsu chosakukō," *DDK*, pp. 782–83.

[15]*T* no. 2458. A study of the *Shingon miketsu* can be found in Shimizutani Kyōjun, *Tendai mikkyō no seiritsu ni kansuru kenkyū*, pp. 95–102.

[16]*DZ* 2: 310–50. Asada Masahiro ["*Shugo kokkaishō* ni okeru shikan," *Bukkyō no jissen genri*, Sekiguchi Shindai, ed. (Tokyo: Sankibō Busshorin, 1977), pp. 515–38] has demonstrated that the *Shikanron* is mainly composed of passages excerpted from the *Yogācārabhūmiśāstra* (*T* no. 1579).

[17]*BZ* 62: 88b. The description of Tokuitsu as an 'eater of rough foods' is found in late biographies. It is undoubtedly based on a derogatory epithet, 'eater of rough foods' 龜食者 which Saichō called Tokuitsu. However, if Tokuitsu actually had eaten rough foods and lived an austere life, Saichō's use of the epithet would have implied praise, not criticism. Saichō probably meant that Tokuitsu ate 'the rough tastes of the Three-vehicle teachings' and not the 'fine tastes of the One-Vehicle teaching' (Tamura, *Saichō jiten*, pp. 148–49.

[18]Ibid., p. 187.

[19]Ui (*Nihon Bukkyō gaishi*, p. 16) claims that Dōchū died in 783. This seems too early though, since he is said to have sent Saichō his disciple Enchō and some books in 798. Perhaps Enchō, Dōchū's disciple, went to study with Saichō in 798 because of his teacher's death.

dates from Saichō's stay in Tōgoku and may have begun when Tokuitsu read a copy of Saichō's *Ehyō Tendaigishū*. On the other hand, perhaps Saichō read Tokuitsu's *Busshōshō* 佛性抄 (Tract on the Buddha-nature) and decided to refute it. Once the controversy began, it continued for the remainder of Saichō's life. It constitutes one of the high points in the intellectual history of Japanese Buddhism.

Tokuitsu wrote the *Busshōshō* 佛性抄 (Tract on the Buddha-nature) sometime before the second month of 817, probably while Saichō was still in Tōgoku. Saichō replied with the *Shōgonjitsukyō* 照權實鏡 (Mirror Illuminating the Provisional and the Real) in the second month of 817.[20] The work is not as well documented as Saichō's later works because it was probably written while he was still in Tōgoku and did not have access to a good library.

The following year after he had returned to Mount Hiei, Saichō expanded his arguments defending the *Lotus Sūtra* and its One-vehicle doctrine in the amply documented four-fascicle work, the *Hokke kowaku* 法華去感 (Vanquishing Misunderstandings about the *Lotus Sūtra*).[21] This work was included in a longer work, the *Shugo kokkaishō* 守護國界章 (Essays on Protecting the Nation) in nine fasicles, also written in 818.[22] The *Shugo kokkaishō* was by far the longest and most detailed of Saichō's works. It refuted Tokuitsu's *Chūhengikyō* 中邊義鏡 (Mirror on Orthodox and Heterodox Doctrine), a work of three fascicles. Tokuitsu is also known to have compiled a twenty-fascicle work, the *Chūhengikyōzan* 中邊義鏡殘, which was probably a collection of quotations supporting the *Chūhengikyō*.

Reconstruction of the *Chūhengikyō* from surviving quotations in the *Shūgo kokkaishō* and other texts indicates that in the first fascicle Tokuitsu criticized the Tendai theories of meditation and classification of doctrines found in Chih-i's *Mo ho chih kuan* and *Ssu chiao i*.[23] In the second fascicle, he attacked the Tendai interpretations of the *Lotus Sūtra* found in the *Fa hua hsüan i* and the *Fa hua wen chü,* Chih-i's two major works interpreting the *sūtra.*

---

[20]*DZ* 2: 1–12. For the date of the work, see pp. 11–12. Tokuitsu's *Busshōshō* is mentioned on page 11. Tamura Kōyū has written a number of articles on the chronology of the controversy. For a chart summarizing his conclusions, see p. 16 of the biography in *Saichō jiten*.

[21]*DZ* 2: 13–150. This work corresponds to the fourth through the sixth fascicles of the *Shugo kokkaishō*.

[22]*DZ* 2: 151–681. For the date of the work see ibid., p. 372.

[23]*T* no. 1929. Tamura Kōyū has reconstructed the table of contents of the *Chūhengikyō* (*Saichō jiten*, pp. 122–23).

Tokuitsu's understanding of Tendai doctrine was more than adequate. He often cited passages from Chih-i's works on his own initiative, not just in response to Saichō's arguments. Yet, since Tokuitsu lived far from the capital, he probably did not have access to Chih-i's works. The Tendai texts brought to Japan by Chien-chen were never widely circulated and the works which Saichō carried back to Japan had only recently been copied. How then did Tokuitsu obtain the Tendai texts? Asada Masahiro 淺田正博 has recently argued that Tokuitsu's knowledge of Tendai doctrine did not come from a study of Chih-i's works, but from a one-fascicle collection of passages from them compiled by Saichō, the *Ichijōgishū* 一乘義集 (Anthology concerning the Doctrines of the One-vehicle).[24] Tamura Kōyū 田村晃祐 has suggested that Tokuitsu relied on a work by Chan-jan's disciple Ming-kuang, the *T'ien t'ai pa chiao ta i* 天台八教大意 (Outline of the T'ien-t'ai Classifications of Buddhism into Eight Teachings).[25] Tokuitsu's *Chūhengikyō* was thus written to refute the doctrines presented in one or both of these anthologies. Tokuitsu also relied on criticisms of T'ien-t'ai doctrines and in interpretations of the *Lotus Sūtra* advanced by two Fa-hsiang patriarchs, Tz'u-en 慈恩 (632–682) and Hui-chao 慧沼 (650–714).[26] In the last fascicle of of the *Chūhengikyō*, Tokuitsu argued against Fa-pao's 法寶 (fl. early 8th c.) *I ch'eng fo hsing chiu ching lun*[27] 一乘佛性究竟論 and was especially concerned with arguments over the Buddha-nature (*Busshō* 佛性). The *Chūhengikyō* appears to have been a *tour de force*.[28] Tokuitsu's

---

[24] The *Ichijōgishū* has not survived [Asada Masahiro, "Tokuitsu no *Chūhengikyō* senjutsu izu," *Bukkyōgaku kenkyū* 31 (1975): 74–99].

[25] *Saichō jiten*, pp. 7, 177–78. The *T'ien t'ai pa chiao ta i* (*T* no. 1930) is a one-fascicle survey of T'ien-t'ai meditation and classification of doctrines. Saichō brought a copy of this work back from China.

[26] Even the title of the *Chūhengikyō* came from a passage in Tz'u-en's *Ta ch'eng fa yüan i lin chang* (*T* 45: 250c–251a) in which Tz'u-en contrasted those who followed the middle way of orthodox Buddhism (*chūshu* 中主) with those who clung to an extreme position (*henshu* 邊主). Tz'u-en is often referred to by the misnomer K'uei-chi 慧窺 [Stanley Weinstein, "Biographical Study of Tz'u-en," *Monumenta Nipponica* 15 (1959): 119–49]. The term 'chūhen' 中邊 (middle and extreme) is also found in the title of Hui-chao's *Neng hsien chung pien hui jih lun* 能顯中邊慧日論 (*T* no. 1863), a text which had a major influence on Tokuitsu.

[27] Unfortunately only the third fascicle of the six-fascicle *I ch'eng fo hsing chiu ching lun* has been published (*Z* 1. 95. 4). The other fascicles were believed to have been lost; however, Etani Ryūkai has announced that he has found manuscripts of the first, second, fourth, and fifth fascicles of the work, as well as a related three-fascicle work by Fa-pao, the *I ch'eng fo hsing ch'üan shih lun* 一乘佛性權實論 (Etani, "Dengyō Daishi wo chūshin to sita Busshō ronsō ni tsuite," *DDK*, p. 96). Publication of these works should clarify a number of problems concerning the debates between Saichō and Tokuitsu. Fa-pao's *I ch'eng fo hsing chiu ching lun* was circulated in Nara. A Japanese monk named Kyōshun 慶俊 (d. 778) wrote a commentary on it, which has not survived.

later work, the *Shaikenshō* 遮違見章 (Essay Blocking Contrary Views) was probably written in response to Saichō's *Shugo kokkaishō*.[29]

Up to this point, Saichō had not taken the offensive in the exchange, allowing Tokuitsu to raise the points to be argued. About 820, Saichō decided to take the initiative in the arguments and sent Tokuitsu a list of twenty questions concerning the exegesis of the *Lotus Sūtra*. Tokuitsu responded, sending his answers through a third party who was undoubtedly used as messenger between the two men. Saichō compiled the exchange and added his final arguments, supporting most of them with quotations from the *Lotus Sūtra*. This work, the *Ketsugonjitsuron* 決權實論 (Treatise on Distinguishing the Real from the Provisional) in one fascicle, was a clear and concise exposition of the key issues in the controversy over the *Lotus Sūtra*.[30] It represented a victory for Saichō insofar as he was able to focus the arguments on the *Lotus Sūtra*. The Tendai School had the most developed tradition of *Lotus Sūtra* interpretation at this time and maintained a position closer to the original meaning of the *sūtra* than that of the Hossō School. Thus Saichō had effectively seized the offensive in the debate and directed it to the topics in which he was best prepared.

In 821, one year before his death, Saichō wrote his final work on the debates, the *Hokke shūku* in three fascicles.[31] Although Saichō directly refuted Tokuitsu on a number of points in the first fascicle, he felt secure enough to digress in the last two. In the second fascicle, Saichō stated that he would review previous arguments on the Buddha-nature in India, China and Japan, but did not actually include a section on Japan. In the last fascicle, Saichō argued for the superiority of the *Lotus* over other *sūtras,* and demonstrated the superiority of Tendai doctrines over those of the Kegon, Sanron, and Hossō schools.

Tendai scholars have often claimed that Saichō decisively won the debates. Although Saichō probably had the advantage at the time of his death, it is difficult to believe that a scholar of Tokuitsu's mettle would have suffered a series of one-sided defeats. Rather, he probably continued to forcefully argue for the Hossō position. A later work, the

---

[28] Scholars such as Sonoda (*Saichō,* p. 496) and Tokiwa Daijō [*Busshō no kenkyū* (Meiji shoin, 1944; reprint Tokyo: Kokusho kankōkai 1972), p. 311] both judge Tokuitsu to have been a very able scholar. In contrast, Asada Masahiro ("*Shugo kokkaishō* ni okeru shikan," p. 537) has carefully examined Tokuitsu's *Shikanron* and argued that they have overrated Tokuitsu's scholarly abilities.

[29] Tamura Kōyū, "Tokuitsu no *Shaikenshō* ni tsuite," *IBK* 18 (1971): 688–93.

[30] *DZ* 2: 685–722.

[31] *DZ* 3: 1–280. The work was divided into five fascicles by a later scholar.

Min'yu benwakushō 愍諭辯惑章, mistakenly attributed to Saichō but actually authored by his disciple Anne 安慧 (795–868), was compiled to refute the doctrines expounded by a scholarly Hossō monk at the Kokubunji (Provincial Temple) in Shimotsuke in 847.[32] This probably referred to Tokuitsu or one of his disciples. Some twenty years later, a Tendai monk named Renkō 蓮鋼, who was active in Kyushu, wrote the *Jōshūron* 定宗論.[33] Although the *Jōshūron* was mainly directed against the Sanron scholar Dōsen's 道詮 (797–876) *Gunkesōron* 群家靜論,[34] Renkō is said to have composed five additional works, one of which refuted Hossō doctrines.[35] After this time, the Tendai School's energies were mainly devoted to competing with the Shingon School. However, the arguments over the Buddha-nature did appear again in Genshin's 源信 (942–1017) *Ichijō yōketsu* 一乘要決.[36]

The Issues in the Debates with Tokuitsu

The dispute between Saichō and Tokuitsu covered a wide range of problems, including the proper method of classifying the Buddha's teachings, the evaluation of Tendai methods of exegesis of the *Lotus Sūtra,* and the criticism of various Tendai doctrines and meditations. Both men offered detailed and penetrating arguments in support of their positions. For example, in the *Chūhengikyō,* Tokuitsu had begun his discussion of the Tendai classification of teachings (*kyōhan*) by explaining that the Hossō (Chin. Fa-hsiang) classification was based on the *Chieh shen mi ching's* (*Saṃdhinirmocanasūtra*) division of the Buddha's preaching into three periods: Hīnayāna, Mahāyāna perfection of wisdom, and Yogācāra.[37] Tokuitsu then questioned the basis for Chih-i's classification of doctrine, and accused Chih-i of having simply invented a classification system without a scriptural basis. Saichō replied by citing passages from the *Nieh p'an ching* (*Mahāparinirvāṇasūtra*) and the *Yüeh teng san mei ching* (*Samādhirājacandrapradīpasūtra*) which

---

[32] *DZ* 3: 444. According to the *Tendai zasuki,* pp. 21–22, debates were held in court in the second month of 868 with Anne, Dōsen, and other Tendai, Hossō and Sanron monks attending.

[33] *T* 74: 313–27 (no. 2369). This work was thought to be lost until it was discovered in 1928. Almost nothing is known about Renkō.

[34] The work has not survived.

[35] Tajima Tokuon, s. v. *Jōshūron, BKD* 6: 44. The other works by Renkō are mentioned in Annen's *Kyōji sōron* (*T* 75: 366a).

[36] *T* no. 2370.

[37] *Shugo kokkaishō, DZ* 3: 153–183.

supported Chih-i's system. Tokuitsu also cited criticisms of the T'ien-t'ai classification system made by Hua-yen scholars such as Fa-tsang and Hui-yüan 慧苑. Tokuitsu's strategy was to show that even other advocates of One-vehicle teachings did not accept Chih-i's classifications. Saichō replied in the *Shugo kokkaishō* by discussing the Hua-yen criticisms in detail.[38] Tokuitsu also attacked specific points in Chih-i's system. For example, Chih-i had noted that the *Hua yen ching* (*Avataṃsakasūtra*) was the first *sūtra* preached after the Buddha's enlightenment and had called it a Sudden teaching 頓教, because the Buddha spoke about his enlightenment without any concern about the ability of his audience to understand his teachings. Tokuitsu criticized these positions maintaining that the *Ti wei po li ching* 提謂波利經 (*Sūtra of Trapuśa and Bhallika*) had been preached first. Tokuitsu also noted that not all of the *Hua yen ching* was composed of Sudden teachings; parts of it were Gradual teachings 漸教.[39] Saichō replied to each of Tokuitsu's charges by citing sources which supported the Tendai position and by criticizing the Hossō position. Saichō argued that the *Chieh shen mi ching* was primarily composed of expedient teachings. Its division of the Buddha's preaching into three periods was of little value, particularly when compared with the Tendai classifications which were based on the ultimate teachings of the *Lotus Sūtra*.

The main focus of the dispute, however, was on the nature of man and on his potential for obtaining Buddhahood. Mahāyāna Buddhist statements on man's potential for obtaining Buddhahood can be divided into two categories.[40] The first category is typified by claims that all sentient beings possess the Buddha-nature and can therefore attain Buddhahood. The second category is typified by statements that not all sentient beings have the Buddha-nature, and thus not all are able to attain Buddhahood. The task of both Saichō and Tokuitsu was to explain and evaluate these conflicting views in such a way that they supported their respective positions.

The Hossō School's position was that two categories of Buddha-nature could be identified:[41] the *ribusshō* 理佛性 which all men possessed

---

[38]Ibid., 183–97.

[39]Ibid., 197–206.

[40]*BD* 5: 4456c.

[41]This classification of the Buddha–nature was advanced by Tz'u–en 慈恩, partly as an attempt to reconcile conflicting statements in the *Nieh p'an ching* 涅槃經 concerning the universality of the Buddha–nature. For a detailed analysis of the problem in the *Nieh p'an ching*, see Tokiwa, *Busshō no kenkyū*, pp. 36–66. Some Fa–hsiang monks, such as Hui–chao

and the gyōbusshō 行佛性 which only a few possessed. The first was the Buddha-nature as absolute. Since the absolute was the basis of all phenomena, and since all sentient beings were ultimately dependent on the absolute, all were said to possess the *ribusshō*. However, Hossō scholars argued that the absolute was static; it did not actively participate in the phenomenal realm. Consequently, the *ribusshō* did not enable a practitioner to attain Buddhahood. When a *sūtra* stated that all sentient beings possessed the Buddha-nature, it indicated only that all had the *ribusshō*, not that all could attain Buddhahood.

The potential of some sentient beings to attain Buddhahood was explained by postulating a second type of Buddha-nature, the gyōbusshō or Buddha-nature of practice. The gyōbusshō consisted of untainted seeds (*muro shuji* 無漏種子) which were stored in the eight or basic consciousness (*arayashiki*, Skt. *ālaya-vijñāna*). These seeds were said to have existed from the beginningless past. If a person possessed them, he could attain Buddhahood. However, if he lacked untainted seeds, he could not create them no matter how diligently he practiced or studied. A person without the gyōbusshō could therefore never attain Buddhahood. Hossō School monks interpreted statements in the *sūtras* that only certain people could attain Buddhahood as referring to the possession of gyōbusshō by those people. Since not everyone had the gyōbusshō, some *sūtras* contained statements that not everyone could attain Buddhahood.

Hossō School scholars maintained the position that besides the untainted seeds for Buddhahood, a practitioner might possess different types of untainted seeds which would enable him to become an arhat or pratyekabuddha. The three vehicles (the teachings enabling one to become an arhat, partyekabuddha or Buddha) were thus separate and real goals which had their basis in three distinct types of seeds.

On the basis of passages in such *sūtras* as the *Chieh shen mi ching* (*Saṃdhinirmocanasūtra*) and the *Leng ch'ieh ching* (*Laṅkāvatārasūtra*), Hossō thinkers argued that any sentient being could be classified in one of five categories according to the presence and type of untainted seeds contained in his *ālaya-vijñāna*. The first category consisted of those who possessed only the seeds which enabled them to become arhats

慧沼, postulated a third type of Buddha–nature, the hidden Buddha–nature (*inmītsu busshō* 隱密佛性). This referred to the passions which must be overcome to attain Buddhahood. They were a hidden cause of Buddhahood, since the struggle against them eventually brought the practitioner to enlightenment. The traditional Hossō view is presented in Saichō's quotations of Tokuitsu in the last three fascicles of the *Shugo kokkaishō* (*DZ* 2: 509–681).

(*shōmonjō jōshō* 聲聞乘定性), the second of those who possessed only the seeds which enabled them to become pratyekabuddhas (*dokukakujō jōshō* 獨覺乘定性), and the third of those who possessed only the seeds which enabled them to become Buddhas (*nyoraijō jōshō* 如來乘定性). People in the three categories were described as those with fixed natures (*jōshō* 定性). Thus someone who possessed only the seeds to become an arhat could never become a Buddha. At death, an arhat or pratyeka-buddha would enter *parinirvāṇa*. No further spiritual progress could occur. The fourth category consisted of those who possessed any two or possibly all three types of the untainted seeds mentioned above. They were said to have an undetermined nature (*fujōshō* 不定性) since they might attain any one of the goals for which they had seeds. In addition, a person with seeds for both Hīnayāna (arhat or pratyekabuddha) and Mahāyāna (Buddha) goals could continue to progress spiritually and become a Buddha even after he had realized a Hīnayāna goal. Finally, the fifth category consisted of those who did not possess any untainted seeds at all (*mushō sendai* 無性闡提). Since they could not develop untainted seeds through practice or study, they were doomed forever to endless cycles of birth and death. Religious practice was not completely in vain for them, however, since it would enable them to be reborn as a man or a god and to avoid rebirth as a lower type of being.

According to Hossō School teachings, there were two other types of beings besides *mushō sendai* who could not attain the goals of Buddhahood, pratyekabuddhahood, or arhathood. All those who could not attain these spiritual goals were called *issendai* 一闡提.[42] It was believed that the *mushō sendai* could never attain salvation but that the two other types of *issendai* could reach it after a much longer period of practice than other sentient beings. The first classification of *issendai* who could eventually attain enlightenment consisted of those who had wrong beliefs (such as not believing in karmic cause and effect) and those who had performed heinous crimes. They were said to be *issendai* who had cut off their instincts to do good (*danzen sendai* 斷善闡提). Their wrong actions, however, did not eliminate any untainted seeds they might possess; thus they could attain spiritual goals after an extremely long period of practice. The second classification of such *issendai* consisted of bodhisattvas who had vowed to postpone their

---

[42]The Sanskrit equivalent for *issendai* is *icchantika*. Tz'u-en claimed that his classification of the three types of *issendai* was partially based on a similar distinction found in Sanskrit terminology. However, the other two Sanskrit terms, *ātyantika* and *acchantika,* may be regional variants of *icchantika* (*BD* 1: 148–49).

enlightenment until they had saved all sentient beings. Since the number of sentient beings was infinite, these bodhisattvas would never attain Buddhahood even though they possessed the untainted seeds to do so. They were called *issendai* of great compassion (*daihi sendai* 大悲闡提).[43] Using this scheme, Hossō scholars could interpret scriptural statements which would normally have supported the Tendai position that all could attain Buddhahood in such a way that they corroborated the Hossō view that not everyone could attain enlightenment. Thus a quotation from a *sūtra* stating that even *issendai* could attain enlightenment might be explained by Hossō scholars as referring to only *danzen sendai,* or by claiming that it was only a provisional teaching.[44]

The Hossō position that man's religious potential was limited by the types of untainted seeds he possessed was based on the Hossō view of the absolute.[45] The absolute was the basis 所依體 of the phenomenal world, but not its essence 當體體. The absolute was seen as eternal and unchanging and thus fundamentally different from the phenomenal world. Because the absolute was static, it did not produce phenomena (眞如凝然不作諸法) and thus could not produce untainted seeds. If one did not have the untainted seeds from the beginningless past, he could not obtain them now. The *arayashiki* (*ālaya-vijñāna*) was tainted by passions 有漏, and therefore could not produce untainted seeds. Most other Buddhist schools did not agree with the Hossō stand. Against them, Hossō monks argued that untainted seeds could not suddenly arise from tainted seeds just because a person had practiced and attained certain spiritual goals. Rather, the untainted seeds must have always been present (*honnu shuji* 本有種子) in the *arayashiki.* Moreover, if tainted seeds could give rise to untainted seeds, then untainted seeds, in turn, could presumably give rise to tainted seeds. According to this reasoning, the untainted seeds of a Buddha could be the causes of tainted seeds, and a Buddha could thus backslide from his exalted state to an impassioned state. The Hossō scholars argued that since their opponents would not want to claim that a Buddha could backslide, they must agree that tainted phenomena could not produce untainted seeds.[46]

---

[43]Tz'u-en recognized that the *daihi sendai* could be classified in the class of those who had the Buddha–nature as well as in the fifth class with the other *issendai*. The *danzen sendai* could also be placed in other categories depending on what types of untainted seeds he possessed.

[44]*Ketsugonjitsuron, DZ* 2: 688–94.

[45]Ibid., pp. 583–88; and Fukaura Seibun, *Yuishikigaku kenkyū,* 2 vols. (Kyoto: Nagata bunshōdō, 1954), 2: 213–14.

[46]*Shugo kokkaishō, DZ* 2: 583–88.

The Tendai School had a more optimistic view of human potential than did the Hossō School. Tendai monks followed the *Lotus Sūtra* in arguing that all sentient beings could eventually attain Buddhahood. No beings were permanently denied Buddhahood. They also argued that the three vehicles did not lead to three separate ultimate goals. Rather, all sentient beings had only one ultimate spiritual goal, Buddhahood. Teachings leading the practitioner to arhathood or pratyekabuddhahood were only provisional teachings designed to encourage those with lesser faculties and lead them onward towards the single ultimate goal for all sentient beings, Buddhahood.

On the basis of these Tendai teachings, Saichō argued that only *sūtras* which presented provisional teachings contained claims that some people could attain Hīnayāna goals but could never attain Buddhahood. The five types of human nature which the Hossō School had presented did not refer to seeds 約種 from the beginningless past, but to stages 約位 which a practitioner might attain and then transcend as he moved onward to higher goals. The five types of human nature were not determined by seeds which sentient beings possessed from the beginningless past, but by the obstacles which men had to overcome on their way to Buddhahood.[47]

Saichō's Sources for his Arguments

In his arguments against Tokuitsu, Saichō carefully referred to debates on the same topics which had occurred in India and China. He often utilized T'ien-t'ai texts to support his position. For example, in the *Tsūrokukushō hahiryōmon* 通六九證破比量文,[48] Saichō referred to Chan-jan's criticisms of Tz'u-en, the founder of the Fa-hsiang School. In the *Ch'eng wei shih lun chang chung shu yao* 成唯識論掌中樞要, Tz'u-en had assembled six quotations from Buddhist scriptures proving that some sentient beings possessed only the seeds necessary to become arhats or pratyekabuddhas and could therefore never attain Buddhahood. Tz'u-en also cited nine scriptural passages which supported the Hossō position that some sentient beings lacked untainted seeds altogether. Chan-jan had refuted Tz'u-en's claims by arguing that the set of six quotations did not prove that those who sought Hīnayāna goals could never become Buddhas. He also maintained that the references to those

---

[47] *Hokke shūku, DZ* 3: 98.
[48] *DZ* 2: 723–48. Tokuitsu criticized Saichō's *Tsūrokukushō hahiryōmon* and Saichō discussed Tz'u–en's quotations again in the *Hokke shūku* (*DZ* 3: 71–109).

without the Buddha-nature did not indicate that they were doomed
forever to that state. Rather, the nine quotations referred to a temporary
stage in the spiritual development of sentient beings.

In many cases, however, T'ien-t'ai sources were of little help to
Saichō in his debates with Tokuitsu. T'ien-t'ai masters had not fully
discussed the Yogācāra theories upon which Tz'u-en and Tokuitsu
had based their positions. Moreover, most of the past debates on the
Buddha-nature had not involved T'ien-t'ai monks. Consequently, Saichō was forced to turn to three scholarly traditions which did discuss
Yogācāra philosophy in order to support his position. His use of these
materials demonstrates Saichō's painstaking scholarship and deep ap-
preciation of the development of Chinese Buddhist doctrine and history.

The first source consisted of literature from the She-lun 攝論 School.
The She-lun School was based on Paramārtha's (499–569) translation of
the *Mahāyānasaṃgraha* (Chin. *She ta ch'eng lun* 攝大乘論). The Yogācāra doctrines propounded in Paramārtha's translations significantly
differed from those held by the Fa-hsiang School which was based on
Hsüan-tsang's translations of the *Mahāyānasaṃgraha* and other Yogācāra works. Paramārtha's translations advocated universal salvation
and maintained that the absolute and phenomenal realms constantly
interacted.[49] Saichō made good use of these differences. In discussing the
Mahāyānasaṃgraha, he always cited and compared all four of the commentaries which were available to him, including translations by both
Paramārtha and Hsüan-tsang.[50]

The second source consisted of Hua-yen texts. The Hua-yen (Jap.
Kegon) School had adopted many Yogācāra doctrines for use in its
teachings. Since Saichō had studied under a disciple of Tao-hsüan, the
Chinese monk credited with transmitting the Hua-yen School from
China to Japan, it is not surprising to find Saichō citing Hua-yen authors.
In addition, Hua-yen thought had made a deep impression on the sixth
T'ien-t'ai patriarch Chan-jan. Since Saichō had brought many of Chan-

---

[49] A discussion of some of the differences between the She–lun and Fa–hsiang positions
can be found in Stanley Weinstein, "Imperial Patronage in the Formation of T'ang Buddhism," in *Perspectives on the T'ang,* ed. Arthur Wright and Dennis Twitchett (New Haven:
Yale University Press, 1973), pp. 291–97. Weinstein's "The Concept of Ālaya–vijñāna in
Pre–T'ang Chinese Buddhism" [*Yūki kyōju shōju kinen: Bukkyō shisōshi ronshū* (Tokyo:
Daizō shuppansha, 1964), pp. 33–50] focusses on the Ti–lun position, but includes information
on Paramārtha.

[50] *Shugo kokkaishō, DZ* 2: 640, and *Hokke shūku, DZ* 3: 21–26, 86–87. The four texts
which Saichō cited were three translations of a commentary on the *Mahāyānasaṃgraha* by
Vasubandhu (*T* no. 1595–97) and a translation of a commentary by Asvabhāva (*T* no. 1598).

jan's works back to Japan and studied them, he was also influenced by the inclusion of Hua-yen doctrines in those T'ien-t'ai works. Saichō and Tokuitsu both cited works by Fa-tsang, the de facto founder of the Hua-yen School, in discussions of the T'ien-t'ai classification of Buddhist doctrine into four teachings.[51] Finally, Saichō passionately defended the Hua-yen One-vehicle position against Tokuitsu's attacks.[52]

Saichō's third source of texts which would support his position was a series of works by monks who had studied under Hsüan-tsang, the renowned translator of Yogācāra texts, but had disagreed with Hsüan-tsang's insistence that not all sentient beings could attain Buddhahood. After Hsüan-tsang's death, bitter debates occurred between Tz'u-en, founder of the Fa-hsiang School, and some of Hsüan-tsang's disciples who disagreed with Tz'u-en's interpretation of the Yogācāra texts. Saichō utilized these debates extensively in his refutation of Tokuitsu. For example, he quoted Hsüan-tsang's Korean disciple Wŏnch'ŭk 圓測 (612–696) in support of his argument that those who followed the two Hīnayāna vehicles eventually would convert to Mahāyāna teachings and attain Buddhahood.[53]

In addition, Saichō cited criticisms of Hsüan-tsang's translations by Ling-jun 靈潤 (d. 650?), one of Hsüan-tsang's earliest collaborators after his return from India. Ling-jun was one of the foremost exponents of the One-vehicle teachings of the *Nirvāṇa Sūtra,* but had also extensively studied *She-lun* and *Ti-lun* doctrines. He was thus well versed in both One-vehicle and Yogācāra thought. Ling-jun pointed out fourteen ways in which Hsüan-tsang's translations differed from those of Paramārtha. Another of Hsüan-tsang's collaborators, Shen-t'ai 伸泰, refuted Ling-jun's criticisms. I-jung 義榮 then criticized Shen-t'ai's views. Saichō discussed these exchanges extensively in the *Hokke shūku.*[54] Elsewhere, Saichō discussed the work of one of Hsüan-tsang's most able students, Fa-pao 法寶, author of one of the three standard commentaries on Hsüan-tsang's translation of the *Abhidharmakośa.* Fa-pao argued that the One-vehicle doctrine was the true teaching (*jitsukyō* 實教) and that

---

[51] *Shugo kokkaishō, DZ* 2: 184f.

[52] Ibid., pp. 608–30.

[53] Ibid., pp. 544, 551. Inoue Mitsusada "*Tōiki dentō mokuroku* yori mitaru Nara jidai sōryo no gakumon," *Shigaku zasshi* 57 (1964): 218–220] claims that Wŏnch'ŭk's works were used only as incidental reference works by Nara monks; however, Saichō's use of them indicates that at least some Japanese monks were acutely aware of the controversies between Wŏnch'ŭk and Tz'u-en [Sonoda Kōyū, "Saichō no ronshō wo tsūjite sita Nanto kyōgaku no keikō," *Shirin* 42 (1959): 589–91].

[54]*Shugo kokkaishō, DZ* 2: 572; and *Hokke shūku, DZ* 3: 154–240.

the three vehicles were only expedient teachings (*gonkyō* 權教). He believed that all sentient beings had the Buddha-nature and utilized the T'ien-t'ai system for classifying the Buddha's doctrines. He was criticized by another of Hsüan-tsang's students, Hui-chao 慧沼 (649–714), the second Fa-hsiang patriarch. Hui-chao was the author of the *Hui jih lun* 慧日論, a work cited by Tokuitsu in support of his arguments.[55]

These Yogācāra and Hua-yen texts proved to be very effective weapons for Saichō. At times Saichō was able to cite some of the most fundamental Hossō texts to refute or question Tokuitsu's statements. For example, Saichō relied on Fa-pao's treatises and the doctrines of the Hua-yen School to argue against the Hossō conception of the absolute. On the basis of Hua-yen doctrines, Saichō argued that the absolute was not separate and isolated from the phenomenal world. Rather the phenomenal arose from the absolute 眞如緣起. The absolute and phenomenal merged and interpenetrated.[56]

On the basis of Fa-pao's arguments, Saichō was able to point out a passage in the *Yü ch'ieh shih ti lun* (*Yogācārabhūmiśāstra*), one of the Hossō School's most important texts, which indicated that untainted seeds arose from the absolute when a person had attained a certain stage in his practice.[57] Fa-pao's works supported Saichō's contention that man's potential to attain Buddhahood did not depend on his possession of untainted seeds from the beginningless past. Rather, the absolute was immanent in everything. Man could produce the seeds of enlightenment through practice. Hence, there could be no class of beings doomed to endless cycles of birth and death because they lacked an active connection with the absolute. The Hossō classification of the Buddha-nature into an absolute and a practical type, according to Saichō, was simply not true.

The Exegesis of the Lotus Sūtra

The debates with Tokuitsu often centered on the evaluation and

[55]*Shugo kokkaishō, DZ* 2: 510, 588. Saichō also criticized Fa-pao's work (ibid., p. 528; *Hokke shūku, DZ* 3: 191). Hui-chao's *Hui jih iun* corresponds to *T* no. 1863.

[56]Yūki Yoshifumi, "Saichō ni okeru Kegon shisō no eikyō," *Nanto Bukkyō* 32 (1974): 17–23.

[57]*Shugo kokkaishō, DZ* 2: 574–83. See Kuge Noburu's study of this problem, "*Shugo kokkaishō* ni okeru Tōshamon Hōbō no busshōron," *Bukkyō daigaku kenkyū kiyō* 59 (1975): 15–39. Although Saichō relied on Fa-pao's writings, he was also critical of Fa-pao at certain points in his discussion.

exegesis of scriptural passages. Each monk would in turn argue that the texts on which he based his interpretation reflected the Buddha's ultimate teaching while those which his opponent used presented only provisional teachings. In its later stages, the debate focussed on the exegesis of the *Lotus Sūtra,* the most authoritative scripture for the Tendai School.

Saichō often referred to his own school as the Tendai Hokkeshū, the Tendai School of *Lotus Sūtra* interpretation. It was not the only school which interpreted the *Lotus Sūtra,* since both the Hossō and Sanron schools had long traditions of exegesis of the *Lotus Sūtra.* Thus Saichō's task was to show that the Tendai interpretation was the most authoritative one.

Tokuitsu followed the orthodox Hossō interpretation, as it was presented in Tz'u-en's (632-682) commentary, the *Fa hua hsüan tsan.*[58] According to Tz'u-en's writings, the Buddha had a hidden purpose 密意 in preaching the *Lotus Sūtra.* He wanted to encourage people of undetermined nature 不定性 to strive to become bodhisattvas, rather than being content with merely becoming or striving to become arhats or pratyeka-buddhas. The One-vehicle doctrine was an expedient teaching (*gonkyō*) directed toward those of undetermined nature. The claims of the *Lotus Sūtra* that it was the ultimate teaching (*jitsukyō*) were an expedient designed to encourage this particular class of practitioner and were not to be considered as teachings which were universally valid. Predictions in *sūtras* that certain people would attain Buddhahood 授記 were said to refer to the individual's possession of the *gyōbusshō* 行佛性 and to not have any general significance. Statements that all beings had the Buddha-nature, such as that by the bodhisattva Jōbukyō (Never-disparaging), were said to refer only to the inactive *ribusshō* 理佛性.

In contrast to the Hossō position presented above, Saichō believed that the *Lotus Sūtra* was the Buddha's ultimate teaching, a direct revelation of the Buddha's enlightenment which was valid for all men and not just intended for one particular group. Saichō supported his arguments by referring to passages in the *Lotus Sūtra* which stated that the *sūtra* was indeed the Buddha's ultimate teaching, by defending the Tendai classification of Buddhist doctrine, and by attacking the Hossō classification of Buddhist doctrine. The defense and exegesis of the

---

[58]*T* no. 1723. Tz'u-en and other Fa–hsiang scholars wrote commentaries concerning the *Lotus sūtra* because of the *sūtra's* great popularity in China, not because it held an authoritative position in the Fa–hsiang doctrinal system. The positions of Tokuitsu and Saichō are presented in the last fascicle of the *Shugo kokkaishō, DZ* 2: 631–80.

Lotus Sūtra occupy an important place in two of Saichō's later works, the *Ketsugonjitsuron* and the *Hokke shūku.*

The teachings of the One-vehicle, the universality of salvation, and the speedy realization of salvation were eventually accepted as standard Buddhist teachings throughout Japan. The new schools of the Kamakura reformation developed out of the Tendai School and adopted the positions which Saichō had defended, though not without changes. Even some Hossō monks such as Ryōhen 良遍 (1194–1252) tried to reconcile the differences between Hossō and Tendai by devising positions which allowed for universal salvation and the quick attainment of salvation.[59]

The Buddha-nature was a controversial topic in India, China and Japan. In his classic study of the long history of these disputes, Tokiwa Daijō 常盤大定 (1870–1945) argued that the debate between Saichō and Tokuitsu represented the culmination of the disputes over the Buddha-nature.[60] The issues were probably more clearly demarcated and discussed by both men than at any other time in East Asian Buddhist history. Many new issues were introduced into the debate and their relation to the subject of the Buddha-nature investigated. Saichō displayed considerable ingenuity and an impressive command of Buddhist literature in drawing upon a variety of sources to formulate and defend his position. At the same time, the debate with Tokuitsu prepared the ground for the controversy over the bodhisattva precepts (*bosatsukai* 菩薩戒) by indicating that the Tendai and Hossō positions were irreconcilable. Saichō's petitions concerning the bodhisattva precepts, discussed in the following chapters, represent his attempt to formulate practices which would reflect the more theoretical statements which he had advanced in his works criticizing Tokuitsu.

---

[59]Kamata Shigeo and Tanaka Hisao, *Kamakura kyū Bukkyō* (Tokyo: Iwanami shoten, 1971), pp. 480–88, 534–545.

[60]*Busshō no kenkyū* pp. 25–27.

CHAPTER EIGHT

THE CONTROVERSY OVER THE BODHISATTVA PRECEPTS

Saichō is best remembered in Japanese Buddhist history for his dramatic struggle to obtain the court's permission to ordain Tendai monks with the *Fan wang* precepts instead of the *Ssu fen lü* precepts. The controversy over Saichō's proposals resulted in a departure from centuries of Buddhist tradition on monastic discipline and decisively affected the future course of the Tendai School and Japanese Buddhism.

Saichō had taken monastic discipline seriously throughout his life. His retreat to Mount Hiei to practice religious austerities and his first work, the *Ganmon* (Vows), are evidence of his intention to observe the precepts more assiduously than his contemporaries. In China, he collected a number of works on the precepts, received a *Fan wang* ordination along with Gishin, and approved of Gishin's *Ssu fen lü* ordination. Nevertheless, Saichō proposed a radical break with traditional monastic discipline. In order to determine the reasons behind Saichō's proposals, the controversy over the precepts is discussed and analyzed chronologically in this chapter. His petitions concerning the precepts, with the exception of the three-fascicle *Kenkairon,* are all translated and annotated.

In traditional Tendai narratives of the controversy, Saichō's proposals on monastic discipline are usually interpreted in the light of his final position.[1] The conflict between Hīnayāna and Mahāyāna values is particularly stressed. In the following account, the focus is placed on the gradual evolution of Saichō's position and the growing antagonism and polarization between the Tendai and Nara schools, particularly over the administration of monasteries and ordinations. Saichō's defense of his position in terms of Buddhist doctrine is discussed in Chapter 9.

The Precepts and the Dispute with Tokuitsu

Both the *Denjutsu isshinkaimon* and the *Eizan Daishiden* relate the events of the dispute over the bodhisattva precepts in great detail;

---

[1] Saichō's three major petitions, the *Rokujōshiki, Hachijōshiki,* and *Shijōshiki,* were often grouped together as a single text, the *Sange gakushōshiki (DZ* 1:11–20), during the last several centuries (*DZ* 5 [*Bekkan*] 1:57, 167; *BZ* 95: 190). The compilation of the petitions into a single text has probably contributed to the tendency to read them as if they reflected a single unchanging point of view.

however, neither work touches on Saichō's disputes with Tokuitsu concerning the Buddha-nature (*Busshō*). Saichō usually discussed the two controversies separately, probably because each involved different antagonists. Modern scholars also have usually treated the two debates separately. Yet the disputes did occur at approximately the same time although the controversy on the Buddha-nature began first. In fact, Saichō probably would not have proposed his radical revision of the precepts had he not been involved in the bitter debate with Tokuitsu. His proposals concerning the bodhisattva precepts represent an attempt to develop the practical implications of the theoretical issues which arose in his debates with Tokuitsu.

Scholars disagree about when the dispute over the precepts began. One scholar has suggested that Saichō may have been influenced by some of Dōchū's 道忠 disciples who, following Chien-chen's 鑑眞 teachings, called for a more open Buddhist order.[2] Others have suggested that on his trips to Kyushu and Tōgoku, Saichō may have gone to see the *kaidan* 戒壇 (precepts platforms) in these two areas, and thus may have been considering reforms as early as 814.[3] Neither of these theories has been proven.

The dispute began in earnest with Saichō's efforts to have the court designate his monastery, Hieizanji, a Mahāyāna temple. On the seventh day of the second month of Kōnin 9 (late 817) Kōjō 光定 reports that Saichō told him that he wanted "to establish a Mahāyāna temple in order to propagate the (Tendai) School." Kōjō seems to have been surprised by Saichō's statement. According to Kōjō's *Denjutsu isshinkaimon*, the following conversation took place:

The disciple (Kōjō) said, "There are no Mahāyāna temples in Japan. Why must we now suddenly establish a One-vehicle temple (*ichijōji* 一乗寺)?"
Our late teacher (Saichō) said, "I will bestow on you the title 'One-vehicle (*ichijō* 一乗)'."[4]

---

[2] Sonoda Kōyū, "Saichō no Tōgoku dendō ni tsuite," *Bukkyō shigaku* 3 (1952): 151–52. Sonoda has not continued to advocate this position since suggesting it in 1952. The position rested upon a controversial interpretation of the Tōshōdaiji precepts platform and on a supposed split among Chien-chen's disciples. Recent scholarship has discredited the interpretation.

[3] Shioiri Ryōchū, *Dengyō Daishi*, pp. 287–91. However, Saichō had little interest in the precepts platform as is indicated later in this chapter.

[4] Saichō's proposal to bestow the additional title of One-vehicle (*ichijō*) on Kōjō may have been based on a similar practice followed by Hsüan-tsang (600–664). Hsüan-tsang bestowed the title of Mahāyāna (*Ta-ch'eng* 大乗) on monks who had received the

His disciple (Kōjō) said, "Since there are no Mahāyāna temples in Japan yet, I will not take the One-vehicle title. Please bestow it on me after we establish a Mahāyāna temple."

Our late teacher said, "In India there are purely Mahāyāna temples, purely Hīnayāna temples and ι..ιxed (Mahāyāna and Hīnayāna) temples."

His disciple said, "If these three types of temples exist, then I ought to take the title. Temples are, after all, only places where monks reside."[5]

At this time, no mention was made of precepts. Exactly what the term 'Mahāyāna temple' or 'One-vehicle temple' designated and how such an institution would differ from the temples in Japan at that time is not specified in the conversation.[6] Probably it was the beginning of an attempt by Saichō to develop a monastic institution which would embody, in a practical way, the issues being debated with Tokuitsu. If the court had recognized Saichō's claim that Hieizanji was a Mahāyāna temple, it certainly would have enhanced the reputation of the Tendai School at the expense of the Hossō and Sanron schools by implying that they did not have purely Mahāyāna temples.

New Plans for Hieizanji

Shortly after this, Saichō began a period of intense activity to realize his plan. In the spring of 818, he is said to have determined the boundaries 結界 of the Tendai establishment on Mount Hiei.[7] At the same time

---

bodhisattva precepts listed in the *Yü ch'ieh shih ti lun* (*Yogācārabhūmiśāstra*), a set which differed from the *Fan wang* precepts. The title was used in front of the monk's name. See Sakaino Kōyō, *Shina Bukkyōshi kōwa*, 2 vols (Tokyo: Kyōritsusha, 1927), 2: 628.

[5] *Denjutsu isshinkaimon, DZ* 1: 532.

[6] In Saichō's works the term "exclusively Mahāyāna temple" (*ikkō daijōji*) first appears in the *Shijōshiki* written by Saichō in 819, well over a year after the conversation recorded in the *Denjutsu isshinkaimon*. The term does not appear in any of Saichō's earlier petitions. Ishida [*Nihon Bukkyō ni okeru kairitsu no kenkyū* (Tokyo: Zaike Bukkyō kankōkai, 1966), p. 124] argues that the term may not have existed at the time of the conversation recorded by Kōjō. Consequently Kōjō may have introduced the term into the conversation in order to make it agree with later events.

[7] Both Sonoda (*Saichō,* p. 503) and Kageyama Haruki [*Hieizan* (Tokyo: Kadokawa shoten, 1966), p. 66] consider this event factual. It is not mentioned, however, in either the *Denjutsu isshinkaimon* or the *Eizan Daishiden*. Sources for it date from the thirteenth and fourteenth centuries, and include the *Eigaku yōki* 叡岳要記 (*GR* 15: 521), *Kuin bukkakushō* 九院佛閣抄 (*GR* 15: 582) and the *Sanbō jūjishū* 三寶住持集 (*DZ* 5: 403, which in turn quotes the *Sange sairyakki*). All three of these sources quote a document which Saichō is said to have written when he determined the boundaries. Differences in wording in the quoted document and its reference to Hieizanji by the name Enryakuji three years before this name was conferred on the Tendai temple raise doubts about the authenticity of the document. However,

he also decided to construct six pagodas which were to be placed in important locations throughout Japan.[8] Each was to contain one-thousand copies of the *Lotus Sūtra*. Shortly before, Saichō had built two pagodas while in Tōgoku, which were to protect the nation in the north and the east. Another pagoda containing copies of the *Lotus Sūtra* had been constructed by Saichō in Kyushu several years before and may have been intended to guard the nation in the south. These three pagodas and one other which was to be built later were to be arranged to protect the country and guarantee peace in each of the four cardinal directions. The remaining two were to be located on Mount Hiei; one was to guard the center, and the second was to unify the other five and thus guard the whole. Before his death Saichō completed at least one of the pagodas on Mount Hiei, the Tōdōin 東塔院 in 821. His plan to establish six pagodas to protect the nation may have been patterned after the Kokubun temple system.

In the year 818, Japan was beset by a severe drought. The spring planting had failed. During the first part of the fourth month, the court commanded various shrines and temples to pray for rain. On the twenty-third the Emperor issued a statement that the drought was due to his unworthiness and that the court would undergo austerities from the twenty-sixth to the twenty-eighth in order to remedy the situation. Temples and shrines were asked to perform ceremonies to bring rain during this time.[9] Meanwhile, on the twenty-first day of the fourth month, a letter from Fujiwara no Fuyutsugu 藤原冬嗣[10] arrived asking Saichō to pray for rain.[11] Two days later Saichō sent his reply, promising to do so. At

---

the wording of the three versions of the quoted documents is sufficiently close that they may have all been based on a single original document. Tendai monks seem to have reinterpreted the boundaries to fit the philosophical needs of their time. Thus the *Sanbō jujishū*, which is attributed to Saichō, but is actually a Muromachi period work, interprets the boundaries as a symbolic representation of the *roku soku* (*DZ* 5: 401–3). Since the events of 818 are consistent with the determination of boundaries, Saichō may well have made such proposals.

The area mentioned in the documents is roughly a square, four kilometers on each side. The boundaries were marked by posts which prohibited women, horses and oxen from entering. Within the boundaries, supplies and food were probably carried by men the rest of the way up the mountain. (Kageyama, *Hieizan*, p. 67).

[8] *Rokushozōhōtō ganmon* 六所造寶塔願門 (*Vow to contruct pagodas at six places, DZ* 5: 373). The work is probably authentic (Tajima Tokuon, *BKD* 9: 323).

[9] Muranaka Yūshō, "Daijōkai teishō to *Kenkairon*," *DDK*, p. 1475.

[10] Fujiwara no Fuyutsugu (775–826) was half–brother to Yoshimine no Yasuyo. A capable man, he rose to the Great Minister of the Left (*sadaijin*) and one of Emperor Saga's most trusted advisors. He established a pharmacy 施藥院 to help the poor and was the founder of the Fujiwara clan college, the Kangakuin 勸學院.

[11] *Denjutsu isshinkaimon, DZ* 1: 532–33.

the same time Kōjō was sent to Fuyutsugu to inquire about the Mahā-yāna temple designation. Fuyutsugu asked Kōjō to wait for a more appropriate time to request the One-vehicle designation for Hieizanji.

Meanwhile, Saichō was planning to expand and reorganize the temple complex on Mount Hiei. On the twenty-sixth day of the fourth month,[12] in conjunction with preparations to pray for rain, he drafted a plan to organize Hieizanji around nine halls, most of which were still to be built. Included was a Precepts Platform Hall (*kaidan'in* 戒壇院). These halls were to be built in part to quiet the vengeful spirits of the late Prince Sawara 早良 and Fujiwara no Yoshiko 藤原吉子 who were believed to be causing the drought.

The nine halls are mentioned in both the *Denjutsu isshinkaimon* and *Hokke chōkō* 法華長講.[13] The latter work is attributed to Saichō but was probably amended by later Tendai monks. Both works use only the term 'nine halls' 九院, without specifying the names of the halls. A later work, the *Kuin bukkakushō* 九院佛閣抄, compiled around the four-teenth century, lists the following:

1. Ichijō shikan'in 一乘止觀院 (One-vehicle Meditation Hall)
2. Jōshin'in 定心院 (Meditation Hall)
3. Sōjiin 總持院 (Dhāraṇī Hall)
4. Shiōin 四王院 (Hall of the Four Guardian Kings)
5. Kaidan'in 戒壇院 (Hall for the Precepts Platform)
6. Hachibuin 八部院 (Hall for the Eight Types of Guardians)
7. Sannōin 山王院 (Sannō [Tendai Shintō] Hall)
8. Saitōin 西塔院 (Western Pagoda Hall)
9. Jōdoin 淨土院 (Pure Land Hall)[14]

Traditionally, this list is assumed to be identical to Saichō's conception of the nine halls; however, the inclusion of a Dhāraṇī Hall, Sannō Hall and Pure Land Hall indicate that the list was amended to coincide with developments that arose after Saichō's death.[15] The inclusion of a Hall for the Precepts Platform is also difficult to explain. Nowhere else did Saichō mention a Precepts Platform. A proposal to build one at

---

[12] Another document, the *Kuinji* 九院事 (*DZ* 5: 575), gives the date as the twenty–first of the seventh month, but is almost certainly a later forgery (Tajima Tokuon, s. v. *Kuinji*, *BKD* 2: 318).

[13] *DZ* 1: 533; and *DZ* 4: 266, 269, 272.

[14] *GR* 15: 586–87. The *Kuin bukkakushō* is representative of a type of historical record that was popular from the late Heian period on. In general, these records are not reliable sources. For a discussion of them, see Hazama Jikō, *Nihon Bukkyō no kaiten to sono kichō*, 2 vols. (Tokyo: Sanseidō, 1948) 2: 245–66.

[15] Tajima Tokuon, *BKD* 2: 318.

this time would certainly not have gone unnoticed by the Nara monks. Moreover, it would have required special permission from the court which Saichō did not request at this time. On the other hand, Kōjō later claimed that Saichō appointed him chief administrator (*bettō* 別當) and Gishin overseer (*chiji* 知事) of the Hall for the Precepts Platform.[16] Saichō's appointment was sufficiently vague, however, that Kōjō stated that he had misunderstood it.[17] The matter was not mentioned again until several years after Saichō's death. At least publicly, Saichō was still confining his activities to the reorganization and expansion of Hiei-zanji. He had given no indication that he was considering a major reform in monastic discipline.

From the twenty-sixth to the twenty-eighth of the fourth month of 818, Saichō and the monks on Mount Hiei meditated, chanted *sūtras,* and lectured on the *Lotus Sūtra,* the *Chin kuang ming ching (Suvarṇapra-bhāsasūtra)* and the *Jen wang ching (Sūtra of the Benevolent King)* in an attempt to end the drought. Meanwhile, Gomyō was leading forty monks in chanting the *Jen wang ching.* On the fifth day of these services rain fell.[18] The success was shared by the entire Buddhist community. Kōjō was rewarded by the court for his efforts as liaison between the court and Mount Hiei with an appointment to the rank of *shugyō man'i* and later, in the ninth month, *dentō man'i.*[19] Shortly after this success,

---

[16] *Denjutsu isshinkaimon, DZ* 1: 637. Earlier in the text (p. 523), Kōjō calls himself the *Kaidan'in chiji.* He was probably appointed to the post after Gishin's death.

[17] Ibid., p. 588.

[18] Ibid., p. 536.

[19] The system of monastic ranks which existed during Saichō s lifetime was proposed by the monk Rōben 良辨 (689–773) and others in 760. The system had four ranks 位, which were divided into thirteen grades 階 as follows:
A.　　*Daihosshii* 大法師位.　equivalent to the third court rank
B. (1)　*Dentō hosshii* 傳燈法師位.　equivalent to the fourth court rank
　 (2)　*Dentō man'i* 伝燈滿位.　equivalent to the fifth court rank
　 (3)　*Dentō jui* 傳燈住位.　equivalent to the sixth court rank
　 (4)　*Dentō nyūi* 傳燈入位.　equivalent to the seventh court rank
C. (1)　*Shugyō hosshii* 修行法師位.
　 (2)　*Shugyō man'i*
　 (3)　*Shugyō jūi*
　 (4)　*Shugyō nyūi*
D. (1)　*Tsūji hosshii* 通持法師位.
　 (2)　*Tsūji man'i*
　 (3)　*Tsūji jūi*
　 (4)　*Tsūji nyūi*
The last rank (*tsūji*) seems to have been abandoned rather early. In 798 the monastic ranks' equivalency to court ranks were specified. At this time, the appelation *dentō* was abandoned and replaced by *shugyō.* Thus Kōjō's *shugyō man'i* was the third highest rank. Relatively few monks received ranks this high at the time; however, later the ranks were conferred with

Saichō presented a copy of the *Jen wang ching* in gold lettering to the court.[20]

Saichō used the opportunity provided by these contacts to have Kōjō press Yoshimine no Yasuyo 良峰安世[21] for the Mahāyāna temple designation. On the eighth day of the fifth month of 818, Kōjō met Yoshimine but was told to wait for a more opportune time to present the request. On the seventeenth Kōjō was informed that Gomyō and other monks had objected to the proposal, arguing that no precedent for Mahāyāna temples existed in India, China, or Japan.[22] No mention of the precepts is made in the *Denjutsu isshinkaimon* account of the negotiations. Unfortunately, it is not possible to determine what Saichō meant by his usage of the term 'Mahāyāna temple' at this time or how Gomyō interpreted the term.

Up to this point, the preceding presentation of Saichō's attempt to expand Hieizanji has primarily followed the account found in the *Denjutsu isshinkaimon*. Kōjō, the author of the *Denjutsu isshinkaimon*, served as liaison to the court for Saichō. After Saichō's death he served as administrator of the precepts platform and finally as the interim administrator (*bettō*) of all of the Tendai establishments on Mount Hiei. Kōjō was vitally concerned with administrative issues within the Tendai School and his narrative reflects this concern.

From this point on, the account of the controversy over the bodhisattva precepts is supplemented by the *Eizan Daishiden* and Saichō's petitions to the court. The *Eizan Daishiden* is a biography of Saichō written several years after his death. In its presentation of the last part

---

greater frequency, until the system was finally amended by Shinga (801–75) in 864. The ranks seem to have carried substantial remuneration. The *Engishiki*, fasc. 21, states that appointments above *man'i* were to be granted by the Office of Monastic Affairs (Sōgō). It is unclear whether this method of appointment was in effect during Saichō's lifetime; however, the Sōgō did try to block his promotion to *daihosshi*, (*BD*, pp. 3028–29).

[20] *Denjutsu isshinkaimon*, *DZ* 1: 537–38. The *Jen wang ching* includes passages on how to prevent the calamities which may befall a state. Saichō quoted the relevant portions of this work in the *Kenkairon* and asked that one–hundred monks be appointed to chant the *sūtra* continuously (*DZ* 1: 125–131).

[21] Yoshimine no Yasuyo (785–830) was the son of Emperor Kanmu. He was also Fujiwara no Fuyutsugu's half–brother; both had the same mother. In 802 he was dropped from the rolls of the imperial family and granted the surname Yoshimine. In 816 he became Controller of the Right (*udaiben*). He was Emperor Saga's half–brother and about the same age as the Emperor. Thus along with Fuyutsugu, he was one of Saga's most trusted advisers. He later concurrently held the posts of Advisor (*sangi*) and Governor of Ōmi. In 828 he was appointed Great Counselor (*dainagon*). He read widely and participated in the compilation of the *Keikokushū* 經國集 and worked together with Fuyutsugu on the compilation of the *Nihon kōki* 日本後紀.

[22] *Denjutsu isshinkaimon*, *DZ* 1: 538.

of Saichō's life, it focuses on the dramatic dispute with the Nara schools over the type of ordination to be used for Tendai monks and ignores many of the administrative issues which concerned Kōjō. Saichō's petitions to the court offer another perspective since they were carefully worded public documents. In the following pages, these three major sources and the differences in their presentations of Saichō's position are analyzed.

The Rejection of the Hīnayāna Precepts

According to the *Eizan Daishiden*, Saichō had decided to abandon the *Ssu fen lü* precepts by 818. In late spring of that year Saichō assembled the teachers and students on Mount Hiei and declared:

I have researched the origins of the Perfect School of the *Lotus Sūtra*. (The Dharma) was preached, studied, and understood in the mountains: first on Vulture's Peak, next on Ta-su 大蘇, and finally on T'ien-t'ai.[23] Students of my (Tendai) school should, therefore, practice and study in the mountains during the first part of their studies. They should do this for the sake of the nation and its people, in order to benefit sentient beings, and so that the Buddha's teaching will flourish. By living in the mountains they shall escape from the criticisms of the mundane world, and the Buddha's teaching will surely grow and prosper.

From now on we will not follow *śrāvaka* ways. We will turn away forever from Hīnayāna (strictures on maintaining) dignity. I vow that I will henceforth abandon the two-hundred fifty (Hīnayāna) precepts.

The great teachers of Nan-yüeh 南岳 and T'ien-t'ai both heard the *Lotus Sūtra* preached and received the three-fold bodhisattva precepts on Vulture's Peak.[24] Since then, these precepts have been transmitted from teacher to teacher. Chih-i conferred them on Kuan-ting 觀頂. Kuan-ting conferred them on Chih-wei 智威. Chih-wei conferred them on Hsüan-lang 玄朗. Hsüan-lang conferred

---

[23] Vulture's Peak is the site where the Buddha preached the *Lotus Sūtra*. Ta-su is the mountain where Hui-ssu practiced, and T'ien-t'ai is the mountain where Chih-i practiced.

[24] Nan-yüeh is the mountain where Hui-ssu, second patriarch of the T'ien-t'ai School practiced. Tendai monks claimed that Hui-ssu and Chih-i received the *Lotus Sūtra's* teachings directly from the Buddha on Vulture's Peak. Thus the Tendai School boasted a lineage that could be traced more directly back to the Buddha than did the Hossō or Sanron schools. The threefold bodhisattva precepts, more commonly known as as the three collections of pure precepts (*sanju jōkai* 三聚淨戒), are discussed in the chapter on Saichō's teachers and predecessors (Chap. 12).

them on Chan-jan. Chan-jan conferred them on Tao-sui. Tao-sui conferred them on Saichō and then on Gishin.[25]

I have read the Buddha's teachings. I know that there are (strictures on) dignity for both the *bosatsusō* (bodhisattva monk) and the *bosatsu* (the lay bodhisattva), and that there are pure Mahāyāna and pure Hīnayāna (teachings). Now, the students of my school shall study Mahāyāna precepts, meditation, and wisdom. They shall abandon inferior Hīnayāna practices forever.[26]

The Rokujōshiki

Saichō may have made this proclamation to his disciples. He was much more cautious, however, when it came to presenting his proposals to the court. He was purposefully vague and ambiguous in his proposals concerning the precepts. He was, after all, challenging the validity of much of the government apparatus designed to regulate monks, since many of the court's regulations for monks were based on the Hīnayāna precepts. Moreover, renouncing the *Ssu fen lü* precepts which had traditionally been followed by monks in China and Japan was equivalent to abandoning the precepts which qualified one as a monk. It was tantamount to returning to the life of a layman. Traditionally, observance of the *Fan wang* precepts alone had never been considered to be sufficient to qualify one as a monk. Needless to say, Saichō and his disciples could not abandon the Hīnayāna precepts without first obtaining government approval for their plan. In the next few years Saichō would have two tasks: (1) obtaining government approval for his proposals, and (2)

---

[25] The lineage given here is almost identical to one found in the *Kechimyakufu* (*DZ* 1: 231–36). The only significant difference is that the *Kechimyakufu* lineage describes the *Fan wang* precepts as transmitted from Birushana Butsu to Shaka Butsu while the *Eizan Daishiden* account omits any mention of Birushana.

[26] *Eizan Daishiden, DZ* 5 (*Bekkan*): 32–33. The authenticity of this speech has been questioned by Fukui Kōjun ("Dengyō Daishi seinenkō shingi," *DDK*, p. 1194). Ishida Mizumaro (*Kairitsu no kenkyū*, p. 125) has mentioned his doubts concerning the speech, but has not arrived at a definite conclusion. The speech appears only in the *Eizan Daishiden*. No reference to it is found in the *Denjutsu isshinkaimon* even though this work describes many less important incidents in detail. In addition, the speech completely rejects the *Ssu fen lü* precepts while later petitions written by Saichō take a more moderate position. The *Eizan Daishiden* makes no reference to the less antagonistic position taken in the *Hachijōshiki* and *Rokujōshiki*, nor does it mention the controversy over the Buddha–nature. Consequently the *Eizan Daishiden* speech is probably an exaggerated dramatic rendering of a speech which Saichō made; however, no conclusive proof for this position has been presented. The stand presented in the speech approximates that of the early Tendai School after Saichō's death, when Saichō's proposal to institute provisional Hīnayāna ordinations (*keju shōkai*) had been abandoned. The *Eizan Daishiden* was compiled several years after Saichō's death.

establishing an educational and legal system which would obviate the need for the *Ssu fen lü* precepts. To this end, in the fifth month of 818, he authored the first of a series of petitions to the court, the *Rokujōshiki* 六條式 (*Regulations in Six Articles*):

REGULATIONS FOR
TENDAI-HOKKE ANNUALLY ALLOTTED STUDENTS[27]

What is the treasure of the nation? It is our religious nature.[28] Thus those who have this religious nature are the treasures of the nation. Long ago a man[29] said, "Ten large pearls do not constitute the nation's treasure, but he who sheds his light over a corner of the country is the nation's treasure."[30] A philosopher of old[31]

---

[27] *DZ* 1: 11–13. This is the work's proper name; however, it is usually called by its shorter name, the *Rokujōshiki* (*Regulations in Six Articles*).

[28] This theme is an old and familar one in China and Japan. The *Lotus Sūtra* (*T* 9: 26) and the *Mo ho chih kuan* (*T* 46: 49a) both refer to the nation's treasure as being a bodhisattva and a teacher of men. A similar entry is found in the *Shoku Nihongi* (Tempyō 15, first month). One of the oldest references is found in *Hsün Tzu* (*Ta lüeh*, no. 27), in which the man who can both act and speak is called the nation's treasure.

[29] Chan–jan's commentary on the *Mo ho chih kuan* (*T* 46: 279b) presents the following story, originally found in *The Spring and Autumn Annals*:

In the twenty–fourth year of King Wei 威 of Ch'i 齊, the King of Wei 魏 asked the King of Ch'i, "Do you have a treasure?" (He) answered, "No." The King of Wei said, "Though my country is small, I have ten pearls one *tsun* (2.25 cm.) in diameter. (They are so brilliant) that they each illuminate the area around twelve chariots. How is it that you have a country with ten–thousand chariots and yet have no jewels?" King Wei (of Ch'i) answered, "What I call a treasure is different from what you call a treasure. I have ministers like T'an Tz'u 檀子 who each guard a corner (of the country). Thus Ch'u, Chao, and Yen would not dare attack. (Within the country) they guard against theft so that even things forgotten on the road are not picked up. Our generals each illuminate one–thousand *li* (1 *li* = 405m.), to say nothing of twelve chariots." The King of Wei was embarrassed and left. The man who can both act and speak is the nation's treasure.

The story takes place during the Warring States Period. It can also be found in *Shih-chi*, fascicle 46. King Wei of Ch'i known as T'ien Yin-ch'i 田因齊, was notorious for arrogating the title of king to himself and for being an ineffectual ruler.

[30] The translation "sheds his light over a corner" (*shōuichigū* 照于一隅) is the traditional translation of this phrase. In the early 1970s, it was being used as the theme of the Tendai School's public relations campaign, with the term 'corner' being interpreted in a more restrictive sense than was probably intended originally (that is, as a small corner of the land rather than as the border or section of the land).

Recently Sonoda (*Saichō*, p. 427) has argued that a manuscript of the work in Saichō's handwriting shows that the passage should read "shed light on a thousand (*li*, and guard the) corner" (*shōsen'ichigu* 照千一隅). The phrase thus refers to two key points from the story quoted in the previous footnote. Tendai scholars, most notably Fukui Kōjun, have argued that the traditional reading should be followed, claiming that Sonoda has failed to recognize that Saichō wrote the character 于(*u*) so that it looked like 千(*sen*) [*Bukkyo taimusu*, Aug. 5, 1974, p. 1; *TG* 16 (1973): 1–17; *TG* 17 (1974): 1–11]. The debate over the correct reading has at times become very acrimonious. In this translation the traditional reading has been followed; however, Sonoda's argument has not yet been effectively refuted. Kimura Shūshō said, "He who can speak but not act is a teacher to the nation.[32] He who can act but not speak is an asset to the nation 國用. He who can both act and speak is a treasure to the nation 國寶. Aside from these three, he who can neither speak nor act is a traitor to the nation."

Buddhists with religious minds are called bodhisattvas in the West, and gentlemen[33] (chün tzu 君子) in the East. They take the bad upon themselves in order to benefit others. This is the height of compassion.[34]

Two types of Buddhist monks exist, the Hīnayāna and the Mahāyāna. Buddhists with a religious nature are of the latter type. Today in Japan only Hīnayāna monks are found; Mahāyāna monks have not yet appeared. Mahāyāna teachings have not yet spread (in Japan); thus it is difficult for Mahāyāna practitioners to arise.[35]

I sincerely ask that in accordance with the late emperor's wish, Tendai yearly ordinands be forever designated Mahāyāna practitioners and bodhisattva monks. Thus the nine (bad) monkeys

has examined the surviving documents in Saichō's handwriting, and arrived at a conclusion agreeing with Sonoda in "Shōu ichigū setsu ni kansuru gimon," *TG* 15 (1973): 52–60.

[31] The reference here is to Mou–jung 牟融 (ca. 60 A. D.), author of the *Mou Tzu* 牟子 or *Li huo lun* 理惑論 in three fascicles. This work is also quoted in Chan–jan's commentary on the *Mo ho chih kuan*, the *Mo ho chih kuan pu hsing ch'uan hung chüeh* (*T* 46: 279a). Saichō's formula differs from that in the *Mou Tzu* by placing the nation's teacher above the nation's asset.

[32] In the *Mou Tzu*, the term 'teacher of the nation' (kuni no shi 國之師) means someone who can teach well. In Japan the term kokushi 國師 was the name of a government position and is translated in this study as 'provincial teacher.'

[33] A chün–tzu was the ideal man according to Confucian teaching. Arthur Waley translates the term as 'gentleman' in *The Analects of Confucius* (New York: Vintage Books, 1938), pp. 34–38. West refers to India and East to China.

[34] This phrase can be found in the seventh major precept of the *Fan wang ching* which concerns praising oneself and slandering others or teaching another person to do so. 'Taking the bad upon himself and turning the good towards others' is the positive side of the precept. It describes the bodhisattva way (*T* 24: 1004b). This precept is also found in many Yogācāra works as the first of the four major precepts.

[35] Saichō's use of Hīnayāna and Mahāyāna are idiosyncratic, and would never have been accepted by the monks of Nara. Although the Kusha and Jōjitsu schools were Hīnayāna Schools, they had no real independent existence. The Kusha School was considered a part of the Hossō School, and the Jōjitsu School part of the Sanron School. Risshū monks usually viewed the Hīnayāna precepts from the perspective of a Mahāyāna practitioner. In addition to studying the *Ssu fen lü*, they also studied the doctrines of a Mahāyāna school and performed ordinations using the bodhisattva precepts.

[36] The story behind this reference is quoted in the *Kenkairon* (*DZ* 1: 165–171). It comes from the *Shou hu kuo chieh chu t'o lo ni ching* 守護國界主陀羅尼經 (*Sūtra Concerning Dhāraṇī to Protect the Ruler*) (*T* 19: 572b). In the *sūtra*, a dream of King Kṛki is described in which nine bad monkeys chase away a good monkey. The monkeys are interpreted as representing bad monks chasing away good monks.

of King Kṛki's dream shall be chased away.[36] Of the five vehicles specified by Mañjuśrī, (the numbers of) those who follow the latter three (the Mahāyāna ones) will increase.[37] With this attitude and desire we shall strive to benefit those who live now and those who come after us throughout the endless eons.[38]

(The regulations for) the two yearly ordinands who were first appointed to spread the Tendai Lotus School by the late Emperor (Kanmu) of Kashiwabara[39] (are as follows):

1.[40] Yearly ordinands of the Tendai Lotus School shall, starting from the ninth year of the Kōnin era (818), be Mahāyāna monks. The title of 'son of the Buddha' shall be conferred upon them, but their original names shall not be removed from the lay register.[41] Bodhisattva novices[42] 菩薩沙彌 shall take the Perfect ten good precepts (enjūzenkai 圓十善戒)[43]

---

[37]The reference is to the *Pu pi ting ju ting ju yin ching* 不必定入定入印經(*Niyatāniyatagati-mudrāvatārasūtra, T* 15: 699c) and is quoted in the *Kenkairon* (*DZ* 1: 62). The *sūtra* consists of a conversation between the Buddha and Mañjuśrī. Five vehicles are mentioned. The first two may backslide from the levels attained through practice. The last three do not backslide. Saichō claimed that the last three vehicles corresponded to the Unique and Perfect Teachings.

[38]The text here reads, "We will not forget (about how Mahādānā labored to) bail the ocean out." The reference is to the *Hsien yü ching* 賢愚經 (*Damamūkanidānasūtra*) *T* 4: 405b. The story describes how Prince Mahādanā was moved by seeing the poverty of the people in his nation. In order to alleviate their suffering, he opened up the country's storehouses. After the storehouses had been emptied, he went to the ocean to preach to the Nāga kings and receive jewels in order to replenish the storehouses. However, after he received the jewels, he fell asleep, and the jewels were stolen by the Nāgas. To retrieve them, he decided he should bail all the water out of the ocean with a turtle shell. Although the gods of the ocean warned him that the task was impossible, he persisted. Finally, the gods took pity on him and were about to aid him when the Nāgas became frightened and returned the jewels. Prince Mahādāna was a former incarnation of the Buddha.

[39] Emperor Kanmu's tomb is at Kashiwabara, Kii–gun, Yamashiro–kuni. Kanmu granted Saichō two yearly ordinands in 806.

[40] The numbers are not in the original text. They have been added in this translation for convenience.

[41] One of Saichō's major objectives was to remove his monks from the jurisdiction of the government offices established to regulate Buddhism. These offices were controlled at the time by Hossō monks such as the *daisōzu* (greater supervisor) Gomyō, head of the Sōgō (Office of Monastic Affairs), and Shin'en 眞苑, head of the Genbaryō (Bureau of Buddhism and Aliens). By excluding Tendai monks from the monastic register, Saichō removed them from the jurisdiction of the Sōgō and Genbaryō and placed them directly under the control of the Dajōdaikan (Chancellor's Office).

[42] The term *bosatsu shami* (*bodhisattva novice*) refers to someone not yet twenty years of age who is in training to become a *bosatsusō* 菩薩僧 (bodhisattva monk). Also see note 44.

[43] The term 'Perfect ten good precepts' is extremely vague. Three possible interpretations exist:
A. The ten major precepts (*jūjūkai* 十重戒) of the *Fan wang ching:*

1. Not to kill living things
2. Not to steal
3. Not to be unchaste
4. Not to lie
5. Not to sell liquor
6. Not to tell others of errors by the four groups (lay and monastic bodhisattvas, monks, and nuns)
7. Not to praise oneself and defame others
8. Not to begrudge others either property or the Dharma (teaching)
9. Not to become angry
10. Not to slander the Three Jewels

B. A Tendai interpretation of the ten precepts normally taken by the Hīnayāna novice (*jūshamikai* 十沙彌戒):
1. Not to kill living beings
2. Not to steal
3. Not to be unchaste
4. Not to lie
5. Not to drink liquor
6. Not to apply perfumes or garlands to oneself
7. Not to watch dancing or listen to singing
8. Not to sit on a high wide bed
9. Not to eat at improper times
10. Not to touch gold, silver or jewels

C. The ten good precepts (*jūzenkai* 十善戒) were one of the earliest formulations of bodhisattva precepts; they were granted to both laymen and monks. They originated from a list of ten actions which produced good karma.
1. Abstention from killing living things
2. Abstention from stealing
3. Abstention from unchastity
4. Abstention from lying
5. Abstention from malicious speech
6. Abstention from harsh speech
7. Abstention from indistinct prattling
8. Abstention from covetousness
9. Abstention from anger
10. Abstention from wrong views

Most modern scholars have interpreted the phrase 'Perfect ten good precepts' as referring to the ten major precepts of the *Fan wang ching*, because such a reading would seem to agree with Saichō's later position (Tamura, *Saichō jiten*, p. 26; and Nakao, *Sange gakushō shiki josetsu*, p. 275). The problem is not nearly so simple, however, since little evidence for this interpretation is found in the *Rokujōshiki* and since historical documents indicate that all three sets of precepts have been used to initiate Tendai novices in the past (Kotera Bun'ei, "En no jūzenkai ni tsuite" *DDK* [*Bekkan*], pp. 157–168). On the basis of passages in the works of Saichō's disciples, Kotera has argued that the term probably was interpreted by Kōjō as referring to the ten major precepts of the *Fan wang ching* and by Ennin and Enchin as referring to the ten good precepts (*ibid.*, pp. 152–59). A group of medieval Tendai monks from Miidera used the traditional precepts for novices (*shamikai*) in their initiations (*ibid.*, pp. 160–62). The history of these interpretations and the reasons for them is still not clear.

The interpretation of this passage was also debated in the Tokugawa period. Keikō 敬光 (1740–95) identified it as the ten precepts for the novice, even though he was arguing against Myōryū 妙立 (1637–90) and Reikū 靈空 (1652–1739), both of whom wanted to use the *Ssu fen lü* precepts for Tendai ordinations (Keikō, *Sanshiki kanchū*, referred to by Sonoda, *Saichō*, p. 428). Shinryū 眞流 (1730?–1772?), another opponent of the *Anrakuritsu* 安樂律 movement to revive the *Ssu fen lü*, claimed that the term referred to the *Fan wang* precepts

at which time we shall ask for governmental approval of their initiation certificates 戒牒.

2. The same year they are initiated,[44] Mahāyāna novices shall be granted the precepts of the disciples of the Buddha,[45] and thus become bodhisattva monks (*bosatsusō*). At this time, governmental approval for their ordination certificates shall be requested. After they have received the full precepts[46] (*daikai* 大戒), they shall reside on Mount Hiei for twelve years and study the two courses. During this period, they shall not leave the confines of the mountain.

3. Everyday throughout the years, those in the Meditation Course (*shikangō*) shall be required to chant extensively, and to lecture on the *Lotus, Chin kuang ming ching, Jen wang ching,*

---

because of its appellation of 'Perfect' (*Gakushōshiki kōben, Tendaishū zensho* 5: 412).

In recent ceremonies on Mount Hiei the ten good precepts have been used, but some Tendai monks would prefer to use the ten major precepts of the *Fan wang ching* (Kotera, "En no jūzenkai ni tsuite," p. 157). The phrase 'Perfect ten good precepts' was ambiguous in Saichō's day and has continued to be so until the present. After a study of the problem, Ishida Mizumaro concluded that the evidence was insufficient to determine what Saichō had intended by the phrase (*Kairitsu no kenkyū*, p. 156). Saichō was probably intentionally ambiguous.

[44] In the "Petition to Establish the Mahāyāna Precepts" (translated below in this chapter), Saichō stated that the same day a candidate became a bodhisattva novice, he would also be given the bodhisattva precepts, making him a bodhisattva monk.

[45] The term 'precepts for disciples of the Buddha'(*Busshikai* 佛子戒) is ambiguous. *Busshi* is a translation of *Buddha putra*, meaning sons or disciples of the Buddha. It is used in the *Fan wang ching* to refer to anyone who follows the *Fan wang* precepts. Thus each precept begins with the words "You disciples of the Buddha." Most scholars have interpreted the term as referring to the *Fan wang* precepts. The term *Busshikai* has not been found, however, in any of the works which Saichō had probably consulted. Ishida (*Kairitsu no kenkyū*, pp. 158f.) has searched the works mentioned in the *Gakushōshiki mondō* for the term, but to no avail.

The term may also refer to the precepts of the *Ssu feu lü*. Although *Busshi* usually had a Mahāyāna connotation, it could also be used to refer to Hīnayāna practitioners. Chi-tsang, in his *Fa hua i su* 法華義疏, referred to five types of Hīnayāna *Busshi* and five types who were both Hīnayāna and Mahāyāna (*BD* 5: 4449). Even more suggestive was Daoxuan's attempt to show that the *Ssu fen lü* teachings were partly Mahāyāna (*buntsū daijō* 分道大乘). The third of five reasons cited by Daoxuan to support his argument is the presence of the word *Busshi* in the *Ssu fen lü* preface [Ui Hakuju, *Bukkyō hanron*, 1 vol. ed., (Tokyo: Iwanami shoten, 1963), p. 111]. Saichō referred to the theory that the *Ssu fen lü* was in substantial agreement with the Mahāyāna position in his *Kenkairon* (*DZ* 1: 80). Also suggestive is an edict issued in 798, in which those who follow the *Ssu fen lü* precepts are called *Busshi* (*Ruijū kokushi, KT* 6: 300).

[46] The term *daikai* 大戒 (literally, great precepts) has two meanings: (a) the full set of precepts used to ordain monks or nuns, as opposed to the smaller sets of precepts taken by lay people or novices and (b) the Mahāyāna precepts (*daijōkai*) as opposed to the Hīnayāna precepts (*shōjōkai*). Although the context of the term shows that the first meaning is more appropriate, there is an element of vagueness in the passage which Saichō probably intended.

Shou hu kuo chieh chu t'o lo ni ching[47] and other Mahāyāna sūtras which protect the nation.

4. Those who study the Esoteric Course (*shanagō*) shall be required to meditate on the *mantras* of the (*Ta p'i lu*) *che na (ching) (Mahāvairocanasūtra), (Fo mu ta) k'ung ch'iao (ming wang ching)* 佛母大孔雀明王經 (*Mahāmāyūrīvidyārājñīsūtra*),[48] *Pu k'ung (chüan so shen pien chen yen ching)* 不空羂索神變眞言經(*Amoghapāśakalparāja*),[49] *Fo ting (ching)* 佛頂經 (*Uṣṇīṣavijayadhāraṇīsūtra*),[50] and other *sūtras* which

---

[47]The *Shou hu kuo chieh chu t'o lo ni ching* 守護國界主陀羅尼經 (*T* no. 997, *Sūtra Concerning Dhāraṇī to Protect the Ruler*) in ten fascicles was translated into Chinese by Prajñā and Muniśrī (d. 806). The work was probably translated into Chinese shortly before Saichō went to China, but was not yet widely disseminated at the time Saichō was in China. Consequently, he returned to Japan without it. Kūkai, however, did obtain a copy (*Goshōrai mokuroku, BZ* 96:30). Kūkai thought highly of the *sūtra* and listed it first in the *zōmitsu* (Mixed Esoteric) section of his list of works that Shingonshū monks should study, the *Shingonshū shogaku kyōritsuron mokuroku* (*BZ* 96: 14). In 801 he petitioned Emperor Saga for permission to use the *sūtra* along with the *Jen wang ching* and the *Fo mu ta k'ung chiao ming wang ching* 佛母大孔雀明王經 (see the following note) to protect the nation (*Shōryōshū*, fasc. 4, *Kōbō Daishi chōsaku zenshū* 3: 183). Two years later, Saichō asked to borrow it (*DZ* 5: 451). The references in the *Rokujōshiki* and *Kenkairon* to the nine bad monkeys are taken from this *sūtra*. The *sūtra* seems to be misplaced here, however, since it is really an Esoteric work with many elements that are precursors to more advanced *ryōbu* Esoteric Buddhist texts (*BKD* 4: 47). In the *Tokugōshiki*, dated only two days later, the work is listed as a text for Esoteric Course students. Perhaps Saichō had not yet thoroughly studied the texts and was uncertain about how to classify it. In 825 Kūkai petitioned the court for permission to lecture on this *sūtra* at the summer retreats each year at Tōji (*Shūizasshū, Kōbō Daishi chōsaku zenshū* 3: 570–72).

[48]The *Fo mu ta k'ung ch'iao ming wang ching* (*T* no. 982) in three fascicles was translated by Amoghavajra (705–774). Earlier translations were made by I–ching (*T* no. 985) and Saṃghabhara (460–524) (*T* no. 984). A one–fascicle version translated by Kumārajīva also exists (*T* no. 988). A *dhāraṇī* in the work is said to protect the country from misfortune. The *sūtra* had appeared in Japan by the time of En no Ozuno, who is said to have recited the *dhāraṇī* during Emperor Jōmei's reign (629–41). Most commentators claim that Saichō was referring to Amoghavajra's translation, although this is not certain. Amoghavajra's translation does not appear in the bibliographies of works which Saichō brought back from China, but does appear in Kūkai's *Goshōrai mokuroku* (*BZ* 96: 28). Saichō may have borrowed it from Kūkai to copy, although no record survives of such a transaction.

[49]The *Pu k'ung chüan so shen pien chen yen ching*(*T* no. 1092) was translated by Bodhiruci (d. 727). This is a thirty–fascicle work with ceremonies and formulae suitable for various occasions. A large number of related translations and excerpts exist, some of which were certainly known in Japan during the Nara period (Misaki, "Nara jidai no Mikkyō," pp. 60, 66–67).

[50]According to Sonoda (*Saichō*, p. 429) and Suehiro (*Yakuchū Eizan Daishiden*, p. 97), *Fo ting* refers to the *Fo ting tsun sheng t'o lo ni ching* 佛頂尊勝陀羅尼經 (*Uṣṇīṣavijayadhāraṇīsūtra*) in one fascicle. A number of translations exist, but the most popular at this time was a version by Buddhapāli done around 676 (*T* no. 907). On the other hand, Sasaki Kentoku [*Sange gakushōshiki shinshaku* (Yamazaki: Hōbundō, 1938), p. 413] and Shioiri Ryōtatsu (*Dengyō Daishishū*, p. 50) claim that *Fo ting* refers to the *I tzu fo ting lun wang ching* 一字佛頂輪王經 in five fascicles translated by Bodhiruci in 708 (*T* nos. 951–52). Translations by

protect the nation.

5. After twelve years, the students of the two courses shall receive appointments in accordance with their achievements in study and practice. Those who can both speak and act shall remain permanently on Mount Hiei to head the order; they are treasures of the nation. Those who can speak but not act shall be teachers of the nation. Those who can act but not speak shall be assets of the nation.

6. As is specified in the Chancellor's directive, the teachers of the nation and those of use to the nation shall spread the Dharma and be appointed as lecturers in the provinces.[51] During their term of office, the provincial lecturers and teachers shall have the robes for their annual summer retreat paid for with funds deposited in the provincial offices.[52] They shall be supervised jointly by provincial and county officials. They are to benefit the nation and its people by repairing reservoirs and irrigation ditches, reclaiming uncultivated land, restoring fallen levees, making bridges and boats, planting trees and ramie, sowing hemp and grasses, digging wells and drawing water.[53]

Amoghavajra in five fascicles (*T* no. 950) and one fascicle (*T* no. 955) exist.

In the *Kechimyakufu* (*DZ* 1: 245), Saichō stated that one of his Esoteric initiations in China was based on a work translated by Bodhiruci. He then quoted a passage from the *K'ai yüan shih chiao lu*, mentioning both the *Pu kung chüan so* and the *I tzu fo ting*. Sasaki's theory thus seems more likely.

[51]*Kōji* 講師 (lecturers) first appear in a 702 edict ordering the appointment of certain monks to the provinces to oversee monks and nuns, and to lecture. At this time, they were called *kokushi* (provincial teacher). In 795 the name of position was changed to *kōji*, and one was appointed to each province. Their duties were mainly limited to lecturing on the *sūtras*. In 805 their term of office was fixed at six years. The numbers and terms of *kōji* varied geatly during the Nara period. For a detailed discussion of the office, see Nanba Toshinari, "Kodai chihō no sōkan ni tsuite," *Nanto Bukkyō* 28 (1972): 30–50.

Kōji appointments at this time were submitted by the Sōgō (Office of Monastic Affairs) to the Dajōdaijin (Chancellor). Since Saichō intended to remove his monks from the Sōgō's jurisdiction, the usual route for securing *kōji* appointments would be closed to him. However, he does not discuss this problem here.

[52]The *Engishiki* includes an account of the government finances for government lecturers and readers (*dokushi* 讀師). Government lecturers and readers were to be supplied by the government offices of the province in which they served. Each was to be supplied with five rolls of low quality silk (1 roll or *hiki* = 2 *tan* = about 14 meters of silk or enough cloth to make clothes for one man). This cloth was to be used to benefit other people. They received other supplies from the government as well as a number of assistants. Each lecturer was also to receive yearly supplies of ten rolls of low–quality silk, twenty *kin* of cotton (1 *kin* = about 1 kg.) and twenty *tan* of flax (1 *tan* = about 12 meters of cloth other than silk; the width was about 9 *sun* or 27 cm.). A reader would receive one–half of this amount (Sonoda, *Saichō*, p. 429; and Sasaki, *Sange gakushōshiki shinshaku*, pp. 423–24).

They should read *sūtras* and cultivate their minds. They are not to engage in private trade or farming.

If these provisions are followed, men with religious minds shall appear one after another in the world, and the way of the gentleman shall never die.

By observing the above regulations in six articles, sentient beings will be led to the Mahāyāna way through the gate of compassion, and the Buddha's teaching will endure forever. The nation shall long remain strong, and the bodhisattva way will not cease.

With profound awe, I submit these regulations for the Tendai School and respectfully request the imperial assent.

The thirteenth day of the fifth month of the ninth year of the Kōnin era (818).

Saichō, the monk who formerly sought the Dharma in China.

The Interpretation of the Rokujōshiki

The most important proposal in the *Rokujōshiki* petition was Saichō's request to remove the Tendai yearly ordinands from the monastic register, a measure which would remove them from the control of the Office of Monastic Affairs. Although Saichō was also clearly interested in the precepts, he did not press this aspect of the petition. Every mention of the precepts was shrouded in ambiguity. The technical terms, especially the 'Perfect ten good precepts,' 'precepts for disciples of the Buddha,' and 'full precepts,' can all be read as referring to either the Mahāyāna or Hīnayāna precepts. The first two terms are especially unusual, with no prior examples of their use to be found. This ambiguity was probably not accidental. Saichō must have been cognizant of the problems that would be caused by a proposal to abandon the Hīnayāna precepts and use only the Mahāyāna ones. Such a plan would have been inconceivable to most of the monastic and governmental leaders of Saichō's time.

Why did Saichō choose to compose the *Rokujōshiki* in this way? No satisfactory answer has yet been proposed by modern scholars.

---

[53] Such activities were usually discouraged by the government because it feared that the monks might incite the people to disorder. However, a long history of such social work does exist in Buddhism. In Japan, Dōshō 道昭 (629–700) and Gyōgi 行基 (668–749) were especially known for such deeds. Chien–chen 鑑眞 also probably engaged in such activities before coming to Japan. Usually such activities assumed one of two forms: (1) supervising the actual work (Saichō may have received training in construction techniques as a youth at his village school), and (2) performing rituals to remove a curse over a construction site and thus encouraging people to work on the project.

Kimura Shūshō 木村周照 has suggested that Saichō was attempting to gradually lead up to a change in the precepts so that he would not deeply offend his former teachers and thereby make the defense of his proposals more difficult.[54] Although Saichō's desire not to offend his former teachers must be considered, Kimura's thesis does not adequately explain the problems in the petition. Ishida Mizumaro 石田瑞麿 has suggested that the *Rokujōshiki* and *Hachijōshiki* (Regulations in Eight Articles) were only work sheets which were never actually submitted to the court.[55] This explanation would help account for the failure of any other early sources, such as the *Eizan Daishiden,* to mention the two works. Although Ishida's suggestion is plausible, most scholars have continued to believe that the *Rokujōshiki* and *Hachijōshiki* were indeed submitted to the court. However, the evidence is insufficient to enable scholars to resolve this aspect of the problem.

An examination of the reasons why Saichō made these proposals helps to elucidate some of the ambiguities in the *Rokujōshiki.* Four important explanations of Saichō's motives have been advanced in the twentieth century. Tsuji Zennosuke 辻善之助, in a well-known essay,[56] suggested that the shock from the defection of Saichō's disciple and close friend Taihan to Kūkai led Saichō to submit his proposals. In fact, the regulation in the *Rokujōshiki* requiring young Tendai monks to spend twelve years on Mount Hiei may have reflected Saichō's desire to keep his other disciples under his direct supervision. However, many of Saichō's other disciples also defected to other schools. Tsuji overemphasized the effects of Saichō's emotional attachment to Taihan. Although Taihan's defection must have seriously disappointed Saichō and have played a major role in Saichō's decision to at least temporarily abandon his efforts to master Esoteric Buddhism, the loss of Taihan does not seem to have been the key factor in Saichō's decision to submit petitions such as the *Rokujōshiki* to the court.

Miura Shūkō 三浦周行 opposed Tsuji's theory with an explanation which stressed the historical inevitability of a clash between the new and rising Tendai School and the older established Nara schools.[57] Miura's

---

[54] Kimura Shūshō, *Dengyō Daishi: Daikai konryū no risō to shinnen* (Tokyo: Nakayama shobō, 1961), p. 38.

[55] Ishida, *Kairitsu no kenkyū*, p. 127. If Ishida's supposition is correct, it would indicate that the Sōgō did not try to stop Saichō by ignoring his first petitions. Rather, the office could not have opposed the proposals because it would not have known about them.

[56] Tsuji Zennosuke, "*Kenkairon* senjutsu no yūrai ni tsuite," *Nihon Bukkyōshi no kenkyū* (Tokyo: Kinkōdō, 1919), pp. 195–209.

[57] Miura, *Dengyō Daishi den,* pp. 233–36.

theory did not take Saichō's personality into account. This is especially evident when Saichō's career is compared to that of Kūkai. Although faced with problems similar to those encountered by Saichō, Kūkai managed to establish the Shingon School while pursuing a policy of cooperation with the Nara schools.

A third view was advanced by Shioiri Ryōchū 塩入亮忠.[58] Shioiri emphasized the doctrinal aspects of Saichō's views on the precepts. His discussion of the relation of the debates on the Buddha-nature to the controversy over the bodhisattva precepts influenced many other modern scholars. He also wrote valuable analyses of Saichō's view of the role of Japan and the Japanese in Buddhist history and how these views affected Saichō's attitudes toward monastic discipline. Shioiri's analysis was primarily based on the *Shijōshiki* and *Kenkairon,* works composed at least a year after the *Rokujōshiki.* In these works, Saichō presented his position on the precepts without the ambiguities found in the *Rokujō-shiki.* Shioiri's analysis is thus helpful in explaining Saichō's fully developed position, but does not adequately explain the ambiguities in the *Rokujōshiki* or the way in which the precepts controversy developed.

More recent scholarship, while taking the previous three positions into account, has focused on Saichō's inability to retain his students.[59] Of crucial importance is a register of Tendai yearly ordinands, the *Tendai hokkeshū nenbun tokudo gakushō meichō* 天台法華宗年分得度學生名帳 (A Register of Yearly Ordinand Students Initiated into the Tendai-Lotus School).[60] In this register, Saichō recorded the names and locations of all his yearly ordinand students from 807 to 818. He noted in the beginning of the list that of twenty-four students only ten remained on Mount Hiei as of 818.

Of those who had left Hieizanji, at least six had defected to the rival Hossō School, one had died, and two were taking care of mothers in ill health. Saichō was not even sure where several students were. Of the ten who remained on Mount Hiei, half were still novices and thus had only recently arrived. Many of his students did not remain on the

---

[58] Shioiri Ryōchū, *Dengyō Daishi,* pp. 264–66; and Shioiri Ryōchū, *Shinjidai no Dengyō Daishi kenkyū,* pp. 91–95. He has also influenced the views of such Tendai scholars as Taira Ryōshō and Kimura Shūshō. Shioiri's views are discussed further in Chapter 9.

[59] For example, see Ishida, *Kairitsu no kenkyū, pp.* 137f.

[60] *DZ* 1: 250–53. Also found in Tsuji, *Nihon Bukkyōshi* 1: 270–74. The work is still extant in Saichō's handwriting. The *DZ* version lists Tokuen's 德圓 teacher as Enshū 圓修. However, as Tsuji indicates, the original text lists Enchō 圓澄 as Tokuen's teacher. Names of the students up to 819 are given. The last two names appear to have been added to the document later.

mountain long enough for Saichō to thoroughly educate them. Saichō mentioned this problem frequently, and in the *Kenkairon*[61] and the *Jōkenkaironhyō*[62] he lamented about how many of his students had left him. A less detailed version of the register is included at the end of the *Kenkairon engi*.[63]

The *Rokujōshiki* and the petitions which followed it must thus be read as attempts by Saichō to formulate an educational program which would retain students on Mount Hiei. Although Saichō was certainly considering a revision in the precepts, he probably did not explicitly state it in the *Rokujōshiki* because he feared that it would doom the rest of his program. If the *Rokujōshiki* had been approved, Saichō probably could not have used it as an authorization to abandon the *Ssu fen lü* precepts and adopt the *Fan wang* precepts for Tendai ordinations. Moreover, approval of the *Rokujōshiki* might have obviated the need to request permission to use an exclusively Mahāyāna set of precepts. The ambiguity of the terminology in the *Rokujōshiki* probably reflected Saichō's indecision about whether to limit his proposals to administrative issues such as the registration of recently ordained monks or to suggest a sweeping change in the precepts used in ordinations.

Petitions Concerning Intermediate Students

During the week after he submitted the *Rokujōshiki,* Saichō wrote two more memorials, adding details about the training program for those who aspired to be yearly ordinands. He proposed a rigorous training course for candidates (called intermediate students or *tokugō gakushō* 得業學生) for the examinations which would qualify them to become government-sponsored yearly ordinands. Saichō was thus both providing his school with able candidates for ordination and responding to the court's attempts to improve the quality of yearly ordinands.

REGULATIONS FOR INTERMEDIATE STUDENTS
OF THE TENDAI-LOTUS HALL ON MOUNT HIEI
(*Heizan Tendai Hokkein tokugō gakushōshiki*[64]
比叡山天台法華院得業學生式)
How difficult it is to reside in conditioned existence, in the cycles

---

[61] *Kenkairon, DZ* 1: 150–51, 181.

[62] *Jōkenkaironhyō, DZ* 1: 256.

[63] *DZ* 1: 296–98. Ishida (*Kairitsu no kenkyū,* pp. 140–41) notes that of the documents in the *Kenkairon engi,* only this one is not issued or certified by the government. The defection of Saichō's students compelled Saichō to include it. However, the *Kenkairon engi* list only goes up to the year 816 and does not note the students' locations or the names of their teachers.

[64] *DZ* 1: 21–22. This work is listed in all the important bibliographies of Saichō's works, and thus is considered to be authentic.

of life and death. Without wisdom, how can we wake from the slumber that is ignorance? (I hear) the faint sound of spring thunder; it is time to be resolute. (I see) the glimmer of summer lightning; time is short.[65] The roots of great compassion may begin to grow this morning. The aspiration to attain enlightenment may arise this very day.

Thus we must permanently establish regulations for our halls which are in this dream-like world. By forever establishing these regulations, we shall open the sources of the Dharma. Above, we shall serve all the generations of emperors. In the middle, we shall protect all the people of the world. Below, we shall save all sentient beings. Thus we would like to install nine[66] intermediate *shikangō* (Meditation Course) students who will lecture and turn[67] the *Lotus Sūtra, Chin kuang ming ching, Jen wang ching* and other *sūtras* daily. They will not miss even one day. We would also like to install nine intermediate Esoteric Course students who will turn and meditate on the *(Ta p'i lu) che na(ching), (Fo mu ta) k'ung ch'iao (ming wang ching), Shou hu (kuo chieh chu t'o lo ni ching)*[68] and other *sūtras* everyday.

Youths who are fifteen years or older, and believers who are twenty-five years or younger should take their identification documents to be verified. Next they should have their names added to the register, be assigned positions, and thus become intermediate students. Those who are able to read three works will form the highest rank. Those who are able to read two will form the middle rank. And those who are able to read only one will form the lowest rank. The top rank shall consist of those with minds of the Middle Way. Among the students, they are the resolute ones, excelling in both ability and achievements.

---

[65] The translation here is not literal. The reference to spring thunder is from the *Nieh p'an ching (Mahāparinirvāṇasūtra,* fasc. 8, *T* 12: 652b), where it is explained that when there is spring thunder, flowers bloom from the tusks of elephants. Such is the time for the bodhisattva's compassionate actions. The reference to summer lightning is also from the *Nieh p'an ching* (fasc. 2, *T* 12: 614c). Lightning is used as a simile for the transiency of life. The passage indicates that now is the time for the bodhisattva's compassion.

[66] In the *Hachijōshiki* the number of intermediate students was changed to six for each course.

[67] *Sūtras* may be read or chanted as part of a religious ceremony in two different ways. If every word of the *sūtra* is read, it is called a 'true reading' 眞讀. However many of the *sūtras* used in ceremonies are too long to chant or read in their entirety in a reasonable amount of time. Consequently only the title or a few selected passages are read. This abbreviated reading is called 'turning the *sūtras*' 轉經.

[68] In the *Rokujōshiki,* the *Shou hu ching* is listed as a text for the Meditation Course.

The students will be tested after nine years and all those who fail the test will be expelled (from the monastery). Those who pass shall reside on Mount Hiei continuously in both body and mind for twelve years. They shall follow the monastery's rules and advance in their studies. (By becoming a) treasure of the nation, a teacher of the nation, or an asset of the nation, they will benefit both themselves and others. They will rapidly advance through the six stages (*roku soku* 六卽)[69] and long reside in the three virtues 三德.[70]

From now on, those who reside in my halls shall purge themselves forever of the three poisons 三毒.[71] They shall follow the rules of the *Lotus Sūtra* and not rely on the sheep or elephant vehicles; rather, they shall board the latter three vehicles.[72]

The fifteenth day of the fifth month of the ninth year of the Kōnin era (818).

Written by Saichō, Head of the Tendai School.

This petition differed from the *Hachijōshiki,* submitted five months later, on several points, the most important being that in the *Hachijōshiki* the number of intermediate students is reduced to six for each course. This earlier petition may actually be only a rough draft that was later revised and incorporated into the *Hachijōshiki.*[73]

The next petition, dated eight days after the *Rokujōshiki,* is directed mainly against Gomyō's objections to the proposal that Hieizanji be designated an 'exclusively Mahāyāna temple.'[74]

PETITION ASKING FOR
PERMISSION TO INSTALL BODHISATTVA MONKS
(*Shobosatsu shukkehyō* 請菩薩出家表)

The monk Saichō states:

From Kashmir west, Mahāyāna and Hīnayāna are practiced separately. From the Hsüan-pu 玄圃 east, Mahāyāna and Hīnayāna

---

[69] See footnote 5 of Chapter 3.

[70] The three virtues which accompany *nirvāṇa* are: (1) embodiment of the absolute, (2) wisdom, and (3) freedom from passions.

[71] The three poisons are covetousness, anger, and ignorance. They are the source of all passions and delusions.

[72] See footnote 37 of this chapter for the five vehicles. The sheep and elephant vehicles are the two lowest ones.

[73] Shioiri Ryochu, s. v. *Hieizan Tendai Hokkein tokugō gakushōshiki, BKD* 9: 94.

[74] The *Denjutsu isshinkaimon* (*DZ* 1: 538–39) describes Gomyō's objections and gives the text of this petition. The petition is also found in *DZ* 1: 22–23.

[75] A large number of the Indian monks who travelled to China were from Kashmir. Hsüan-tsang and other Chinese pilgrims visited there. Saichō relies especially on Hsüan-

are practiced together.[75] Although (Buddhist practice) is different in the east and the west, both have Buddhist wisdom as their objective. The ultimate and complete doctrine, the pure and perfect teaching, (is found in the) *Lotus Sūtra.* (According to this *sūtra,* Mahāyāna monks) may not greet Hīnayāna monks, nor may they be in the lecture hall together.[76] From now on, we shall encourage our students to abide by the rules set out in the *sūtras.*[77]

I humbly think that the virtue of the literary and martial Kōnin Emperor[78] pervades heaven and earth. His brightness is equal to the sun and moon. All precedents pale before his loyalty and filial piety. He renews etiquette and music. He gladdens the myriad nations and converts the barbarians. Heaven and earth respond to him. He presides over (the nation) and determines propriety.

Now, the former emperor's (Kanmu) desire was that the Tendai School (prosper). The language (of the Tendai works) is lofty; few monks have responded to it. Men are weak while the Dharma is profound. As a result this teaching has not yet spread, nor have students pursued it. Thus it is naturally fitting that we encourage (special) rules for this school, and thereby educate and encourage our students. Mahāyāna and Hīnayāna practitioners should live separately and vie with each other in their practice of Buddhism. Those in the mountains and those in the capital should strive in harmony to protect the nation.

Therefore, a Chinese memorial[79] states: "We must control our emotions which run about like monkeys. We must tether our minds which rampage like elephants. But unless we retreat to the mountains, we shall not succeed."

I respectfully request that henceforth Tendai yearly ordinands be initiated in accordance with Mahāyāna (teachings) at the hall on Mount Hiei on the seventeenth day of the third month of every year in honor of the late emperor, and that an imperial messenger be dispatched to certify this ceremony. This is specified in the School's

tsang's travel records in the *Kenkairon* (*DZ* 1: 37–56). Hsüan–pu, a place where immortals are said to dwell, is located on K'un–lun Mountain in west China.

[76] *Lotus Sūtra,* "Anrakugyōbon," *T* 9: 37a.

[77] Namely such *sūtras* as the *Lotus, Fan wang ching,* and *Wei mo ching* (*Vimalakīrtinirdeśa*) which prohibit the Mahāyāna practitioner from consorting with Hīnayānists. See *Kenkairon, DZ* 1: 138–144.

[78] This title is not found in Saichō's other works.

[79] Hsüan–tsang's "Memorial Asking for Permission to Enter Mount Sun," contained in the *Ssu sha men Hsüan tsang piao chi, T* 52: 825c.

regulations. If this is done the Buddha-vehicle we transmit will continue to flourish, and the students that we teach will be pure in practice throughout the years.

With outmost sincerity I reverently submit this memorial and humbly ask His Majesty to grant it.

The twenty-first day of the fifth month of the ninth year of the Kōnin era (818).

Submitted by Saichō, the Head of the Tendai School, the monk who formerly sought the Dharma in China.

This petition again indicates Saichō's reluctance to openly propose that the *Fan wang* precepts be used to ordain monks instead of the *Ssu fen lü* precepts. Above all, it was noteworthy for two things which were not requested, but were to be of crucial importance in the *Shijōshiki* submitted ten months later. Their absence indicated that Saichō was still not prepared to publicly propose that the *Fan wang* precepts be substituted for those of the *Ssu fen lü*. First, Saichō mentioned nothing about the ordination of monks in the above petition. Yearly ordinands, because of their special function of praying for the welfare of the state, were usually initiated in the court. Saichō asked that the location of this ceremony be changed from the court in Kyoto to Mount Hiei, with an imperial messenger attending. This initiation, however, only qualified the practitioner as a novice (*shami*). The full ordination which qualified him as a monk was a separate ceremony performed on the precepts platform in Nara. Saichō did not mention the full ordination in the *Shobosatsu shukkehyō*. Second, Saichō was still vague about which set of precepts he wanted to use to initiate novices. He stated only that they should be, "initiated in accordance with Mahāyāna (teachings)" 依大乗得度, but did not specify that Mahāyāna precepts be used. Saichō's choice of words seems to be deliberately ambiguous. A Nara monk of the time would probably have thought that the phrase referred to an initiation using the ten traditional Hīnayāna precepts for novices (*shamikai* 沙彌戒) interpreted according to Mahāyāna teachings.

The Hachijōshiki

During the next few months, Saichō probably continued his efforts to reorganize and expand Hieizanji. Later sources of dubious authenticity claim that during this time Saichō planned sixteen halls and named the Tendai monks who were to oversee them.[80] In addition to the

---

[80]*Eigaku yōki, GR* 15: 520f.

Precepts Platform Hall (*kaidan'in*), these documents include halls for the four Tendai types of meditation, as well as other halls important to the early Tendai School. Five of the sixteen halls are identical to those found in the list of nine halls which Saichō may have authored several months earlier. One-third of the sixteen buildings were never constructed.

Saichō heard very little or nothing concerning his petitions. Since they were probably submitted to the court through the Office of Monastic Affairs, which was controlled by the Hossō monk Gomyō 護命, the petitions might never have reached the court or the Emperor. Even if they had reached the court, the issues were rapidly becoming so controversial that the court probably did not want to become involved in the dispute. Finally in the eighth month of 818, Saichō submitted another petition, the *Hachijōshiki* 八條式 (Regulations in Eight Articles).

REGULATIONS TO ENCOURAGE TENDAI YEARLY ORDINAND STUDENTS

(*Kanshō Tendaishū nenbun gakushōshiki* 勸奬天台宗年分學生式)[81]

1. (At any one time) there will be twelve intermediate students (*tokugō gakushō* 得業學生).[82] Their period of study will be set at six years. Since the number of students will decrease by two each year, two more should be added (each year).[83] In order to test the intermediate students, the teachers will all gather in the study hall[84] and examine the students on their reading of the *Lotus Sūtra* and the *Chin kuang ming ching* (*Suvarṇaprabhāsasūtra*).[85] If they pass, it

---

[81] Usually this petition is known as the *Hachijōshiki* because it is divided into eight sections. Although there is no numbering in the original text, numbers are added here for convenience.

[82] Intermediate students (*tokugō gakushō*) were students who wished to become Tendai yearly ordinands. Since they were to study for six years before they became yearly ordinands, and twelve years afterwards, the total period of study for a student on Mount Hiei was a long eighteen years. These students were to follow the precepts for laymen until they were ordained as yearly ordinands. Also see the *Regulations for Intermediate Students* (translated above).

[83] Two students were to be initiated each year. These would have to be replaced if the total number of intermediate students was to remain twelve. (See Shioiri, *Dengyō Daishishū*, p. 42). On the other hand, Sonoda (*Saichō, p.* 429) interprets this passage as meaning that if it were impossible to initiate one yearly ordinand into the Tendai Course and one into the Esoteric Course, then it would be permissible to initiate two into either course. In any case, two men were to be initiated. Shioiri's interpretation seems to be the more reasonable one.

[84] The study hall (*gakudō* 學堂) was a building on Hiei. Shioiri Ryōtatsu (*Dengyō Daishishū*, pp. 42–43) notes that this gathering is the forerunner of an annual conference still held on Hiei.

[85] In testing his students on the *Lotus Sūtra* and *the Chin kuang ming ching*, Saichō was following a long tradition which held yearly ordinands responsible for these two *sūtras*. At the same time, Saichō's introduction of study of the *Ta p'i lu che na ching* and *Mo ho chih kuan* as requirements for some yearly ordinands was a significant change from past practices [Ogami Kanchū, "Nenbundosha ni mirareru kashiki seido (jō)," *Nihon Bukkyō* 8 (1960): 24–

will be fully recorded in the register; on the day they fulfill the requirements, the authorities shall be informed. If they pass after six years, they will be added to the ranks of those who have fulfilled the requirements. If they do not pass, they will not be added to the ranks of those who have fulfilled the requirements. If anyone withdraws, his name and the name of the person replacing him will be recorded and reported to the authorities.

2. All intermediate students will provide their own food and clothing.[86] However, if there is someone who is of excellent mind, ability and health, but who lacks sufficient clothing and food, then this hall (the Ichijō shikan'in) will issue him a certificate permitting him to go and beg in the nine directions.[87]

3. If an intermediate student's character is not in accord with the Dharma and he breaks the rules 衆制,[88] then the authorities shall be informed and he will be replaced, as is specified in the regulations 式.

4. Intermediate students will receive the full precepts the same year that they are initiated.[89] Once they have received the full

---

27]. In this passage, only the ability to read the *sūtras* in the Japanese (*kun*) style is mentioned. Previously, the Sino–Japanese (*on*) reading style was also usually required.

[86] Since the intermediate students were not yet monks, they were neither entitled to the temple's provisions nor to government support. Yet it was certainly in Saichō's interest to attract and support able students. The fact that he could not support them is an indication of Mount Hiei's financial problems at this time.

[87] The nine directions are north, south, east, west, northwest, northeast, southwest, southeast, and the center. The restrictions on begging illustrate Saichō's determination to maintain strict control over his students even before they were ordained as monks.

[88] This reference to a set of rules is one of the few passages which indicate how Saichō planned to resolve problems not covered by the precepts. The *Fan wang* precepts alone were not sufficient to govern the order; these precepts were idealistic and did not specify penalties for transgressions. The rules mentioned here were probably temple rules designed to solve specific problems which arose on Mount Hiei but which were not covered by the *Fan wang* precepts. One such list of rules is found in Saichō's will [*DZ* 5 (*Bekkan*): 39] which is translated later in this chapter. Shortly after Saichō's death, another list was compiled by his disciples Ninchū, Enchō, and Gishin (*Enryakuji kinseishiki*, in *Tendai kahyō*, fasc. 5A, *BZ* 42: 4–5). Later, other sets of rules were compiled. One of the earliest extant sets is by Ryōgen, the Tendai *zasu*, compiled around 970 (*Heian ibun* 2: 431–39). Sets of rules to supplement the precepts were often compiled in China. For an analysis of rules compiled by such monks as Tao–an and Chih–i, see Tsuchihashi, "Chūgoku ni okeru kairitsu no kussetsu," *Ryūkoku daigaku ronshū*, no. 393 (1970), pp. 27–60.

[89] Normally there was no set period of time between initiation and ordination. The two ceremonies might be given at the same time, or a period of years might intervene. But in all cases a candidate had to be initiated as a novice before he was ordained as a monk. At the time of this petition, Saichō did not allow Tendai novices to receive the full ordination pending the outcome of the controversy with the Nara schools over the Tendai School's right to use the *Fan wang* precepts to ordain monks.

precepts, they will not leave the confines of the mountain for twelve years and will devote themselves to their studies and practices. For the first six years, they will learn mainly through lectures. Secondary emphasis will be placed on contemplation and the practice (of meditation).[90] Each day two-thirds of their studies will concern Buddhism and one third will concern other subjects.[91] Extensive lecturing will be their training; preaching the Dharma will be their discipline. During the last six years, contemplation and the practice (of meditation) will be stressed. Secondary emphasis will be placed on lectures. Those in the (Tendai) Meditation Course will thoroughly practice the four types of meditation. Those in the Esoteric Course will thoroughly practice chanting and meditation on the *sanbu* 三部.[92]

5. Tendai yearly (ordinand) students and any others who wish to practice in the One-vehicle Meditation Hall[93] will not have their names removed from their original temple's register.[94] Their names will be entered in (the register of one of) the temples of Ōmi which

[90]Listening to lectures, thinking, and practicing form a group known as the three types of wisdom (*san'e* 三慧).

[91]No list of the non–Buddhist works which Tendai monks were to study is found in Saichō's writings. However, Saichō's writings do contain a number of passages based on Confucian and Taoist sources which Saichō had probably studied as a youth (Uchino Kumaichirō, "Dengyō Daishi chōsaku shōsoku bunchū no geten shōku tekisetsu," *DDK* [*Bekkan*], pp. 61–70). Tendai monks were probably expected to study the Chinese classics. According to the *Ken pen shuo i chieh yu pu p'i na yeh tsa shih* (T 24: 332, *Mūlasarvās-tivādavinayaksudrakavastu*), only intelligent monks were to be allowed to study non–Buddhist texts and only one-third of their time was to be devoted to non–Buddhist subjects.

[92] The term *sanbu* is ambiguous in this passage. It probably refers to the three divisions of the Taizōkai, namely the Buddha (Butsubu), Lotus (Rengebu) and Daimond (Kongōbu). Sonoda (*Saichō*, p. 198) claims that it may refer to the three Esoteric *sūtras* mentioned in the *Regulations for Intermediate Students*.

[93] The One-vehicle Meditation Hall (Ichijō shikan'in 一乘止觀院) was the center of activities on Mount Hiei during Saichō's lifetime. Later accounts such as the *Eigaku yōki* claim that Saichō built the Konpon chūdō 根本中堂 (Main Hall), installed a statue of Yakushi Nyorai (Bhaiṣajyaguru Tathāgata) which he had carved himself as the central image, and called it the Ichijō shikan'in in 788, only three years after he sequestered himself on Mount Hiei. The name of the hall, the One-vehicle Meditation Hall, reflects a commitment to Tendai which Saichō probably did not have at that time. In earlier literature, the hall is first mentioned in the *Eizan Daishiden* [*DZ* 5 (*Bekkan*): 7] in reference to a meeting held in 801, in which the hall is called a small thatched hut. It was big enough, however, to house the temple's collection of *sūtras* (*Gokyōzō mokuroku, DZ* 4: 434). The name of the hall is also found in the lists of nine and sixteen halls. It is probably the place where Saichō died (Sonoda, *Saichō*, pp. 429–30).

[94] The reference to monks other than Tendai yearly ordinands is a significant change from the *Rokujōshiki*. Saichō is gradually widening the scope of his regulations. During Saichō's lifetime, there was no separate register for Hieizanji. Even Tendai yearly ordinands were registered at temples in Nara, most often at Kōfukuji.

receives a sufficient stipend of food.[95] That temple will send them food. Robes, however, for the summer and winter will be obtained by going out and begging in different places in accordance with Mahāyāna teachings.[96] Thus they will be able to clothe themselves and will not backslide in their practice. From now on, they will strictly adhere to these customs. They will make thatched huts their abodes and use bamboo leaves as their seats. They will disregard their own needs and respect the Dharma. Thus will the Dharma long endure, and the nation be protected.

6. With the exception of yearly ordinands from other schools,[97] any monk who has been initiated and received the full precepts, and who comes of his own accord and wishes to remain on the mountain for twelve years to practice the two courses, will note the name of his temple and teacher, obtain a certificate from the hall on Mount Hiei and deposit it with the governmental authorities. When he has spent twelve full years on the mountain, he will be granted the rank of *hosshi* (Dharma Teacher) along with the yearly ordinand students of this school.[98] If he does not follow the rules of the school, he will be sent back to his former temple.

7. After a student has completed twelve years on the mountain, studying and practicing in accordance with the regulations, he will be granted the rank of *daihosshi* 大法師 (Great Dharma Teacher). If his studies are incomplete, but he still has spent a full twelve years on the mountain without leaving, then he will be granted the rank *hosshi*. If a student of the School does not follow the rules or stay

---

[95] This article reflects the poverty of Mount Hiei. Saichō was petitioning the government for food from temples which may have opposed him. It is doubtful that this proved very satisfactory. Eventually the government ordered the Kokubunji in Ōmi to supply Mount Hiei with food for twenty-four monks, the number of yearly ordinands who were to live on Mount Hiei under Saichō's plan (*Engishiki,* fasc. 20, included in Umeda, *Nihon shūkyō seidoshi: Jōdaihen,* p. 459). Each monk was to be allotted two *masu* of rice.

[96] While yearly ordinands probably received robes from the government, other monks had no such source. Exactly how this precept was to be put into practice is unclear. Presumably monks not restricted to Mount Hiei for twelve years of training did all the begging. 'Begging in accordance with Mahāyāna teachings' implies that no element of self-seeking enters one's mind. Minor precepts 26–28 of the *Fan wang ching* (*T* 24: 1007a) are concerned with the proper attitude when receiving invitations and begging.

[97] The exclusion of yearly ordinand students from other schools probably reflects Saichō's concern over having his own yearly ordinand students lured away by the Nara Schools. The defection of yearly ordinands may have resulted in changes in the government's financial support of the schools affected; however, the evidence on this point is scanty and inconclusive.

[98] *Hosshi* (or *dentō hosshi*) is the second highest grade. *Daihosshi* is the highest.

in the mountain halls, or if he remains on the mountain but repeatedly breaks the rules, or if the number of years (spent on the mountain) is not sufficient, his name will be permanently removed from the Tendai School's official registers and he will be sent back to his former temple.

8. Two lay administrators[99] (*zoku bettō* 俗別當) will be appointed to the Tendai School's Hall. They will take turns supervising the order, and also be responsible for prohibiting theft, liquor, and women (on the mountain). They will uphold the Buddha's Dharma and protect the nation.

The above eight articles uphold the Buddha's Dharma, benefit the nation, draw sentient beings to the true teaching, and encourage future students to do good.

I humbly ask for His Majesty's judgment.

The twenty-seventh day of the eighth month of the ninth year in the Kōnin era (818).

Submitted by Saichō, the monk who formerly went to China in search of the Dharma.

Nothing seems to have come of Saichō's petitions. About seven months after the petitions were submitted, Saichō decided to press for approval of them once again. According to the *Denjutsu isshinkaimon*, on the third day of the third month of 819 he summoned Kōjō and told him of his plan to use the Mahāyāna precepts to ordain monks.[100]

This passage is the earliest reference to the Mahāyāna precepts in the *Denjutsu isshinkaimon*. It dates Saichō's concern with the bodhisattva precepts almost one year later than the 818 date found in the *Eizan Daishiden*. This discrepancy may be explained by the fact that the *Denjuttsu isshinkaimon* is concerned with the Tendai School's external relations

---

[99] The *bettō* was to be the chief administrator of the temple and was in charge of building, repairs, and monastic discipline. The earliest record of the office is Rōben's appointment as *bettō* of Tōdaiji in 752. After this, *bettō* were appointed at various other temples. During the Heian period a number of distinctions in the rank and method of appointing *bettō* developed, but the system was still relatively simple at the time of Saichō's petitions (*BD* 5: 4523). Saichō's proposal was unique, however, in asking that laymen be appointed to serve as a direct liaison between the Council of State (Dajōkan) and the Tendai School. Saicho's proposal may have been influenced by the system devised by his patron, Fujiwara no Fuyutsugu, to oversee the private college established for the Fujiwara family in 821, the Kangakuin [Furukawa Eishun, "*Gakushōshiki* ni okeru Tendai shūdan no dokuritsu to sono riyū ni tsuite," *TG* 3 (1961): 14], or by Amoghavajra's petitions concerning 'commisioners of religion' (*kung–te–shih* 功德使). The office of lay adininistrator is discussed further in Chapter 14.
[100] *DZ* 1: 552.

with the government while the *Eizan Daishiden* focusses more on the School's internal affairs. Saichō may have taken a more extreme stance when he was talking to Tendai monks than when he was presenting his ideas to outsiders. However, the *Denjutsu isshinkaimon*'s separate treatment of the debate over the Mahāyāna temple designation and the dispute over the bodhisattva precepts suggests that Saichō's concern with the precepts almost certainly developed as a consequence of the disputes over the temple designation and the proposals for an end to the juridsiction of the Office of Monastic Affairs over the Tendai School. The ambiguity of Saichō's references to the precepts in his earlier petitions suggests that he was considering a reform of the precepts, but had not yet decided to ask that the *Fan wang* precepts be substituted for the *Ssu fen lü* precepts in ordinations. If the court had approved his earlier petitions, Saichō might never have pressed for a change in the precepts. Removing his monks from the jurisdiction of the Sōgō might have satisfied him. However, when the Sōgō ignored his early petitions, Saichō felt compelled to take a more extreme position and suggest a change in the precepts used for ordinations and monastic discipline. Surely the Sōgō could not ignore such a suggestion.

After Saichō told Kōjō about his plan to use the *Fan wang* precepts in ordinations, he asked Kōjō to take the relevant petitions to Gomyō, the *sōzu* (supervisor) who resided at Nodera in Kyoto, and obtain his signature before the petitions were submitted to court. In doing so, Saichō was following the procedure stated in the Yōrō Legal Code (compiled in 718):

> Monks and nuns who present memorials concerning temple affairs directly to the government or who importune the households of officials with improper petitions, instead of going through the proper channels, shall be punished by hard labor for fifty days; and if the offense is repeated, for one hundred days. This shall not apply to the *bona fide* statement of a case where through an unfair decision of the civil or ecclesiastical authorities justice has been denied or delayed.[101]

The proper official channel meant that the petitions would go from the Sōgō (Office of Monastic Affairs) to the Genbaryō (Bureau of Buddhism

---

[101] Quoted in Umeda, *Nihon shūkyō seidoshi: Jōdaihen*, pp. 230–31. The English translation is based on George Sansom, "Early Japanese Law and Administration," *Transactions of the Asiatic Society of Japan*, new series, 11 (1934): 129. Commentaries differ as to whether the article refers to private and/or temple affairs.

and Aliens), then to the Jibushō (Ministry of Civil Administration), and finally to the Dajōkan (Council of State). But since both the Sōgō and Genbaryō were controlled by monks of the Hossō School who were hostile to Saichō, his petitions had little chance of being approved. For this reason, Kōjō suggested that they bypass the usual route and submit the proposals directly to the Emperor through the *udaiben* (Controller of the Right), Yoshimine no Yasuyo. Saichō agreed to Kōjō's suggestion.

The Shijōshiki

Yoshimine also agreed to this plan. On the fifteenth day of the third month of 819, he presented the Emperor with Saichō's two petitions along with three Mahāyāna *sutras*, the *Ch'eng tsan ta ch'eng kung te ching* 稱讚大乘功德經, *Shuo miao fa chüeh ting yeh chang ching* 說妙法決定業障經, and the *Ta fang kuang shih tzu hou ching* 大方廣師子吼經 (*Siṃhanādikasūtra*).[102] In the main petition, the *Shijōshiki* 四條式 (Regulations in Four Articles), was a proposal that each year on the anniversary of Kanmu's death the Tendai School be allowed to ordain monks using the Mahāyāna precepts. The first possible occasion for such an ordination would come only two days after the petition was submitted to the Emperor. In the memorial accompanying the *sutras* Saichō stated:

> A Perfect and Sudden mind arose in the Emperor Kanmu, who established the Lotus One-vehicle School in Japan in order to benefit sentient beings. (Thirteen years) after His Majesty passed away, on the seventeenth day of the third month of the tenth year of the Kōnin era (819), I respectfully copied these three Mahāyāna *sutras*. In order to repay the late Emperor's virtue and with the hope that he will not tarry on the narrow roads of Hīnayāna's roundabout teachings, but will take the Mahāyāna Great Direct Path (*daijiki-dō* 大直道), I humbly present these *sutras* . . .[103]

Yoshimine and Kōjō were obviously hoping for quick approval of their proposals before any opposition could surface. According to

---

[102] *Denjutsu isshinkaimon, DZ* 1: 540–41. The *sutras* correspond respectively to *Taishō* numbers 840, 841, and 836. All three are one fascicle each. The first two are translations of the same *sutra* with slight variations, no. 840 being by Hsüan–tsang, and no. 841 by Chih–yen (trans. in 721). Saichō probably submitted them because they warn against slandering Mahāyāna teachings and consorting with Hīnayāna adherents. Numbers 840 and 841 are quoted in the *Kenkairon, DZ* 1: 58–61.

[103] *Denjutsu isshinkaimon, DZ* 1: 541. For Kōjō's description of the events surrounding the Emperor's refusal to consider the request, see ibid., p. 544.

this strategy, the court would have accepted a major change in monastic policies as part of the ceremonies honoring the late Emperor Kanmu. Kōjō described the Mount Hiei monks as expectantly waiting for approval on the seventeenth; however, their wait was in vain.

The two petitions Saichō submitted at this time are translated below.

REGULATIONS FOR TENDAI-LOTUS YEARLY ORDINANDS AND FOR THOSE WHO WISH TO TURN AWAY FROM HĪNAYĀNA TEACHINGS TOWARDS MAHĀYĀNA TEACHINGS

(*Tendai Hokkeshū nenbundosha eshō kodai shiki*
天台法華宗年分者回小向大式)

Composed of four articles in all.[104]

A. There are three types of Buddhist temples:

1. Exclusively Mahāyāna temples where beginning bodhisattva monks[105] live.

2. Exclusively Hīnayāna temples where exclusively Hīnayāna *risshi*[106] live.

3. Temples in which both Hīnayāna and Mahāyāna Buddhism are practiced[107] and where advanced bodhisattva monks[108] live.

Now after Tendai-Lotus yearly (ordinand) students and those beginning students who have willingly turned from Hīnayāna to Mahāyāna teachings have spent twelve years practicing at the

---

[104] *DZ* 1: 16–20. Of the three petitions included in the *Sange gakushōshiki*, only this one included the number of articles at the beginning of the petition. The popular name of this petition, the *Shijōshiki* (*Regulations in Four Articles*), comes from the term *shijō* (four articles). The names of the other two petitions, the *Rokujōshiki* (*Regulations in Six Articles*), and *Hachijōshiki* (*Regulations in Eight Articles*), were then patterned after the *Shijōshiki*.

[105] For Saichō, a beginning bodhisattva monk (*shoshugō bosatsusō* 初修業菩薩僧) is one who although a Mahāyāna adherent is still in danger of backsliding towards Hīnayāna teachings. Thus he must be isolated from Hīnayāna practitioners. The classification of three types of temples is based on travel diaries by Chinese pilgrims in India such as Hsüan-tsang.

[106] A *risshi* 律師 or *vinaya*–master is a monk who keeps and remembers the precepts. In its usage here, it should not be confused with the Nara and Heian period monastic office of the same name, though from Saichō's perspective both usages had Hīnayāna connotations.

[107] This category appears to include those temples in which monks kept the Hīnayāna precepts with a Mahāyāna mind. Thus it would describe the temples in Nara.

[108] Advanced bodhisattva monks (*kushugō bosatsusō* 久修業菩薩僧) are those who are no longer in danger of backsliding. They may associate with Hīnayāna practitioners and live in temples where both Hīnayāna and Mahāyāna practices are performed.

[109] The four types of meditation are found in the *Mo ho chih kuan*, fasc. 2A, *Chūge gōhen Tendai Daishi zenshu* (hereafter cited as *TZ*), 11 vols. (Tokyo: Nihon Bussho kankōkai, 1969), *Mo ho chih kuan* 1: 395–555. They are: (a) meditation done while constantly sitting, (b) meditation done while constantly walking, (c) meditation done while half–sitting and half–walking, and (d) meditation done while neither walking nor sitting. A description of these meditations can be found in Hurvitz, *Chih-i* pp. 321–28. Saichō had planned to

chapels for the four types of meditation[109] deep in the mountains and have completed their courses (*tokugō* 得業), they will be permitted to provisionally receive a Hīnayāna ordination in order to benefit others.[110] They may then live in temples where both Hīnayāna and Mahāyāna Buddhism are practiced.

B. Both Hīnayāna and Mahāyāna seats of honor (*jōza* 上座) have been established in Buddhist temples:

1. The exclusively Mahāyāna temple installs the bodhisattva Mañjuśrī (Jap. Monjushiri) as *jōza*.[111]

2. The exclusively Hīnayāna temple installs the preceptor

---

construct four chapels, one for each type of meditation. However, he died before they could all be built (Kageyama, *Hieizan,* pp. 71, 185–86). Unlike his earlier petitions, Saichō here implies that students of both the Meditation and Esoteric courses would undergo training in Tendai meditation.

[110] In previous petitions, the term *tokugō* referred to those who had passed the requirements qualifying them to become Tendai yearly ordinands. Here, however, it probably refers to monks who had completed twelve years of confinement on Mount Hiei. Tendai monks have long disagreed about the level of proficiency a practitioner must demonstrate in order to qualify as having completed the course. Kakuhō 覺寶 (1808–1890), in the *Gakushōshiki kōben* stated that a 12-year period on Mount Hiei was sufficient to complete the course (*Tendaishū zensho* 5: 418). In contrast, Ryōten 克碩 (1760–1791) claims that unlesss the practitioner has attained a stage at which his six senses are pure and he will no longer backslide, he has not fulfilled the requirements for *tokugō* (*Enkai jūyō, Tendaishū zensho* 8: 38–39). The definition of this term is one of the key problems in later Tendai thought, particularly during the *Anrakuritsu* controversy in the Tokugawa period. Whether or not Tendai monks would be required to take the *Ssu fen lü* ordination depended on the definition of the term *tokugō.*

[111] In this case, the term *jōza* refers to the Buddhist image installed in dining halls. Before monks eat, they offer a portion of food to the *jozā* (also known as *shōsō* 聖僧). The term has several other meanings: (a) to refer to monks who have spent a certain number of years in the order, usually twenty or more; (b) to refer to the place of honor at the head of the monastic assembly which was usually occupied by the worthy monk with the most seniority, although at times it might be given to a lay patron; and (c) a monastic office.

Mañjuśrī, the personification of the wisdom which leads to Buddhahood, is said to be the teacher of innumerable Buddhas, including Śākyamuni (T 15: 451a). Mañjuśrī also played an important role in Esoteric Buddhism, occupying the chamber above Śākyamuni in the Womb-realm (Taizōkai) *maṇḍala.* Mañjuśrī is mentioned prominently in the *Lotus Sūtra* and plays a major role in the *Fan wang* ordination ceremony. By honoring Mañjuśrī, Saichō was tying together the various traditions which he had combined under the heading of Tendai and showing that Hieizanji was indeed a Mahāyāna temple.

Saichō's proposal to use Mañjuśrī as *jōza* was based on a similar proposal made by Amoghavajra in 769 (*Kenkairon, DZ* 1: 102–105). The worship of Mañjuśrī was one of the central themes in Amoghavajra's Esoteric Buddhism. Amoghavajra translated eight texts on Mañjuśrī and founded temples or halls dedicated to Mañjuśrī in various places, including Wu-t'ai-shan 五台山, the Chinese mountain where Mañjuśrī was believed to reside. Even earlier, the Hua-yen master Fa-tsang 法藏 (643–712) had noted that Mañjuśrī was regarded as the *jōza* (elder) in Mahāyāna temples in India and Central Asia (*Fan wang ching p'u sa chieh pen shu* T 40: 605b). More information about Mañjuśrī can be found in E. Lamotte, "Mañjuśrī," *T'oung pao* 48 (1960): 1–96; and Stanley Weinstein's chapter on "Buddhism under the T'ang" in the *Cambridge History of China,* forthcoming.

(*wajō*) Piṇḍola (Jap. Binzuru) as *jōza*.[112]

3. The temple in which both Mahāyāna and Hīnayāna are practiced installs both Mañjuśrī and Piṇḍola as *jōza* 上座.[113] On the Hīnayāna *upavasatha* (*fusatsu* 布薩) day, Piṇḍola is *jōza* and the monks sit in Hīnayāna order. On the Mahāyāna *upavasatha* day, Mañjuśrī is *jōza* and the monks sit in Mahāyāna order.[114] This (Mahāyāna) order has not yet been used in

---

[112] Binzuru harada, (Skt. Piṇḍola-bhāradvaja), one of the sixteen arhats, was famous for his wisdom and compassion. The tradition of installing Piṇḍola as elder (*jōza*) and offering food to him can be explained by referring to two sets of stories about him. According to a number of accounts, Piṇḍola had been a glutton as a lay man, but overcame his desire for food after he became a monk. The name 'Piṇḍola' is interpreted as meaning 'alms-getter' or 'alms receptacle.' According to another set of stories, Piṇḍola mastered certain superhuman powers, but broke the precepts by displaying his powers, before laymen. As a result, Śākyamuni Buddha forbade Piṇḍola from entering *nirvāṇa* until Maitreya appeared. During that time, Piṇḍola was to serve the Buddhist order and to act as a field of merit for both laymen and monks.

The traditions that Piṇḍola enjoyed food and that he served the order were probably combined to make Piṇḍola the recipient of offerings of food. Since Piṇḍola had been alive from the time of Śākyamuni, he was clearly qualified to be the senior monk (*jōza*). The tradition of installing Piṇḍola as elder probably began in India, but was particularly widespread in China, because, according to some stories, he had been exiled from India to other lands. Ui Hakuju notes that some texts claim that his exile was later lifted (*Shaku Dōan no kenkyū* [Tokyo: Iwanami shoten, 1956], p. 28).

His appearance in China is first mentioned in the *Kao seng chuan* (fasc. 5, *T* 50: 353b), where he appeared in a dream to Tao–an and indicated that Tao–an's commentaries were accurate. He told Tao–an that he should be offered food; however, Tao–an did not recognize him. After Tao–an's death, the *Shih sung lü* 十誦律 (*Sarvāstivāda vinaya*) was translated. On the basis of this work (see *T* 23: 268c–269b), Tao–an's disciple Hui–yüan identified the old man in his teacher's dream as Piṇḍola and installed an altar dedicated to him in the dining hall. In 457, the *Ch'ing pin t'ou lu fa* 請賓頭盧法 (*T* no. 1869), a work describing the ritual of offering food to Piṇḍola, was translated.

Since Piṇḍola had not yet died, only an empty place was prepared for him at first and offerings made at his seat. Various ways were devised to determine if Piṇḍola had come. According to one tradition, a monk was able to determine whether Piṇḍola had manifested himself as a *nirmāṇakāya* or as a *saṃbhogakāya,* an interesting feat for a figure not permitted to enter *nirvāṇa*. Images of him are said to have been first drawn by Fa–yüan 法願 (414–500) and Fa–ching 法鏡 (437–500) around 470. After this, the practice of making images of him was widespread.

In Japan, temple records indicate that Piṇḍola was installed as *jōza* at several temples in Nara (*BD* 3: 2675b–2676c, and 5: 4333c–4335a: and John Strong, "The Legend of the Lion–roarer: A study of the Buddhist Arhat Piṇḍola Bhāradvaja," *Numen* 26 1979 : 50–88).

[113] Temples existed in China and Central Asia in which both Piṇḍola and Mañjuśrī were installed (Ono Katsutoshi, *Kōki no kenkyū* 2: 424). In Japan, the Shitennōji seems to have adopted this system following Saichō's petitions (*Shitennōji engi,* quoted in *BD* 2: 1747c). However, eighteenth century Shitennōji records list only Mañjuśrī (*Shitennōji meishakushū,* referred to in *BD* 3: 2676c).

[114] The *fusatsu* or *upavasatha* (Skt.) is the fortnightly meeting at which the *saṃgha* assembles and recites the precepts. The *fusatsu* is mentioned in the *Fan wang ching* in several places (*T* 24:1004a, 1005b, 1008a). In China, *fusatsu* using bodhisattva precepts were popular because they served as an occasion for monks and laymen to meet and practice together.

Japan.

C. There are two types of Buddhist precepts:

1. The Mahāyāna full precepts consist of the ten major and forty-eight minor precepts.

2. The Hīnayāna full precepts consist of the two-hundred fifty precepts.

D. There are two types of Buddhist ordinations:

1. (The ordination for) the Mahāyāna precepts.

The three teachers and the witnesses are invited as is specified in the *Kuan p'u hsien ching* 觀普賢經.[115] Śākyamuni Buddha is asked to be the preceptor for the bodhisattva precepts. The bodhisattva Mañjuśrī is asked to be the

---

Fusatsu based on bodhisattva precepts may have been based in part on the Hīnayāna Buddhist custom of allowing laymen to assemble at temples to fast and observe the eight precepts (*hassaikai*) for a day every fortnight. For a discussion of pre–Sung documents concerning *fusatsu* based on the bodhisattva precepts, see Tsuchihashi Shūkō, "Tonkōhon ni mirareru shuju no bosatsukaigi," in *Rekishi to bijutsu no shomondai,* vol. 6 of *Saiiki bunka kenkyū* (Kyoto: Hōzōkan, 1963), pp. 95–171 *passim.*

Since the precepts for different schools varied slightly, monks of one school probably did not participate in the *fusatsu* of another school. Thus pilgrims such as Hsüan–tsang make no mention of participating in *fusatsu* during their travels.

Because some of the *Fan wang* precepts specifically prohibit contact with Hīnayāna practitioners, the *Fan wang fusatsu* was usually not performed along with the Hīnayāna *Ssu fen lü fusatsu.* Although it is difficult to find examples of mixing the *fusatsu* in China, Chien–chen apparently did introduce such a practice into Japan. See the *Shinsen Tōdaiji kaidan jukai hōki* by Chien–chen's disciple Fa–chin, contained in the *Tōdaiji yōroku,* ed. Tsutsui Eishun (Osaka: Zenkoku shobō, 1944), pp. 334–37. The *Ssu fen lü fusatsu* was probably held on the 14th and 29th of the month, and the *Fan wang fusatsu* on the 15th and 30th. Other sources indicate that they might be performed on the same day or in the reverse order [Ishida Mizumaro, *Bonmōkyō,* Butten kōza, vol. 14 (Tokyo: Daizō shuppansha, 1971), p. 223]. Although according to the *Fan wang ching* the *fusatsu* should be performed in front of the image of a Buddha or bodhisattva (*T* 24: 1008a), Saichō seems to be the first person to specify that the bodhisattva be Mañjuśrī [Ishida Mizumaro, "Ganjin ni okeru fusatsu no igi," *Nanto Bukkyō* 21 (1968): 5–8].

[115] T 9: 393c. An English translation of the passage is found in Katō et. al., *The Threefold Lotus Sūtra* (New York: Weatherhill–Kōsei, 1975), pp. 367–68. The *Kuan p'u hsien ching* ordination is for conferring the precepts on oneself (*jisei jukai* 自誓受戒). Two sets of precepts mentioned in Yogācāra works, the six major and eight major precepts, are conferred in the ceremony. Although these precepts differ from the *Fan wang* precepts and although the ceremony described on the *Kuan p'u hsien ching* was for conferring the precepts on oneself, the idea of having the Buddhas and bodhisattvas participate in the ordination was so attractive that T'ien–t'ai masters such as Chan–jan incorporated elements from the *Kuan p'u hsien ching* in their ordination manuals describing how a teacher could transmit the precepts to others (*jūtajukai* 從他受戒). Since Chih–i had designated the *Kuan p'u hsien ching* as the capping *sūtra* (*kekkyō* 結經) for the *Lotus Sūtra,* Chan–jan and Saichō could incorporate parts of it into the *Fan wang* ordination ceremony even though the *Kuan p'u hsien ching* specified that major precepts in Yogācāra texts were to be used in the ordination. The roles played by the three teachers and the witnesses are described below in note 118.

karma ācārya 羯磨阿闍梨 for the bodhisattva precepts. The bodhisattva Maitreya is asked to be the instructor *ācārya* 教授阿闍梨 for the bodhisattva precepts. All of the Buddhas of the ten directions are asked to be witnesses 證師 for the bodhisattva precepts. All of the bodhisattvas of the ten directions are asked to be fellow students 同學等侶 of the bodhisattva precepts.

(A person who is qualified) and able to transmit the precepts is asked to serve as the teacher who is present (and presides over the ceremony).[116] If no teacher is present who is able to transmit the precepts, the candidate should search for one within one-thousand *ri*.[117] If no one who is able to confer the precepts (can be found) within one thousand *ri,* the candidate should confess (*sange* 懺悔) with utmost sincerity. He shall surely receive a sign 好相 from the Buddha and may then administer the precepts to himself by oath 自誓受戒 in front of an image of the Buddha.

Beginning Tendai yearly ordinand students and beginning students (of other schools) who have turned away from Hīnayāna to Mahāyāna teachings shall be granted the above-mentioned Mahāyāna precepts 大乘戒 and thereby become fully-ordained monks 大僧.

2. (The ordination for) the Hīnayāna precepts.

Ten teachers[118] are asked to be present and to perform

---

[116] This is the first of two types of Mahāyāna ordinations mentioned in the *Shijōshiki.* In this one, a qualified person is physically present to conduct the ceremony and transfer 傳 the precepts even though the actual conferral 授 of the precepts is done by invisible Buddhas and bodhisattvas. This type of ceremony is mentioned in the *Fan wang ching* (T 24: 1006c). It is preferred over the next type, conferring the precepts on oneself (*jisei jukai*), because a special sign from the Buddha is not required to certify that an ordination conducted by a qualified teacher is valid.

[117] The second type of ordination consisted of conferring the precepts upon oneself. It is mentioned in many Mahāyāna *sūtras* containing sections on the bodhisattva precepts. It usually consisted of a period of prolonged confession and the taking of vows. The ceremony culminated in a sign such as a dream or vision of the the Buddha which certified that the ordination was valid. This type of ordination has been popular at times in Japanese history, particularly when the validity of ordinations conferred by monks was questioned. Saichō relies on the *Fan wang ching* for his description (T 24: 1006c).

[118] Hīnayāna ordinations were usually performed with ten monks presiding (five monks if the ordination was held in outlying districts). The candidate asked a qualified monk to be his preceptor 和上. If the preceptor agreed, he would then be responsible for asking other monks to participate in the ordination and for training the new monk. A second monk served as *karma*–master 羯磨阿闍梨. He was responsible for correctly conducting the ordination. A third monk served as the teacher 教授阿闍梨 and asked the candidate questions which

a ceremony 白四羯磨 consisting of one statement of the motion 白 and three calls for agreement 羯磨. Ten worthy monks who have been pure in keeping the precepts are asked to serve as the three teachers and seven witnesses. If one monk is missing, the ordination may not be performed.

Now, Tendai yearly ordinand students and beginning students who have turned from Hīnayāna to Mahāyāna shall not be permitted to take these (Hīnayāna) precepts; however, an exception shall be made for advanced practitioners.[119]

I have pondered upon how the *Lotus Sūtra* calls the bodhisattva the nation's treasure[120] and how the Mahāyāna *sūtras* preach the Mahāyāna practice of benefiting others. If we do not employ Mahāyāna *sūtras* to prevent the seven calamities[121] which afflict the world, then what shall we use? If the great disasters to come are not vanquished by the bodhisattva monks 菩薩僧 then how will they be forestalled? The virtue of benefiting others and the power of great compassion is that which the Buddhas extol and that in which gods and men rejoice. The hundred monks (who chant the) *Jen wang ching*[122] draw upon the power of wisdom (*hannya*). The eight worthies who practice *The Sūtra Used in Asking for Rain* (*Ch'ing yü ching* 請雨經)[123] follow the Mahāyāna precepts. If the

---

determined his eligibility to enter the order. The seven other monks (two in outlying districts) served as witnesses 證明. They testified to the validity of the ordination if any problems arose later. Since the teachers were apt to be older men, at least one of the witnesses had to be young so that after the older teachers had died, a witness would still survive. The whole Hīnayāna ceremony was designed to initiate the candidate into the order in a way which maintained the harmony of the order, provided for the candidate's later training, and avoided any conflict with lay society.

The most important part of the Hīnayāna ordination occurred when a motion (*jñapti* 白) was made to the order that the candidate be accepted as a fully ordained monk. The monks were then asked three times if they agreed to the motion. The vote was called the *karman* 羯磨. The candidate remained silent and passive during this part of the ceremony. In the Tendai *Fan wang* ordination ceremony conducted by a qualified teacher, the question was put to the candidate three times (*DZ* 1: 331). The candidate thus played a more active role in the *Fan wang* ordination than he did in the *Ssu fen lü* ordination.

[119] Saichō's attitude toward the Hīnayāna precepts is discussed in Chapter 10.

[120] *T* 9: 2b.

[121] The seven types of calamity are described in the *Jen wang ching* (*T* 8: 843a). Saichō quotes the *sūtra* and Liang-pen's 良賁 (717–777) commentary (*T* 33: 513c) in the *Kenkairon* (*DZ* 1: 120f.). The seven types of disaster are those arising from (1) the sun and moon, (2) the stars, (3) fires, (4) the seasons, (5) the winds, (6) droughts, and (7) war and banditry.

[122] *T* 8: 840a. At times of disaster, the court might ask one-hundred monks to chant the *Jen wang ching*. This ceremony was used in China. The *Shoku Nihongi* indicates that it was also popular during the Nara period (*KT* 2: 210, 217, 226, 239, 270, 274, 404).

[123] The Ch'ing yü ching (*Mahāmeghasūtra*) describes a ceremony in which *dhāraṇī* are

bodhisattva is not the treasure of the nation or the benefactor of the nation, then who is? In Buddhism he is called a bodhisattva; in the secular world he is called a gentleman. These precepts are broad and extensive; they have the same import for layman and monk (*shinzoku ikkan* 眞俗一貫).

Two types of bodhisattva are mentioned in the *Lotus Sūtra*. The bodhisattva Mañjuśrī and the bodhisattva Maitreya are both bodhisattva monks. Bhadrapāla[124] and the five hundred bodhisattvas are lay bodhisattvas 在家菩薩. The *Lotus Sūtra* fully presents both types of men but considers them to be one group. It distinguishes them from Hīnayāna monks and considers them to be Mahāyāna practitioners. However, this type of bodhisattva has not yet appeared in Japan. I humbly ask His Majesty to establish this Great Way and transmit the Mahāyāna precepts beginning from this year in the Kōnin era and continuing forever, and thus benefit (the people and the nation).

This proposal shall be inscribed on the outside of the great bell[125] and transmitted through the ages. Thus I submit the School's regulations and respectfully ask for His Majesty's judgment.

The fifteenth day of the third month of the tenth year of the Kōnin era

Submitted by the Tendai-Hokke monk Saichō, who formerly traveled to China

---

recited to cause the Nāgas to send rain at times of drought. Saichō probably relied on the translation by Narendrayaśas (*T* no. 991) which specifies that eight worthies perform the ceremony (*T* 19: 498b). Tamura Kōyū suggests that he relied on a translation by Amoghavajra (*T* no. 989, *Saichō jiten* p. 128).

[124] Bhadrapāla is included in the groups of sixteen and eight bodhisattvas. He and his group of five hundred bodhisattvas were said to have kept the five precepts of a householder and to have been skilled in meditation.

[125] The *Gakushōshiki kōben* (*Tendaishū zensho* 5: 423) notes that the idea of transmitting a teaching to future generations by inscribing it on a bell is also found in China, and cites a memorial by Ts'ao Chih 曹植 of the Wei Dynasty as an example of the practice. Around the time when Saichō submitted the *Shijōshiki*, he proposed that a bell be cast which would be symbolic of the propagation of the Tendai School. After consultations with Fuyutsugu, he decided to postpone ordering the bell until permission to use the *Fan wang* precepts for ordinations had been granted. The bell was finally cast in 827, five years after Saichō's death. Fujiwara no Natsutsugu 藤原夏嗣 composed the inscription for the bell which was then calligraphed by the retired Emperor Saga (*Denjutsu isshinkaimon, DZ* 1: 545–48).

[126] Texts can be found in the (a) *Eizan Daishiden, DZ* 5 (*Bekkan*): 33–34; (b) *Denjutsu isshinkaimon, DZ* 1: 567–68; and (c) *Shoryu daijōkaihyō, DZ* 1: 248–49. The *Eizan Daishiden* text is followed in this translation.

PETITION ASKING FOR PERMISSION TO USE
THE MAHĀYĀNA PRECEPTS (*Shōryū daijōkaihyō* 請立大乗戒表)[126]

The monk Saichō states:

Saichō has heard that the Buddha's precepts vary according to the faculties of the person who follows them. The aims of people differ according to whether they are Hīnayāna or Mahāyāna practitioners. The place of honor (*jōza*) differs according to whether it is occupied by Mañjuśrī or Piṇḍola. The ordination ceremony differs according to whether one or ten teachers participate.

The late Sagely Emperor Kanmu supported the Lotus School and established it anew here. The virture of His Majesty, the Sagely, Literary and Martial Kōnin Emperor, pervades heaven and earth. His brightness is equal to the sun and moon. His literary genius surpasses the old. His calligraphy is fresh. He gladdens the hearts of the myriad nations and converts the barbarians. He rules the nation and regulates propriety.

Now, at this time, I sincerely request that the monks of both courses turn away from Hīnayāna rules and firmly adhere to Mahāyāna rules, and that in accordance with the *Lotus Sūtra,* Mahāyāna rules not be mixed with the Hīnayāna ones. In the third month of every year, on the anniversary of the late emperor's death, we shall initiate those who have been pure in their practice as bodhisattva novices on Mount Hiei. We shall also confer the full bodhisattva precepts 菩薩大戒 and ordain them as bodhisattva monks. Then they shall live and practice on the mountain for twelve years. They shall be guards for the nation and shall benefit the people. They shall be the nation's treasure and shall benefit the nation as is specified in the School's regulations.

If the Emperor graciously grants this request, the late emperor's wish (that the Tendai School) will prosper over the years (will be fulfilled), and the Mahāyāna precepts will be followed purely throughout the years. Originating with the Kōnin era, the Mahāyāna precepts will be transmitted. The good from transmitting the precepts will in turn protect His Majesty.

With the utmost sincerity, I humbly submit this petition, and respectfully ask for His Majesty's approval...

The fifteenth day of the third month of the tenth year in the Kōnin era (819)

The monk Saichō

In addition Kōjō recorded the following short speech which Saichō delivered about the time the *Shijōshiki* was submitted:

Now, my Mountain School shall rely on the teachings set forth in the *Anrakugyōbon* (Chapter on Comfortable Conduct) of the *Lotus Sūtra*, It shall follow the Mahāyāna precepts rather than the Hīnayāna precepts. It shall be based on the doctrines of the *Lotus Sūtra*... From beginning to end, we shall follow the bodhisattva precepts and be bodhisattva monks. We shall practice the three studies which are pure and complete in themselves (*jishō shōjō sangaku* 自性清浄三學). We shall not tarry on indirect ways, but shall go straight to the treasure and attain the fruits of Buddhahood. How do we know this? In the *Chu fa wu hsing ching* 諸法無行經 (*Sarvadharmāpravṛttinirdeśasūtra*) Kikon 喜根 is called a bodhisattva monk, and in the *Lotus Sūtra* Jōbukyō 常不輕 (Never-Disparaging) is also called a bodhisattva monk...[127] The Venerable Master Tso-ch'i's 左溪[128] memorial stone is inscribed with the words: "In the Liang and Wei Dynasties, there was a bodhisattva monk named Bodhidharma..."[129]

Opposition from the Nara Monks

Emperor Saga was aware of the storm of protest that approval of Saichō's petitions would bring and referred the petitions back to Shin'en, head of the Genbaryō (Bureau of Buddhism and Aliens) and to the Sōgō (Office of Monastic Affairs), directing them to take whatever measures they deemed appropriate. Saichō's attempt to bypass the proper authorities had failed. When Gomyō discovered that Saichō had tried to circumvent the Sōgō, he surely would not be pleased. In a last-minute effort to salvage the situation, Saichō sent Kōjō to ask Gomyō for his signature on the petitions. Kōjō recorded the following conversation which occurred when Gomyō rejected Saichō's request.[130]

Gomyō: There are no bodhisattva monks in China. Nor have there been bodhisattva monks who take only the bodhisattva precepts (*betsuju bosatsusō* 別受菩薩僧); however, there are bodhisattva monks who take both the Hīnayāna precepts and

---

[127] The roles of the *Lotus Sūtra* and the *Chu fa wu hsing ching* in Saichō's views of the precepts are discussed in Chapters 9, 10, and 11.

[128] Tso-ch'i was the home of Hsüan-lang 玄朗, the fifth Patriarch of T'ien-t'ai.

[129] *Denjutsu isshinkaimon, DZ* 1: 566–67.

[130] Ibid., pp. 570–71.

the bodhisattva precepts (*tsūju bosatsusō* 通受菩薩僧).

Kōjō: I do not understand what you mean when you claim that there are no bodhisattva monks who take only the bodhisattva precepts but that there are those who take both the bodhisattva precepts and the Hīnayāna precepts.

Gomyō: According to the Mahāyāna (precepts), a person need not shave off his hair, but according to the Hīnayāna precepts, a monk or novice must shave off his hair. There are monks who take the Hīnayāna (precepts) and then take the bodhisattva precepts, but there is no monk who does not take the Hīnayāna (precepts) and does take the bodhisattva precepts.... Therefore I will not agree to your petition.

When Kōjō climbed Mount Hiei and reported the conversation, Saichō complained that Gomyō had not read all the *sūtras* and their commentaries.

Saichō and Gomyō had found definite grounds to argue on. Up to this point, the Tendai patriarch's petitions had been too vague to draw the Nara monks into a confrontation; but now Saichō seemed to be espousing a defenseless and groundless position. His proposals were unprecedented. The *Fan wang* precepts were not sufficiently detailed to regulate the monks on Mount Hiei, and thus Saichō was open to criticism that he would not be able to maintain order in his monastery. His proposals concerning bodhisattva monks (*bosatsusō*) must have seemed especially strange to the monks in Nara. Since bodhisttvas were usually portrayed as householders, the very term 'bodhisattva monk' seemed to be inviting violations of the Hīnayāna precepts.

Gomyō lost no time in attacking Saichō. He related the contents of Saichō's proposals to eminent monks in the seven great temples in Nara, and received answers[131] from Chōe 長慧, Sehyō 施平,[132] Buan豊安, Shūen 修圓, and Taien 泰演.[133] He also received a work entitled the *Meihō shishōron*迷方示正論 by the Risshū monk Yōjin 影深 of Tōdaiji.[134]

---

[131] The petitions are listed in the table of contents of the *Kenkairon engi* (*DZ* 1: 266), but unfortunately have not survived. Chōe (d. 826) was appointed *risshi* (*vinaya* master) in 810. He was *shōsōzu* (lesser supervisor) at the time of the petitions, and eventually rose to be *daisōzu* (greater supervisor).

[132] Sehyō (d. 832) was a Hossō monk from Gankōji. He was appointed *risshi* in 816. In 827 he participated in a meeting at court (*Honchō kōsōden*, fasc. 5, *BZ* 63: 46).

[133] Taien was a Hossō scholar associated with both Gankōji and Saidaiji. He was Shōgo's pupil and was known for his skill in debating (*Honchō kōsōden*, fasc. 5, *BZ* 63: 46).

[134] The *Meihō shishōron* is listed in the contents of the *Kenkairon engi*, but has not survived. Yōjin, a Tōdaiji Risshū monk, had served as preceptor at Kōjō's *Ssu fen lü* and

This work pointed out twenty-eight flaws in Saichō's argument. Gomyō and Shin'en were about to submit these to the court when Yoshimine stopped them on the grounds of improper procedure. Gomyō rewrote the objections in the form of a memorial and resubmitted it on the nineteenth day of the fifth month of 819.[135] Besides the abovementioned monks, Saichō's old friend Gonsō agreed with the petition opposing Saichō, although he did not sign because he was away in the provinces.[136]

The petition was placed in the library (fudono). Meanwhile, Emperor Saga ordered Fuyutsugu's nephew Fujiwara no Koreo 藤原是雄, who was the head of the Bureau of Carpentry (takumi no kami), to inform Saichō of the contents of the memorial. Koreo related this to Kōjō. When Kōjō in turn told Saichō, Saichō asked to see the petition itself. He received it on the twenty-seventh day of the tenth month and was also allowed to read Yōjin's treatise.[137] After Saichō had studied the objections, he was relieved to find that the petitions included no scriptural references in support of their arguments.

The next few months must have been very busy ones for Saichō. In the space of four months, he finished compiling the Kechimyakufu, the Kenkairon, and the Jōkenkaironhyō. On the twenty-ninth day of the second month of 820, he submitted these three works to the throne. The Kenkairon 顯戒論 (Treatise Revealing the Precepts) was a detailed refutation of the Nara monks' criticisms of the Shijōshiki (Regulations in Four Articles). The Kechimyakufu (full title: Naishō Buppō sōjō kechimyakufu 內證佛法相承血脈譜) consisted of lineages which traced Saichō's Zen, Tendai, Fan wang ordination and Esoteric Buddhist teachings back to their Indian and Chinese origins, and thereby demonstrated their orthodoxy. Since these two works are discussed in detail elsewhere in this study,[138] only the Jōkenkaironhyō (On Submitting the Kenkairon) is translated here. Several versions of this work exist. The translation below, based on the Eizan Daishiden version, is supplemented

---

bodhisattva precepts ordinations in Nara. He also lectured occasionally on Daoxuan's Hsing shih ch'ao 行事鈔 (T no. 1804; Denjutsu isshinkaimon, DZ 1: 528–29).

[135] Denjutsu isshinkaimon, DZ 1: 544–45. The memorial is quoted in the Kenkairon, DZ 1: 33–36.

[136] Gonsō was at Sayama ike 狹山池 (in Osaka-fu). Inoue Kaoru has suggested that Gonsō may have been supervising repairs on buildings built by Gyōgi and his followers. See "Sayama ikesho to Gonsō," Bukkyō shigaku 12, no. 3 (1966): 33–38.

[137] Eizan Daishiden, DZ 5 (Bekkan): 136. Yōjin's treatise is quoted in the Kenkairon (DZ 1: 56), indicating that Saichō must have had access to it.

[138] These works are discussed in Chapters 9 and 13.

with several passages which are found in the *Denjutsu isshinkaimon* version.[139] These passages are set apart by brackets.

ON SUBMITTING THE *KENKAIRON*
(*Jōkenkaironhyō* 上顯戒論表)

Saichō states:

Last year (819) on the twenty-seventh day of the tenth month, the Sōgō's petitions were brought by the monk Kōjō and shown to me. The rains have fallen, causing all to flourish; the withered trees have revived. I am overcome with humility at receiving His Majesty's favor. Saichō is truly overcome with fear and awe, and filled with respect and happiness.

Saichō has heard that in South India, Nāgārjuna set forth the eight negations in order to refute wrong doctrines.[140] In Eastern India, Aśvaghoṣa set forth the doctrine of One-mind and opened the way.[141] Dharmapāla wrote a commentary on (Vasubandhu's) verses and defeated the wrong apprehension of nonsubstantiality (*śūnyatā*).[142] Bhāvaviveka wrote a treatise to cut off all craving.[143] Vasubandhu authored a treatise to purge the five errors.[144] Sāramati

---

[139] The *Jōkenkaironhyō* explains Saichō's reasons for submitting the *Kenkairon* and gives a brief summary of the *Kenkairon's* major points. Four versions of the work exist: (a) *Eizan Daishiden, DZ* 5 (*Bekkan*): 36–38; (b) *Denjutsu isshinkaimon, DZ* 1: 554–58; (c) *Ken'yō daikairon, DZ* 1: 257–61; and (d) *Tendai kahyō, DZ* 1: 254–57. The first two versions are the earliest. Differences in wording, dates, and the number of yearly ordinands mentioned in the first two versions indicate that the *Denjutsu isshinkaimon* version was an earlier draft of the *Eizan Daishiden* version (Sonoda, *Saichō*, p. 157). However, Tajima Tokuon (*BKD* 6: 3–4) has argued that the *Eizan Daishiden* version may have been tampered with by later scholars. Since the *Eizan Daishiden* text has fewer textual errors, it has been used for this translation.

The *Denjutsu isshinkaimon* version includes several important passages not found in the *Eizan Daishiden*, which have been included in this translation. The *Ken'yō daikairon* version appears to be an attempt by Ennin or a later scholar to reconcile discrepancies between the two earlier versions. The *Tendai kahyō* version is close to the *Eizan Daishiden* version.

[140] Nāgārjuna was the third century founder of the Mādhyamika School. The eight negations appear at the beginning of the *Mādhyamikakārikā:* not birth, not death, not impermanence, not permanence, not identical, not different, not coming, and not going.

[141] Aśvaghoṣa lived around the second century. The *Ta ch'eng ch'i hsin lun (Awakening of Faith, T* nos. 1666–67) is attributed to him, but is probably a fifth century Chinese work. Saichō regards him as a Yogācāra patriarch. The One–mind doctrine presented in this text postulates a One–mind that is the basis of phenomena and the absolute.

[142] Dharmāpala was the sixth century monk from Māgadha who taught Śīlabhadra, Hsüan–tsang's teacher. He died at 32. He was critical of Mādhyamika; the phrase 'wrong apprehension of *śūnyatā*' is found in the *Ch'eng wei shih lun (T* 21: 39b). The commentary referred to is on Vasubandhu's thirty verses.

[143] Bhāvaviveka was a sixth century South Indian Mādhyamika monk. He criticized the *ālaya-vijñāna* theories of the Yogācāra philosophers.

[144] Vasubandhu was the fifth century author of the *Abhidharmakośa* and of numerous

wrote a treatise showing the one ultimate.[145] Among Mahāyāna treatises, Asaṅga's *Ken'yō*,[146] and among Hīnayāna treatises, Saṃghabhadra's *Kenshū*,[147] refuted heresies and revealed the true teaching. There are so many similar treatises of this kind that even a cart could not carry all of them.

In China Fa-lin 法琳 of the T'ang dynasty refuted Fu-i's 傅奕 wrong teachings.[148] Seng-chao 僧肇 of the Ch'in dynasty demonstrated that wisdom (*prajñā*) is No-knowledge.[149] The venerable Fa-pao 法寶 wrote the *Fo hsing lun.*[150] Hui-chao 慧沼 of Tzu-chou wrote the *Hui jih lun* 慧日論.[151] There have been many such monks throughout the ages.

I humbly know that His Majesty has received the mandate of Heaven and has ascended the throne. He renews sagely government in the country of the true Dharma. Heaven and earth are in harmony.

[In the second fascicle of the *P'u sa ying lo pen yeh ching* 菩薩瓔珞本業經, it states:

If a Dharma-master teaches, initiates and confers the bodhisattva

important Yogācāra works. The five errors found in his *Fo hsing lun (Buddhatvaśāstra?)* are the errors from which the Buddha sought to save men by preaching the doctrine of the Buddha-nature. They are: (1) a feeling of inferiority, (2) looking down upon on others, (3) clinging to the unreal, (4) slandering the absolute, and (5) clinging to the concept of self (*T* 31: 787a).

[145] Sāramati was a sixth century Central Indian monk. The *Mahāyānottaratantraśāstra* (*Chiu ching i ch'eng pao hsing lun*, *T* no. 1611) is attributed to him. This work greatly influenced later thought on the doctrines concerning the One-vehicle and the Buddha-nature.

[146] Asaṅga, a fifth century Indian monk, was Vasubandhu's elder brother. Both are important patriarchs of the Yogācārins. The work referred to here is the *Hsien yang sheng chiao lun* (T no. 1602) in 20 fascicles. The first fascicle consists of verses by Asaṅga, while the remaining fascicles are a commentary on them by Vasubandhu.

[147] Saṃghabhadra was a fifth century monk from Kashmir known for writing the *A p'i ta mo shun cheng li lun* (*T* no. 1562, *Abhidharmanyāyānusāraśāstra*) and the *A p'i ta mo tsang hsien tsung lun* (*T* no. 1563, *Abhidharmakośaśāstrakārikāvibhāṣya*). The first work argues against Sautrāntika tendencies in Vasubandhu's *Kośa;* the second explains the correct doctrine. They are both large works, numbering 20 and 40 fascicles respectively.

Saichō probably mentions the works by Asaṅga and Saṃghabhadra because the titles contain the character 顯 (Chin. *hsien*, Jap. *ken*), the same character with which the title of the *Kenkairon* begins.

[148] Fa-lin (572–640) is famous for his defense of Buddhism against Fu-i's proposals.

[149] Seng-chao (384–414) was one of Kumārajīva's disciples. The *Chao lun* (*T* no. 1858), a collection of treastises by Seng-chao, contains a work entitled *Wisdom Is No-Knowledge* (*Pan jo wu chih lun* 般若無知論).

[150] Fa-pao is discussed in chapter 7. See footnote 27 of that chapter for information on the *I ch'eng fo hsing chiu ching lun* 一乘佛性究竟論.

[151] Hui-chao (650–714) studied under Hsüan-tsang and Tz'u-en and became the third patriarch of the Fa-hsiang (Jap. Hossō) School. In the *Hui jih lun* (*T* no. 1863) he argues against Fa-pao's position on the Buddha-nature.

precepts on just one person in the world, then the merit gained by that Dharma-master is greater than if he had built 84,000 *stūpas*. How much more so (if he grants the precepts) to two, three, hundreds or thousands? His merit is indescribable. Married couples and relatives may take each other as their teacher and confer the precepts. The recipient of the precepts enters the realms of the Buddhas and is counted among the bodhisattvas. He passes out of the sufferings of the realm of life and death in the past, present, and future. Thus you should take these precepts. It is better to take the precepts and break them than not to take them and follow them. (One who takes the precepts and) breaks them is called a bodhisattva; (one who does not take them and) does not break them is still called a non-believer. He who takes just one precept is known as a one-precept bodhisattva, and so on with two, three, or four precepts. He who takes all ten is known as one with the full precepts.[152]]

The Lotus School was established for the benefit of the nation by the late Emperor Kanmu. Its two (yearly) ordinands are to be Mahāyāna monks of the Lotus School. Its Sudden and Perfect students do not seek the three vehicles outside the gate.[153] Of what use would the rules on dignity for the sheep vehicle be to them? They do not desire the castle in the middle of the road.[154] How

---

[152] *T* 24: 1021b. Saichō is said to have conferred the *Fan wang* precepts on one person at this time to illustrate this passage (*Denjutsu isshinkaimon, DZ* 1: 554).

[153] In the *Lotus Sūtra* [*Scripture of the Lotus Blossom of the Fine Dharma*, tr. Leon Hurvitz (New York: Columbia University Press, 1976), pp. 58–64], the Buddha uses the following story to explain that the three vehicles are only expedient teachings and that all shall become Buddhas.

The mansion of a rich man suddenly caught fire. His children were absorbed in their play and did not flee. Although the man called to them warning them of the danger of the fire, they did not understand and continued to play. He then devised a stratagem to lure them outside. He told them that a sheep–cart, a deer–cart, and an ox–cart were waiting outside the gate for them. This time they came running out, but the promised carts were not there. However, their father gave them each a lavish cart drawn by a white ox. They were overjoyed.

The implication of Saichō's statement is that Tendai monks have no need for expedient teachings, and no need for the sheep–vehicle (*śrāvaka*) precepts.

[154] In the *Lotus Sūtra* (Hurvitz tr., pp. 148–49), there is a a parable concerning some travellers on a long journey in search of a cache of jewels. Eventually, they became so tired and discouraged that they were about to abandon their quest. At this point, their leader caused a castle to appear in the road so that they could relax and refresh themselves. After they had rested, the leader told them that the jewels which they sought were near and that he had conjured up the castle so that they could rest and continue their quest.

The castle represents the expedient Hīnayāna teachings, and the jewels represent the

much less would they be likely to take a round-about detour? Tomorrow when they are given riches, they will know their father and know that they are his sons. What need is there to be a stranger (in their own house)? Or to sweep up dung?[155] On the night when (the king) extolls (his troops') deeds, he undoes his topknot and gives them his pearl.[156] Why should one wish for a mansion? Why should one search for a castle? I know that there is nothing in the past or present to compare with this teaching in which the late Emperor believed. It protects the nation and benefits sentient beings. How pale (Hīnayāna practices) which require many *kalpas* (are when compared to the ultimate teaching).

[Literature pertaining to the *Fan wang* precepts has not yet been sufficiently translated in China; but the spiritual essence of *prātimokṣa* has long been transmitted.][157]

Now, the Mountain School has set forth the three Perfect Studies (morality, meditation and wisdom) for bodhisattva monks. I respectfully ask for the Emperor's ruling (permitting us to carry these plans out). We have submitted a petition in four articles to the Sōgō and asked for the cooperation of the other schools. But the monastic leaders (*sōtō*), intending to protect the Dharma and wielding their swords of knowledge, wrote papers attacking us and wish

---

true teaching. The long detour Saichō mentions represents the eons of practice necessary for the Hīnayāna practitioner to attain his goal.

[155] The story referred to here is from the *Lotus Sūtra* (Hurvitz trans., pp. 85–100). A youth once left his home to go travelling. Years later he returned but recognized neither his former home nor his father. The father recognized his son, but also realized that his son's manners and preferences had changed and become coarse. He thus devised the stratagem of employing his son as a servant to sweep up dung without telling his son that they were related. The son gradually rose in station until he became manager of all the property, but still regarded himself as only an employee. His father finally called a meeting of all the relatives at which he revealed the identity of his son and deeded the son his property. The father's stratagems are equivalent to the Buddha's provisional teachings. The son, even though he is already qualified by birth to receive his father's belongings, must still be led to a point where he is able to do so. In the same way, although people already possess the Buddha–nature, they must be led to a point where they can recognize it.

[156] In the *Lotus Sūtra* (Hurvitz trans., pp. 218–19) the story is told of a king who gave away all of his possessions, except for the pearl in his topknot, to his troops in order to encourage them. Finally he was so pleased by his troops' exploits that he even gave them his pearl. In a similar way the Buddha encourages his disciples with provisional teachings, and then reveals the ultimate teaching, that of the *Lotus Sūtra*.

[157] Saichō is probably referring here to a tradition which claims that the *Fan wang ching* was originally part of a 120–fascicle work, only two of which were translated. Saichō may well have believed that translation of the remaining parts of the work would strengthen his position.

to debate. They submitted their petitions to the court and secretly asked for the Emperor's decision. But the Emperor's mind is broad and fair. Thus he ordered the petitions of the monastic leaders sent to Mount Hiei and bestowed upon us new hope.

I have respectfully read the *sōtō*'s petitions. They are the words of Hīnayāna Buddhists, not of the practitioners of the sagely teaching. Because they have not read widely, they deny that there might be three types of temples in Japan. Because they have not looked at (Emperor Tai-tsung's) new regulations, they try to prevent the installation of Mañjuśrī as elder (*jōza*). They ring the bell calling monks to the universal 無遮 assembly but stint on food.[158] They speak of the Order as the Dharma-realm 法界, but have already fallen deeply into the error that Hsien warned about.[159] Though they censure me as nonsensical, they actually speak ill of their Preceptor (Chien-chen).[160] Theirs is the stumbling block of wrong teaching; they go against the tradition of their teachers.

The five items that Mahādeva proposed long ago were not in accordance with the Buddha's teaching; but the four articles we on Mount Hiei propose are in accordance with Buddhist

---

[158] The *sōtō* (government–appointed leaders of the monastic order) argued that Saichō wanted to establish a separate order of monks. Such actions violated the Hīnayāna precepts which required monks to ring a bell announcing meals or the distribution of gifts, so that all monks could partake of the food or gifts. Saichō replied that the Nara monks had already violated these rules by establishing registers which limited the number of monks and by restricting the amount of food which monks could beg or receive. Athough the Nara monks rang the bell announcing meals, their assemblies were not open to all who wished to attend (*Kenkairon, DZ* 1: 57).

[159] The *sōtō* compared the monastic establishment with the Dharma–realm (*hōkai*). The *sōtō* argued that Saichō was making arbitrary distinctions in the Dharma–realm by suggesting that three types of temples existed. Saichō replied that the Dharma–realm was the realm of meditation. Monasteries were in the phenomenal realm and therefore were subject to distinctions. If the *sōtō* abolished all distinctions, the regulations concerning the proper location for temples would lose all their meaning. The restrictions on travelling by monks during the rainy season retreat would cease to be applied. Saichō then cited a passage from Fa-hsien's 法銑 commentary on the *Fan wang ching* which warned against comparing the rainy season retreat with the Dharma–realm and thereby rendering the regulations concerning the rainy season retreat meaningless (*Kenkairon, DZ* 1: 57–58).

[160] The *sōtō* attacked Saichō's proposal that Tendai monks be permitted to receive the *Ssu fen lü* ordination only after they had received the *Fan wang* ordination and completed their course of study on Mount Hiei. Saichō replied that Chien–chen, the Chinese monk who had presided over the first orthodox *Ssu fen lü* ordinations in Japan, had first received an ordination of the *Fan wang* precepts, and only later the *Ssu fen lü* ordination. In fact, Chien–chen probably received the *Fan wang* ordination first because he was not old enough to receive the *Ssu fen lü* ordination at the time. Consequently, Saichō's interpretation of Chien–chen's ordinations was not very convincing (*Kenkairon, DZ* 1: 78–79).

teachings.[161] If you ask (the Nara monks) about the precepts, they will say, "We are Mahāyāna Buddhists." Yet they insist on retaining Piṇḍola as *jōza*.[162] (They) have criticized (me for studying) in the provinces; but then how can one believe (their own scholars who study) at Hiso 比蘇?[163] If they do not recognize provisionally named bodhisattvas (*kemyō bosatsu* 假名菩薩),[164] then who do they recognize as being a true (bodhisattva)?[165]

I believe that the five schools[166] which receive yearly ordinands should be the guardians of the nation and a resource for the people. They should (serve as) boats to cross the oceans of birth and death,

---

[161] The *sōtō* accused Saichō of attempting to divide the Order just as Mahādeva had done centuries earlier. In defending himself, Saichō noted that Mahādeva was motivated by the fear that his inadequacies and wrongdoings would be discovered. In contrast, Saichō claimed that he was motivated by his desire to defend the true teaching (*Kenkairon, DZ* 1: 82–86).

[162] The controversy concerning the installation of the *jōza* in the dining hall is discussed in footnotes 111–112 of this chapter, and in the *Kenkairon, DZ* 1: 102–6.

[163] The *sōtō* noted that Saichō had studied only in the provinces in China, not in the capital Ch'ang-an. Therefore he was not qualified to claim that the temples in China had replaced Piṇḍola with Mañjuśrī in their dining halls. Saichō replied that criticisms of monks because they had studied in the provinces applied equally to Hossō monks who travelled to the mountains in order to perform Esoteric Buddhist practices which were supposed to improve the memory (*Kenkairon, DZ* 1: 106). Saichō was probably referring to Gomyō in this passage [Sonoda Kōyū, "Kodai Bukkyō ni okeru sanrin shugyō to sono igi," *Nanto Bukkyō* 4 (1957): 46–47]. Tokiwa Daijō has argued that Saichō was referring to Tao–hsüan in this passage [*Nihon Bukkyō no kenkyū* (Tokyo: Shunjūsha, 1943), pp. 456–58; also see Tamura, *Saichō jiten*, pp. 113–114]. However, this interpretation is not very convincing, since Saichō would be pointing out that one of the men whom he included in his Zen lineage studied in the country rather than arguing that his opponents also performed religious practices in the country.

[164] The term *kemyō bosatsu* (one who is provisionally called a bodhisattva) is used in opposition to the term *shin bosatsu* or *shinjitsu bosatsu* 眞實菩薩 (true bodhisattva). A *kemyō bosatsu* is a bodhisattva in name only; he does not yet possess the wisdom or power of a true bodhisattva. In the *Kenkairon* (*DZ* 1: 125), Saichō defined *kemyō bosatsu* as anyone who had not yet attained the stage of *sōji soku*. A *shinjitsu bosatsu* is someone who has attained the stage of *bunshin soku*. For definitions of *sōji soku* and *bunshin soku* see footnote 5 of Chapter 3.

[165] In the *Shijōshiki* Saichō had claimed that Tendai bodhisattva monks could help the nation avoid calamities in the future. The *sōtō* replied that if Saichō's monks were true bodhisattvas (*shin bosatsu*), they could indeed prevent calamities; however, Tendai monks could only provisionally be called bodhisattvas (*kemyō bosatsu*) because they had not yet attained the status of true bodhisattvas. They had not been able to prevent starvation and drought in the past, and would not be able to prevent disasters in the future. Saichō replied to the *sōtō*'s charges by noting that some types of disasters were due to evil deeds committed in the past. Even the Buddha could not prevent such calamities from occurring. However, other disasters were not caused by such grave deeds and could be prevented by *kemyō bosatsu* (*Kenkairon, DZ* 1: 125–30). Saichō followed a plan proposed by Amoghavajra in suggesting that one-hundred monks installed on a mountain to chant the *Jen wang ching* would be able to prevent some disasters.

[166] Hossō, Sanron, Kegon, Ritsu and Tendai.

and as steps leading to the other shore. Thus when the schools practice and work together, they should blend as harmoniously as salt and plums. When the monks preach or teach together, their voices should be like the golden speech of the Buddha. How then can monks support only their own school and suppress other schools? The monastic leaders in Nara respect only what enters the ears and (immediately) comes out of the mouth. They do not try to cultivate their minds at all.

If no one practices purely and selflessly, then how can we prevent calamities from occurring? We are currently debating about which of the Buddha's teachings are Perfect and which are provisional. This is the time for the (true) way to arise; it is the day to choose the correct practice. Now, the Hīnayāna precepts are for those who follow Hīnayāna or Common teachings. The threefold *Fan wang* precepts[167] are for those who follow the Unique or Perfect teachings.

Now, when novices of the Perfect School are compelled to take the Hīnayāna precepts, they forget about the Perfect threefold precepts and vie for fame and profit. Thus they all backslide in their practice. From the second year of the Daidō era to the eleventh year of the Kōnin era, a total of fourteen years, we have had twenty-eight monks in our two courses. But for a variety of reasons, they have scattered and gone to different places. Not even ten remain on Mount Hiei. Because the Perfect precepts have not yet been put into effect, the foundation for proper meditation does not exist. When we see the mistakes of our predecessors, we should correct them in order to benefit those yet to come.

Thus in this, the eleventh year of the Kōnin era, in order to transmit the Perfect precepts, I wrote the *Kenkairon* in three fascicles and the *Buppō kechimyaku* in one fascicle. I respectfully submit them to His Majesty. Again I ask that in accordance with the teachings of our School, the students of both courses of the Tendai Perfect School be permitted to receive the precepts of the Perfect teaching and be called bodhisattva monks. In order to encourage bodhisattva practices, the monks shall not leave Mount Hiei for a period of

---

[167] The fifty–eight precepts of the *Fan wang ching* are conferred in the ordination ceremony as the three collections of pure precepts (*sanju jōkai* 三聚淨戒, *Jubosatsukaigi, DZ* 1: 320–21). The *sanju jōkai* formula emphasizes three aspects of the the precepts: preventing evil, promoting good, and benefiting sentient beings.

twelve years. During this time, they shall cultivate the four types of meditation. In this way, the One-vehicle precepts and meditation will be transmitted in our land forever, and practice in the mountains will continue throughout the ages. The virtue (of the precepts) will banish all misfortune. With (this virtue) may His Majesty live forever. Receiving the (benefit of the precepts), may the people be pure and tranquil.

Saichō's knowledge does not compare with that of I-hsing, nor does his learning compare with that of Chan-jan. Filled with foreboding, I humbly and foolishly submit this. If His Majesty agrees to this petition, I ask that approval come straight from the court (without going through the normal channels). Because the full import of transmitting the precepts has not yet been realized, I submit my petitions and ask that they be granted.

[The twenty-ninth day of the second month in the
eleventh year of the Kōnin era (820)
The monk Saichō][168]

Kōjō waited in Kyoto. He hoped to have Saichō's proposals approved within the next three weeks, thus enabling Saichō to perform ordinations on the anniversary of Kanmu's death, the seventeenth day of the third month. On the tenth day of the third month, Kōjō accompanied Fujiwara no Fuyutsugu to the court. After a short wait, he was summoned to appear before Emperor Saga, who had the *Kenkairon* in front of him. Also present was the assistant director of the Genbaryō (Bureau of Buddhism and Aliens), Ōmiwa no Funekimi 大神船公. Like Shin'en 眞苑, the director of the Genbaryō, Funekimi was also a supporter of the Hossō School. He and Kōjō debated the relative merits of Tendai and Hossō doctrine that day, but unfortunately did not have time to discuss the bodhisattva precepts and the *Kenkairon*.[169]

After Saichō submitted his works, the accuracy of his quotations from other texts was verified by the assistant director of the Bureau

---

[168] The signature and date are not found in the *Eizan Daishiden* version. They are added here following the *Tendai kahyō* version. The date agrees with a passage preceding the *Jōkenkaironhyō* in the *Eizan Daishiden* [*DZ* 5 (Bekkan): 35]. The *Denjutsu isshinkaimon* gives the date of submission as the twenty-first day of the tenth month of the tenth year of the Kōnin era (*DZ* 1: 554), three months earlier than the *Eizan Daishiden* date. The *Denjutsu isshinkaimon* version mentions twenty-four yearly ordinands, not the twenty-eight of the *Eizan Daishiden* version. These discrepancies indicate that the *Denjutsu isshinkaimon* version is probably a preliminary draft of the text.

[169] *Denjutsu isshinkaimon, DZ* 1: 602-3.

of Books and Drawings, Tamazukuri 玉作. Finding them correct, he forwarded them to the Sōgō (Office of Monastic Affairs). The *Eizan Daishiden* reports that the Sōgō was completely overwhelmed by Saichō's arguments and unable to reply.[170] In fact, Gomyō had already decided to fight Saichō's proposals through the normal channels, challenging them in the Sōgō and Genbaryō, rather than engaging in a public debate.

A year passed without any action being taken on Saichō's petition. In the third month of 821, Saichō collected 33 documents and edited them into a work entitled the *Kenkairon engi* 顯戒論緣起 (Materials Concerning the *Kenkairon*) which he submitted to the secretary 史記官 of the Council of State (Dajōkan).[171] Since some of the monks in Nara had questioned the orthodoxy of Saichō's teachings, much of the *Kenkairon engi* was devoted to establishing Saichō's credentials. Although the exact date of presentation is not known, it was probably submitted to coincide with the anniversary of Kanmu's death.

The *Kenkairon engi* was divided into two fascicles. The first, which survives, primarily contained official documents concerning Saichō's studies in China and a request for yearly ordinands for the Tendai School. Of special importance is a document attesting to Gishin's Hīnayāna ordination in China. The second fascicle of the work contained documents concerning the controversy over the bodhisattva precepts, including petitions by Saichō's opponents. This fascicle unfortunately has been lost. Thus the only extant primary source material written by Saichō's opponents is found in the passages which Saichō quoted in the *Kenkairon*.

That same year, Saichō also completed the *Hokke shūku* 法華秀句 (Elegant Words on the Lotus Sūtra), his last work dealing with the interpretation and classification of the *Lotus Sūtra*.

Meanwhile Kōjō was active in the capital urging approval of Saichō's proposals. In 810 Saichō had been granted the second highest monastic rank, that of *dentō hosshi*. In 819 Kūkai had received the highest rank, that of *dentō daihosshi,* while Saichō had been disregarded, presumably because of opposition from the Sōgō, even though he was seven years older than Kūkai. Kōjō discussed this with the *udaijin* (Grand Minister of the Right), Fujiwara no Fuyutsugu. As a result, Emperor

---

170 *DZ* 5 (*Bekkan*): 35.
171 *DZ* 1: 263–98. Though Saichō claims to have included 37 items in the work, the table of contents lists only 33 items.

Saga granted Saichō the rank of *dentō daihosshi* in the second month of 822 without waiting for a recommendation from the Sōgō. The Emperor, in an unusual act, wrote the certificate himself.[172]

Saichō's Death

Saichō's health was failing, and by the third month of 822 he was on his death bed. Once again on the anniversary of Kanmu's death, Kōjō went before the Emperor to press for approval of the proposals concerning the precepts, emphasizing that Saichō would not live much longer. If the petition were not granted, Saichō would die without seeing the Tendai School properly established. The director of the Genbaryō, Shin'en, was also present at the audience and suggested that Saichō come to the Nara temple Saidaiji to debate the proposals. Emperor Saga rejected this plan, arguing that it would not be fair to the ailing Saichō.[173]

Late that day, the Emperor and Kōjō agreed upon a compromise solution to the controversy. The Emperor mentioned that the leaders of the six Nara schools would not agree to Saichō's proposals, since approval would result in the abolition of the Sōgō. Although Saichō's first petitions had been presented as rules applying to the Tendai School only, he had argued later in the *Kenkairon* that the Sōgō should be abolished.[174] Kōjō replied that the petitions should apply only to the Tendai School and that the Sōgō could remain intact as long as it did not oversee the Tendai School.[175] This solution was eventually used; however, opposition to Saichō's proposals continued for several more months.

The *Eizan Daishiden* reports that in the fourth month of 822 Saichō called his disciples together and said:

> I will not live much longer. After my death you must not mourn (for me).[176]

---

[172] *Eizan Daishiden, DZ* 5 (*Bekkan*): 39; and *Denjutsu isshinkaimon, DZ* 1: 574–75.

[173] *Denjutsu isshinkaimon, DZ* 1: 583–84. The text reports that the Emperor was concerned about Saichō's physical safety if he travelled to Nara. The passage hints that Saichō might have been physically attacked if he had gone; however, the implied threat is probably an attempt to vilify the Nara monks. Shioiri Ryōchū (*Dengyo Daishi*, p. 431) questions the passage, but comes to no conclusion.

[174] See *Kenkairon, DZ* 1: 179–80.

[175] *Denjutsu isshinkaimon, DZ* 1: 520.

[176] The *Eizan Daishiden* [*DZ* 5 (*Bekkan*): 39] gives only the character *fuku* 服. Two interpretations of the character exist:
(a) The *Konpon Daishi rinjū yuigon* (*DZ* 1: 299) expands the term to mean lay clothing 俗服. Since the *Fan wang ching* mentions clothing only briefly, Saichō might have wanted to explicitly prohibit monks from wearing lay clothing (*Kenkairon, DZ* 1: 119–20).

Furthermore, my fellow monks on Hiei, the Buddha's precepts state that you may not drink liquor. Anyone who breaks (this rule) is not my fellow monk, nor is he a disciple of the Buddha. He should be expelled immediately and should not be allowed to step foot within the boundaries of the mountain. Nor is anyone who uses liquor as medicine to be allowed within the mountain temple's confines.[177]

Women may not come near the temple and certainly may not enter its sacred precincts.

You should lecture extensively on the Mahāyāna *sutras* everyday. You must carefully perform your religious practices in order that the Dharma may endure forever. You must diligently strive to benefit the nation and save sentient beings. My fellow monks, you must not tire in your practice of the four types of meditation. Esoteric initiations and the *goma* 護摩 (Skt. *homa,* Esoteric fire ceremony) should be performed at the appropriate times. You should return your debt of gratitude to the nation by helping the Buddha's teachings to prosper.

Saichō predicted that he would be reborn in Japan and continue to propagate the One-vehicle teaching. Fourteen of his disciples, including Ennin and Ninchū, pledged to work and practice with him in future lives. Gishin and Enchō were not mentioned in the *Eizan Daishiden* account of this pledge, probably because they were not on Mount Hiei at that time.

Saichō also left the following six admonitions for his disciples:

1. Monks should sit according to the order in which they received the Mahāyāna precepts. On days when there is a general assembly (which includes monks who have received the Hīnayāna precepts), Tendai monks should conceal their bodhisattva practices and behave as Hīnayāna monks, sitting together with the

---

(b) The term has also been explained as referring to mourning clothes and thus to a prolonged period of seclusion for mourning. Katsuno Ryūshin convincingly argues that this meaning is the original one, and that the first interpretation was a later development used to contend with problems arising in the latter half of the Edo Period ["Shūso *Goyuikai* ni okeru fuku no mondai," *TG* 3 (1961): 2–11]. Both Chih–i and Amoghavajra asked their disciples not to mourn for them. Saichō might very well have patterned his request after statements by these two men (Kiuchi, *Dengyō Daishi,* p. 195).

177 Buddhists have traditionally distinguished between liquor used for enjoyment 毒酒 and liquor used for medicine 藥酒. The first was strictly prohibited while the second was permitted by most authorities [Michihata Ryōshū, *Chūgoku Bukkyōshi no kenkyū* (Kyoto: Hōzōkan, 1970), pp. 247–56].

Hīnayāna monks in the position of novices. An exception to this[178] rule is allowed when one monk defers to another.[178]

2. A monk's frame of mind should be as though he were first entering the Buddha's room, later wearing the Buddha's robes, and finally sitting in the Buddha's place.[179]

3. For robes, the man of higher faculties uses dirty rags found at the side of the road. The man of medium faculties uses rough cloth,[180] and the man of lower faculties uses robes (of cotton or flax) received from lay donors.

4. For food, the man of higher faculties begs, but without any thought about what he receives. The man of medium faculties begs while strictly adhering to the precepts. The man of lower faculties obtains his food from lay believers.[181]

5. For his cell, the man of higher faculties uses a thatched hut made of bamboo brush. The man of medium faculties uses a three-room wooden house, and the man of lower faculties uses the whole monastery.[182] You should obtain materials for building or for repairs by begging in the autumn, receiving one *masu* of rice in the provinces and one *mon* of coin in the towns.

6. For his bedding, the man of higher faculties uses bamboo brush and straw. The man of medium faculties uses one straw mat

---

[178] *Eizan Daishiden, DZ* 5 (*Bekkan*): 40–41. In a mixed assembly, the Tendai monks were to sit below the Nara monks together with the novices. Novices sat according to their ages. If several novices were the same age, their seating order was to be determined by the order in which they had taken the precepts. Exceptions to these rules were made if a senior monk deferred to a monk who was his junior because of the latter's learning or virtue. Seating was an important problem in the early Tendai order. It is discussed in Chapter 10.

[179] This rule refers to a passage in the *Lotus Sūtra* (Hurvitz trans., p. 180) in which the Buddha describes the attitudes that should be held by those who preach the *Lotus Sūtra* in later times. They are to take great compassion as their dwellings, tolerance and patience as their clothing, and the wisdom that all *dharmas* are nonsubstantial as their seats. These rules are for monks, nuns, laymen and laywomen.

[180] This refers to a cloth also called *tani* which was too rough to be used for paying taxes. It was mainly worn by people in underdeveloped areas.

[181] The man of lower faculties receives his food without begging, by attending feasts given for monks.

[182] The order of the types of rooms used by the men of medium and lower faculties is reversed in the *Konpon Daishi rinjū yuigon* (*DZ* 1: 299). Following this reading, *hōjō* 方丈 would refer to a one *jō* (ten–foot) square room rather than a whole monastery (Suehiro, *Yakuchū Eizan Daishiden*, p. 94). Since the *Eizan Daishiden* version of Saichō's admonitions is the more reliable text, it is followed in this translation. The ambiguity concerning the term *hōjō* is probably due to its use in describing Vimalakīrti's small room, which was able to miraculously accomodate several thousand monks and bodhisattvas. *Hōjō* thus could be interpreted as being either a small room or a monastery which could accomodate many monks. The latter definition is rarely found.

(*mushiro*) and one reed mat (*komo*). The man of lower faculties uses one bordered mat (*tatami*) and one straw mat.

We do not have the means to purchase large tracts of land, nor do we receive rich stipends of food. We do not dwell in the monasteries administered by the government-appointed monastic leaders. On the day when Śākyamuni, Prabhūtaratna (Tahō 多寶) and their manifestations assemble, they answer Mañjuśrī's question saying that bodhisattvas may not greet *śrāvakas,* nor may they assemble in the same lecture hall or practice walking meditation in the same place as *śrāvakas.*[183] In the morning, you should beg for food. After offering a little (to the hungry ghosts), you should then present it to those practicing on the mountain. In the autumn, you should beg for a little cloth to cover your cold bodies.[184] You should want nothing other than food and clothing.

Those who go out into the world in order to preach shall be exempted (from these rules).

Saichō also admonished his followers not to use coarse speech and to treat the acolytes 童子 well.[185] These boys, after all, would become monks.

Saichō's admonitions are important in understanding his use of the *Fan wang* precepts. Since the *Fan wang* precepts traditionally had been conferred on monks, nuns, laymen and laywomen, Saichō could have been expected to be tolerant of women. In fact, by barring women from Mount Hiei and forbidding his monks from leaving the mountain temple's precincts for twelve years, he imposed much stricter rules than were found in either the *Ssu fen lü* or the *Fan wang ching.* In restricting his followers to Mount Hiei for twelve years, Saichō was making a clear distinction between the lay and monastic worlds even though the bodhisattva precepts applied to both. Far from loosening the restrictions imposed by the precepts, Saichō was reforming them by adopting a shorter and more relevant set, and then supplementing it with his own directives and rules. The exemption from the rules for monks who traveled and preached did not permit such monks to drink or consort with

---

[183] Śākyamuni, Prabhūtaratna and their manifestations assemble when the *Lotus Sūtra* is about to be preached (Hurvitz trans., pp. 185–88). The rules against associating with Hīnayāna Buddhists are found in the *Lotus Sūtra* (ibid., pp. 209–10). Śākyamuni preaches these rules in response to a question by Mañjuśrī.

[184] Traditionally, monks went out begging for robes after the summer rainy retreat.

[185] *Eizan Daishiden, DZ* 5 (*Bekkan*): 40.

women. Rather it relaxed the austerities which the monks underwent on Mount Hiei in order to allow them to be more effective in their preaching to the populace. Under Saichō's rules, these preachers were to take the 250 precepts of the *Ssu fen lü,* and thus be bound by the extensive Hīnayāna rules.

Early in the fourth month, poems were exchanged between Saichō, the Emperor, and various officials.[186] Several of them were authored and calligraphed on special paper by Emperor Saga himself. The poems praise Saichō's efforts on behalf of Buddhism and express concern over his illness. They indicate that the court was aware of Saichō's deteriorating health.

Before he died, Saichō was left with one more task, that of naming his successor. Ten years earlier when he had been ill, he had named Enchō head of the Tendai School. At the time Gishin had been in Sagami. One year later, in 813, he had returned. In 822 Saichō named Gishin as head of the Tendai School. Saichō probably changed the appointment because Gishin had accompanied him to China and had received the bodhisattva precepts as well as other transmissions there. At a time when the orthodoxy of Saichō's teachings was being questioned, a successor who had also been to China could not be easily ignored. Nevertheless, the change in succession created difficulties. Kōjō questioned Saichō about what was to be done concerning the two successors. Saichō replied that the senior monk, in this case Gishin, should become head of the order. In addition, Ninchū 仁忠 was to act as presiding officer (*jōza*), and Jun'en 順圓 as head lecturer on the *Lotus Sūtra.*[187]

On the fourth day of the sixth month of 822, Saichō died. His most influential lay patrons, Minister of the Right (*udaijin*) Fujiwara no Fuyutsugu 藤原冬嗣, Vice Councillor (*chūnagon*) Yoshimine no Yasuyo 良峰安世, Provisional Vice Counciller (*gonchūnagon*) Fujiwara no Mimori 藤原三守 and Vice Controllor of the Left (*sachūben*) Ōtomo no Kunimichi 大伴國道, submitted a petition to the Emperor requesting approval of the *Shijōshiki* (Regulations in Four Articles).[188] Seven days after he died, Saichō's request was granted.

---

[186] *DZ* 5 (*Bekkan*): 117–19. Emperor Saga's poems were included in the *Bunka shūreishū,* an anthology compiled by Fujiwara no Fuyutsugu and others at the request of Emperor Saga. They are considered authentic.

[187] *Eizan Daishiden, DZ* 5 (*Bekkan*): 41; and *Denjutsu isshinkaimon, DZ* 1: 640.

[188] *Eizan Daishiden, DZ* 5 (*Bekkan*): 41–42. However, the *Denjutsu isshinkaimon* (*DZ* 1: 576) states that the petition was submitted by Fujiwara no Tsunenaga 藤原常永. No satisfactory explanation for this discrepancy has been advanced. The text of the edict granting Saichō's request is also found in the *Eizan Daishiden.*

The Approval of Saichō's Proposals

Saichō's death had presented Fuyutsugu and Saichō's other supporters with a chance to press for approval of the *Shijōshiki*. In addition, it had presented the court with an opportunity to grant Saichō's request as a token of its grief at his passing. Thus the court was able to honor Saichō without allowing the Tendai School an undue advantage over the Nara schools. Approval of Saichō's requests during his lifetime would have been the equivalent of court recognition of Tendai superiority.

Saichō's requests were probably granted at this time because many of his lay supporters had risen to high court positions by the time of Saichō's death. A list of the highest court officials in 821 indicates the power that Saichō's lay supporters had obtained by this time.[189]

Office	Name		Age
Udaijin	Fujiwara no Fuyutsugu	藤原冬嗣	47
Dainagon	Fujiwara no Otsugu	藤原緒嗣	48
Chūnagon	Bun'ya no Watamaro	文室綿麻呂	57
Chūnagon	Yoshimine no Yasuyo	良峰安世	37
Chūnagon	Fujiwara no Sadatsugu	藤原貞嗣	63
Gonchūnagon	Fujiwara no Mimori	藤原三守	37
Sangi (Adviser)	Harubara no Ioe	春原五百枝	62
Sangi	Tajihi no Imamaro	多治比今麻呂	69
Sangi	Tadayo Ō	直世王	46

In 822 Ono no Takamori and Tachibana no Tsuneo were added as *sangi*. In the years preceding 822, the composition of the court had changed rapidly because of deaths and political incidents, with Emperor Saga consolidating his power. Fuyutsugu rose rapidly, being appointed *udaijin* in 821; he was certainly one of Emperor Saga's most trusted advisers. In addition, Fujiwara no Mimori and Yoshimine no Yasuyo had been appointed *sangi* in 816, and had risen rapidly to powerful positions. Thus, Saichō's position had the active backing of a young and influential group of court nobles, highly favored by the Emperor. Furthermore, one of the new *sangi* appointed in 822, Ono no Takamori 小野岑守, had helped Saichō with arrangements for the *kanjō* (Esoteric consecration or *abhiseka* ceremony) on Mount Takao years before.

Very little is known of Saichō's relationship with other top ranking court officials. However, his relations with the Fujiwara family should be

---

[189] Kawasaki Tsuneyuki, "Saga Tennō to Saichō Kūkai," in *Nihon jinbutsu shi taikei*, 7 vols. (Tokyo: Asakura shoten, 1959–61), 1: 136–69.

mentioned. The Fujiwara clan temple was Kōfukuji, a temple with close connections to the Hossō School. At the same time, monks with different scholarly interests also practiced at Kōfukuji. Although sectarianism was increasing, Kōfukuji still was probably not an exclusively Hossō temple. In the *Gakushō meichō* (Register of Students) the twenty-two Tendai yearly ordinands are registered as Kōfukuji monks,[190] suggesting that Saichō had close relations with the temple and probably with the Fujiwara clan. Half of the twenty-eight lay patrons listed in the *Eizan Daishiden* are from the Fujiwara clan.[191] Thus the Hossō connections of Kōfukuji did not seriously constrain the Fujiwaras from supporting Saichō. Unreliable sources compiled several centuries after Saichō's death suggest that Saichō received substantial aid from the Fujiwaras. The *Dengyō Daishi yuisho* 傳教大師由緒, said to have been compiled by Fujiwara no Hikomura 藤原彦村 in 934, claims that Saichō's mother was named Fujiwara no Fujiko 藤原藤子.[192] In addition, later sources such as the *Kuin Bukkakushō* 九院佛閣抄 note that many Kōfukuji monks were present at the first ceremony performed at the Konpon chūdō (Main Hall) and the dedication of the Monjudō (Mañjuśrī Hall). Although these later sources are not reliable, they may indicate that Saichō did, in fact, have close connections with the Fujiwara clan. Fujiwara no Muchimaro 藤原武智麻呂 (680–737) and his son Nakamaro 藤原仲麻呂 (706–764) both served as governors of Ōmi, and had connections with Mount Hiei before it became a center for the Tendai School. Thus the Fujiwara clan probably did not oppose Saichō's petitions.[193]

Besides Fujiwara patronage, several other factors which contributed to Saichō's victory must be mentioned.[194] Saichō's proposals were in accordance with religious trends already evident. Buddhism in Nara had been growing increasingly sectarian for several decades when Saichō made his proposals. This sectarianism was reflected in the rivalry between the Hossō and Sanron schools. Temples were already beginning to be associated with certain schools. Both Saichō and Kūkai supported and developed this sectarian tendency on the basis of what they had seen in

---

[190] *DZ* 1: 250–53.

[191] *DZ* 5 (*Bekkan*): 46; and Suehiro, *Yakuchū Eizan Daishiden*, pp. 104–5.

[192] *DZ* 5 (*Bekkan*): 96; and Tsuruoka Shizuo, *Kodai Bukkyōshi kenkyū* (Tokyo: Bungadō shoten, 1967), p. 217.

[193] Much of the material on the Fujiwaras is taken from Tsuruoka, "Saichō to Fujiwarashi," *Kodai Bukkyōshi kenkyū*, pp. 205–29.

[194] The following explanation follows Sonoda, *Saichō*, pp. 512–14.

China. Shortly after Mount Hiei was granted its independence from the Sōgō's control, Kūkai requested that Tōji be designated an exclusively Shingon institution. In 838, following the example set by the Tendai School, the Shingon School requested that it too no longer be subject to supervision by the Sōgō.

Saichō's personality was crucial to his eventual success. In his retreat to Mount Hiei, his voyage to China, his debates with Tokuitsu and his pursuit of independence for the Tendai School, Saichō exhibited a singleminded seriousness of purpose. Throughout his life he stressed the importance of strict adherence to monastic discipline. In his quest for approval of the *Shijōshiki* and other petitions, he repeated his request almost every year. In approving his proposals, the court recognized that there was no element of self-seeking in Saichō's reforms. A less serious monk would probably never have succeeded in obtaining approval for such a major revision of the precepts against so much opposition.

The system of monastic control which Saichō was challenging was already decaying. Originally, it had been planned as a system which would place the monks firmly under government control while still allowing elder monks and teachers control over the selection, ordination, and training of monks under their supervision. However, sectarianism had made the system partial to the monks of certain schools. Because Tendai yearly ordinands were initiated in court and then ordained at Tōdaiji in Nara, many of them defected to temples in Nara. The Sōgō and Genbaryō, which were to oversee the registration of the new monks, were controlled by monks hostile to Saichō who used their authority in partisan ways. This was most evident in their biased treatment of Saichō's petitions. By proposing that the Tendai School be removed from the jurisdiction of the Sōgō and Genbaryō and placed under the jurisdiction of the Council of State (Dajōkan), Saichō tried to eliminate some of the abuses in the existing system.

In conclusion, Saichō did not initially set out to change the set of precepts used to ordain monks. His early petitions to the court concerned the training of Tendai monks and their removal from the jurisdiction of the Nara monastic leaders. References to the precepts were purposefully vague. Only after these petitions had failed to achieve their goal did Saichō clearly suggest that the *Fan wang* precepts be substituted for the *Ssu fen lü* precepts.

PART TWO

SAICHŌ'S VIEW OF THE PRECEPTS

CHAPTER NINE

THE ROLE OF THE PRECEPTS IN SAICHŌ'S THOUGHT

When Saichō submitted his petitions to the court calling for reforms in monastic discipline and the ordination system, he was primarily
concerned with insuring the future of the Tendai School through the
revision of the administrative procedures used by the government to
supervise Buddhist institutions. His petitions were clear descriptions of
the bureaucratic changes he envisioned. After his death, Saichō's proposals were carefully put into effect by his disciples.

In the previous chapter, the administrative problems which threatened the existence of the Tendai School and Saichō's attempts to resolve
them were discussed. In this chapter, Saichō's doctrinal justification for
his proposals are analyzed. Saichō could not make the unprecedented
suggestion that the *Fan wang* precepts be substituted for the Hīnayāna
precepts in full ordinations without defending his proposals with respect
to Buddhist doctrine. However, Saichō did not have sufficient time to
develop a systematic and comprehensive statement of his position on
the precepts. He died before his proposals had been approved. His
major work on the precepts, the *Kenkairon,* was a detailed and vigorous
defense of the proposals presented in the *Shijōshiki* against the charges
of the monastic leaders of Nara. It was never intended to be a reasoned,
systematic presentation of his position on the precepts.

The terminology in Saichō's petitions and the *Kenkairon* reflected
the unfinished quality of his thought on the precepts. Saichō referred
to the precepts and to the ideal Tendai practitioner with terms which
were many and varied.[1] Saichō seemed to be searching for a new
set of terms to present his ideas. He devised new systems for classifying teachings and practices, but often did not discuss their relationship
to each other or to the classification systems devised by Chih-i. Concepts
such as the Direct Path (*jikidō* 直道) to enlightenment and Perfect faculties (*enki* 圓機) were discussed briefly in his works, rather than with the
detail they merited. If Saichō had lived longer, he probably would have
written further about many of these concepts.

---

[1] For a list of the terms, see Takeda Chōten,"Dengyō Daishi ni okeru risōteki ningenzō,"
Taishō daigaku kenkyū kiyō 61 (1975): 28–29.

Saichō believed that he was living at a time in history which required radical changes in Japanese Buddhism. His proposal to base monastic practice on the *Fan wang ching* was only one part of a larger plan to reform Tendai Buddhism. Saichō envisioned Mount Hiei as an institution which would dispatch monks to the provinces to spread Tendai teachings as well as training them so that they could realize enlightenment during their current lifetime (*sokushin jōbutsu* 即身成佛).

In the *Hokke shūku* Saichō argued that the *Lotus Sūtra* was the Buddha's ultimate teaching and that it was appropriate for the Japanese people. In the following passage, Saichō mentioned some of the factors which he believed should be considered in determining the right doctrine and practice for the Japanese people.

> If we speak of the age in which we live, it is the end of the Period of the Imitated Dharma and the beginning of the Period of the End of the Dharma. If we inquire about the land in which we live, it is to the east of China (in other words, Japan).... If we ask about the people to whom this teaching is to be preached, it is to those who are born in a time of strife during the period of the five defilements (*gojoku* 五濁).[2]

These same three factors, the age in which Saichō lived, the Japanese nation, and the capabilities of the Japanese people, decisively influenced Saichō's understanding of the role which the precepts should play in Japanese Buddhism and led him to formulate a new interpretation of the precepts for Heian period Japan. In this chapter, Saichō's view of the precepts will be discussed in terms of these three factors. Finally, Saichō's view of Buddhist practice and the role of the precepts within it will be considered.

Saichō's View Of Buddhist History: The Decline Of The Buddha's Teaching

Saichō frequently referred to the decline of the Buddha's teaching in his writings. In the *Kenkairon* he cited a number of scriptures which described friction within the Buddhist order and the deterioration of Buddhist practice which would come after the Buddha's death.[3] During

---

[2] DZ 3:251. The five defilements (*gojoku*) are described in the *Lotus Sūtra* (Hurvitz trans., p. 31). They consist of five characteristics of an age in decline. First, the age or *kalpa* itself was defiled. The time was such that the other four defilements tended to come into being. Second, passions (*kleśa*) such as covetousness, anger and ignorance arose in people. Third, all sentient beings who lived at such a time were defiled; because of past wrongdoings, people possessed inferior faculties and had weak bodies. Fourth, people maintained wrong religious views. They believed in heterodox teachings such as in the existence of an eternal soul. Fifth, the lifespan of people gradually shortened.

this time Buddhist monks would be jealous of each other and fight among themselves. Monks who seriously wanted to practice religious austerities would be persecuted by decadent monks and be unable to do so. In addition, various natural disasters such as floods, droughts, and earthquakes would occur. Heterodox teachings would flourish, and people would commit terrible crimes.

Predictions of the decline of the Buddhist teaching had played an important role in Indian and Chinese Buddhism. In China these predictions had been crucial to the development of Pure Land Buddhism and the Sect of the Three Stages. Buddhists representing these movements had argued that a new age in Buddhist history required new teachings. Other Chinese monks, such as Daoxuan, had responded to the threat of a decline in Buddhism by calling upon monks to faithfully follow established Buddhist practices, especially those specified in the precepts.[4]

In Japan the idea of a decline in Buddhist teachings and practices was familiar to Japanese monks as early as the Nara period. Particularly popular was a theory which classified the deterioration of Buddhism into three stages: the Period of the True Dharma (*shōbō* 正法), the Period of the Imitated Dharma (*zōhō* 像法) and the End of the Dharma (*mappō* 末法).

Of the various theories concerning the length of these periods, two were particularly well-known in China and Japan. According to the first, the Period of the True Dharma lasted five-hundred years and the Period of the Imitated Dharma lasted one-thousand years. By the eighth century, the Chinese and Japanese usually dated the death of the Buddha as occurring in 949 B. C.;[5] thus the Nara and Heian periods corresponded to *mappō*. This theory had been advocated by Dōji 道慈, a monk who had studied in China. Dōji had written the section of the *Nihon shoki*

---

[3] *DZ* 1:154–56, 164, 170–72.

[4] Predictions of the decline of the Buddha's teaching were a major factor in Daoxuan's call for renewed rigor in observing the precepts [Miyabayashi Akihiko, "Dōsen no mappōkan to kaigaku," *Taishō daigaku kenkyū kiyō* 61 (1975): 17–26]. For a good discussion of Indian theories of the decline of Buddhism, see David Chappell, "Early Forebodings of the Death of Buddhism," *Numen* 27 (1980): 122–154.

[5] During the Six Dynasties, Chinese Buddhists moved the date of the death of the Buddha back in time from the fifth century B. C. to 949 B. C. in order to counter Taoist charges that the arrival of Buddhism had caused Chinese dynasties to be shortlived and to prove that the Buddha had lived before Lao Tzu. Eventually the date of 949 B. C. was accepted as the date of the Buddha's death by most Chinese. By claiming that Buddhism had arrived in China shortly after the Buddha's death, Chinese monks could argue that Buddhism had been taught in China during the long Chou Dynasty and thus had not adversely affected the longevity of Chinese dynasties.

describing the introduction of Buddhism to Japan. Unlike earlier scholars who had dated the introduction of Buddhism into Japan as 538, Dōji had dated it as 552, the first year of *mappō*. Tamura Enchō 田村圓澄 has suggested that Dōji may have wanted to demonstrate that Japanese Buddhism could flourish during *mappō*, even though Chinese Buddhism was exhibiting signs of deterioration.[6]

The second theory maintained that the periods of the True Dharma and Imitated Dharma had each lasted one-thousand years. Japan during the Nara and Heian periods would thus have been in the Period of the Imitated Dharma. Statements to this effect were included in the *Shoku Nihongi*.[7]

Saichō believed that many of the descriptions of the decline of the Buddha's teaching accurately depicted the corruption among Buddhist monks in Nara. The monks of Nara vied for fame and profit, rather than exerting themselves to attain enlightenment. They jealously criticized and persecuted any monk who seriously practiced Buddhist austerities. Saichō saw himself as the persecuted monk and the Nara monks as the corrupt Buddhists described in the *sūtras*.[8]

Although Saichō referred to the theories describing the decline of Buddhism in three periods, he did not attempt to reconcile the discrepancies between the various accounts of the decline. Nor did he discuss the chronology of the decline of Buddhism in his writings.[9] Saichō's disciple Kōjō, however, included a passage in the *Denjutsu isshinkaimon* which did give a chronology for the decline.[10] The Period of the True Dharma (*shōbō*) lasted one-thousand years, and the Period of the Imitated Dharma (*zōhō*) would also last one-thousand years. Thus Kōjō noted that 806, the year Emperor Kanmu granted yearly ordinands to the Tendai School, was 1747 years after the Buddha's death. Only two-

---

[6] See Tamura Enchō, *Asuka Bukkyōshi kenkyū* (Tokyo: Hanawa shobō, 1969), pp. 166–77, for a discussion of the two chronologies and their roles in early Japanese Buddhism. Tamura's thesis has been questioned by Nakamura (*Miraculous Stories from the Japanese Buddhist Tradition*), p. 12.

[7] Ibid.

[8] This aspect of Saichō's argument is expressed vividly in a quotation from the *Shou hu kuo chieh chu t'o lo ni ching* (*Kenkairon, DZ* 1:165–71); for a description of the passage, see footnote 36 of Chapter 8.

[9] In a quotation from the *Ta pao chi ching* (*Mahāratnakūṭa*) in the *Kenkairon* (*DZ* 1: 171–72), Saichō also referred to a description of the decline of Buddhism in five stages of five-hundred years each. Other sources which he quoted referred only to the period of decline after the Buddha's death without giving a chronology (ibid., pp. 154–56).

[10] *DZ* 1:540–41. This chronology is also referred to in the *Jubosatsukaigi* and in Enchin's notes on it (*DZ* 1:309–10).

hundred years remained before the final period of decline, that of *mappō*. Kōjō's mention of a significant event in Saichō's life, the bestowal of yearly ordinands, in his chronology suggests that Saichō also accepted this time table.

Saichō justified several of his proposals by referring to predictions of the decline of Buddhism. He argued that the changed circumstances of the current age required new forms of Buddhism. In proposing that Mañjuśrī should replace Piṇḍola as elder (*jōza*) in the dining halls, Saichō noted that:

> At the end of the Period of the Imitated Dharma (*zōmatsu* 像末), the four groups[11] violate the Hīnayāna and Mahāyāna precepts and turn against the Buddha's teachings. The Hīnayāna *jōza* (Piṇḍola) does not have enough power (to accomplish such feats as vanquishing the karmic consequences of wrongdoings). If you do not install Mañjuśrī as *jōza* in the dining halls, then you ignore the Dharma in India and go against the laws of China. To whom will you turn to escape the consequences of your violations of the precepts? How will you escape the fierce flames of Avici Hell?[12]

Elsewhere Saichō argued that serious monks should withdraw to the mountains to meditate. After quoting a passage from the *Fa mieh chin ching* 法滅盡經 which described the complete degradation of Buddhism, Saichō asked, "If it is known that it is the time (of the decline of Buddhism), who would not go to the mountains (in order to practice in peace)?"[13]

Saichō was one of the first Buddhist monks in Japan to argue that certain of his teachings were better suited to the period of the decline of Buddhism than those of his opponents. He did not, however, use the advent of *mappō* as the primary factor in justifying his reforms as did some monks in the late Heian and Kamakura periods. For example, Saichō never argued that the *Fan wang* precepts should replace the *Ssu fen lü* precepts precisely because it was the Period of the End of the Dharma (*mappō*).[14]

---

[11] The term 'four groups' probably refers to monks, nuns, laymen and laywomen, but it might also refer to monks, nuns, male novices and female novices. The term *zōmatsu* was borrowed from Ming-kuang's 明曠 commentary on the *Fan wang ching* (*T* 40:586a). It can also be translated as the Period of the Imitated Dharma (*zōhō*) and the Period of the End of the Dharma (*mappō*). The translation of *zōmatsu* as the end of the Period of the Imitated Dharma is based on a passage from the *Shugo kokkaishō* (*DZ* 2:349).

[12] *Kenkairon, DZ* 1:101–2.

[13] Ibid., p. 156.

[14] According to the *Mappō tōmyōki* 末法燈明記 (*DZ* 1:415–427), a work attributed to

The Fan Wang Precepts And Saichō's View Of Japan

In the following pages, two of the ways in which Saichō's view of the Japanese nation influenced his position of the precepts are discussed. First, Saichō believed that Japanese Buddhism was at a crucial point in its history. The Buddha's ultimate teaching, the One-vehicle doctrine of the *Lotus Sūtra,* had just been recognized by the Japanese court with the allocation of Tendai yearly ordinands by Emperor Kanmu. If this teaching was to flourish it had to be further encouraged. The *Fan wang* precepts played a key part in Saichō's defense of the Tendai School. Second, Japanese Buddhism had traditionally been patronized by the court, and in turn, had performed ceremonies to protect the nation and court. Saichō redefined Nara state Buddhism by establishing the autonomy of the Tendai School and increasing the number of people to whom Buddhism appealed. The *Fan wang* precepts played a significant role in Saichō's efforts to reform church-state relations.

Saichō sometimes referred to Japan by the honorific title *Dainipponkoku* 大日本國. He usually used this title in conjunction with the parallel one for China, *Daitō* 大唐. In this way he gave Japan a status equal to that of China, the country to which Japan had looked for cultural and religious leadership during the past several centuries. Yet Saichō's own activities reveal that in many ways he still viewed China as the model for Japanese Buddhism. He had traveled to China in order to study Buddhism and later used his transmissions in China as the basis for his argument that his teachings were orthodox.[15] Many of the reforms proposed in the *Kenkairon* were based on practices in China. His proposals for installing Mañjuśrī as *jōza* and for installing one-hundred monks in a mountain temple to chant the *Jen wang ching* in order to protect the country were based on precedents found in Amoghavajra's recommendations to the Chinese court.[16] Saichō's substitution of lay administrators (*zoku bettō*) for the Sōgō (Office of Monastic Affairs) and the Genbaryō

Saichō, the precepts could no longer be followed precisely because Japan was about to enter *mappō*. Most modern scholars believe the work was compiled after Saichō's death since attitudes differing from those in many of Saichō's works are included in it; however Ienaga Saburō (*Jōdai Bukkyō shisōshi kenkyū*, pp. 188–217) has argued that the work was written by Saichō. Summaries of current scholarship on the text can be found in Asaeda Zenshō, *Heian Bukkyōshi kenkyū*, pp. 204–219, and Tsuruoka Shizuo, *Nihon kodai Bukkyōshi no kenkyū*, pp. 157–198. The *Mappō tōmyōki* played a key role in the formation of Kamakura Buddhism. For an English translation of the text, see Robert F. Rhodes, "Saichō's *Mappō Tōmyōki*: The Candle of the Latter Dharma," *Eastern Buddhist* n. s. 13 (1980): 79–103.

[15] The *Kenkairon engi* and *Kechimyakufu* amply document Saichō's reliance on Chinese teachers.

[16] *DZ* 1:103–6 130–31, 150–59.

(Bureau of Aliens and Buddhism) was based on the Chinese office of Commissioner of Good Works (*kung te shih* 功德使).[17]

Yet at the same time Japanese Buddhism could not simply imitate China; it had to develop in its own way, though it was still to be based on Chinese and Indian precedents. Saichō had an acute sense of the flow of Buddhist history. In his debates with Tokuitsu, Saichō had discussed the history of the conflict between the One-vehicle and Three-vehicle interpretations of the Buddha's teachings. Both interpretations had arisen in India and been transmitted to China. Chih-i had advanced the correct interpretation of the *Lotus Sūtra's* One-vehicle teaching, but the T'ien-t'ai School had been eclipsed by the popularity of the Fa-hsiang School and its Three-vehicle teachings. However, even at the height of the Fa-hsiang School's popularity and influence, Chinese monks who were versed in Yogācāra doctrine, such as Fa-pao and Ling-jun, had argued for a One-vehicle interpretation of Buddhism. Eventually, the One-vehicle teachings of Fa-tsang's Hua-yen School and the One-vehicle Esoteric teachings of Śubhakarasiṃha and Vajrabodhi received the support of the state, and the Three-vehicle teachings were vanquished. As Saichō declared in the *Shugo kokkaishō:* "The years during which the expedient (Three-vehicle teachings flourished) have already set with the western sun. The sun of the ultimate (teaching of the One-vehicle) will rise in the east (Japan)."[18]

Saichō dated the rise of the One-vehicle teaching in Japan with the allocation of yearly ordinands to the Tendai School in 806.[19] The date suggests that Saichō believed that he was the messenger who had brought the new teaching to Japan and that he was responsible for defending it.[20] Saichō's proposals concerning the *Fan wang* precepts were an important part of his efforts to propagate and defend the One-vehicle Tendai teaching in Japan. In addition, Saichō probably believed that the rise of the

---

[17] See the discussion of *zoku bettō* in Chapter 14. The office of Commissioner of Good Works was first filled by one of Amoghavajra's lay disciples, Li Yüan-ts'ung 李元琮, who was Commander of the Lung-wu Imperial Guard Army of the Right.

[18] *DZ* 2:234.

[19] *DZ* 1:197.

[20] The *Lotus Sūtra* contained many passages which encouraged people to preach and must have contributed to Saichō's sense of his mission. Although Saichō did not identify himself with any of the personages in the *sūtra*, he did call Chih-i an 'emissary of the Buddha' (*nyoraishi* 如來使), a term which referred to anyone who preached the *Lotus Sūtra* (*Ehyō Tendaishū, DZ* 3:364; *Hokke shūku, DZ* 3:243–44; *Shugokokkaishō, DZ* 2:289, 291, 301; Hurvitz, *Lotus,* p. 175). Since Chih-i was the de facto founder of the T'ien-t'ai School and Saichō was the founder of the school in Japan, Saichō probably considered himself to be an emissary of the Buddha.

One-vehicle teaching in Japan justified innovations such as using the *Fan wang* precepts to ordain monks.

Even a cursory glance at Saichō's biography and writings reveals that like most of his contemporaries, Saichō considered the protection of the state to be one of Buddhism's chief functions. Japanese scholars during the first half of the twentieth century often emphasized the nationalistic side of Saichō's belief, largely because of the incorrect view that Saichō was the very first person to use the honorific title *Dainipponkoku* for Japan.[21]

Nara Buddhism had emphasized the protection of the state. The court expected this type of service from Buddhism, and Saichō did not disappoint the court officials. His petitions emphasized that Tendai monks would perform various activities to protect the nation and guard it from calamities, as the following passage from the *Kenkairon* demonstrates:

> Thus I clearly know that contemplation, chanting, turning and reading (the *sūtras*) will serve as able generals who will protect the nation. I sincerely request that the two Japanese Tendai yearly ordinands (be allowed to) receive the bodhisattva precepts and thus become the treasures of the nation 國寶.[22] As for the Esoteric teachings (based on the *Ta jih ching*), permit us to establish a building in which to perform Esoteric consecrations and practices. There we shall always chant and meditate on the *sūtras* to guard the state, as well as perform the *goma* 護摩 ceremony.[23] For Mahāyāna practices, we shall establish halls for the four types of (Tendai) meditation (*shishu sanmai* 四種三昧).[24] Allow us to turn the *sūtras* for the nation, and to lecture on *prajñāpāramitā*.[25] If these proposals are approved, then the One-vehicle precepts of the Buddha 一乘佛戒 will not cease (being transmitted) over the years, and the students of the Perfect (Tendai) School will flourish. One hundred bodhisattva

---

[21] Sakamotō Taro, "Dengyō Daishi to Dainippon no kokugo," *DDK*, pp. 485–500. Sakamoto examines Saichō's use of the term and lists Japanese precedents for its use. He also discusses the Chinese term upon which it is based.

[22] For the term 'nation's treasure,' see footnote 28 and the translation of the *Rokujōshiki* in Chapter 8.

[23] The *goma* (Skt. *homa*) ceremony is an Esoteric ceremony involving the use of a fire. It probably had its origins in Vedic fire sacrifices.

[24] The four types of meditation are discussed in footnote 109 of Chapter 8.

[25] The *Prajñāpāramitā sūtras* were often chanted in order to protect the state during the Nara period. Saichō was especially interested in the *Jen wang ching,* a Perfection of Wisdom *sūtra* compiled in China.

monks will be installed on the mountain.[26] Eight worthies who hold the precepts will pray for rain and easily obtain good results.[27]

In return for their efforts to protect the nation, Saichō and the Tendai School received financial aid and patronage from the nobility. However, Saichō's view of church-state relations did differ from that of the Nara monks in two important ways.

First, Saichō worked for a more autonomous Buddhist order. Since the *Sōniryō* (*Regulations for Monks and Nuns*) had been composed, it had been periodically supplemented in order to tighten state control over the Buddhist order. Many new regulations concerning the order were issued in the late eighth century during the reigns of emperors Kōnin and Kanmu as the court attempted to cope with the abuses that had occurred while the monk Dōkyō was in a position of power. Although Saichō agreed with many of the reforms made, he was dissatisfied with the bureaucracy which supervised Tendai monks. In the *Kenkairon* Saichō pointed out that the *Jen wang ching,* one of the most important *sūtras* chanted to protect the nation, stated that establishing a monastic register and installing monastic officials to control the Buddhist order would surely bring about the decline of Buddhism.[28] The monks who served as officials in the Sōgō and in the Genbaryō had originally been appointed to control the order, while still allowing Buddhist monks to have a voice in their relations with the government. However, from Saichō's point of view they were only obstacles in his quest to establish the Tendai School. In place of the Sōgō and Genbaryō, Saichō proposed that lay administrators (*zoku bettō*) serve as direct liasons between Mount Hiei and the Dajōkan (Council of State). Since the *zoku bettō* who were eventually installed were also high ranking officials at court,

---

[26] Saichō proposed that one-hundred monks be installed on Mount Hiei to constantly chant the *Jen wang ching* (*Sūtra on the Benevolent King*) and thereby protect the nation from calamities. His proposal was based on a similar plan submitted to the Chinese court by Amoghavajra (*DZ* 1:151–53).

[27] *Kenkairon, DZ* 1:131. Saichō had previously performed ceremonies to bring rain for the Japanese court. Such ceremonies were among the first rituals performed in China by Buddhist monks (Ōchō, *Chūgoku Bukkyō no kenkyū* 1:339). The *Ch'ing yü ching* (*Sūtra Used in Asking for Rain, T* 19:498b) specified that eight men be used in the ceremony.

[28] *DZ* 1:179–80. Although the *Jen wang ching* is probably a Chinese compilation, two 'translations' exist. Saichō quoted both in this instance. The earlier translation, attributed to Kumārajīva, prohibited any registration of monks or the installation of officially appointed monks to oversee the order. Amoghavajra compiled a 'new translation' and changed the passage so that only unreasonable government control of the order was warned against. This later translation is closer to Saichō's attitude than the earlier one.

the Tendai School had more effective representation at court than if it had used the traditional bureaucratic channels of the Sōgō and Genba-ryō.

Saichō did not ask for complete autonomy for the Tendai School. Although he criticized the bureaucracy controlling the Buddhist schools, he readily accepted the principles of government control over the number of monks, government examination and certification of candidates for the order, and government issuance of identification certificates for novices and monks. The lay administrators (*zoku bettō*) too were appointed by the government, which could have resulted in direct government supervision of the Tendai School by laymen.

Saichō certainly could have criticized such supervision by the court as infringements on the autonomy of the Tendai School, but chose not to do so, probably because he was more concerned with the interference of Nara monks in Tendai affairs than with the possibility of interference from the court.

One of Saichō's most important achievements in church-state relations was his clear demarcation of the areas in which monks could live and act. The testing, initiation, and ordination of prospective Tendai monks was no longer to take place in Nara and Kyoto but on Mount Hiei, where the new monks were required to spend the next twelve years.[29] Tendai monks were to be concerned with religious, not political affairs; thus they would not give the court cause to interfere in monastic affairs.

Secondly, Saichō tried to broaden Buddhism's popular base in Japan. During the Nara period the court had promoted Buddhism as a religion of the elite. To a large extent, the Nara schools had not objected. In fact, the Hossō teaching that only some sentient beings possessed the seeds necessary for enlightenment contributed to these elitist attitudes. Monks were directed to stay in their temples and practice. The court believed that unrestricted contact with the populace could be subversive and thus discouraged it. The fifth article in the *Sōniryō* stated:

> Monks or nuns who are not residents of a monastery or temple and who set up (unauthorized) religious establishments and preach to congregations of the people . . . shall be expelled from holy orders. Officials of provinces and districts, who are aware of such conduct but do not prohibit it shall be punished in accordance with the law. Persons desiring to beg for food must submit an application

---

[29] Ibid., pp. 180–81.

supported by the joint seals of their superiors through the provincial or district offices. The authorities may grant permission after they are satisfied that true ascetic practice is intended.[30]

The twenty-third article read:

Monks, nuns, and others who send lay persons from house to house to exhort people with prayers and images shall be punished with one hundred days hard labor; the lay persons shall be dealt with according to the law.[31]

The *Sōniryō* date from the early eighth century. In subsequent years they were supplemented by edicts under a number of emperors including Kanmu. In Saichō's time, although the above two articles were still laws, they were largely ignored. Such sources as the *Nihon ryōiki*, compiled in the early ninth century, provide ample evidence that Buddhism was already spreading among the common people. The Nara monks did not choose to challenge Saichō's plan to send Tendai monks out to the provinces to preach and assist with public works such as bridge building.[32] They too were interested in this type of activity.

Saichō's proposals led to government recognition of trends already present in Buddhism and thus enabled monks to approach the people even more closely. His efforts to defend the doctrinal basis for the participation of the common people in Buddhism were a crucial part of this change. In his works directed against Tokuitsu and the Hossō School, Saichō argued that all people had the Buddha-nature and could attain Buddhahood. Receiving the *Fan wang* ordination and adhering to the precepts were religious practices open to anyone. Anyone could receive a *Fan wang* ordination and anyone who had been correctly ordained could in turn confer the *Fan wang* precepts on others. The universal scope of the *Fan wang* precepts was due to the universality of the Buddha-nature.

Saichō envisaged a system in which Tendai monks would be trained for twelve years on Mount Hiei and then go to live in the provinces in order to perform good works, to preach, and to confer *Fan wang* ordinations. Saichō himself made two such trips: the first to Kyushu and the second to Kōzuke and Shimotsuke. On the second trip he is said to

---

[30] Sansom, "Early Japanese Law and Administration," *Transactions of the Asiatic Society of Japan* 11 (1934):128.

[31] Ibid., p. 133.

[32] The one case where the *sōtō* and Saichō did argue over a specific rule in the *Sōniryō* concerns whether Saichō had followed the correct procedure in submitting the *Shijōshiki*. See the *Kenkairon, DZ* 1:196, and footnote 101 in chapter 8.

have performed ordinations. In addition, Mount Hiei was to be the center of a matrix of pagodas and temples which were to protect the emperor and the nation from harm. Observance of the *Fan wang* or Perfect precepts was to be a universal practice which could be used by the entire Japanese population. Thus the nation would be protected through the spread of the Perfect precepts (*denkai gokoku* 傳戒護國).[33]

Perfect Faculties

If a religious teaching is to be effective, it must be suited to the abilities and faculties of those to whom it is preached. If it is too profound for its listeners, they may be frightened by it and thus doubt their own abilities, or they may leave the assembly at which it is being preached.[34] Even the earliest *sūtras* contain the idea that the Buddha adapted his teachings to fit the capabilities of his audience. The Buddha was often compared to a doctor who administered medicine to the sick. If the medicine (or doctrine) was not suited to their needs, it would not cure them. The *Lotus Sūtra* and the *Hua yen ching* (*Avataṃsakasūtra*) both contain passages which describe *śrāvakas* and *pratyekabuddhas* who did not have faculties sufficiently mature to understand the Buddha's more advanced teachings. These passages played key roles in Chih-i's systems of classification of Buddhist teachings. The *Hua yen ching* was criticized because it made no allowances for the faculties of its listeners. It was thus considered an ineffective teaching for most people, leaving them as if they were 'deaf and dumb.' The *Lotus Sūtra*, in contrast, did consider the faculties of its audience. According to the *Lotus Sūtra*, the Buddha waited until his listeners were ready to hear his ultimate teaching before preaching the *Lotus Sūtra*. Despite this, five-thousand people left the assembly at which the Buddha preached the *Lotus Sūtra* because of their 'overweening pride.' On the basis of this passage, Chih-i was able to argue that the *Nieh p'an ching* (*Mahāparinirvāṇasūtra*), traditionally regarded in China as the Buddha's last sermon, had the function of saving these five-thousand monks and nuns. Chih-i thus classified the *Nieh p'an ching* in the same period of the Buddha's life as the *Lotus Sūtra* and noted that the *Nieh p'an ching* included elements

---

[33] *Kenkairon*, *DZ* 1:26 (opening verses of the *Kenkairon*). See Takeda Chōten, "Shūso ni okeru denkai to gokoku," *DDK*, pp. 687–709. Ordinations conferring the bodhisattva precepts had long been associated with the protection of the emperor and the nation in China (Ōchō, "Chūgoku Bukkyō ni okeru kokka ishiki," *Chūgoku Bukkyō no kenkyū* 1:333, 341–42, 351).

[34] Hurvitz, *Chih-i*, pp. 231–32, 237–241. Also see the *Lotus Sūtra* (Hurvitz trans.), p. 29.

of the Perfect Teaching.

One of the central teachings of the *Lotus Sūtra* is that during most of his life the Buddha preached expedient teachings for those with lesser faculties, but waited until the faculties of people had matured sufficiently before he preached his ultimate teaching, the Perfect teaching of the *Lotus Sūtra,* at the end of his life. As Saichō stated in the *Hokke shūku,* "The basic teaching of the One-vehicle (is not preached) until the proper time has arrived and (the audience) has the proper faculties. Only when their faculties have matured and the appropriate time has come does the Buddha preach it. Thus the Buddha waited until the Sudden faculties (*tonki* 頓機) of people had matured before preaching the One-vehicle Sudden Teaching."[35]

Chih-i categorized the maturation of man's faculties and subsequent enlightenment in three stages.[36] First, the karmic seeds connecting a person to Buddhism had to be planted (*geshu* 下種). Although everyone possessed the Buddha-nature, a person first had to be exposed to the Buddha's teachings in order to begin to realize this basic truth. He had to listen to elementary teachings which gradually drew him on to more profound teachings until his faculties matured (*jōjuku* 調熟). In the second stage, his faculties had matured and he was ready to hear the Buddha's ultimate teaching, the *Lotus Sūtra.* Finally, in the last stage, the process was completed; freed (*gedatsu* 解脱) from his sufferings, he had achieved perfect enlightenment. For Chih-i this system was to be applied on an individual basis. One person might be at an advanced stage, while his neighbor might be at a lower stage.

Saichō used the concept of the maturing of people's faculties in a different way than Chih-i. Rather than applying the idea to individuals, Saichō argued that the Japanese people as a group possessed mature faculties. Saichō utilized Japan's place in Buddhist history and the teachings concerning the decline of Buddhism to support his views. In the preface to the *Ehyō Tendaishū* dated 816, Saichō first presented this idea in several enigmatic, short sentences: "In Japan the Perfect faculties (*enki* 圓機) of the people have already matured. The Perfect teaching has finally arisen."[37] Several years later in his *Shugo kokkaishō,* Saichō further explained his view:

Now men's faculties have all changed. There is no one with

[35] *DZ* 3:17.
[36] *Fa hua hsüan i,* fasc. 1A, *TZ* 1:216–27; and *Fa hua wen chü,* fasc. 1A, *TZ* 1:59.
[37] *DZ* 3:343.

Hīnayāna faculties. The Period of the True and of the Imitated Dharma have almost passed, and the age of *mappō* is extremely near. Now is the time for those with faculties suitable for the Hokke One-vehicle teaching. How do we know this? Because of what the *Anrakugyōbon* 安樂行品 teaches about the latter days of the decline of the Dharma.[38]

Saichō's view of the Perfect faculties of the Japanese people was partly based on statements in the *Lotus Sūtra* that the Buddha's supreme teaching could be preached during the "latter evil age."[39] Saichō believed that the faculties of the Japanese people had matured and that they were ready to hear him expound the Buddha's ultimate teaching found in the *Lotus Sūtra*. Although the Sanron and Hossō interpretations of the *Lotus Sūtra* had been studied previously in Japan, Saichō argued that they did not represent the correct interpretation of the *Lotus Sūtra*. The Tendai teachings concerning the *Lotus Sūtra*, transmitted directly to Saichō by Chinese T'ien-t'ai masters, were the only explanations of the *sūtra* which fully revealed it as the Buddha's ultimate teaching. In order to stress this point, Saichō often referred to his school as the Tendai Hokkeshū (Lotus School), and thus closely linked the terms Tendai and *Lotus Sūtra*.

Chien-chen had brought the first T'ien-t'ai texts to Japan, but had not actively attempted to spread Tien-t'ai teachings. Instead, he had devoted himself to conducting *Ssu fen lü* ordinations. As a result T'ien-t'ai teachings were virtually forgotten several decades after Chien-chen's death. In contrast, Saichō succeeded in spreading T'ien-t'ai teachings throughout Japan. By Saichō's time the faculties of the Japanese people had matured. They were ready to listen to the Tendai interpretation of the *Lotus Sūtra*.[40]

Saichō did not explain the difference between his own times and those of Chien-chen by referring to a deterministic theory, such as the number of years which had passed since the death of the Buddha. Rather, Saichō seems to have believed that a major factor was the difference in the objectives of the two men. Saichō's primary mission in life was to preach the Tendai interpretation of the *Lotus Sūtra*. Chien-chen was

---

[38] *DZ* 2:349. The *Anrakugyōbon* is the Chapter on Serene and Pleasant Activities in the *Lotus Sūtra*. Its role in Saichō's thought is discussed in Chapter 11.

[39] *Anrakugyōbon*, Hurvitz, tr., *Lotus*, p. 208.

[40] This type of explanation is found in such documents as a letter by Ōtomo no Kunimichi (*Tendai kahyō*, fasc. 2A, *BZ* 41:256), and in a memorial to the court by Ennin (ibid., fasc. 5B, *BZ* 42:7).

principally interested in teaching the *Ssu fen lü* precepts. Saichō believed, however, that the Hīnayāna precepts taught by Chien-chen caused people to backslide away from the goal of enlightenment. As the next section of this chapter indicates, Saichō maintained that only exclusive adherence to the *Fan wang* precepts would allow people to realize the full potential of their Perfect faculties.

Saichō's View Of Buddhist Practice: The Direct Path To Enlightenment (*jikidō* 直道)

In his writings Saichō frequently mentioned traditional Tendai classifications of Buddhist doctrine, such as the division of the Buddha's teaching into five periods and eight types of teaching (*goji hakkyō* 五時八教).[41] In addition, he developed a number of new systems of classification which were designed to reveal various aspects of the superiority of Tendai teachings over those of other schools. Even before studying in China, Saichō had divided Buddhist schools into two categories, those based on *sūtras* (the words of the Buddha) and those based on *śāstras* (works by Buddhist monks).[42] Using this classification, Saichō criticized the two preeminent Buddhist schools in Japan, the Hossō and Sanron, because they were based on works (*śāstras*) by Buddhist monks rather than on the words of the Buddha. Twenty years later in the *Hokke shūku* he further refined this system by dividing the schools based on *sūtras* into two groups: the Tendai School which was based on the *Lotus Sūtra* and all other schools based on *sūtras*, such as the Kegon School.[43]

Saichō's most innovative classification systems were devoted to revealing the differences between the practices advocated by the various Buddhist schools. One of the most important of these systems was based on a hierarchical classification of five types of bodhisattva found in the *Pu pi ting ju ting ju yin ching* 不必定入定入印經 (*Niyatāniyatagatimu-*

---

[41] For an example of Saichō's use of these classification systems, see the *Shugo kokkaishō, DZ* 2:183–281, 289–301. The *goji hakkyō* system of classifying Buddhist teachings is described in Hurvitz, *Chih-i,* pp. 229–71. Sekiguchi Shindai has expressed doubts about whether Chih-i or Saichō actually used the *goji hakkyō* as a comprehensive system for evaluating Buddhist teaching. For a summary of many of Sekiguchi's points, see David Chappell, "Introduction to the *T'ien t'ai ssu chiao i,*" *Eastern Buddhist,* new series 9 no. 1 (1976): 72–86. Although the term '*goji hakkyō*' does not appear in Saichō's writings, the various elements of this system do appear in close conjunction with each other. (For an example, see *Shugo kokkaishō, DZ* 2:214). Consequently, Sekiguchi's insistence that Saichō did not use the *goji hakkyō* system must be questioned [Nakao Shunpaku, "Dengyō Daishi Saichō no kyōhan," *IBK* 24 (1975): 276–79].

[42] *Eizan Daishiden, DZ* 5 (*Bekkan*): 11–12.

[43] *DZ* 3:273.

drāvatārasūtra). Each type was compared with a man who was attempting to travel to a distant place. If the man boarded the wrong type of vehicle, he would never arrive at his destination because winds and storms would constantly delay him and force him to turn back. If he chose a more suitable vehicle, he would eventually arrive at his destination, but only after a very long period of time. If he rode the best vehicle, he would quickly arrive at his destination. The five types of bodhisattvas described in the *sūtra* and their vehicles were:

1. The bodhisattva who followed sheep vehicle practices (*yōjōgyō* 羊乘行)
2. The bodhisattva who followed elephant vehicle practices (*zō-jōgyō* 象乘行)
3. The bodhisattva who followed the practices of the vehicle which endowed him with superhuman powers enabling him to reach the sun and moon (*gatsunichi jinzū jōgyō* 月日神通乘行)
4. The bodhisattva who followed the practices of the vehicle which endowed him with the superhuman powers of a *śrāvaka* (*shōmon jinzū jōgyō* 聲聞神通乘行)
5. The bodhisattva who followed the practices which endowed him with superhuman powers like those of the Buddha (*Nyorai jinzū jōgyō* 如來神通乘行).[44]

The *sūtra* did not describe the actual practices which each vehicle represented. Rather, the main theme of the *sūtra* was that not all religious practices were of the same efficacy. Some practices enabled a person to advance rapidly towards his religious goal without any danger of backsliding. Others, especially Hīnayāna practices, caused him to regress, removing him further away from his goal than ever. Although the sheep vehicle and the elephant vehicle were both subject to backsliding, the other three vehicles were not.

In the *Kenkairon* Saichō quoted this *sūtra* at length[45] and then applied its teachings to the precepts:

I clearly understand that from among the five types of bodhisattvas,

---

[44] Much of the terminology in this *sūtra* (*T* no. 645) is unusual and is not found in either the standard Buddhist dictionaries or in other *sūtras*. Although it warns against consorting with Hīnayāna practitioners, the second highest category of bodhisattva is said to have superhuman powers like those of a *śrāvaka*. Even the lowest category of practitioner, the follower of the sheep vehicle who is identified by Saichō as a Hīnayāna practitioner, is called a bodhisattva. The differences between the three types of superhuman powers are not clarified in the *sūtra*.

[45] *Kenkairon*, *DZ* 1:62–73. The passage quoted corresponds to *T* 15:699c–701c, and consists of the first one-third of the *sūtra*.

some will not regress and will be assured of enlightenment while others will backslide. They will regress because they practice together with Hīnayāna adherents. The precepts of the Hīnayāna and Common teachings are followed by inferior bodhisattvas without wings.[46] (The bodhisattvas of) the three vehicles with super-human powers are assured that they will attain Buddhahood. They follow the precepts of the Unique and Perfect teachings. They are bodhisattvas who follow the Direct Path (*jikidō*) to enlightenment. Japan is a country where Mahāyāna teachings are studied. How can you (the monastic leaders of Nara) cling to Hīnayāna practices and obstruct the Mahāyāna (teachings) which should be kept distinct (from the Hīnayāna tradition)?[47]

In the *Kenkairon* Saichō classified the five bodhisattvas into two major categories, those who backslid and those who did not. In the *Ketsugonjitsuron* Saichō further developed the classification by matching the five types of bodhisattvas with the four categories (*kehō shikyō* 化法四教) of Chih-i's classification of the contents of Buddhist teachings.[48] The five types can be summarized as follows:

1. The bodhisattva who followed the practices of the sheep vehicle was equivalent to the Buddhist described in the *Abhidharmakośa* who required over three great *kalpas* to attain Buddhahood.
2. The bodhisattva who followed the practices of the elephant vehicle corresponded to the practitioner of Common teachings 通教, represented in this case by the *prajñāpāramitā* (Perfection of Wisdom) teachings.
3. The bodhisattva who followed the practices of the vehicle which endowed him with superhuman powers enabling him to reach the sun and moon corresponded to the practitioner of the fifty-two stages outlined in the *Ying lo ching* 瓔珞經, and thus was equivalent to one form of the Unique teaching (*bekkyō* 別教).
4. The bodhisattva who followed the practices of the vehicle which endowed him with the superhuman powers of a *śrāvaka* corresponded to the practitioner of another form of the Unique

---

[46] A person who follows Hīnayāna practices will backslide as surely as a wingless bird will fall to earth.

[47] *DZ* 1:72–73.

[48] The four types of Buddhist teaching (*kehō shikyō*: Hīnayāna, Common, Unique and Perfect) and the four methods of conversion (*kegi shikyō* 化儀四教: sudden, gradual, secret indeterminate and express indeterminate) make up the eight types of teachings (*hakkyō*) mentioned at the beginning of this section.

teaching, the follower of the forty-one stages presented in the *Hua yen ching* (*Avataṃsakasūtra*).

5. The bodhisattva who followed the practices of the vehicle which endowed him with the superhuman powers of the Buddha corresponded to the practitioner of the Perfect teaching (*engyō* 圓教). Saichō noted that this bodhisattva was like the eight-year old Nāga girl described in the *Lotus Sūtra* who turned into a man and immediately attained enlightenment.[49]

Saichō died before he could further develop this classification[50] and discuss such problems as how Esoteric Buddhism would fit into the system. However, the reasons for Saichō's interest in this classification system are clear. It enabled him to discuss Buddhist practices in terms of the speed with which they would enable a practitioner to attain enlightenment without backsliding. These same concerns are evident in Saichō's discussion of the Direct Path (*jikidō* 直道) to enlightenment, an important element in another classification system which Saichō devised in order to categorize Buddhist practice.

Besides preventing a person from backsliding, the most advanced practices, those of the Perfect teaching (*engyō*), enabled him to take the Direct Path to supreme enlightenment. In fact, if a person possessed superior abilities, he might attain enlightenment in this very existence (*sokushin jōbutsu* 即身成佛). If he did not attain enlightenment during his present life, Saichō argued that he would surely attain it in one of his next two lives.[51]

Concern with attaining Buddhahood in this life is one of the distinguishing features of Buddhism during the early Heian period. Both Saichō and Kūkai were actively concerned with this possibility, although almost no evidence exists indicating any exchange of ideas between them on the subject. In fact, the two men based their theories on very different sources. Saichō argued almost entirely from the discussion in the *Wu*

---

[49] Summarized from *DZ* 2:715. The *Ying lo ching*, compiled in China, is *T* no, 1485. The story in the *Lotus Sūtra* concerning the Nāga girl is found in Hurvitz trans., *Lotus*, pp. 199–201.

[50] This classification was utilized by some of Saichō's successors. Ennin used it in the *Ken'yō daikairon* (*T* 74:672c–78b). Annen also adopted it, but changed it considerably to fit his own needs [Asai, *Jōko Nihon Tendai*, pp. 771, 862 (note 20)].

[51] *Hokke shūku, DZ* 3:264–66, 280. Saichō borrowed this idea from the Kegon *sanshō jōbutsu* 三生成佛 theory of enlightenment within three lifetimes (*Shugo kokkaishō, DZ* 2: 275–76). He also based it on a passage from the *Kuan p'u hsien ching* (*Hokke shūku, DZ* 3: 266). Kūkai did not accept the *sanshō jōbutsu* (attainment of Buddhahood within three lives) theory, however; nor was it found in the writings of most Taimitsu scholars (Asai, *Jōko Nihon Tendai*, p. 187).

liang i ching 無量義經 on the Direct Path and from the story in the *Lotus Sūtra* about the Nāga girl.[52] In contrast, Kūkai based his theories solely on Esoteric sources. Saichō was probably the first of the two men to espouse the theory. The author of the *Eizan Daishiden* stated that Saichō had discussed the teaching in the Takaosanji lectures before he studied in China.[53]

The doctrine of sudden enlightenment had a long history in China and was a major issue in Chan-jan's defense of the T'ien-t'ai School against the Hua-yen School.[54] Saichō studied under Chan-jan's disciples and brought back eighteen of Chan-jan's works from China. Thus it is not surprising that he was concerned with sudden enlightment. Saichō's terminology and thought differed from that of Chan-jan, however, partly because Saichō had been decisively influenced by Kegon and Esoteric Buddhist teachings. The term *sokushin jōbutsu* (the attainment of Buddhahood in this very existence) was found only once in Chan-jan's writings and only a few times in some Esoteric works translated by Amoghavajra.[55] The term, in fact, did not occupy a prominent place in East Asian Buddhist thought until Saichō and Kūkai began using it. Kūkai especially favored the term and awarded it an important place in his Esoteric writings. In contrast, Saichō used the term *jikidō* (Direct Path). Although the term *jikidō* had appeared in the *Wu liang i ching*,[56] it too had not been commented on by scholars before Saichō's time.

While Kūkai systematically discussed the theory and the practice of the attainment of Buddhahood in this existence in such works as the *Sokushin jōbutsugi* 即身成佛義,[57] Saichō mainly used the concept as a

[52] *Shugo kokkaishō, DZ* 2:282, 395–96. The *Wu liang i ching* is *T* no. 276.

[53] *Eizan Daishiden, DZ* 5 (*Bekkan*): 9. See Katsumata, *Mikkyō no Nihonteki tenkai,* pp. 173–74, and Asai, *Jōko Nihon Tendai,* pp. 180–90 for comparisons of the positions of Saichō and Kūkai on *sokushin jōbutsu.*

[54] For a discussion of early Chinese thought on the quick attainment of Buddhahood, see Ōchō Enichi, "Sokushitsu jōbutsu no shisō," *Hokke shisō no kenkyū,* pp. 84–95. Treatments of the debates between Tendai and Kegon monks on meditation and enlightenment can be found in Andō Toshio, *Tendaigaku;* Ishizu Teruji, *Tendai jissōron no kenkyū* (Tokyo: Kōbundō, 1947); and Hibi Nobutada, *Tōdai Tendaigaku kenkyū* (Tokyo: Sankibō Busshorin, 1975).

[55] Chan-jan, *Fa hua wen chü chi, T* 34:314b. For Amoghavajra's use of the term, see the *Chin kang ting yü ch'ieh chung fa a nou to lo san miao san p'u t'i hsin lun* 金剛頂瑜伽中發阿耨多羅三藐三菩提心論, *T* 32:572c; and *Ju i pao chu chuan lun pi mi hsien shen ch'eng fo chin lun chou wang ching* 如意寶珠轉輪秘密現身成佛金輪呪王經, *T* 19:333c, 337a.

[56] For an English translation, see Katō, *The Threefold Lotus Sutra,* p. 19. Ōchō Enichi has argued that the *Wu liang i ching* was composed in China during the latter part of the fifth century, possibly by Liu Ch'iu 劉虯 to support the position that it was possible to attain enlightenment rapidly through certain practices (Ōchō, *Hokke shisō no kenkyū,* pp. 68–83).

[57] *T* no. 2428. For an English translation see Hakeda, *Kūkai,* pp. 225–34.

means of classifying and evaluating doctrines, as the following example demonstrates.

In the third fascicle of the *Shugo kokkaishō*, Saichō had defended Chih-i's description of meditation against Tokuitsu's attacks. Tokuitsu had claimed that Chih-i's instructions for meditation had no scriptural basis. As part of his response, Saichō extensively quoted a work by Tokuitsu on meditation. Saichō then proposed a classification system for Buddhist practice. Since Tokuitsu's text on meditation fit none of the classifications, Saichō argued that it was merely a mixture of disharmonious elements. Moreover, it was a teaching which no one could practice because Tokuitsu had ignored the religious faculties of people in Japan. Tokuitsu also had not chosen teachings which were suitable for people living in the Period of the End of the Dharma (*mappō*). In contrast, Saichō considered these factors in his writings. He stated,

Now I (Saichō) will criticize the meditations presented by (Tokuitsu) 'the eater of rough foods,' according to whether they are Hīnayāna or Mahāyāna. The 'eater of rough foods' has searched the one main treatise and the ten works[58] which clarify its meaning in order to establish classifications of three parts and ten parts (which explain meditation)[59] .... (However, his work) contradicts the *sūtras* and *śāstras*. He gives us bows and arrows but does not teach us how to use them. He collects medicine (to cure us of our spiritual ills), but does not decide upon a measure with which to weigh it. Without knowing our faculties and abilities, he administers an antidiarrheal drug 黄湯. The provisional teachings of Hīnayāna and Mahāyāna, as well as the ultimate Mahāyāna teaching, are distinct....

There are (three) paths which may be followed in Buddhist practice: the roundabout path (*ue* 迂回), the path requiring many eons (*ryakukō* 歷却), and the Direct Path (*jikidō*). The practitioners who follow these paths (can also be classified into three types): he who walks on the roundabout path, he who walks on the path requiring many eons, and he who flies along the Direct Path. The

---

[58] The one main treatise is the *Yü ch'ieh shih ti lun* 瑜伽師地論 (*Yogacarabhūmiśāstra*). The ten works which clarify its meaning are listed in Sonoda, *Saichō*, pp. 247–48. Asada Masahiro has demonstrated that Tokuitsu's treatise was largely excerpted from the *Yü ch'ieh shih ti lun* ("*Shugo kokkaishō* ni okeru shikan," in *Bukkyō no jissen genri*, pp. 515–38).

[59] Tokuitsu's treatise on meditation was divided into three main sections: explanation of focussing and quieting the mind (*śamatha* or *shi* 止), discussion of insight (*vipaśyanā* or *kan* 觀) and explanation of concentration and insight together (*shikan*). The ten parts may refer to the subdivisions of the first two parts of Tokuitsu's treatise on meditation.

Hīnayāna meditations explained by (Tokuitsu), 'the eater of rough food,' are generally like a walk on a roundabout path. Most of the bodhisattva practices (he describes) are comparable to a walk of many eons. Although he teaches these two pedestrian paths, no one actually follows them.[60]

Saichō argued that Hīnayāna and Hossō practices all required eons, but that the Japanese could not actually follow them because they were not suited to their faculties. In contrast, the *Lotus Sūtra* taught a direct path; instead of walking (*hogyō* 歩行) upon the path, the practitioner flew (*higyō* 飛行) directly to his goal. The path requiring eons was descriptive of Mahāyāna doctrines and practices ranging from those of the Sanron and Hossō Schools to those of the Kegon School. In the *Hokke shūku*, Saichō characterized the differences between Kegon and Tendai One-vehicle teachings in terms of their efficacy in leading to enlightenment. Kegon practice was described as leading to sudden enlightenment only after eons of training (*ryakukō shugyō tongo* 歴劫修行頓悟). Kegon doctrines had not yet fully revealed the ultimate teaching of the Buddha, nor had they been purged of provisional teachings. The teachings of the *Lotus Sūtra*, however, led directly to sudden enlightenment (*jikishi dōjō tongo* 直至道場頓悟).[61] An adherent of the *Lotus Sūtra* had no need for eons of preparatory practice and provisional teachings.

Saichō sometimes also distinguished between the Great Direct Path (*daijikidō* 大直道) and the Direct Path (*jikidō*). The Great Direct Path consisted of the Perfect teachings preached in the *Lotus Sūtra,* while the Direct Path consisted of the Perfect teachings mixed with the provisional teachings which were preached before the *Lotus Sūtra*.[62]

Saichō died before he could develop his theory of a Direct Path and a Great Direct Path to enlightenment beyond anything more than a means of classifying doctrines. The task of further developing the *jikidō* theory was left to his followers. Their first attempts to elaborate upon the *jikidō* theory appeared in a set of questions that were sent to China by Kōjō and Tokuen, two of Saichō's disciples who were especially interested in Esoteric Buddhism. The answers given by Chinese T'ien-t'ai monks were not very satisfactory to the Japanese, however, because the issue was primarily a Japanese concern. The Japanese monks asked such questions as whether attaining Buddhahood in this very existence

---

[60] *DZ* 2:348–49.
[61] *DZ* 3:37.
[62] *Chū Muryōgikyō, DZ* 3:606; Asai, *Jōko Nihon Tendai*, pp. 74, 77–78.

(*sokushin jōbutsu*) meant that a person actually became a Buddha with the šame body that had previously been subjected to ignorance and passions, or whether he somehow received a new untainted body just before he attained Buddhahood.[63]

The Perfect Precepts

What were the practices for the Perfect Teaching which enabled a person to follow the Direct Path to enlightenment? One of the earliest and most common classifications of Buddhist practice was the threefold learning (*sangaku* 三學), or the practices of precepts, meditation, and wisdom. In Hīnayāna Buddhism the threefold learning was usually regarded as a progression of practices which led to the final goal of liberation. The precepts provided the moral basis for meditation; meditation provided the basis for wisdom, and wisdom led to liberation. Although the precepts served as the basis for the entire structure, they were ranked lower than the other two types of learning.

The Chinese *Ssu fen lü* master Daoxuan (596–667) had used the classification of Buddhism into three types of learning to argue that the precepts were the basis of all Buddhist practice. He criticized the tendency of many Chinese monks to concentrate on meditation or lecturing on the *sūtras* (wisdom) while they ignored monastic discipline (precepts). Such one-sided practice could not succeed because it overlooked the most basic practice of all, the observance of the precepts.[64]

Daoxuan also criticized monks who ignored the *Ssu fen lü* precepts because of their Hīnayāna origins.[65] These monks argued that they were Mahāyāna monks and should not be bound by Hīnayāna precepts. Daoxuan defended the *Ssu fen lü* precepts by arguing that they were, in fact, partially Mahāyāna (*buntsū daijō*). T'ien-t'ai monks such as Chan-jan (711–782) noted that the attitude of the practitioner, not the origin of the precepts, determinined whether a person's practice was Hīnayāna or Mahāyāna.[66] Thus T'ien-t'ai monks almost always advocated adherence to the *Ssu fen lü* precepts.

The onus which some Chinese monks attached to the *Ssu fen lü* precepts because of the Hīnayāna origins of the *vinaya* may have been partly due to the incompatability of precepts composed in sixth century

---

[63] *Tōketsu, Nihon daizōkyō* 46:415–16, 422–25.

[64] Miyabayashi Akihiko, "Dōsen no sangakukan," in Sekiguchi, ed., *Bukkyō no jissen genri,* pp. 189–91.

[65] *Hsü kao seng chuan, T* 50: 621 b.

[66] *Chih kuan fu hsing ch'uan hung chüeh, TZ, Mo ho chih kuan,* 2:529.

B. C. India with life in China one-thousand years later.[67] In addition, although Mahāyāna literature concerning meditation and wisdom had developed impressively and replaced its Hīnayāna counterparts, monks in India and China still adhered to the Hīnayāna precepts. A Mahāyāna version of the full *vinaya* had never been composed. The bodhisattva precepts were included in *sūtras* rather than in a *vinaya*. Descriptions of the bodhisattva precepts in *sūtras* were usually brief and did not contain nearly as much detail as could be found in the *Ssu fen lü* and other full *vinayas*. Consequently, the bodhisattva precepts did not replace the *Ssu fen lü* precepts in China as Mahāyāna meditations and wisdom had replaced their Hīnayāna counterparts. The bodhisattva precepts were used by monks primarily to supplement the Hīnayāna ordinations; it was still the *Ssu fen lü* ordination which qualified the candidate as a monk.

Chinese T'ien-t'ai masters such as Chih-i and Chan-jan were more interested in meditation and doctrinal issues than in the precepts. In the *Mo ho chih kuan*, Chih-i discussed the precepts as a preliminary practice for meditation, a position which was consistent with traditional theories of the threefold learning.[68] He also applied the Tendai *kaie* 開會 (reveal and harmonize) mode of exegesis to the *Ssu fen lü* precepts in order to explain their significance for Mahāyāna practice. Chan-jan argued that the attitude of the practitioner, not the Hīnayāna origin of the precepts, was the crucial factor in the interpretation of *Ssu fen lü* ordinations.

Saichō was deeply dissatisfied with these interpretations. Previous efforts to interpret the *Ssu fen lü* precepts as a form of Mahāyāna monastic discipline or to supplement them with the bodhisattva precepts were unconvincing to Saichō. What was needed, he argued, was a set of precepts which were exclusively Mahāyāna. He stated his position in the *Kenkairon*:

Although the ten major precepts (of the *Fan wang ching*) have been transmitted before, this was in name only; their (true) meaning was not transmitted. How do I know that their (true) meaning was

---

[67] Some of the conflicts between the *vinaya* and Chinese attitudes are discussed in Kenneth Ch'en's *The Chinese Transformation of Buddhism*. The historical Buddha, Śākyamuni, gave his disciples permission to alter the minor precepts shortly before he died. The monks voted not to change the precepts at the First Council, however, because they feared that they would be criticized for abandoning some of the Buddha's precepts too soon after his death. Their decision marked the beginning of a conservative attitude toward change in the precepts which persisted for centuries in many Buddhist countries and still survives in the Theravāda tradition today.

[68] *TZ* 2:525 ff.

not transmitted? Because their Perfect meaning has not yet been understood and because they have been followed together with the Hīnayāna precepts.[69]

Saichō explained his reasons for stressing that the *Fan wang* precepts must be practiced without reference to the *Ssu fen lü* precepts in the following passage:

The monastic leaders (*sōtō*) state: The *Lotus Sūtra* teaches that one should not consort with anyone who seeks Hīnayāna goals, but in Japan there are no monks who seek Hīnayāna goals.

Saichō replies: Although (those who board) the sheep vehicle or elephant vehicle do not seek Hīnayāna rewards, still they backslide to the realms of the two (Hīnayāna) vehicles and take 80,000 *kalpas* to recover (and attain Buddhahood). Although no monks in this country seek Hīnayāna goals, they do follow the Hīnayāna rules of conduct and thus follow Hīnayāna practices. How can this not lead to a Hīnayāna result (in the end)?[70]

Saichō believed that his students were defecting to the Nara schools because their *Ssu fen lü* ordinations and practices caused them to backslide away from the Perfect teaching. In order to remedy the situation, he proposed to establish a Perfect threefold learning which would not mislead his students. In the concluding lines of the *Kenkairon,* Saichō stated:

Although One-vehicle monks have appeared year after year, the threefold learning of the Perfect teaching (*engyō sangaku* 圓教三學) is still incomplete. Although two (of the three types of learning) are beginning to appear, the learning with respect to the (Perfect) precepts has not yet arisen. Thus I presume upon his majesty to request (that he approve my proposal to authorize) the Perfect precepts.[71]

Saichō was clearly dissatisfied with the traditional T'ien-t'ai position that monks should be ordained with the *Ssu fen lü* precepts, but practice them with a Mahāyāna spirit. The precepts needed to be reformed as thoroughly as meditation and wisdom had been. For Saichō the

---

[69] *Kenkairon, DZ* 1:109.

[70] Ibid., p. 137.

[71] Ibid., p. 197. This passage is found in the verses which conclude and summarize the *Kenkairon.* Saichō's statement that 'two (of the three types of learning) are beginning to appear' may indicate that he was considering changes in Tendai meditation and doctrines as well as the precepts.

Perfect threefold teaching consisted of the *Fan wang* precepts as the Perfect precepts, the four types of Tendai meditation (*shishu sanmai* 四種三昧) as Perfect meditation, and the study of the Perfect teachings expounded in such texts as the *Lotus Sūtra* as Perfect wisdom.[72] By following Perfect practices Saichō claimed that "even a person with the dullest faculties would surely receive some sign (from the Buddha that his efforts were effective) after spending twelve years (on Mount Hiei)."[73]

There are several important reasons why Saichō was particularly concerned with the precepts. First, although Chih-i and his successors had systematically discussed Mahāyāna meditations and doctrines, they had not yet developed a convincing Tendai view of the precepts. Both Chih-i and Chan-jan had followed the *Fan wang* precepts along with the Hīnayāna precepts. Chan-jan's disciple Ming-kuang 明曠 had formulated a position on the precepts which would have allowed T'ien-t'ai monks to abandon the *Ssu fen lü* precepts, but his teachings were never put into practice in China. Consequently, Saichō believed that the task of formulating an exclusively Mahāyāna view of the precepts had fallen to him. The Hīnayāna ordinations conferred in Nara had resulted in the defection on many of his students to the Nara schools.

Second, the precepts could be practiced by anyone. Even people who were too slowwitted to understand doctrine or who did not have enough time to practice meditation could observe the precepts. Saichō repeatedly argued in the *Kenkairon* that the *Fan wang* precepts and the *Anrakugyō* were for everyone, including monks and nuns, laymen and laywomen.[74] They could even be conferred between husband and wife.[75] If people with Perfect faculties (*enki* 圓機) would follow Perfect practices, then they would be able to ameliorate the calamities which might befall the state.[76] Conferring the Perfect precepts would protect the nation (*denkai gokoku* 傳戒護國).

Since the precepts were the basis of the other two practices, meditation

---

[72] Passages linking the precepts with the Direct Path to enlightenment (*jikidō*) can be found in ibid., pp. 73, 149–150. In the *Shugo kokkaishō*, Saichō described the four types of meditation, as well as some Esoteric practices, and associated them all with *jikidō* (*DZ* 2:349). In the *Kenkairon, DZ* 1:73–74, he defended the four types of meditation as Perfect meditations (*enkan*) suitable for practitioners during the Period of the Decline of the Dharma. In the *Hokke shūku* (*DZ* 3:258–67), Saichō discussed the *Lotus Sūtra* and *jikidō*. The petitions translated in Chapter 8 of this study also describe Saichō's training program.

[73] *Kenkairon, DZ* 1:154

[74] Ibid., pp. 124–25, 137, 139–42, 181.

[75] Ibid., p. 133.

[76] Ibid., pp. 125–30.

and wisdom, the precepts potentially contained the other two. In China this idea had been emphasized and developed in the works of Daoxuan, as well as in treatises by such T'ien-t'ai scholars as Chih-i, Chan-jan, and Ming-kuang.[77] On the basis of their thought and the ideas suggested in the *Fan wang ching,* Saichō developed a theory which emphasized the fundamental identity of the separate elements of the threefold learning.[78]

The Perfect precepts were much more than mere rules of conduct. All elements of the Perfect threefold learning were essentially expressions of the Buddha. They were grounded in one's own inherently pure nature (*jishō shōjō* 自性清淨). Complete adherence to the precepts would result in complete mastery of meditation and wisdom. Perfect observance of the precepts in which the practitioner would never even be tempted to violate a rule would necessarily entail a profound understanding of the nonsubstantiality of all things. In such a case the practitioner's observance of all three elements of the threefold learning would be immovable and unhindered (*kokū fudō* 虛空不動) by any obstacle.

The *Ssu fen lü* precepts had been formulated by the historical Buddha, Śākyamuni, in response to specific situations. The *Fan wang* precepts, in contrast, were said to be eternal and universal, the precepts of a thousand Buddhas. Saichō considered them to be the source from which all Buddhas and bodhisattvas proceeded. Moreover, they were based in the Buddha-nature which everyone possessed and thus were called the *Busshōkai* 佛性戒 (Buddha-nature precepts).[79] Everyone could and and should follow these precepts. Holding the precepts made one a true disciple of the Buddha and allowed him to enter the ranks of the Buddhas. Thus the *Fan wang* precepts were considered to be the ultimate teaching, not a provisional one. The *Fan wang* precepts enabled the practitioner to enter the Direct Path (*jikidō*) to enlightenment without any danger of backsliding.

---

[77] See the discussion of the T'ien-t'ai position on the precepts in chapter 12.

[78] This theory was emphasized by medieval and modern Tendai scholars. It was often referred to as 'the single essence of the threefold learning' or *sangaku ittai* 三學一體 (Fukuda Gyōei, *Tendaigaku gairon,* pp. 615–25). In fact, Saichō does not refer to it in any of his petitions or the *Kenkairon,* probably because these works were concerned with practical problems rather than with more theoretical issues. The most important primary sources for Saichō's *sangaku ittai* theory are the *Denjutsu isshinkaimon* (*DZ* 1:580, 636) and the *Chū Muryōgikyō* (*DZ* 3:583). Saichō's position and terminology were influenced by Tao-hsüan (*Denjutsu isshinkaimon, DZ* 1:618).

[79] *Kenkairon, DZ* 1:107–8. Saichō based these statements on passages found in the *Fan wang ching* (*T* 24:1003c, 1004a, 1009a).

CHAPTER TEN

THE PROVISIONAL HĪNAYĀNA ORDINATION
(*KEJU SHŌKAI* 假受小戒)

In the *Shijōshiki* Saichō proposed that Tendai monks be ordained with the *Fan wang* precepts at the beginning of their twelve-year training period. He also asked that they be allowed to receive *Ssu fen lü* ordinations at Tōdaiji after they had completed their training on Mount Hiei. Thus while the *Fan wang* ordination qualified the candidate to be a Tendai monk, the *Ssu fen lü* ordination was taken only as an expedient measure to benefit other sentient beings,[1] not for any spiritual qualification it might bestow on the Tendai monk. The *Ssu fen lü* ordination would enable Tendai monks to live in harmony with the monks of Nara and to avoid disputes over monastic discipline, seniority, or the procedures for holding assemblies. Because the *Ssu fen lü* ordination did not qualify a person to be a Tendai monk and was taken primarily to smooth relations with other sentient beings, Saichō called it a 'provisional Hīnayāna ordination' (*keju shōkai* 假受小戒).

Saichō died before the court had agreed to his proposals and thus never saw them put into effect. Administering *Ssu fen lü* ordinations to Tendai monks proved to be unworkable and was quickly abandoned by his successors. After the bitter debates which had occurred between Saichō and the Nara schools, the monks of the two sides could not forget their differences so readily. The very concept of a provisional *Ssu fen lü* ordination provoked heated arguments between the Tendai and Nara monks.[2] The terms 'provisional' and 'Hīnayāna' implied that the *Ssu fen lü* ordination was inferior.

If Saichō's proposal for provisional Hīnayāna ordinations had been adopted, it would have placed Tendai monks at a disadvantage in their relations with Nara monks. From the point of view of the Nara schools,

---

[1] Many Chinese and Japanese monks called the *Ssu fen lü* precepts Hīnayāna precepts (*shōjōkai*) because they primarily helped the person who was ordained with them. However, the *vinaya* master Daoxuan had argued that the *Ssu fen lü* precepts were consistent with Mahāyāna practice and could be taken for the purpose of benefiting others (Miyabayashi Akihiko, "Dōsen no sangakukan," *Bukkyō no jissen genri*, p. 199). Saichō's argument that the *Ssu fen lü* ordination should be taken in order to help others thus relied partly on Daoxuan's arguments. Daoxuan, however, would never have agreed with Saichō's position that the *Fan wang* precepts could replace the *Ssu fen lü* precepts in full (*gusokukai* 具足戒) ordinations.

[2] *Kenkairon, DZ* 1:79–82.

Tendai monks could not be considered full-fledged monks until they had taken the *Ssu fen lü* ordination. Thus the twelve or more years which Tendai monks spent on Mount Hiei would not count towards their monastic seniority. Arguments could easily arise when monks from Nara and Mount Hiei sat together at large state-sponsored assemblies, since seniority determined seating order. To prevent such an occurrence, Saichō had asked the Tendai monks to defer to the Nara monks and sit with the novices who had been initiated in accordance with the *Ssu fen lü* whenever Tendai and Nara monks met in joint assemblies.[3] Consequently a Tendai monk who had been ordained with the *Fan wang* precepts ten years earlier might be required to sit in an inferior position to a Nara monk who had just received his full *Ssu fen lü* ordination. This arrangement obviously did not win much support from the Tendai monks. Furthermore, Saichō's plan would have worked to the disadvantage of Tendai monks in their competition with the Nara monks for government honors and offices since seniority was an important consideration in these awards.

In order to remedy some of these problems, Saichō's disciple Kōjō asked Ōtomo no Kunimichi, councilor at court and lay administrator for the Tendai School, to make certain changes in Saichō's plan.[4] As a result of Ōtomo's efforts, Tendai and Nara monks were not permitted to take each other's ordinations. When they sat together, Tendai monks were to mark their seniority from the date of their *Fan wang* ordination. Nara monks would count their seniority from the date of their *Ssu fen lü* ordination as before. Because the two groups of monks were to sit together at court-sponsored meetings, neither group was treated as if it were superior to the other. The prohibition on Tendai monks receiving *Ssu fen lü* ordinations effectively ended any possibility of provisional Hīnayāna ordinations for Tendai monks. These decisions were made shortly after Saichō's death, sometime between 823 and 828.[5] Prohibitions on monks receiving both sets of ordinations were again issued by the court in 877.[6] At that time the court was not very worried about possible trouble between the two groups of monks; rather, it was concerned with controlling and registering the monks who were ordained. Two sets of records with two separate procedures for maintaining them

---

[3] See footnote 178 of Chapter 8 and *DZ* 1:112–13.

[4] *Denjutsu isshinkaimon*, *DZ* 1:596–98.

[5] Ishida, *Kairitsu no kenkyū*, pp. 306–7.

[6] Takagi, *Heian jidai Hokke Bukkyōshi kenkyū*, p. 26; the *Engishiki* edict is quoted in Umeda, *Nihon shūkyō seidoshi: jōdaihen*, p. 458.

would have allowed many unauthorized people into the orders unless bureaucratic procedures were very strict.

With very few exceptions, Tendai monks never did receive *Ssu fen lü* ordinations. One isolated case is that of Shūei 宗叡 (809–884).[7] At age fourteen he climbed Mount Hiei and was initiated. Although no record of a *Fan wang* ordination for Shūei during this period has survived, he must have received one since he remained on Mount Hiei until he was past the age of twenty. When he was twenty-three he traveled to Nara where he received a *Ssu fen lü* ordination. He then studied Hossō doctrines under Gien 義演 at Kōkōji 廣岡寺. Several years later he returned to Mount Hiei, received a second *Fan wang* ordination and studied Tendai doctrines again. Later he became a Shingon monk and studied in China. Although nowhere did Shūei specifically state that he received a provisional Hīnayāna ordination (*keju shōkai*), his earlier stay and subsequent return to Mount Hiei suggest that he might have taken the *Ssu fen lü* ordination as an expedient measure to aid him in studying Hossō doctrine. However, Shūei did not precisely follow the procedure suggested by Saichō because he received the *Fan wang* precepts a second time after he had studied Hossō teachings.

The only other recorded case of a provisional ordination from the early Heian period which has come to light concerns the Tendai yearly ordinands who were to serve at the Kamo 賀茂 and Kasuga 春日 shrines.[8] A proposal by Kansei 觀栖 dated 887 suggested that they be allowed to take Hīnayāna ordinations. Unfortunately, it is unclear whether Kansei's proposal was ever put into practice and whether it consisted of a Hīnayāna ordination which was taken after the *Fan wang* ordination. These two obscure cases represent the only examples of monks attempting to put Saichō's plan for provisional Hīnayāna ordinations into effect during the ninth century.

This alteration of Saichō's plans left later Tendai monks with a difficult problem. How could they justify their abandonment of provisional *Ssu fen lü* ordinations? In the late seventeenth century, a group of monks at the Anrakuin 安樂院 Chapel on Mount Hiei led by Myōryū 妙立 (1637–1690) and Reikū 靈空 (1653–1739) attempted to reintroduce the *Ssu fen lü* precepts into Japanese Tendai practice. At that time, the interpretation of Saichō's proposal of 'provisional Hīnayāna ordinations' became a major issue. Eventually the dissident factions of the Tendai

---

[7] *BD* 3:2212–13; Ishida, *Kairitsu no kenkyū*, p. 321.

[8] This incident is discussed further in Chapter 14.

School returned to the traditional use of the *Fan wang* ordination and abandoned their attempt to institute the provisional Hīnayāna ordination. However, confusion and controversy have continued to surround this aspect of Saichō's proposals.

These controversies concern two major issues: when a monk should receive the *Ssu fen lü* ordination and why Saichō proposed that Tendai monks receive the *Ssu fen lü* ordination.

The question of when a Tendai monk was to take the *Ssu fen lü* ordination traditionally focussed on the definition of the term *tokugō* 得業. In the *Shijōshiki* the term probably referred to the completion of the twelve-year training period on Mount Hiei. Some Tokugawa period Tendai scholars, however, insisted that this interpretation was a superficial one which distorted Saichō's true intentions. They claimed that a careful reading of the *Kenkairon, Ganmon,* and *Yuikai (Final Admonitions)* indicated that Saichō intended *tokugō* to be understood as the attainment of *rokukon sōji* 六根相似 (the stage when all six of the practitioner's faculties or senses were pure).[9] Since this was an advanced stage which few, if any, monks could attain during the Latter Period of the Dharma (*mappō*), the performance of provisional Hīnayāna ordinations became a theoretical, not a practical problem. Tendai monks could thus claim that they were following Saichō's instructions even though they did not actually grant the Hīnayāna ordination.

Arguments supporting this position usually depended upon forced interpretations of the texts. Passages from the *Shijōshiki, Kenkairon,* and *Denjutsu isshinkaimon* all used the term *tokugō* to refer to the completion of the twelve-year course of study on Mount Hiei.[10] Saichō had argued that at the end of twelve years of training, even a monk with the dullest of faculties would have some spiritual merit to show for his efforts.[11] Completing the training course indicated that the Tendai monk was no longer a bodhisattva monk in the early states of his training (*shoshugō bosatsusō* 初修業菩薩僧); rather he had become a bodhisattva monk of long standing (*kushugō bosatsusō* 久修業菩薩僧). Thus he was no longer in danger of backsliding and could receive the *Ssu fen lü* ordination without fear of being adversely affected by the Hīnayāna precepts.

The second problem concerns Saichō's reasons for proposing that

---

9 For a definition of *rokukon sōji* see footnote 5 of Chapter 3
10 The term *tokugō* is discussed in footnote 110 of Chapter 8.
11 *Kenkairon, DZ* 1:153–54.

Tendai monks provisionally receive *Ssu fen lü* ordinations. A number of practical reasons are evident. The *Ssu fen lü* ordination had traditionally been used to confer monkhood in China and Japan. The *Ssu fen lü* precepts provided the advanced Tendai practitioner with a detailed set of provisions to govern his conduct once he had left Mount Hiei. In contrast, the *Fan wang* precepts were not as detailed and traditionally had not been used as the primary regulations for monastic conduct.

Seniority was counted from the time of a monk's *Ssu fen lü* ordination. Appointments as lecturer (*kōji*) or reader (*dokushi*) required that the appointee be conversant with the Hīnayāna precepts.[12] In addition, Saichō may have been attempting to bridge some of his differences with the Nara monks by including *Ssu fen lü* precepts and ordinations in his proposals. In the *Kenkairon,* Saichō attempted to indicate similarities between his proposals and Chien-chen's teachings on the precepts.[13] Some modern Tendai scholars such as Fukuda Gyōei 福田堯穎 and Kimura Shūshō 未村周照 have suggested that Saichō's proposal that the *Ssu fen lü* ordination be used as an expedient was primarily a conciliatory gesture to the Nara monks.[14] They have argued that once circumstances changed, the Tendai School could abandon provisional Hīnayāna ordinations without violating Saichō's proposals.

Their position ignored an important aspect of Saichō's thought. In making his proposals, Saichō may also have been trying to reconcile some differences between his plan and the position of the Chinese T'ien-t'ai School. Chih-i and Chan-jan had maintained that if a candidate received the Hīnayāna precepts with a Mahāyāna mind, he could observe those precepts as a Mahāyāna practitioner. Since the *Ssu fen lü* precepts ultimately were devised to lead people to Buddhahood, they potentially revealed that final goal. This explanation was called the *kaie* 開會 (revealing and harmonizing) interpretation of the precepts.

The term *kaie* refers to the One-vehicle teaching of the *Lotus Sūtra.* According to this teaching the Buddha's statements about the Three Vehicles in other *sūtras* can all be revealed to be in harmony with the teaching of the one ultimate vehicle which leads to Buddhahood. Chih-i used the principle of *kaie* as a basic mode in his classifications of the Buddha's teachings. All of the Buddha's teachings, even Hīnayāna

---

[12] Ibid., pp. 150–51.
[13] Ibid., pp. 78–81.
[14] Kimura Shūshō, "Keju shōkai ni tsuite," *TG* 8 (1968): 35; and Fukuda, *Tendaigaku gairon,* p. 604.

doctrines, pointed towards and could be shown to potentially contain the Buddha's final teaching which was fully revealed in the *Lotus Sūtra*. When this teaching was applied to the precepts, it resulted in a rationale which enabled monks who considered themselves to be Mahāyāna Buddhists to observe the *Ssu fen lü* precepts. Although the precepts had Hīnayāna origins, they could still be observed by Mahāyāna monks because they ultimately pointed towards Buddhahood.

Nowhere did Saichō clearly state that he used a *kaie* interpretation of the *Ssu fen lü* precepts. Since Chien-chen and Tao-hsüan had both interpreted the precepts using elements of the *kaie,* this type of exegesis had become influential among Nara scholars.[15] In fact Saichō argued against an attempt by the Nara monks to use a *kaie* interpretation of the *Ssu fen lü* based on the *Lotus Sūtra*.[16] Saichō claimed that the Nara interpretation would require a monk to spend eons following Hīnayāna practices rather than striving to attain the Mahāyāna goal of Buddhahood in the immediate future.

On the basis of such evidence, Ishida Mizumaro 石田瑞麿 argued that Saichō completely abandoned the *kaie* interpretation of the *Ssu fen lü* precepts and relied primarily on a strict and literal reading of the *Fan wang ching's* prohibition of Hīnayāna teachings.[17] Ishida supported his argument by proving that the *Lotus Sūtra* played only a secondary role in Saichō's position on the precepts. As a consequence, he maintained that Saichō's proposal for provisional *Ssu fen lü* ordinations for Tendai monks was derived solely from a concern to help others and was not influenced by the *kaie* style of interpretations.

Ishida's position suffered from two shortcomings. First, he was very selective in the evidence which he considered. At the same time Saichō was composing the *Kenkairon,* he was also writing extensively about the *Lotus Sūtra* and Tendai teachings. These works included passages which referred to *kaie* theory.[18] It is unlikely that Saichō would have applied *kaie* theory in one case but not in the other. For example, in the *Hokke shūku* Saichō discussed the importance of Mahāyāna precepts

---

[15] Chien-chen's view of the precepts involves a number of complicated problems, but many scholars believe that he was significantly influenced by T'ien-t'ai teachings. See Ishida, *Kairitsu no kenkyū,* pp. 55–104, and Tokuda Myōhon, "Ganjin wajō no Risshū," *Nanto Bukkyō* 24 (1970): 39–49. Tao-hsüan's commentary does not survive; however it is quoted in the *Kenkairon* (*DZ* 1:134–35).

[16] *Kenkairon, DZ* 1:149.

[17] Ishida, *Kairitsu no kenkyū,* pp. 195–217.

[18] *Hokke shūku, DZ* 3:18; *Shugo kokkaishō, DZ* 2:171. Also see Taira Ryōshō's critique of Ishida, "Enkai no en," *TG* 8 (1968): 3–11.

and then noted that all of the Buddha's provisional teachings potentially contained his ultimate teaching.[19] Saichō's lengthy citations of the *Chu fa wu hsing ching* 諸法無行經 (*Sarvadharmāpravṛttinirdeśasūtra*) in the *Kenkairon* shed further light on his view of the *Ssu fen lü*.[20] This *sūtra*, translated by Kumārajīva, expounded the nature of things as they really are (*shohō jissō* 諸法實相). Episodes from it were incorporated into the *Ta chih tu lun* (*Mahāprajñāpāramitopadeśa*), and Chih-i mentioned it in the *Fa hua hsüan i* and the *Mo ho chih kuan*.[21] Although the contents of the *sūtra* were potentially important for T'ien-t'ai doctrine, it was in fact rarely referred to in T'ien-t'ai works until Saichō quoted it extensively in the *Kenkairon*. Saichō cited it in his reply to the attempts of the monastic leaders of Nara to judge the depth of Tendai monks' practices. The passages quoted concerned the nonsubstantiality of all practices. According to the text, a monk should not rejoice at hearing about strict observance of the precepts, nor should he feel repugnance at hearing about violations of monastic discipline. He should not reject the Hīnayāna and cling to the Mahāyāna. Since all such concepts are nonsubstantial, they are equal. This teaching was consistent with a *kaie* interpretation of the precepts, but not with an outright and complete rejection of *Ssu fen lü* precepts. Included in the *sūtra* was a warning that its teachings were not suitable for bodhisattvas in the early stages of practice (*shinbotchi* 新發意) because the teachings could adversely affect beginning bodhisattva monks.[22] Thus the teachings of the *Chu fa wu hsing ching* were only appropriate for the advanced bodhisattva monk who had provisionally received a *Ssu fen lü* ordination. The advanced monk was capable of understanding a *kaie* interpretation of the precepts. For such a monk the *Ssu fen lü* could even serve as a Mahāyāna document. By following the practices described in it, he could benefit others.

Secondly, Ishida's reading of the *Kenkairon* was, at times, almost too literal. Although he correctly noted that Saichō had not specifically advocated a *kaie* interpretation of the *Ssu fen lü* precepts, his assertion that Saichō had completely rejected this interpretation must be questioned. The *Kenkairon* was a polemical work, written to refute the charges raised by the monastic leaders of Nara (*sōtō*). Perhaps because the *sōtō* did not wish to argue points of Tendai doctrine with the leading advocate

---

[19] *DZ* 3:272–73.
[20] *T* no. 650; *DZ* 1:145–48, 181–95. The quotations comprise about one-tenth of the *Kenkairon*.
[21] *TZ, Mo ho chih kuan* 2:36; and *TZ, Fa hua hsüan i* 4:180.
[22] Quoted in *Kenkairon, DZ* 1:182.

of it in Japan, Saichō, they did not dwell upon the issue of Saichō's seeming neglect of the *kaie* interpretation of Buddhist teachings.[23] In addition, the *sōtō* were not confident of their mastery of the T'ien-t'ai works which had only recently been copied and distributed to the temples in Nara. Since Saichō's position on the precepts differed significantly from the traditional Chinese T'ien-t'ai position, he probably did not raise the subject of the *kaie* interpretation himself. An extensive discussion of the *kaie* exegesis of the precepts might have involved Saichō in an embarrassing discussion of the orthodoxy of his interpretation of T'ien-t'ai teachings.

Sixty years before Saichō submitted his proposals to court, Chien-chen and his disciples had introduced the *kaie* interpretation of the precepts to Nara.[24] During Saichō's lifetime, Risshū monks in Nara were still influenced by the *kaie* view of the *Ssu fen lü* precepts. Saichō and the Risshū monks both used elements of the *kaie* method of exegesis. What then were the major differences between the positions of Saichō and the Nara monks?

First, Saichō argued that the *Fan wang* ordination was sufficient to qualify the ordinand as a monk. In accordance with Chinese Buddhist tradition, the Nara monks believed that only a properly performed *Ssu fen lü* ordination could qualify a candidate as a monk. Saichō's position thus drastically reduced the importance of the *Ssu fen lü* ordination. Instead of being the basis of monastic practice, the Hīnayāna ordination was treated as an option which an advanced monk might take in order to benefit others.

Second, Saichō deferred use of the *kaie* interpretation of the precepts until a monk was sufficiently advanced to understand it and was no longer in danger of backsliding toward Hīnayāna tendencies. In contrast, the Nara monks maintained that a person could take the *Ssu fen lü* precepts with a Mahāyāna mind and not be in any danger of backsliding because of the Hīnayāna origins of the precepts.

Third, Saichō's repeated references to the *Ssu fen lü* precepts as Hīnayāna precepts angered the monks of Nara. In China and Japan almost all monks had considered themselves Mahāyāna Buddhists. Even monks who studied Hīnayāna works such as the *Chü she lun*

---

[23] The arguments of the *sōtō* exist only as quotations in the *Kenkairon*. These quotations are sufficiently extensive, however, to demonstrate that the *sōtō* referred only briefly to the *kaie* interpretation of the precepts (see footnote 16 of this chapter) in their attacks on Saichō.

[24] For Tendai elements, in Chien-chen's thought, such as the *kaie* method of exegesis, see Ishida, *Kairitsu no kenkyū*, pp, 55–104.

(*Abhidharmakośa*) considered themselves to be Mahāyāna practitioners. *Ssu fen lü* masters such as Daoxuan, Chien-chen, and Buan had long argued that the *Ssu fen lü* precepts were at least partly Mahāyāna (*buntsū daijō* 分通大乘). When the term 'Hīnayāna' was applied to a tradition in China and Japan, it was almost always used in a derogatory fashion. For example, the Ch'eng-shih (Jap. Jōjitsu) tradition declined in China after the San-lun master Chi-tsang 吉藏 convincingly argued that it consisted of Hīnayāna teachings. The systems with which the Tendai, Hossō, Sanron and Kegon schools classified Buddhist teachings (*kyōhan* 教判) all considered Hīnayāna Buddhism to be the least profound form of Buddhism. Consequently, when Saichō insisted that the *Ssu fen lü* precepts were Hīnayāna precepts, he attacked the validity of the religious practices followed by the monks of Nara.

The difference between the positions of Saichō and the Nara monks may also be attributed to a difference in their approach to the classification of Buddhist doctrines (*kyōhan*). Chinese T'ien-t'ai masters used both affirmative and negative interpretations of *kyōhan* to describe the relationship of the ultimate teaching (*jitsukyō* 實教) to provisional teachings (*gonkyō* 權教).[25] The affirmative approach was called 'opening the provisional to reveal the ultimate' (*kaigon kenjitsu* 開權顯實). Since there was only one ultimate goal, all other Buddhist teachings eventually led to it and could be considered as being potentially Perfect. Chih-i relied heavily on this interpretation in devising a system which would encompass the various schools and movements of Chinese Buddhism which existed during his lifetime. Chien-chen's view of the precepts was almost certainly influenced by Chih-i's inclusive approach towards Buddhist teachings. However, this approach had a hidden danger. If applied indiscriminately, it encompassed all teachings, and the distinction between Perfect and provisional teachings could be blurred and lost.

Consequently, Chih-i devised a negative approach to emphasize the difference between the various teachings which was called 'discarding the provisional and establishing the ultimate' (*haigon ryūjitsu* 廢權立實). This approach was later used extensively by Chan-jan to defend the T'ien-t'ai School against the claims of the Fa-hsiang and Hua-yen schools. Chan-jan also argued that the *Lotus Sūtra* was superior to all other

---

[25] See Andō Toshio [*Tendai shōgu shisōron* (Kyoto: Hōzōkan, 1953), pp. 38–56] for a discussion of Chih-i's use of the two approaches to *kyōhan*. The two approaches were sometimes used to characterize the difference between Chinese and Japanese Tendai, with Chinese T'ien-t'ai being more positive toward other teachings, while Japanese Tendai was more negative (Andō Toshio, *Tendaigaku,* p. 4).

sūtras and that its teachings surpassed the eightfold classification system (the four methods of conversion and the four Dharmas of conversion) which Chih-i had formulated. Saichō studied under two of Chan-jan's disciples while in China. The influence of their sectarianism appeared in Saichō's exchanges with Tokuitsu[26] and in the proposals in the *Shijōshiki*. But this approach, if excessively applied, might lead a person to postulate an unbridgeable gap between the Perfect and provisional teachings.

In order to formulate his interpretations of the precepts, Saichō had to balance the exclusive and inclusive forms of Tendai exegesis. His proposal for a provisional Hīnayāna ordination (*keju shōkai*) was probably an attempt to move from a position which excluded the *Ssu fen lü* precepts toward a more inclusive formulation of the precepts. However, only after Tendai monks were sufficiently prepared to withstand any temptations the Nara Schools might offer, was Saichō prepared to reveal to them the Mahāyāna potential of the *Ssu fen lü* precepts.

In conclusion, when Saichō submitted his petitions concerning the *Fan wang* precepts, his most immediate concern was to insure the future of the Tendai School by removing it from under the jurisdiction of the Sōgō (Office of Monastic Affairs). At the same time, he was also concerned with reformulating Tendai Buddhist practices so that they might lead directly to Buddhahood during the practitioner's lifetime. To achieve this end he wanted to sequester Tendai students on Mount Hiei for twelve years of intensive practice.

During the last years of his life, Saichō focussed his attention on the precepts, the most basic element of the threefold learning (precepts, meditation, wisdom). He believed that if he could purge all Hīnayāna elements from the precepts, he would eliminate a major reason why Tendai monks backslid in their practice and defected from the Tendai School. Saichō intended his reforms of monastic discipline and administration to be the first and most basic step in his program to reformulate all the practices of his school so that they would reflect the doctrines of the Perfect teaching. In addition to reforming the precepts, Saichō probably intended to revise the traditional Tendai meditation and doctrinal systems, possibly by supplementing them with Esoteric practices and teachings. However, he died before he could complete his plans.

Saichō's rejection of the Hīnayāna *Ssu fen lü* precepts was not absolute. Like many of his Chinese T'ien-t'ai predecessors, Saichō believed

---

[26] *Shugo kokkaishō. DZ* 2:203–4, 214.

that the *Ssu fen lü* precepts could be used in Mahāyāna practice. However, he differed from most other T'ien-t'ai thinkers by insisting that the use of *Ssu fen lü* precepts and ordinations be postponed until the Tendai monk was so advanced in his practice that he would not be adversely affected by the Hīnayāna origins of the *Ssu fen lü*.

Saichō interpreted the *Fan wang* precepts in accordance with the teachings of the *Lotus Sūtra* and Tendai Buddhism; consequently, he referred to the *Fan wang* precepts as the Perfect precepts (*enkai*). Several centuries after Saichō's death, a movement began in the Tendai School to deemphasize the role of the *Fan wang* precepts as Tendai precepts in favor of the more ambiguous formless precepts of the *Lotus Sūtra*.[27] This interpretation, however, ignored the importance which Saichō had placed on strict adherence to the *Fan wang* precepts.

Saichō defended his proposals by arguing that the teachings and practices advocated by the Nara schools were no longer valid for the period in Buddhist history during which he lived. Moreover, Saichō argued that the religious faculties of the Japanese people had sufficiently matured so that they no longer required the provisional teachings advocated by the Nara schools. New practices which reflected the Perfect teachings of the Tendai School had to be instituted.

Saichō's statements concerning the importance of Tendai teachings and practices for the Japanese people are found in both the *Kenkairon* and in Saichō's works criticizing Tokuitsu. The unifying theme in the works written during the last decade of Saichō's life lies in Saichō's concern with the defense and formulation of Tendai practices and doctrines. Saichō's works criticizing Tokuitsu defend Tendai meditation and teachings. The *Kenkairon* defends Saichō's proposals concerning the precepts. Together, these works define Saichō's position on the threefold learning of the Tendai School.

---

[27] See chapter 11.

CHAPTER ELEVEN

SAICHŌ'S SOURCES FOR THE PERFECT PRECEPTS:
THE *LOTUS SŪTRA* AND THE *FAN WANG CHING*

Saichō's thought on the precepts was mainly derived from two *sū-tras*. The first was the *Fan wang ching*. In the *Shijōshiki*, Saichō clearly indicated that the ten major and forty-eight minor precepts of the *Fan wang ching* were to replace the two-hundred fifty precepts of the *Ssu fen lü* as the basis of Tendai monastic discipline.[1] In the *Kenkairon*, the *Fan wang ching* was quoted thirty-one times and mentioned three additional times. Many of the quotations appeared at key points in Saichō's argument. For example, Saichō cited the *sūtra* to prove that Tendai monks must not follow Hīnayāna teachings, that anyone might receive the *Fan wang* precepts, and that those precepts were followed by all Buddhas. Thus, the *Fan wang ching* played a vital role in shaping Saichō's thought.[2]

The second *sūtra* was the *Lotus Sūtra*. Saichō quoted it ten times and mentioned it three other times in the *Kenkairon*, placing it second only to the *Fan wang ching* in frequency of citation. The *Lotus Sūtra*, however, was not quoted at crucial points in his argument as was the *Fan wang ching*. Rather, its prominence in the *Kenkairon* was due to the central role it played in Tendai thought, not because it was directly applicable to the problems which Saichō was discussing.

The *Lotus Sūtra* includes a number of passages which could be read as advocating correct behavior and thus as a form of precepts. In order to understand Saichō's use of the *Lotus Sūtra* and the ways in which later scholars interpreted his references to it, these passages must be considered. Medieval Tendai scholars maintained the position that these passages described four types of precepts.[3] First were the

---

[1] *DZ* 1:17.

[2] For example, see *Kenkairon, DZ* 1:107–10. For a survey of Saichō's use of the *Fan wang ching*, see Ishida, *Kairitsu no kenkyū*, pp. 195–213. Ishida did not give the role of the *Lotus Sūtra* the attention it deserved, however.

[3] These categories are discussed in Chih-i's works; however Chih-i does not seem to have regarded them as precepts (Ishida, *Kairitsu no kenkyū*, pp. 170–72). The four categories as precepts are mentioned in the *Tendai Hokkeshū gakushōshiki mondō* (*DZ* 1:363).

The *Tendai Hokkeshū gakushōshiki mondō* (*DZ* 1:335–414) is an eight-fascicle work written in the form of a commentary on Saichō's *Rokujōshiki*. The text traditionally was attributed to Saichō; however, its authenticity has been questioned since the Tokugawa period (Ishida Mizumaro, "*Gakushōshiki mondō* no gisen ni tsuite," *IBK* 8 [1960]: 495). Ishida has

eternal unconditioned precepts which provided the foundation for all other sets of precepts, called the Lotus One-vehicle precepts (*Hokke ichijōkai* 法華一乘戒) or the Unmanifested Diamond precepts (*musa kongōhōkai* 無作金剛寶戒). These precepts were formless, without definite content, and based mainly on the second chapter of the *Lotus Sūtra*.[4] No direct reference to these precepts was found in Saichō's works.

In contrast to these formless precepts, the other three types did have definite contents. The second type concerned the behavior of those who preached the *Lotus Sūtra*. It was referred to in Saichō's *Final Admonitions* (*Yuikai*).[5]

The third type consisted of four requirements for people who would devote themselves to upholding the *Lotus Sūtra* (*jikyō* 持經) after the Buddha's death. They were to:

1. Be under the guardianship of the Buddhas.
2. Plant the roots of a multitude of virtues.
3. Enter the various correct concentrations.
4. Aspire to save all living beings.[6]

This list did not play an important role in Saichō's thought, and was referred to only in works by later scholars.

The fourth and most important type of precepts was found in the chapter on serene and pleasing activities (*Anrakugyōbon*) in the *Lotus Sūtra*.[7] This chapter described the ways in which bodhisattvas were to practice during the period of the decline of the Buddha's teaching. These practices consisted of general instructions for preaching and for adhering to the teachings of the *Lotus Sūtra* rather than actual rules. They were grouped into four categories: action, word, thought and vow. Saichō was concerned mainly with the actions which the *sūtra* recommended. These were divided into two sets. The first set was a description of the religious practices which a devout person should follow, such as quietly

---

pointed out differences in terminology and content between the *Mondō* and Saichō's works (ibid., pp. 495–99). The role of the *Lotus Sūtra* is emphasized in the *Mondō* while the *Fan wang* precepts are assigned a lesser place, a position which would de-emphasize the importance of strict adherence to the precepts. Because this position is found in some Tendai *hongaku* (Original Enlightenment) texts, Ishida suggested that the work had been written during the Nanboku Period (1331–1392). Recently Tamayama Jōgen has studied a manuscript from Tōji dated 1206 and argued that the *Mondō* was composed early in the thirteenth century (Tamayama Jōgen, "*Tendai Hokkeshū gakushōshiki mondō* [Tōji-hon] no shiteki kachi," *DDK*, pp. 739–763).

[4] Uesugi, *Nihon Tendaishi*, p. 652.
[5] See footnote 179 in Chapter 8.
[6] *Lotus* (Hurvitz trans.), pp. 332–33, with changes.
[7] Ibid., pp. 208–24.

meditating on things as they are 實相. The second set was a list of the many types of people whom a Mahāyāna Buddhist was to avoid. Commentators traditionally divided this set into ten types of people, the fifth of which consisted of those who sought Hīnayāna goals.

These precepts, usually called the *anrakugyō* 安樂行 (serene and pleasing activities), have long played as important role in T'ien-t'ai thought. They were among the teachings which Hui-ssu was said to have transmitted to Chih-i, and the subject of Hui-ssu's *Fa hua ching an lo hsing i* 法華經安樂行儀. Hui-ssu classified the *anrakugyō* as attributeless practices and believed that they were based on a permanent state of trance which affected all of a practioner's actions. The meditation which arose with the *anrakugyō* was thus very different from normal types of meditation which involved specific postures and actions.[8]

Saichō was interested in the *anrakugyō* for the same reason as his T'ien-t'ai predecessors. The *Anrakugyōbon* recommended retiring from the secular world and living a life of quiet meditation in a period when the Dharma was declining. When Saichō referred to the *Lotus Sūtra* in the *Kenkairon,* he usually cited the *anrakugyō* prohibition on consorting with those who sought Hīnayāna goals.[9] He also mentioned similar prohibitions found in the *Fan wang ching.*[10] Thus Saichō's use of the *anrakugyō* only reinforced the *Fan wang* precepts.[11]

The exact relationship between the *Lotus Sūtra* and the *Fan wang ching* was not discussed by Saichō or any of his immediate followers. By the Kamakura period, however, many scholars were vitally concerned with clarifying the relationship between the two works. Although even a causal reading of the *Kenkairon* revealed Saichō's extensive citations of the *Fan wang ching,* this text did not hold the highest position in the traditional Tendai classification of *sutras.* Because of its similarities

---

[8] Hui-ssu's work corresponds to *T* no. 1926. Studies of it can be found in: Ōchō Enichi, "Nangaku Eshi no Hokke zanmai," *Hokke shisō no kenkyū,* pp. 276–78; Yūki Reimon, "Nangaku Tendai to Shianrakugyō," *Tōhō shūkyō* 1, no. 6 (1954): 16–27; Hurvitz, *Chih-i,* pp. 86–100, 108–10.

[9] *Kenkairon, DZ* 1:73, 88, 133–43.

[10] Ibid., pp. 109–10.

[11] The *anrakugyō* were identified with the Perfect precepts by the Jōdo monk Ninkū 仁空 (1309–88) in his *Bonmōkyō giki monsho.* Before Ninkū, scholars apparently were not very interested in the topic. Recently Kotera Bun'ei ("Enkai to Shianrakugyō," *Bukkyō no jissen genri,* pp. 605–17) has argued that Saichō may also have identified the *anrakugyō* with the Perfect precepts. He based his argument on quotations from the *Rōzan hotsuganmon* 籠山發願 門 which Ninkū included in his work (*Tendaishū zensho* 15:11, 47, 594). Although Ninkū claimed that the *Rōzan hotsuganmon* was written by Saichō, the authenticity of the work is questionable.

with the *Hua yen ching* (*Avataṃsakasūtra*), Chih-i had considered it to be the capping *sūtra* for the *Hua yen ching*. In Tendai terms, this meant that it was a mixture of Unique and Perfect teachings (*betsuengyō* 別圓教) and thus inferior to the solely Perfect (*jun'en* 純圓) teachings of the *Lotus Sūtra*.

Since the *Lotus Sūtra* included no detailed rules which could adequately serve as precepts, certain factions of medieval Tendai monks claimed that the *Lotus Sūtra* taught formless precepts (*rikai* 理戒) or the essence of the Precepts (*kaitai* 戒體), while the precepts with form (*jikai* 事戒 or *kaisō* 戒相) were taught in the *Fan wang ching*.[12] These theories were in part a further development of Tendai theories on the *anrakugyō*. However, such an interpretation relegated the *Fan wang* precepts to a position of secondary importance. The formless precepts arose through the cultivation of proper attitudes and views. They were thus much more ambiguously defined than precepts with form, such as the *Fan wang* precepts, which consisted of specific and clearly defined rules. Too much emphasis on the formless precepts easily led to laxness in the observance of precepts.[13]

Scholars who awarded the preeminent role in the precepts to the *Lotus Sūtra* often emphasized the Ryōzen 靈山 (Vulture's Peak) lineage with Śākyamuni at the source of the precepts, and deemphasized the role of Rushana. For example, the Kamakura period work, the *Gakushōshiki mondō* attributed to Saichō, set forth a lineage originating with a transmission from Śākyamuni in Tahō (Prabhūtaratna) Nyorai's pagoda, and completely eliminated the role of Rushana.[14]

The relative emphasis placed on the *Lotus Sūtra* and the *Fan wang ching* was an important topic in the Tendai School during the Tokugawa period. The Tendai monk Keikō 敬光 (1740–1795) presented the various positions in his *Enkai fudan* 圓戒膚談. Monks of Rozanji 廬山寺 stressed the importance of the *Fan wang ching* while monks in the Kurodani 黑谷 lineage emphasized the importance of the *Lotus Sūtra*. Keikō believed that both positions were one-sided. He maintained that the *Lotus Sūtra* should be given precedence in discussions of the absolute formless precepts (*rikai* 理戒), but that the *Fan wang ching* should be

---

[12] Asai Endō, "Dengyō Daishi to Hokke shisō no renkan," in *Hokekyō no shisō to bunka,* ed. Sakamoto Yukio, *Hokekyō* kenkyū, vol. 1 (Kyoto: Heirakuji shoten, 1965), p. 581.

[13] Ishida, *Kairitsu no kenkyū*, pp. 232–33.

[14] *DZ* 1:369–75. The Ryōzen lineage is also discussed in Chapter 13.

[15] Ishida, *Kairitsu no kenkyū*, pp. 218–20.

given precedence in discussions of the precepts with form (*jikai* 事戒).[15] The relative importance of the two *sūtras* in Saichō's view of the Perfect precepts is still a matter of controversy among modern Japanese scholars.[16]

How did Saichō use the *Lotus Sūtra* and the *Fan wang ching* in his discussions of the precepts? Since the *Kenkairon* was a polemical work and was not concerned with presenting a detailed analysis of the precepts, advocates of the various positions discussed above have relied on forced interpretations and readings of certain passages in the text. The opening verses of the *Kenkairon* have often been subjected to this type of exegesis. Several centuries of debate have failed to produce a consensus on the proper interpretation of these lines.[17] In the following discussion, the roles and relations of the two *sūtras* will be analyzed from the broader perspective of how they were used in Saichō's works on the precepts.

Saichō clearly advocated strict adherence to the *Fan wang* precepts. Later attempts to substitute the *Lotus Sūtra's* precepts for them were in violation of Saichō's intention. His only reference in the *Kenkairon* to the precepts of the *Lotus Sūtra* concerned the *anrakugyō* proscription on consorting with Hīnayāna practitioners. Saichō thus awarded the *Fan wang ching* a higher status than had Chih-i, who relegated it to the status of Kegon teachings, a mixture of Unique and Perfect teachings. In contrast, Saichō followed Ming-kuang in regarding the *Fan wang* precepts as solely Perfect precepts.[18] Saichō had studied the *Fan wang* precepts and read Tao-hsüan's commentary on the *Fan wang ching* when he was younger. Saichō's first work, the *Ganmon,* had been influenced by the *Fan wang ching.* Saichō was thus ready to follow Ming-

---

[16] Fukuda (*Tendaigaku gairon,* pp. 568–76) has argued that Saichō relied mainly on the *Lotus Sūtra* for his position on the precepts. Ishida (*Kairitsu no kenkyū,* pp. 222–25) has criticized Fukuda, arguing that Saichō mainly relied on the *Fan wang ching.* Taira ["Enkai no en ni tsuite," *TG* 8 (1968): 3–11] and Kotera ["*Kenkairon* kikyōge kō," *Ryūkoku daigaku Bukkyō bunka kenkyū kiyō* 7 (1968): 105–8] have in turn criticized Ishida. The position taken in the following discussion is closest to that of Taira and Kotera. Saichō's disciple Kōjō also tended to de-emphasize the role of the *Fan wang ching*; see chapter 15 for a description of Kōjō's position.

[17] See footnote 16 for references.

[18] Taira, "Enkai no en," p. 4. Chih-i and Ming-kuang are discussed in Chapter 12. In the *Shugo kokkaishō* (*DZ* 2:608–30), Saichō defended the Kegon One-vehicle teaching. However, he clearly distinguished between the doctrines of the *Lotus Sūtra* and the *Hua yen ching* in the *Hokke shūku* (*DZ* 3:38, 244). Although Saichō often referred to the *Fan wang* precepts as the Perfect precepts (*enkai*), he also occasionally called them the Unique and Perfect precepts (*betsuenkai*), indicating that he was aware of their relationship to the Kegon tradition (*Kenkairon, DZ* 1:133). For some of the traditional Tendai criticisms of the Kegon tradition, see Hurvitz, *Chih-i,* pp. 231–32, 245–46, 262–67.

kuang in considering the *Fan wang* precepts to be Perfect precepts.

Saichō realized that in Japan the *Fan wang* precepts had traditionally been taken by monks after they had received the *Ssu fen lü* precepts. Only by applying the Perfect teachings (*engyō* 圓教) of the Tendai School to the *Fan wang* precepts did Saichō arrive at his interpretation of the precepts. In the *Kenkairon* Saichō stated his position:

> The government-appointed monastic officials declare in their petition: "The Mahāyāna precepts have long been transmitted. The eminent monks of China and the famous monks of Japan have transmitted them without a break until today."

> I (Saichō) answer: "Although the *Fan wang* precepts were transmitted in times past, those who have taken them in Japan have not understood them in the Perfect sense (*en'i* 圓意). They have used the *Fan wang* rules with the *śrāvaka* precepts. When the (*Fan wang* precepts) are used with the *śrāvaka* rules, how can a person help but violate (the *Fan wang* precept prohibiting one from thinking of Hīnayāna subjects for even) an instant?[19] The famous monks in this country have taken the Mahāyāna precepts, but they do not observe the Mahāyāna rainy season retreat.[20] Although they have a Mahāyāna assembly fortnightly, they do not separate themselves from those who have not yet taken the (bodhisattva) precepts.[21] Nor have they installed Mañjuśrī as elder (*jōza*) or transmitted the Unique and Perfect (*Fan wang*) rules (*betsuen no igi* 別圓之威儀)..."

> The monastic officials state in their petition: "What are these new precepts that are to be transmitted? What is wrong with the precepts which have been transmitted by our eminent monks? Why should we adopt the precepts conferred by this troublemaker (Saichō)?

> I (Saichō) reply: The precepts transmitted by the new (Tendai) School are the Perfect *Fan wang* precepts. (The teacher of the Perfect precepts) should possess the five Perfect virtues in order to be able to benefit those with Perfect One-vehicle faculties. You should know that unless you use the T'ien-t'ai commentary (by Chih-i), you will be hard pressed to explain the Perfect precepts

---

[19] *Fan wang ching, T* 24:1007 b.

[20] The Mahāyāna rainy season retreat is mentioned in the *Fan wang ching T* 24:1008a, and in Ming-kuang's commentary (*T* 40: 597a).

[21] See footnote 114 in Chapter 8 of this study; *Fan wang ching*, minor precept 37, *T* 24:1008a.

(*enkai*圓戒), Perfect seniority (*enrō* 圓臘), Perfect understanding (*enzō* 圓藏), Perfect meditation (*enzen* 圓禪), and Perfect wisdom (*en'e* 圓慧).[22]

The *Fan wang* precepts could not be understood as Perfect precepts until they had been interpreted according to the teachings of the *Lotus Sūtra* and the Tendai School. Such a view is not surprising since Saichō was defending the *Lotus Sūtra* in works such as the *Shugo kokkaishō* at the same time he was composing the *Kenkairon*. Saichō emphasized the role of the *Lotus Sūtra* by naming Śākyamuni Buddha the preceptor in the ordination ceremony[23] and by asserting that the Ryōzen lineage was valid for the precepts. Five years after his death, Saichō's disciples constructed a precepts platform with Śākyamuni and a Tahōtō (*stūpa* for Prabhūtaratna Tathāgata) occupying the central places on it.[24]

The *Fan wang ching* played the key role in the practice and interpretation of the Perfect precepts. However, the interpretation of the precepts was not complete until the Perfect sense of the *Lotus Sūtra* had been applied to them.[25] This did not mean, however, that the *Fan wang ching* could be ignored. Rather the *Fan wang ching* specified the contents of the precepts. Saichō did not elaborate on the relative value of the two *sūtras* because he believed that the two texts contained Perfect teachings preached by Buddhas who were essentially the same. Elements from the *Lotus Sūtra* and its capping *sūtra*, the *Kuan p'u hsien ching*, could be harmoniously combined with precepts from the *Fan wang ching* because the Perfect purport of all three works was the same.

---

[22] *DZ* 1:133–34. Other references to the Perfect significance of the precepts are found in ibid., pp. 109, 137. According to the *P'u sa chieh i su* attributed to Chih-i (*T* 40:568a), a monk who administered the precepts was expected to: (1) observe the precepts, (2) have at least ten year's seniority as a monk, (3) understand the texts on precepts, (4) be well-versed in meditation, and (5) thoroughly comprehend the profundities of literature on wisdom.

[23] *Jubosatsukaigi, DZ* 1:306–7; and *Kenkairon, DZ* 1:123–24.

[24] Asai, *Jōko Nihon Tendai,* p. 108.

[25] However, see Ishida, *Kairitsu no kenkyū,* pp. 201–6, for an argument that Saichō's use of the term 'Perfect' depends more on the *Fan wang ching* than on the *Lotus Sūtra*.

CHAPTER TWELVE

THE MAJOR INFLUENCES ON SAICHŌ'S
VIEW OF THE PRECEPTS

Many of Saichō's arguments in the *Kenkairon* were devoted to showing that his ideas had precedents in India, China and Japan. Because Saichō's proposals represented a break with traditional Buddhist attitudes towards monastic discipline, modern scholars also have devoted much effort to determining which traditions or scholars influenced Saichō. Their efforts have been complicated by the number of sources which Saichō cited and the way in which he used them to support his arguments.

In the second section of the *Kenkairon,* Saichō summarized the contents of the travel diary by Hsüan-tsang and quoted the travel diary by I-ching in an attempt to prove that "purely Mahāyāna temples" had previously existed in India.[1] These passages are typical of Saichō's method of argument and use of sources in the *Kenkairon.* Saichō's quotations were usually long and accurate, and to his credit, he rarely quoted a passage out of context in order to twist or obscure the meaning of the text. However, he sometimes did ignore relevant information which would have weakened his position. For example, I-ching noted that both Hīnayāna and Mahāyāna practitioners used the Hīnayāna precepts. Although this passage is found in the diary shortly after the section quoted in the *Kenkairon,* Saichō ignored it, and thus implied that monks at purely Mahāyāna temples used only Mahāyāna precepts.[2]

Saichō cited the travel diaries by Hsüan-tsang and I-ching in the *Kenkairon* only to support his contention that exclusively Mahāyāna temples had previously existed. Other aspects of his proposals were supported by quotations from other works. Saichō referred to a total of forty-seven different texts in the *Kenkairon.* While using each work to support a particular aspect of his argument, Saichō never relied exclusively on any one work to bring the various elements of his position together. The result was a very effective defense. Saichō marshalled an

---

[1] *DZ* 1:37–56.

[2] *DZ* 1:55–56. The relevant passage in I-ching's diary is translated by Takakusu Junjirō in *A Record of the Buddhist Religion as Practiced in India and the Malay Archipelago* (London: Clarendon Press, 1896; reprinted in Delhi: Munshiram Manoharlal, 1966), p. 14.

impressive array of sources to support his points. At the same time, he did not give his opponents àn easy target to attack since he never allowed his whole argument to rely on one particular work. By analyzing his opponents' attacks and by replying to various aspects of those attacks, Saichō was also able to avoid discussing the vulnerable aspects of his position. For example, Saichō argued that Mahāyāna monks existed and that they should have nothing to do with Hīnayāna teachings, supporting his position with quotations from the Buddhist canon; at the same time, however, he conveniently avoided a discussion of whether taking the *Fan wang* precepts alone were sufficient to qualify them as Mahāyāna monks.

Despite the care with which Saichō supported his arguments with precedents and scriptural references, he was aware that his overall position was, in fact, a departure from the past. In the *Kenkairon* he stated:

> Although the ten major precepts (of the *Fan wang ching*) have been conferred in times past, this has been in name only. Their (true) significance has not yet been transmitted. How do I know that their (true) significance has not been transmitted? Because people have not understood their Perfect meaning, and because people still practice them together with the Hīnayāna precepts.[3]

Elsewhere Saichō stated:

> The Perfect teaching's (*engyō*) interpretation of the three studies (precepts, meditation, wisdom) is still not complete. Although two of the studies have beginnings at least, no (Perfect explanation of the) precepts has yet emerged.[4]

When modern scholars began examining Saichō's works for the important influences on his thought, they were troubled by the variety of sources which he had used, and his seemingly ambivalent attitude toward precedents and predecessors. In addition, Saichō died before his proposals were approved, and thus never had an opportunity to explain the full implications of his proposals. Consequently, scholars have often had to base their discussions concerning Saichō's teachers and predecessors on forced interpretations of a few words or lines in polemical works such as Saichō's *Kenkairon* or Kōjō's *Denjutsu isshinkaimon*.

Modern scholars have advanced arguments attributing elements of

---

[3] *Kenkairon, DZ* 1:109.
[4] Ibid., p. 197.

Saichō's views on the precepts to a number of different teachers and sources. Among the most significant analyses advanced earlier in this century were Tokiwa Daijō's claim that Tao-hsüan's thought had a decisive influence on Saichō.[5] Another was Hosokawa Kōshō's theory that Saichō was influenced by Chien-chen's supposed opposition to government supervision of the monastic order and ordinations.[6] The arguments presented by Tokiwa and Hosokawa were based on insufficient evidence and are not widely accepted today.

In the remainder of this chapter, three other possible sources of Saichō's views on the precepts are considered. The first is the tendency in some early Mahāyāna texts and sets of bodhisattva precepts to denigrate the Hīnayāna tradition. The second is Chinese T'ien-t'ai views of the precepts, particularly those of Ming-kuang. Third is a trend among some Buddhist practitioners during the Nara period to ignore or criticize government ordinations. Although these were not the only influences on Saichō's views on the precepts, they are the ones which have best withstood the test of scholarly analysis.

Mahāyāna Criticisms of Hīnayāna Practice

Saichō did not cite any cases in which the bodhisattva precepts alone had been used to qualify an ordinand as a monk. However, recent research has indicated that some groups of early Mahāyāna believers may have used bodhisattva precepts to ordain themselves. Hirakawa Akira has argued that the early Mahāyāna groups probably developed around *stūpas* in India.[7] The leaders of these groups called themselves

---

[5] Tokiwa's argument is found in his book *Nihon Bukkyō no kenkyū* (Tokyo: Shunjūsha, 1943) pp. 369–499. Ishida Mizumaro has convincingly criticized Tokiwa's argument in *Kairitsu no kenkyū*, pp, 255–270.

[6] Hosokawa Kōshō, "Ganjin no ikkōsatsu," *Rekishi chiri* 76 (1940): 235–61. The Buddhist order had struggled to maintain its autonomy against the government in India and China. For a good survey of the problem, see Kenneth Ch'en, *The Chinese Transformation of Buddhism* (Princeton: Princeton University Press, 1973), pp. 65–124. Hosokawa maintained that Chien-chen hoped to preserve at least some of the order's autonomy. However, his evidence was scanty. Criticisms of Hosokawa's arguments are found in Ishida, *Kairitsu no kenkyū*, pp. 55–73; Andō Kōsei, *Ganjin* (Tokyo: Yoshikawa kōbunkan, 1967), pp. 191–206; and Tokuda Myōhon, "Tōshōdaiji kaidan kō," *Nanto Bukkyō* 24 (1959): 30–45. Although Tokuda is critical of Hosokawa's view of the precepts platform, he views Hosokawa's opinions on Chien-chen's concerns for the autonomy of the Buddhist order more favorably than do Andō and Ishida (Tokuda, *Risshū gairon*, pp. 543–47, 557–60).

[7] Hirakawa's discussions of the early Mahāyāna order can be found in: "Daijō Bukkyō kyōdan no kyōdanshiteki seikaku," in Miyamoto Shōson, ed. *Daijō Bukkyō no seiritsuteki kenkyū*, (Tokyo: Sanseidō, 1954), pp. 447–82; "Shoki daijō Bukkyō no kaigaku to shite no jūzendō," in Yoshimura Shūki, ed., *Bukkyō kyōdan no kenkyū* (Tokyo: Hyakkaen, 1968),

bodhisattvas, and recognized a distinction between lay (*zaike bosatsu* 在家菩薩) and monastic bodhisattvas (*shukke bosatsu* 出家菩薩). While lay bodhisattvas pledged their faith in the three refuges and observed the five lay precepts, monastic bodhisattvas began developing sets of rules of their own, the bodhisattva precepts.

Early versions of the bodhisattva precepts were based on the ten virtuous actions 十善, a list of ten practices conducive to wholesome behavior which first appeared in Hīnayāna literature. Early Mahāyāna practitioners then interpreted the ten virtuous acts as precepts or injunctions, and thus produced one of the earliest sets of bodhisattva precepts. The ten virtuous precepts 十善戒 are:

(1) abstention from taking life
(2) abstention from taking what is not given
(3) abstention from wrong conduct as regards sensuous pleasures
(4) abstention from lying speech
(5) abstention from malicious speech
(6) abstention from harsh speech
(7) abstention from indistinct prattling
(8) abstention from covetousness
(9) abstention from ill will
(10) abstention from wrong views[8]

This list of restrictions included many elements that were also found in the *Fan wang* precepts, the set of fifty-eight precepts which Saichō proposed to follow. Although the *Fan wang* precepts were compiled much later than the ten virtuous precepts, the two sets shared certain characteristics. Both sets were primarily concerned with moral issues. Little attention was paid to issues of dress, decorum and manners, subjects which had been treated at great length in the Hīnayāna precepts. Although subjects such as appropriate clothing for monks were discussed in the *Fan wang ching,* the work was more concerned with moral issues such as lying. In fact, Saichō had to point out to the monastic leaders of Nara that the *Fan wang* precepts would require Tendai monks

---

pp. 167–203; and *Shoki daijō Bukkyō no kenkyū* (Tokyo: Shunjūsha, 1969). An important article by Hirakawa has been translated into English by Unno Taitetsu under the title "The Rise of Mahāyāna Buddhism and Its Relationship to the Worship of Stūpas," *Memoirs of the Research Department of the Tōyō Bunko,* no. 22, pp. 58–106. Shizutani Masao has summarized and criticized Hirakawa's work in "Daijō kyōdan no seiritsu ni tsuite," *Bukkyō shigaku* 13 (1969): 146–74, 200–18; and 14 (1970): 32–49.

[8] Edward Conze, tr., *The Perfection of Wisdom in Eight Thousand Lines* (Bolinas, California: Four Seasons Foundation, 1973), p. 200. Hīnayāna precedents of the ten virtuous actions are discussed in Hirakawa, "Kaigaku to shite no jūzendō," pp. 117–78.

to shave their heads and wear robes.[9]

The Hīnayāna precepts were designed to fit the needs of certain classes of people. According to the *Ssu fen lü,* the *vinaya* most often followed in China, monks were to adhere to a set of 250 precepts, nuns a set of 348, novices a set of ten, probationary nuns a set of eight, and laymen and laywomen a set of five. In contrast, the ten virtuous precepts could be applied to any group of practitioners. There were differences in interpretation, however. For example, the third precept was sometimes formulated to state that all sexual activity was banned, a restriction which applied only to clergy. At other times, it banned only illicit sexual activity and thus applied only to laymen and laywomen since sexual intercourse between married couples was permitted. The ten virtuous precepts were usually viewed as rules which were concerned with moral and religious activity for all people, not as a set of precepts suited only for people of a certain social group, such as monks.

Although some later works on the bodhisattva precepts distinguished between precepts for the clergy and laity, the *Fan wang ching* did not do so. Instead, it mixed precepts which were suitable for only monks and nuns with those suitable for only laymen. For example, the fifth major precept in the *Fan wang ching* prohibited the selling of liquor, a restriction which was applicable only to laymen since monks were not allowed to touch gold or silver.[10] The forty-sixth minor precept prescribed the proper decorum to be observed when lecturing to others, a subject directed towards monks since laymen had few opportunities to preach.[11] The majority of *Fan wang* precepts were suitable for both monks and laymen. Because the *Fan wang* precepts included precepts directed towards a variety of audiences, they were often administered to both laymen and monks as a supplement to ordinations involving the Hīnayāna precepts.[12] One of Saichō's major tasks in the *Kenkairon* was to prove

[9] *Kenkairon, DZ* 1:117–21. Many other differences between the bodhisattva and Hīnayāna precepts could be mentioned. A summary of them can be found in Tsuchihashi, "Daijōkai to shōjōkai," Nihon Bukkyō gakkai (ed.), *Bukkyō ni okeru kai no mondai* (Kyoto: Heirakuji shoten, 1967) pp. 112–28.

[10] *T* 24:1004c. Chih-i (*JZ* 15:841) claimed that this precept applied to both monks and laymen, but gave no explanation as to how it would apply to monks.

[11] *T* 24:1009c. Chih-i's commentary (*JZ* 15:867) claims that this precept applied only to monks, nuns and novices. Sakaino Kōyō [*Shina Bukkyō seishi* (Tokyo: Sakaino Kōyō hakase ikō kankōkai, 1935), pp. 842–43] lists the *Fan wang* precepts according to whether they apply to laymen, monks or both groups. However, commentaries on the *Fan wang ching* often did not agree about the status of many of the precepts.

[12] The *Fan wang* precepts were still conferred as a supplement to the Hīnayāna precepts in China earlier this century. See Holmes Welch, *The Practice of Chinese Buddhism* (Cambridge: Harvard University Press, 1967) pp. 285–296, 381–85.

that the *Fan wang* precepts could be administered in such a way that they differentiated between clergy and laity.[13]

Some of the early Mahāyāna practitioners in India who compiled the first lists of bodhisattva precepts may have administered the precepts in a manner similar to that advocated by Saichō. Hirakawa has argued that these people probably used the bodhisattva precepts, and not the Hīnayāna precepts, to ordain themselves as monastic bodhisattvas. Since the bodhisattva precepts differed substantially from the traditional Hīnayāna precepts, the monastic bodhisattvas must have differed considerably from Hīnayāna monks. The early Mahāyāna practitioners probably combined lay and monastic elements in their practices, and thus by Hīnayāna standards could not be called monks. Early Mahāyāna groups were usually connected with a *stūpa*. Since some Hīnayāna *vinayas* did not permit monks to be affiliated with a *stūpa*, they would not have considered the Mahāyāna practitioners to be monks. In addition, *stūpa* worship often involved music and dancing, activities which Hīnayāna monks were not even permitted to watch.[14] The early Mahāyāna practitioners were also not laymen, however, since they wore robes and shaved their heads. From the perspective of a traditional monk, these early Mahāyāna practitioners could be called neither laymen nor monks.

The Hīnayāna monks responded to the early Mahāyāna practitioners with calculated indifference. Consequently, Hīnayāna writings rarely mentioned Mahāyāna Buddhism. In contrast, Mahāyāna writings condemned Hīnayāna Buddhists with great vigor. In the *Shih chu p'i p'o sha lun* (*Daśabhūmika-vibhāsa?*) attributed to Nāgārjuna, it was stated:

> If one falls into *śrāvaka-bhūmi* and *pryatyekabuddha-bhūmi,* this is called the death of the bodhisattva. That is, all benefits will be lost. Even if one falls into hell, one will not have such great fears.[15]

Some of the polemics and terminology against Hīnayāna Buddhism used by Saichō in the *Kenkairon* reflected this stage in the development of the Mahāyāna literature.[16]

Eventually, some of the rivalry between the Hīnayāna and Mahāyāna groups seems to have abated. Hīnayāna monks were converted to Mahāyāna teachings, and brought their studies of the *abhidharma* and *vinaya* with them to the Mahāyāna orders. By doing so, they were

---

[13] *DZ* 1:107–15.

[14] Hirakawa, "The Rise of Mahāyāna," pp. 98–100.

[15] *T* 26:41a.

[16] For examples, see *Kenkairon, DZ* 1:138–44.

contributing to the development of Mahāyāna doctrine and practice. Eventually the Hīnayāna precepts became the standard of behavior followed by Mahāyāna monks,[17] though the Hīnayāna precepts were probably often supplemented by various forms of the bodhisattva precepts. The Mahāyāna adoption of the Hīnayāna *vinaya* helped to resolve many of the problems concerning dress and decorum which had not been adequately discussed in the bodhisattva precepts.

As time passed, formulations of the bodhisattva precepts appeared in numerous Mahāyāna writings.[18] Some of these formulations contained passages critical of Hīnayāna practice and doctrine while other formulations integrated the Hīnayāna and bodhisttva precepts. These two approaches to the relation between Hīnayāna and Mahāyāna precepts were often illustrated by referring to a doctrinal classification system called the three collections of pure precepts (*sanju jōkai* 三聚淨戒). The three collections were precepts for: (1) the prevention of evil 攝律儀戒 (2) the promotion of good 攝善法戒, and (3) the salvation of sentient beings 攝衆生戒. According to a number of works in the Yogācāra tradition, the Hīnayāna precepts could be identified with the prevention of evil while the Mahāyāna bodhisattva precepts could be identified with the promotion of good.[19] Variations of this system were sometimes used in Chinese and Japanese ordination ceremonies to explain the relation of the precepts of the *Ssu fen lü* and *Fan wang ching*.

Another interpretation of the three collections of pure precepts was eventually developed in East Asia. This interpretation was based on a passage in the *Ying lo ching*,[20] a text compiled in China and closely related to the *Fan wang ching*. In the *Ying lo ching* description of the three collections of pure precepts, the Hīnayāna precepts were not identified with any of the elements of the *sanju jōkai* formula. The *Ying lo ching* interpretation of the *sanju jōkai* formula could be used to argue that the Hīnayāna Precepts were not an essential factor in Mahāyāna monastic discipline. Eventually, the T'ien-t'ai thinker Ming-kuang did use the *Ying lo ching* interpretation in such a manner. As is

[17] See Hirakawa Akira, "*Kegonkyō* ni mirareru shoki daijōkyōto no shūkyō seikatsu," in Nakamura Hajime, ed., *Kegon shisō* (Kyoto: Hōzōkan, 1960). Hirakawa compared five translations of the chapter on pure practices of the *Hua yen ching* to demonstrate that the ordination ceremony described in them gradually approached that used by Hīnayāna monks.

[18] For a detailed analysis of this literature, see Ōno Hōdō, *Daijō kaikyō no kenkyū* (Tokyo: Risōsha, 1954).

[19] *Ti chih ching* (*Bodhisattvabhūmi*, *T* 30:910b–c) *and Yü ch'ieh shih ti lun* (*Yogācārabhūmiśāstra*, *T* 30:511a).

[20] *T* 24: 1020b–c.

demonstrated in the following section, Ming-kuang's views on the precepts significantly influenced Saichō.

The Precepts in the T'ien-t'ai Tradition: Chih-i and Ming-kuang

As the founder of the Japanese Tendai School, Saichō was obviously concerned with Chinese T'ien-t'ai attitudes towards the precepts. He must have been aware that Chih-i and Chan-jan had maintained that the *Ssu fen lü* precepts could be the basis of Mahāyāna practice, a position which differed from that maintained by Saichō in the *Shijōshiki*. However, another T'ien-t'ai thinker, Ming-kuang 明曠, was a major influence on Saichō's thought on the precepts. In this section, the views on the precepts of Chih-i, Chan-jan and Ming-kuang are discussed and their influences on Saichō are considered.

CHIH-I. For Chih-i (538–597), the de facto founder of the T'ien-t'ai School, the performance of ordinations with bodhisattva precepts was an important way of spreading Buddhism. Chih-i conferred the bodhisattva precepts on monks and laymen throughout China.[21] He also performed ordinations using the bodhisattva precepts for Emperor Hsien (r. 568–82) of the Ch'en Dynasty and Crown Prince Yang Kuang of the Sui Dynasty.[22] Chih-i quoted the *Fan wang ching* only four times in his three major works, the *Mo ho chih kuan, Fa hua hsüan i,* and *Fa hua wen chü.*[23] Although no record of any lectures by Chih-i on the *Fan wang ching* is to be found in his biographies, the brief references to the *Fan wang ching* in his works suggest that these were the precepts which Chih-i conferred.[24]

Chih-i's view of the relationship between the Hīnayāna and the Mahāyāna precepts has been the subject of controversy among modern scholars examining Chih-i's influence on Saichō. Chih-i did not specifically mention the three collections of pure precepts (*sanju jōkai*) in his three major works (*Tendai sandaibu*) although certain passages in his works indicate that he was aware of this classification of the precepts. Hence, the three collections of pure precepts do not serve as an adequate indication of Chih-i's views on the relationship between

---

[21] *Hsü kao seng chuan T* 50:568a.

[22] Hurvitz, *Chih-i,* pp. 135, 145; and Satō Tatsugen, "Bosatsukai no ikkōsatsu," p. 9. The *Sui T'ien t'ai chih che ta shih chuan* (*T* 50:195) does not identify the type of bodhisattva precepts conferred; however, it does identify them with filial piety, a formula found in the *Fan wang ching* (*T* 24:1004a).

[23] Satō Tetsuei, *Tendai Daishi no kenkyū* (Kyoto: Hyakkaen, 1960), p. 414.

[24] *T* 46:481c. Also see footnote 22 above. The *P'u sa chieh i su,* a commentary on the *Fan wang ching,* is discussed later in this chapter.

the Hīnayāna and Mahāyāna precepts.[25]

In many of his works, Chih-i based his discussion of the precepts on the ten classifications of the precepts (*jikkai* 十戒), a system which was based on the *Ta chih tu lun* (*Mahāprajñāpāramitopadeśa*).[26] Although Chih-i's analysis of the ten classifications of precepts changed during his lifetime, his discussion of this classification system always began with the full Hīnayāna precepts, progressed to the Mahāyāna precepts, and concluded with the precepts which naturally accompanied meditation 定共戒 or the attainment of a certain stage on the path to enlightenment 道共戒. A typical example of Chih-i's analysis of the ten classifications is found in the *Mo ho chih kuan:*

1. The unbroken precepts 不缺戒. This refers to the observance of the precepts which are instinctive to all men 性戒 and to the observance of the four *pārājika*... When these precepts are violated, they are like a vessel which has been lost and cannot be used. (One who violates them) is no longer a Buddhist...

2. The precepts without cracks 不破戒. This refers to the observance of the thirteen *saṃghādiśeṣa*... When these precepts are violated, they are like a vessel with a crack (that is, it can be repaired with much effort).

3. The precepts without holes 不穿戒. This refers to the observance of the *pratideśanīya* and the lesser precepts. If these precepts are violated, they are like a bowl with a hole (that is, it can be repaired with effort)...

4. The precepts without deviation 不雜戒. This refers to the precepts held while a person is meditating 定共戒. When a person observes the precepts but thinks of violating them, it is called a deviation. However, since his mind is controlled while he meditates and no desires arise, he holds the precepts without deviation...

---

[25] Kotera Bun'ei, "Enkai ni okeru sanjusetsu no tenkai," *TG* 9 (1967): 17. However, Tonegawa Kōgyō ["*Tendai kaisho no jikkai*," *IBK* 23 (1974): 171] argues that Chih-i may have used the *sanju jōkai* in a work no longer extant.

[26] The ten classifications (*jikkai*) probably originated from the practice of meditating on the virtues of moral behavior. A list of eight subjects similar to the *jikkai* is found in the *Aṅguttara-nikāya* and is commented on by Buddhaghosa in the *Visuddhimagga* [Buddhaghosa, *The Path of Purity,* tr. Bhikkhu Nyānamoli, 2 vols, (Berkeley: Shambala, 1976) 1:240]. Chih-i's list of the *jikkai* is based on a list of seven subjects for meditation from the *Ta chih tu lun* (*T* 25:225c), which has been supplemented with three subjects taken from a list of ten subjects found in the *Ta p'in pan jo ching* (*T* 8:386a, *Pañcaviṃśatisāhasrikāmahāprajñāpāramitāsūtra*).

5. The precepts which arise in accordance with the path 隨道戒. When a person acts in accordance with the truth, the wrong views which can be destroyed through insight 見惑 are vanquished.

6. The precepts without attachment 無著戒. The practitioner perceives the truth and becomes a sage. He is no longer contaminated by any of the illusions which can only be destroyed through practice 思惟惑.

7-8 The precepts praised by the wise 智所讚戒 and the precepts which embody freedom 自在戒. These concern the bodhisattva's efforts to save others. These (precepts) are praised by the Buddhas. The bodhisattva acts with complete freedom in the phenomenal world, but when his actions are viewed by those ensconced in the world, the bodhisattva appears to be observing the precepts.

9-10. The precepts which arise in accordance with the *śuraṃgama* meditation[27] 隨定戒 and the full precepts 具足戒. Though the practitioner does not emerge from his trance of cessation 滅定, he still manfests all forms of normal behavior. He manifests his form in the ten realms[28] in order to lead sentient beings (to salvation). Though he acts, he is by nature always quiet. Thus these are called the precepts arising from meditation.... Among these precepts of the middle way, there are none which are incomplete. Thus they are called the full precepts. (The practitioner) observes the precepts which are the supreme truth of the middle way.[29]

Chih-i equated the ten classifications of the precepts (*jikkai*) with various stages on the path to Buddhahood and consequently integrated the Hīnayāna precepts with Mahāyāna practices. In the following passage from the *Mo ho chih kuan,* no specific set of bodhisattva precepts was mentioned. However, in an earlier discussion of the *jikkai,* Chih-i equated the *Fan wang* precepts with the seventh category of the precepts.[30]

---

[27] The *śuraṃgama-samādhi* can only be attained by bodhisattvas of the tenth land. It encompasses all other meditations performed by bodhisattvas. The meditation required to hold these precepts is thus more advanced than that described in the precepts without deviation, the fourth classification.

[28] The ten realms are those of Buddhas, bodhisattvas, *pratyekabuddhas, śrāvakas,* gods, men, *asuras,* animals, hungry ghosts and the denizens of hell.

[29] *TZ, Mo ho chih kuan* 2:525–28.

[30] *Shih ch'an po lo mi tz'u ti fa men, T* 46:484.

1–3. The first three classifications (of the ten) are all called precepts which prevent wrongdoing 律儀戒. They encourage good and prevent evil.... The ordinary person with a distracted mind can observe all of these precepts.

4. Next are the precepts without deviation. The mind is controlled through meditation; its blind movements are suppressed. The body and mouth are also quiet.... These are the precepts which accompany meditation. When a person is meditating, (his mind) naturally is devoid of any wrong thoughts. When he emerges from meditation, the body and mind are still flexible and without wrong inclinations. If an ordinary man meditates, he can observe these precepts.

5. The precepts are observed when the stream-winner (*srotapānna*) perceives his own true nature and thus becomes a sage. These are precepts which are observed by sages, but not by ordinary men.

6. The precepts without attachment can be observed by a non-returner (*anāgāmin*), but cannot be observed by the stream-winner.

7–8. The precepts praised by the wise and the precepts embodying freedom are held by the bodhisattva who benefits others, but not by followers of the two (Hīnayāna) vehicles.

9–10. The precepts which arise from (the highest) meditation and the full precepts are observed by those with (superior) Mahāyāna faculties, but not by the bodhisattva who follows Common teachings (*tsūgyō*) and practices the six perfections. How then could ordinary men or followers of the two Hīnayāna vehicles observe these (superior precepts)?[31]

Chih-i's discussion of the ten classifications indicates that he followed the precepts used by many earlier Chinese monks, and combined the *Fan wang* and the Hīnayāna precepts into a harmonious system.[32]

In the above quotation, Chih-i described only the precepts held by bodhisattvas who performed 'gradual' practices 漸行菩薩 which allowed them to slowly advance along the path to Buddhahood. However, in other works, Chih-i described bodhisattvas who performed 'Sudden

---

[31] *TZ, Mo ho chih kuan* 2:531–32.

[32] Hirakawa has shown that Chih-i probably followed the precepts of the *Shih sung lü* (*T* 1435, *Sarvāstivādavinaya*?) rather than those of the *Ssu fen lü* ("Chigi no kaitairon ni tsui-te," In *Okuda Jiō sensei kiju kinen: Bukkyō shisō ronshū* [Kyoto: Heirakuji shoten], p. 758). After Daoxuan popularized the *Ssu fen lü* precepts, T'ien-t'ai monks followed them. Chan-jan, for example, had a *Ssu fen lü* ordination.

religious practices' which enabled them to attain Buddhahood in an instant 頓行菩薩.[33] This type of bodhisattva was able to perfect all aspects of the precepts in an instant. Consequently, he could progress to Mahā-yāna practices without first taking the Hīnayāna precepts. Chih-i's concept of a bodhisattva who performed Sudden practices presaged Saichō's claim that the Perfect precepts were suitable for the bodhisattva who could take a direct path (*jikidō* 直道) to enlightenment.[34] However, a crucial difference remained between the views of Chih-i and Saichō. Chih-i never attempted to reject the Hīnayāna precepts, nor did he argue that ordinations with bodhisattva precepts should precede full Hīnayāna ordinations. In the *Fa hua hsüan i*, he stated that the Hīnayāna precepts should be explained in a way which revealed their Mahāyāna contents.[35] According to Chih-i, the bodhisattva who followed Sudden practices perfected and encompassed both the Hīnayāna and Mahāyāna precepts. Consequently, the concept of sudden practices did not imply that the Hīnayāna precepts were to be rejected. Moreover, since both Chinese and Japanese Risshū monks wrote about Sudden practices and Sudden enlightenment, Chih-i's concept of a bodhisattva who perfected the precepts in a instant was not unique to the T'ien-t'ai School.[36]

Besides the concept of a bodhisattva who performed Sudden practices, Chih-i also introduced another concept utilized by Saichō, the Perfect precepts (*enkai* 圓戒). The term 'Perfect precepts' referred to Chih-i's classification of Buddhist doctrine into four categories, and designated the precepts appropriate for followers of the Perfect teaching. Chih-i equated the Perfect precepts with the precepts of the Buddha. They were realized through meditation, practice, and the development of a mind which was free from passions and thus able to perceive things as they really are (*jissōshin* 實相心).[37] The Perfect precepts were usually not

---

[33] *Shih ch'an po lo mi tz'u ti fa men,* T 46:485a; and *TZ, Fa hua hsüan i* 3:187.

[34] The term *jikidō* appears in the *P'u sa chieh i su* JZ 15:815) and the term *daijikidō* in the *Fa hua hsüan i*, (*TZ* 3:195). For an explanation of these terms see Chapter 9.

[35] *TZ, Fa hua hsüan i* 2:565.

[36] Tsuchihashi Shūkō ["Dōsen no bosatsukai," *IBK* 15 (1966): 132–33] claims that in times of trouble Daoxuan did not require his followers to take the precepts in the hierarchical order prescribed in the *Yü ch'ieh shih ti lun* (*Yogācārabhūmiśāstra*), beginning with the three refuges and culminating in the full precepts or bodhisattva precepts. However, it should be noted that due to the paucity of Daoxuan's writings on the bodhisattva precepts much of Tsuchihashi's argument is based on the writings of Tao-shih 道世 (d. 668?), a contemporary of Daoxuan who studied under the same teacher. Of course, the abilities of the recipient also played a role in determining whether he could receive the bodhisattva precepts in a 'Sudden' fashion without first receiving all the required Hīnayāna ordinations. For the views of Japanese Risshū monks on 'Sudden' practices, see Tokuda, *Risshū gairon*, pp. 34–35.

[37] *TZ, Fa hua hsüan i* 3:185.

identified in Chih-i's writings with any particular set of rules such as the precepts of the *Fan wang ching,* Hīnayāna sets or even with the *anrakugyō* (Serene and Pleasant Activities) of the *Lotus Sūtra.* Elsewhere, however, Chih-i stated that adherence to the *Lotus Sūtra* (*jikyō* 持經) was equivalent to holding the most profound precepts 第一義戒.[38] Such precepts were called absolute (*rikai* 理戒) and were free of specific content. They were realized in two ways. A monk or nun might gradually practice precepts of increasing subtlety until the Perfect precepts were attained, or he or she might attain them in an instant through Sudden practices.

Chih-i's depiction of the Perfect precepts emphasized their absolute character. They were not to be limited by identifying them with a specific set of precepts. How then did the precepts of the *Fan wang ching* fit into this scheme? Although Chih-i did not discuss the *Fan wang* precepts much in his later major works (*Tendai sandaibu*), he did quote the *Fan wang ching* in the *Mo ho chih kuan* in such a way as to imply that they might be used as Perfect precepts.[39] Elsewhere he called them precepts for practitioners of both the Unique and Perfect teachings,[40] but did not clarify the difference between their Unique and Perfect interpretations. The *Fan wang* precepts never assumed the position of being solely Perfect (*jun'en* 純圓) precepts for Chih-i, probably because he considered the *Fan wang ching* to be the capping *sūtra* for the *Hua yen ching* (*Avataṃsakasūtra*), the main source for the Unique teaching (*bekkyō*).[41] Moreover, the concept of Perfect precepts was too abstract to be limited to any particular set of precepts.

The foregoing discussion was based on works of unquestioned authenticity by Chih-i and his disciple Kuan-ting. The *P'u sa chieh i su,* a commentary on the *Fan wang ching* traditionally attributed to Chih-i, must also be mentioned. The authenticity of this text has been questioned in recent years by Satō Tetsuei.[42] Chih-i usually divided his commentaries into five major topics; however, the *P'u sa chieh i su* employed only

---

[38] *Fa hua wen chü, T* 33:138a.

[39] *TZ, Mo ho chih kuan* 2:539.

[40] *TZ, Fa hua hsüan i* 2:561. The reading of this controversial passage is discussed in Ishida, *Kairitsu no kenkyū,* pp. 191–92.

[41] *Fa hua wen chü, T* 33:128a. In China and Japan, a major *sūtra* was sometimes associated with two shorter *sūtras.* One of these was lectured on before the major *sūtra* was discussed, and was consequently called an opening *sūtra* (*kaikyō*). The other was lectured on after the major *sūtra* and was called a capping *sūtra* (*kekkyō*). The *Fan wang ching* was associated with the *Hua yen ching* because Rushana Butsu played a major role in both *sūtras* and the doctrines preached in the *sūtras* were similar.

[42] Satō Tetsuei, *Tendai Daishi no kenkyū* (Kyoto: Hyakkaen, 1960), pp. 412–15.

three topics.[43] Chih-i wrote about the essence of the precepts[44] (kaitai 戒體) as a mental factor in most of his works, but in the *P'u sa chieh i su* its physical aspect was emphasized.[45] Since the *kaitai* was a major subject of controversy among monks who studied the precepts, Chih-i probably would not have advocated a new position in the *P'u sa chieh i su* without explaining the reasons for the change. The *P'u sa chieh i su* is not referred to in any documents dating from Chih-i's time, nor was it mentioned in Daoxuan's *Ta t'ang nei tien lu,* a major bibliography compiled in 664. The earliest reference to it in Chinese Buddhist literature

---

[43] The organization of Chih-i's commentaries is discussed below in the section of this chapter on Ming-kuang.

[44] The concept of 'the essence of the precepts' (Ch. *chieh-t'i,* Jap. *kaitai*) has its origins in Indian discussions of *karma.* When a person was ordained, his promise to observe the precepts would influence his future actions. Indian monks were vitally interested in explaining the way in which ordinations and vows affected a person's actions. Consequently, Indian *abhidharma* masters analyzed the influences of ordinations, vows, promises and other activities with karmic consequences according to such factors as whether they corresponded to mental or physical *dharmas.*

Despite Indian interests in explaining the functioning of *karma,* no Sanskrit term corresponding to the concept of 'the essence of the precepts' has been found. The *kaitai,* however, was an important topic among Chinese Buddhists during the Six Dynasties Period. The concept may have developed in the course of Chinese discussions of the precepts and ordinations, which were influenced by Indian studies of *karma.* These discussions would have been stimulated by the dissemination of the translations of the full *vinayas* and the compilation in China of such works as the *Fan wang ching* and *Ying lo ching* (*T* 1485).

Discussions of the *kaitai* were also influenced by Neo-Taoist theories about the essences (Ch. *t'i* 體, Jap. *tai*) and functions (Ch. *yung* 用, Jap. *yō*) of various things. As a result, the *kaitai* was identified with teaching, faith, and truth. The concepts of essence and function were also applied by Chinese Buddhists to the exegesis of Buddhist *sūtras,* as well as to discussions of the precepts. Consequently, the concept of *kaitai* was probably developed through the interaction of Chinese Neo-Taoist ideas with Indian *abhidharma* studies. For more information on the *kaitai* see Ōno Hodō, "Kaitai ni tsuite," *Nanto Bukkyō* 5 (1958): 1–13; and Aoki Kōshō, "Chūgoku Bukkyō ni okeru kaitaikan ni tsuite no ikkōsatsu," *IBK* 20 (1972): 776–80; and Hirakawa, *Genshi Bukkyō no kenkyū* (Tokyo: Shunjūsha), pp. 165–222.

Some Chinese monks believed that the *kaitai* arose when the Three Refuges were recited in ordinations. Daoxuan argued that the *kaitai* was received when the precepts were explained to the candidate (*Chieh mo su, Z* 1. 64. 4. 365b). Daoxuan thus viewed the *kaitai* as representing the karmic functioning of the precepts. The argument that the *kaitai* arose when the Three Refuges were recited remained popular, however. In Japan, some ordinations were performed in which no precepts were granted; yet they still conferred a *kaitai* (Tsuchihashi, "Jukai reigi no hensen," *Bukkyō kyōdan no kenkyū,* pp. 275–76). The concept of the *kaitai* used in such ordinations was close to the Neo-Taoist concept of *t'i* and represented an ineffable essence of the precepts rather than their karmic functioning.

[45] *JZ* 15: 821. Chih-i's view of the *kaitai* has been the subject of a number of essays, particularly by members of the Tendai School who have argued that no contradiction exists between the two views of the *kaitai.* See, for example, Takeda Chōten, "Shōmusakeshiki no kaitairon," *TG* 4 (1962): 12–16. The best essay on the subject, even though the author is not a scholar of Tendai, is Hirakawa Akira's, "Chigi no kaitairon ni tsuite." Hirakawa argues that there is no contradiction between the two views, but reserves judgment on the authorship of the *P'u sa chieh i su.*

dates back to the early eighth century.[46] Consequently, the work was not generally known in China until over a century after Chih-i's death. Satō outlined his doubts concerning the commentary's authenticity, but arrived at no final conclusion concerning the problem. Instead, he called on other scholars to do further research on the authenticity of the *P'u sa chieh i su.*

Saichō brought the *P'u sa chieh i su* back from China, and believed that it was by Chih-i.[47] He referred to it several times in the *Kenkairon* and the *Shugo kokkaishō.*[48] The commentary played an important role in the lineage for the *Fan wang* precepts which Saichō included in the *Kechimyakufu.*[49] Many of the practical details concerning the *Fan wang* precepts and ordinations which were not mentioned in Chih-i's major works were discussed in the *P'u sa chieh i su.* Consequently this text provided Saichō with additional details for his treatment of the *Fan wang* precepts. However, the *P'u sa chieh i su's* discussion of the relationship between the Hīnayāna and Mahāyāna precepts did not differ significantly from that found in Chih-i's major works. The *P'u sa chieh i su* followed the same interpretation of the ten classifications of the precepts (*jikkai*) as the *Mo ho chih kuan.*[50] Although the three collections of the pure precepts (*sanju jōkai*) were introduced into the discussion of the *Fan wang* precepts and although the *Ying lo ching* passage which excluded the Hīnayāna precepts from the *sanju jōkai* formula was quoted,[51] a formula harmoniously combining the *Fan wang* with the Hīnayāna precepts was still generally advocated by the compiler of the *P'u sa chieh i su.* Consequently, this commentary on the *Fan wang ching* does not appear to have played an important role in Saichō's decision to ordain Tendai monks with the *Fan wang* precepts.

In conclusion, Chih-i's writings contributed two important elements to Saichō's thought on the precepts. First, Chih-i's concept of a bodhisattva who performed Sudden practices was a forerunner of Saichō's association of the *Fan wang* precepts with the Direct Path (*jikidō*) to enlightenment. Secondly, Chih-i's use of the term 'Perfect precepts' (*enkai*) suggested that certain precepts were suited for those who followed

---

[46] Taira Ryōshō, "Dengyō Daishi no nittō denkai ni tsuite," *DDK*, p. 638. One of the earliest citations of the work is found in Chan–jan's *Fa hua wen chü chi* (*T* 34: 330c), but Chan–jan does not identify it as a work by Chih-i.

[47] *Taishūroku, BZ* 95: 229b.

[48] *Kenkairon, DZ* 1: 113, 122; and *Shugo kokkaishō, DZ* 2: 287.

[49] Taira, "Dengyō Daishi no nittō denkai ni tsuite," *DDK* p. 640.

[50] *JZ* 15: 816–17.

[51] Ibid.

the Perfect teachings of the *Lotus Sūtra* and that those precepts might be distinct from the Hīnayāna precepts.

Chih-i's position on the precepts differed from that of Saichō in several ways. First, Chih-i advocated the harmonious combination of the Hīnayāna and Mahāyāna precepts. Even when the precepts were realized through Sudden practices, they still encompassed the Hīnayāna precepts. Secondly, Chih-i's concept of the Perfect precepts was abstract. He did not identify the Perfect precepts with a specific set of rules. The *Fan wang* precepts represented a mixture of Unique and Perfect teachings, not solely Perfect (*jun'en*) teachings. The purely Perfect precepts could only be observed by the Buddha. Before the doctrinal foundation for Saichō's proposals would be complete, the Perfect precepts would have to be identified with the *Fan wang* precepts and freed of the onus of incorporating Hīnayāna or Unique teachings. These innovations would finally appear in the writings of Ming-kuang.

CHAN-JAN.   After Chih-i's death, the T'ien-t'ai School went through a period during which it was eclipsed by such new schools as the Hua-yen and Fa-hsiang. Chan-jan (711–782) revived the T'ien-t'ai School during the eighth century. Traditional biographies state that Chan-jan had thoroughly studied the *Ssu fen lü* and was ordained by the *Ssu fen lü* master T'an-i 曇一 (692–771).

Among Chan-jan's numerous works are commentaries on Chih-i's three major works. His treatment of the Perfect precepts in these commentaries is much like that of Chih-i with one important change in emphasis. While Chih-i stressed the abstract, formless qualities of the absolute precepts (*rikai*), Chan-jan argued that the *rikai* were only complete when they had actual rules (*jikai*) as their contents. Moreover, Chan-jan maintained that if the absolute, formless quality of the *rikai* were overemphasized, monks would be more apt to violate the precepts.[52] Chan-jan argued that the *Fan wang* precepts could be considered the contents of the Perfect precepts.[53] In doing so, he gave the *Fan wang* precepts a greater practical role than Chih-i had given them in his three major works.

This shift in emphasis reflected the growing popularity of the *Fan wang ching* in China since Chih-i's time. Such eminent scholars as Fa-

---

[52] *Chih kuan fu hsing ch'uan hung chüeh,* fasc. 4A, *TZ, Mo ho chih kuan* 2: 533.

[53] *Fa hua hsüan i shih ch'ien,* fasc. 3B, *TZ, Fa hua hsüan i* 2: 562; and *Fa hua wen chü chi,* fasc. 9A, *T* 34: 319b.

tsang 法藏 (643–712) and Chih-chou 智周 (556–622) had already written commentaries on the *Fan wang ching,* and the T'ien-t'ai master Hui-wei had written an ordination manual for it. However, Chan-jan still did not classify the *Fan wang* precepts as solely Perfect (*jun'en*). Because of their association with the *Hua yen ching* (*Avataṃsakasūtra*), he followed Chih-i's interpretation and regarded the *Fan wang* precepts as a mixture of Unique and Perfect teachings.[54]

Since the *Fan wang* precepts occupied only one fascicle of the *Fan wang ching,* they were not very detailed. Chan-jan maintained that they therefore should be supplemented with the more detailed Hīnayāna precepts. The Hīnayāna precepts were regarded as expedient precepts when used in this way; yet at the same time, they were necessary to clarify many of the contingencies not covered by the *Fan wang* precepts. If a monk did not observe the Hīnayāna precepts, he could not properly observe the *Fan wang* precepts and the whole concept of Perfect precepts would lose its practical significance.[55] When a monk followed the Perfect precepts, he was not to concern himself with such distinctions as Hīnayāna and Mahāyāna.[56] Rather he was to observe the *Ssu fen lü* precepts with a mind unaffected by their Hīnayāna origins.

Chan-jan's emphasis on the practical application of the *Fan wang ching* is also illustrated by his ordination manual, which later became the basis of the *Fan wang* ordination ceremony performed by the Japanese Tendai School. His ordination manual incorporated elements from both the *Ying lo ching* 瓔珞經 and *Ti chih ching* 地持經.[57] No criticisms of the *Ssu fen lü* precepts were included in the manual.

MING-KUANG. While the term 'Perfect precepts' appeared in the writings of Chih-i, and while the *Fan wang* precepts were assigned a paramount position in Chan-jan's pronouncements on monastic discipline, neither Chih-i nor Chan-jan suggested that the Hīnayāna precepts could be abandoned as the basis of monastic ordinations. Although Saichō quoted the writings of the two T'ien-t'ai masters in the *Kenkairon,* he rarely cited them at crucial points in his arguments,[58] probably because

---

[54] Ishida, *Kairitsu no kenkyū,* p. 182.

[55] *Chih kuan fu hsing ch'uan hung chüeh, TZ, Mo ho chih kuan* 2: 503.

[56] Ibid., p. 529.

[57] *Shou p'u sa chieh i, JZ* 15: 872.

[58] In the *Kenkairon,* Saichō cited the *Mo ho chih kuan* (*DZ* 1: 73–74) once, Chih-i's commentary on the *Wei mo ching* once (ibid., pp. 75–78), the commentary on the *Fan wang ching* once (ibid., p. 113) and the *Fa hua wen chü* once (ibid., p. 140). Chan-jan's commentary

he realized that their writings could be used against him very effectively.[59]

A position similar to that of Saichō finally emerged in the writings of Chan-jan's disciple Ming-kuang. Little is known about Ming-kuang's life. Although some traditional histories and catalogues list him as a disciple of Kuan-ting (561–632),[60] today he is recognized as a disciple of Chan-jan (711–782). He may have succeeded Chan-jan as the head of a temple in Ching-chi (in Kiangsu Province).[61] Ming-kuang is credited with the authorship of a number of works, at least three of which were brought back to Japan from China by Saichō.[62]

Among Ming-kuang's works is the *T'ien t'ai p'u sa chieh su* 天台菩薩戒疏, a commentary on the *Fan wang ching* authored in 777.[63] Although the commentary is not listed among the works which Saichō brought back from China, Saichō did quote from it twice in the *Kenkairon*,[64] suggesting that he probably brought it with him from China. The first citation supported Saichō's contention that bodhisattva monks could be ordained with the *Fan wang* precepts and thus were distinct from Hinayāna monks. It also discussed the practical problem of the order in which monks and laymen were to be seated after they had been ordained with the *Fan wang* precepts. The second citation indicated that bodhisattva monks should wear monastic robes. After Saichō's death when a question arose over the proper seating order, Kōjō indicated that Ming-kuang's commentary was to be used as an authority to settle the dispute.[65] Elsewhere, Kōjō stated that Saichō relied heavily on Ming-kuang's work.[66] Ming-kuang's ideas also significantly influenced Kōjō's own writings on the precepts.[67] Ming-kuang's commentary thus played a seminal role in the development of the ideas of both Saichō and Kōjō on the precepts. It also aided the early Tendai School in resolving some

---

on the *Fa hua wen chü* (ibid., pp 140–42) was cited twice. The quotations from Chan–jan concerned the *anrakugyō*, and were the only quotations from the works of Chan–jan and Chih–i which played an important role in the *Kenkairon*.

[59] In their debates with Saichō, the Nara masters did not cite the works of Chih–i and Chan–jan, perhaps because they felt insecure about using T'ien–t'ai sources which they had not mastered. By the Kamakura period, however, monks of the Nara schools were using the writings of Chih–i and Chan–jan to question the Tendai position (Kuno, "Saichō wo shūten to suru *Jubosatsukaigi* no seiritsu katei," *Bukkyō ronsō*, p. 116).

[60] *Tōiki dentō mokuroku, BZ* 95: 10; and *Fo tsu t'ung chi, T* 49: 201a.

[61] *Taishūroku, BZ* 95: 228.

[62] Ibid., pp. 225–26.

[63] *T* 40: 602.

[64] *DZ* 1: 113, 121.

[65] *Denjutsu isshinkaimon, DZ* 1: 596–97.

[66] Ibid., p. 614.

[67] Ibid., pp. 629–30. Kōjō quoted from Ming–kuang's subcommentary without identifying it.

of the practical problems which arose from Saichō's proposals.

In the *T'ien t'ai p'u sa chieh su,* Ming-kuang stated that he was writing a work which would supplement and remedy the shortcomings found in previous T'ien-t'ai works on the *Fan wang* precepts.[68] The *Fan wang ching* commentary attributed to Chih-i seemed inadequate to Ming-kuang in several ways. Chih-i had usually used a fivefold exegetical system (*gojū gengi* 五重玄義) when writing commentaries, dividing his discussion into five sections: (1) explanation of the title, (2) analysis of the scripture's substance, (3) clarification of its fundamental principles, (4) discussion of its practical manifestations, and (5) evaluation of its place in the total scheme of the Buddha's doctrine. Yet the commentary on the *Fan wang ching* attributed to Chih-i had utilized only a threefold approach: (1) explanation of the title, (2) analysis of the scripture's substance, and (3) explanation and analysis.[69] Ming-kuang tried to correct this shortcoming by using a sevenfold system in his commentary: (1) explanation of the title of the scripture, (2) discussion of the scripture's practical uses and fundamental principles, (3) evaluation of its place in the scheme of the Buddha's teaching, (4) explanation of the ordination procedure, (5) description of the translation of the work, (6) a section of questions and answers, and (7) a line-by-line commentary on the text of the *Fan wang ching.*[70] Ming-kuang presented his explanation of the substance 體 as well as the title of the *Fan wang ching* in the first section of his commentary; as a result he was able to discuss all five categories of Chih-i's *gojū gengi* in the first three sections of his commentary. The last four sections of Ming-kuang's commentary were reserved for discussions of topics, such as the ordination ceremony, which were not readily incorporated into the T'ien-t'ai fivefold exegetical system. In Chart 4 the differences and similarities between the three exegetical systems are diagrammed.

Ming-kuang abandoned the traditional T'ien-t'ai position of treating the *Fan wang* precepts as precepts belonging to the Kegon class of teachings, a classification which combined Perfect with Unique (*betsuen* 別圓) teachings. Instead, he interpreted the *Fan wang* precepts as solely Perfect (*jun'en* 純圓) precepts, thereby elevating the *Fan wang ching* to the same status as the Perfect teachings of the *Lotus Sūtra.*[71] In doing so, he raised the *Fan wang ching* to a higher position in the T'ien-t'ai

---

[68] *T* 40: 580b.

[69] *JZ* 15: 815.

[70] *T* 40: 580c.

[71] Ibid., pp. 580b, 581c, 582b.

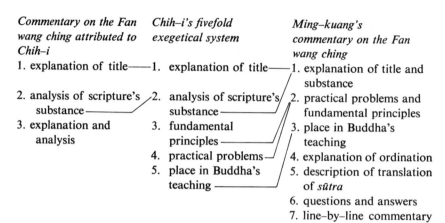

Commentary on the Fan wang ching attributed to Chih–i	Chih–i's fivefold exegetical system	Ming–kuang's commentary on the Fan wang ching
1. explanation of title	1. explanation of title	1. explanation of title and substance
2. analysis of scripture's substance	2. analysis of scripture's substance	2. practical problems and fundamental principles
3. explanation and analysis	3. fundamental principles	3. place in Buddha's teaching
	4. practical problems	4. explanation of ordination
	5. place in Buddha's teaching	5. description of translation of *sūtra*
		6. questions and answers
		7. line–by–line commentary

Chart **4.** Comparison of the differences between the exegetical systems followed in the commentary on the *Fan wang ching* attributed to Chih–i, the *gojū gengi* found in most of Chih–i's commentaries, and Ming–kuang's commentary on the *Fan wang ching*.

classification of teachings than it had been given by earlier T'ien-t'ai writers. While earlier T'ien-t'ai masters had formulated a single interpretation to explain the observance of the *Fan wang* precepts for those who followed the Unique and Perfect teachings, Ming-kuang advanced separate interpretations of the *Fan wang* precepts, distinguishing between the precepts practiced by followers of the Unique teaching and those practiced by followers of the Perfect teaching. Ming-kuang based his new interpretations of the *Fan wang* precepts on Chih-i's distinction between bodhisattvas who followed gradual practices 漸行菩薩 and bodhisattvas who followed Sudden practices 頓行菩薩. The follower of the Unique teaching gradually practiced and mastered the various sets of precepts, including the Hīnayāna precepts.[72] In contrast, the follower of the Perfect teaching mastered all the precepts in an instant.[73] Thus he did not necessarily have to master the Hīnayāna precepts before progressing to the *Fan wang* precepts. Ming-kuang's analysis effectively purged the *Fan wang* precepts of any onus resulting from the association of the *Fan wang ching* with the *Hua yen ching*. The idea of a Sudden realization of the precepts was fundamental to Saichō's identification of the Perfect precepts with the direct path 直道 to enlightenment.

Ming-kuang's concept of the perfection of the precepts in an instant also obviated the need for the practitioner to observe both the Hīnayāna

[72] Ibid., p. 584a.
[73] Ibid., p. 581a.

and Mahāyāna precepts. Ming-kuang did, in fact, reject the Hīnayāna precepts, as is shown by his discussions of the ten classifications of the precepts (*jikkai*) and the three collections of pure precepts (*sanju jōkai*).

Whereas Chih-i had used the *jikkai* classification to organize the Hīnayāna and Mahāyāna precepts into a hierarchy which would both encompass and transcend the Hīnayāna precepts, Ming-kuang did not identify any of the categories of the *jikkai* with the Hīnayāna precepts. The first three classifications of the *jikkai* were equated with the fifty-eight *Fan wang* precepts instead of the full set of Hīnayāna precepts, as the following passage from Ming-kuang's commentary demonstrates:

1. The unbroken precepts are the ten good precepts 十善性戒 and the ten major precepts (of the *Fan wang ching*). If they are violated, they are like a vessel which is so badly broken that it can not be (repaired and) used.

2–3. The precepts without cracks and the precepts without holes correspond to the forty-eight minor precepts. If they are broken, they are like a vessel with a crack or a hole (that is, it can be repaired and used).[74]

By substituting the *Fan wang* for the Hīnayāna precepts in the first three classifications, Ming-kuang removed any trace of Hīnayāna influence from the *jikkai* system. If Hīnayāna influence was absent from the first and most basic classifications of the *jikkai*, then it would also be absent from the remaining classifications since they represented even more advanced levels of the precepts. Consequently, Ming-kuang did not equate the various classifications of the *jikkai* with the levels of spiritual attainment of Hīnayāna and Mahāyāna practitioners as did Chih-i. Instead of treating the *jikkai* as a series of stages to be ascended, Ming-kuang insisted that the *"jikkai* could be assembled in an instant."[75]

Ming-kuang's desire to exclude the *Ssu fen lü* precepts from his analysis of the *Fan wang* precepts was further illustrated in his discussion of the three collections of pure precepts. Chih-i and Chan-jan had ignored the difference between the *sanju jōkai* formula in the *Ti chih ching* (*T* 1581, *Bodhisattvabhūmi*) which included the Hīnayāna precepts, and the formula in the *Ying lo ching* (*T* 1485) which excluded them. Ming-kuang, in contrast, clearly followed the *Ying lo ching* formula by

---

[74] Ibid., p. 581a. Ming–kuang's discussion of the seven remaining classifications is similar to that found in the *Mo ho chih kuan* (*TZ, Mo ho chih kuan* 2: 527–28) translated above in the discussion of Chih–i's position on the precepts.

[75] *T* 40: 581a.

declaring that the *sanju jōkai* had no relation to the Hīnayāna precepts.[76]

Ming-kuang analyzed and developed the *sanju jōkai* formula much further than had any of his T'ien-t'ai predecessors. In Chih-i's three major works the formula was barely mentioned. Although Chan-jan's ordination manual had depicted the bestowal of the *sanju jōkai* as the climax of the ordination ceremony, his discussion of the formula itself was very brief.[77] In contrast, Ming-kuang borrowed theories developed by the Hua-yen master Fa-tsang and the *Ssu fen lü* master Daoxuan in order to elaborate his own views on the *sanju jōkai*. The *sanju jōkai* were identified with the three bodies of the Buddha 三身, the three views 三觀, and the four bodhisattva vows 四弘誓願.[78] By equating the precepts with the essential qualities of Buddhahood and bodhisattvahood, Ming-kuang elevated the status of the precepts. The precepts were no longer the elementary and basic practice upon which other, apparently more difficult and profound practices, such as meditation and doctrinal study, were based. Instead, the precepts were as important and as profound at meditation and wisdom.[79] Ming-kuang identified the essence of the precepts (*kaitai*) with the mind which perceived all things as they really are (*jissōshin*).[80] For the practitioner of the Perfect precepts (*enkai*), complete observance of the precepts was synonymous with deep meditation or a profound understanding of religious truths.

For Ming-kuang, the Perfect precepts or an advanced understanding of the three collections of pure precepts (*sanju jōkai*) were not to be identified solely with the formless absolute precepts (*rikai* 理戒). Ming-kuang argued that each element of the *sanju jōkai* contained and harmonized with the other two elements, and moreover, that the *sanju jōkai* were contained in, and harmonized with, each of the fifty-eight *Fan wang* precepts. These precepts were called the bodhisattva precepts

---

[76] Ibid., pp. 580c–81a, 599c.

[77] *Shou p'u sa chieh i, JZ* 15: 875–76.

[78] *T* 40: 580c, 584b. Similar views are found in the writings of Fa-tsang and Daoxuan (Kotera, "Enkai ni okeru sanjusetsu no tenkai," p. 21). Saichō used these ideas in his *Chū Muryōgikyō* (*DZ* 1: 583). The three bodies of the Buddha are the *dharmakāya, saṃbhogakāya* and the *nirmāṇakāya*. The three views or truths are the nonsubstantiality of all phenomena, the provisional reality of all things despite their nonsubstantiality, and the lack of contradiction between the first two views. The four bodhisattva vows are to save all sentient beings, to cut off all passions, to study all Buddhist teachings, and to attain supreme enlightenment.

[79] *T* 40: 584a–b.

[80] *T* 40: 584a. This passage is quoted in the *Denjutsu isshinkaimon DZ* 1: 629–30. Ming-kuang thus rejected the idea that the essence of the precepts was a form of physical *dharma*, which had been expounded in the commentary on the *Fan wang ching* attributed to Chih-i. Tendai monks generally accept the identification of the essence of the precepts with the mind.

in Perfect Harmony 圓融.[81] By including all three elements of the *sanju jokāi* in the precepts consisting of rules (*jikai* 事戒), Ming-kuang brought the Perfect precepts within reach of the ordinary person since anyone could attempt to follow the rules of the *Fan wang ching*. In contrast, Chih-i had called the Perfect precepts (*enkai*) the Buddha's precepts (Bukkai 佛戒) because only the Buddha could faithfully adhere to them.[82]

Ming-kuang had formulated a rationale which would have permitted him to abandon the *Ssu fen lü* ordination. He never did reject it, however, probably because this ordination ceremony was already an established part of Chinese Buddhist practice. Instead, Ming-kuang regarded the *Ssu fen lü* ordination simply as a means of qualifying one to be a monk. After the ordination, the *Ssu fen lü* precepts were to lose their importance as guides to conduct.[83] The Tendai monk's practice was to be based on the *Fan wang* precepts; they qualified him as a bodhisattva monk.[84] It was not until Saichō's time, however, that anyone carried Ming-kuang's ideas to their logical end and abandoned the Hīnayāna precepts as the basis of the full ordination conferring monkhood.

In conclusion, Ming-kuang provided Saichō with much of the doctrinal justification for his proposals. In the process of remedying inadequacies which he perceived in the commentary on the *Fan wang ching* attributed to Chih-i, Ming-kuang freed the *Fan wang ching* from the onus of being closely associated with the *Hua yen ching*. He insisted that the *Fan wang* precepts could be considered as solely Perfect (*jun'en*) precepts, not merely as precepts reflecting a mixture of Unique and Perfect teachings. At the same time, he also argued that the Perfect precepts were separate and distinct from the Hīnayāna precepts, a position which Saichō later adopted in the *Shijōshiki*. Ming-kuang was probably the first Chinese monk to formulate a position on the precepts which developed the full implications of the *Ying lo ching's* exclusion of the Hīnayāna precepts from the *sanju jōkai* formula. In addition, Ming-kuang's discussions of the 'Sudden' acquisition of the Perfect precepts and his development of the doctrines concerning the (*sanju jōkai*) provided a rationale for elevating the precepts from being used as a stepping stone to the more advanced practices of meditation or wisdom, to a practice equal to, and essentially identical with, meditation and wisdom.

---

[81] *T* 40: 584b. A similar idea is found in the *Jubosatsukaigi, DZ* 1: 317–18.
[82] *TZ, Fa hua hsüan i* 3: 185.
[83] *T* 40: 599c.
[84] Ibid., p. 593a.

Saichō and Kōjō both adopted Ming-kuang's treatment of the *sanju jōkai* in their writings. Finally some of the terminology which Saichō used in his petitions may have been taken from Ming-kuang's commentary. For instance, Saichō believed that he was living at "the end of the period of the counterfeit *Dharma*" (*zōmatsu* 像末). This phrase was probably borrowed from Ming-kuang's commentary.[85] Ming-kuang also suggested that a monk who had received the *Fan wang* precepts be called a monastic bodhisattva (*shukke bosatsu* 出家菩薩).[86] Saichō used this term in the same way as Ming-kuang had.

Gyōgi and the Bodhisattva Monk Tradition

Gyōgi 行基 was born in 668 into a family descended from Korean nobles. At the age of fifteen, he left home to become a Buddhist novice and subsequently studied Hossō doctrine, probably under the Japanese Hossō monk Dōshō 道昭 (d. 700). Dōshō had studied in China under Hsüan-tsang and after returning to Japan had supervised construction projects in various provinces which benefited the villagers and townspeople.

From 704 to 712 Gyōgi is said to have devoted himself to supporting his aged mother and then to mourning her death.[87] However, during this time he also had begun to travel to various parts of Japan in order to supervise construction projects which would benefit the local populace. Some of the projects which Gyōgi directed were building bridges, ponds, and canals, establishing ferries, and setting up rest houses for travelers and those on their way to do corvée labor. Many of these projects were managed by Gyōgi's disciples, pious laymen and laywomen. Although they were not ordained as monks and nuns, these lay followers apparently adopted some monastic practices such as begging and performing religious austerities. Gyōgi segregated his followers by sex, establishing thirty-four chapels for men and fifteen for women.[88] Many of Gyōgi's disciples came from the large numbers of people who attended his sermons and were attracted by his virtuous deeds.[89]

---

[85] Ibid., p. 588a. For a discussion of this term, see Chapter 9.

[86] Ibid., p. 593a.

[87] Futaba Kenkō has expressed his doubts concerning the traditional view that Gyōgi spent the years from 704 to 712 caring for his mother ["Gyōgi no shōgai to hanritsuryō Bukkyō no seiritsu," *Nanto Bukkyō* 5 (1961): 19].

[88] Nakai Shinkō, *Nihon kodai no Bukkyō to minshū*, Nihonjin no kōdō to shisō, vol. 22 (Tokyo: Hyōronsha, 1973), p. 127.

[89] Some scholars have maintained that Gyōgi's followers were from the upper classes; however, Futaba has effectively argued that most of them were from the lower classes ("Gyōgi

Gyōgi's activities were not approved of by the court, as they violated many of the *Regulations for Monks and Nuns* (*Sōniryō* 僧尼令).[90] These regulations required monks and nuns to remain in their temples except when they were permitted to travel to the mountains to meditate. No unauthorized monastic establishments were to be set up. Nor were monks to preach to the masses or falsely expound the doctrine of karmic retribution. Although many of the rules in the *Sōniryō* might be overlooked, Gyōgi's actions were too flagrant to be ignored by the court. As early as 712 the court had criticized Gyōgi. An edict issued by the court in 717, read:

> These days the streets are filled with an ordinary monk named Gyōgi and his followers. They preach the karmic retribution of good and evil irresponsibly and mislead people by organizing groups and burning fingers and elbows as they abuse the Buddha's teaching to ask for donations. They cause disturbances among both monks and laymen, as well as bring the four classes of people (warriors, farmers, artisans, merchants) to abandon their work. They violate the Buddha's teachings and break the nation's laws.[91]

Preaching irresponsibly to the people was a serious violation punishable by the laicization of the monk. Yet despite the edict's specific mention of Gyōgi by name, he does not seem to have been seriously persecuted by the government. The edict may have been meant as a general warning to Gyōgi since no specific instances of violations were indicated, perhaps Gyōgi was mentioned only as an example of the type of monk the court wished to discourage. By the time of the proclamation, many of the regulations in the *Sōniryō* were no longer being enforced.[92] Whatever the reason was for the court's hesitation to act, Gyōgi did not respond to the government's orders by diminishing his activities. Rather, the rate at which he established chapels increased.

Government pressure on Gyōgi began to decrease in 731, when the court permitted his male disciples above sixty-one and female disciples above fifty-five to be ordained as monks and nuns. In subsequent years, government documents referred to Gyōgi with honorific terms

---

no shōgai," pp. 40–41).

[90] The *Sōniryō* have been translated by George Sansom, "Early Japanese Law and Administration," *Transactions of the Asiatic Society of Japan,* second series 11 (1934): 127–34.

[91] *Shoku Nihongi,* Yōrō 1. 4. 23. The English translation is based in part on Nakamura, *Miraculous Stories from the Japanese Buddhist Tradition,* p. 24.

[92] Nakai, *Nihon kodai no Bukkyō to minshū,* pp. 80–85.

such as teacher 師位 or venerable 大德, an indication that Gyōgi was regarded with favor by at least some of the officials at court.[93] The government's attitudes towards Buddhism were changing. It could no longer confine monks and nuns to temples and call upon them only for court ceremonies. Some compromises with popular religious movements had to be made. Gyōgi and his followers were motivated by religious zeal, not the desire to avoid taxes or corvée labor requirements. Their willingness to live in groups segregated according to sex was a measure of their earnestness. Thus by granting Gyōgi's older disciples the right to be ordained, the court was responding to the more serious religious interests of the masses. At the same time, the court would not be deprived of much economically since older people were taxed at lower rates.[94]

By 743 Gyōgi was highly esteemed at court. Emperor Shōmu (r. 724–49) respected him and received the bodhisattva precepts from him.[95] Moreover, Gyōgi was appointed to a position in the Sōgō in 745. The extraordinary post of *daisōjō* 大僧正 (great chief executive), the highest position in the Sōgō, was created especially for him. His appointment to it, even though he had not held any of the lower-ranking posts in the Sōgō, was dramatic evidence of the emperor's favor.

One of the major problems of interpretation in modern biographies of Gyōgi has been explaining the reasons for the change in the court's treatment of him. Had court expectations of Buddhism changed to the extent that Gyōgi's activities were approved? Or had Gyōgi renounced the activities for which he had previously been criticized in order to be appointed *daisōjō*? Had both sides compromised?[96]

Scholars such as Kitayama Shigeo and Kawasaki Tsuneyuki have offered the explanation generally accepted today. They argued that Gyōgi had been awarded the post of *daisōjō* after he had encouraged the common people to support Emperor Shōmu's plan to construct a giant image of the Buddha (Daibutsu) in Nara and thus saved the foundering project from failure. Yet Gyōgi's support of the Daibutsu project is not mentioned in any of his early biographies. Consequently, Gyōgi probably gave only token encouragement to the undertaking out

---

[93] Ibid., p. 81; and Futaba, "Gyōgi no shōgai," p. 45.

[94] Sansom, "Early Japanese Law and Administration," p. 135.

[95] Futaba, "Gyōgi no shōgai," pp. 53–54.

[96] Tsuruoka Yasuo has summarized the opinions of modern scholars concerning this and several other problems pertaining to Gyōgi's activities. See his *Nihon kodai Bukkyōshi no kenkyū*, pp. 56–68; and *Kodai Bukkyōshi kenkyū*, pp. 444–50. He notes that recent scholarship has favored the view that Gyōgi's attitudes did not change when he was appointed *daisōjō*.

of respect for the emperor. If he had actively supported the construction of the Daibutsu, he would have been advocating a project which
required more labor from the very same commoners whom he had spent
his life aiding. Gyōgi received the post of *daisōjō* as an indication of
Emperor Shōmu's respect for him. It may also have been given to him
with the futile hope that it would encourage him to mobilize the people
to participate in government-sponsored projects such as the construction of the Daibutsu.[97]

During his tenure as *daisōjō,* Gyōgi continued to work on projects
which would benefit the common people. Historical records do not
indicate that he played an active role in the Sōgō or initiated any new
government policies to supervise the clergy.[98] Consequently, the change
in the government's treatment of Gyōgi appears to have been brought
about by a shift in the court's attitudes, not any reversal in Gyōgi's attitudes or activities.

The court still regarded Buddhism primarily as a tool to be used for
the court's benefit. Buddhist monks were summoned to pray for rain or
for the cure of the sick, just as before. The main difference in the court's
attitude was that it now perceived Buddhism as a potential tool to pacify
restive commoners. The court was impressed by Gyōgi's ability to mobilize
men and had hopes that Gyōgi's abilities could be utilized to defuse some
of its problems with a populace which balked at the heavy taxes and corvée
labor duties imposed upon it. Some members of the courts may have
been particularly impressed by Gyogi's seemingly superhuman ability
to observe and effectively handle large numbers of people.[99]

In contrast to the court's self-centered goals, Gyōgi and his followers
attempted to benefit all men through their projects, not just themselves.[100]
Their view of Buddhism was much closer to the ideals expressed in
Mahāyāna *sūtras* than those of the court. Consequently Gyōgi did not
oppose the government out of revolutionary fervor. Rather, he violated
the *Sōniryō* (Regulations for Monks and Nuns) because these regulations
limited his activities and contacts with the populace and thereby prevented him from acting on his Mahāyāna ideals. When the government

---

[97] Futaba, "Gyōgi no shōgai," pp. 46–49.

[98] Ibid., p. 54.

[99] The *Nihon ryōki* includes a number of stories concerning Gyōgi's almost superhuman
powers of observation (Nakamura, *Miraculous Stories from the Japanese Buddhist Tradition,*
pp. 170, 201–2). Although these stories were recorded fifty years after Gyōgi's death, they
may relate the types of powers which Gyōgi and other holy men (*hijiri*) were thought to have
even during their lifetimes (ibid., pp. 76–80).

[100] Futaba, "Gyōgi no shōgai," pp. 60–62.

softened its stand on the *Sōniryō*, Gyōgi was willing to accept the post of *daisōjō* in order to spread his teachings to even more people, including the members of the court. Ultimately, the differences between the court's expectations of Buddhism and Gyōgi's views of Buddhism were too great for long-lasting cooperation to result.

Kimura Shōshū has argued that Gyōgi provided Saichō with a model of the ideal Tendai practitioner, the *bosatsusō* 菩薩僧 or bodhisattva monk.[101] Saichō planned to train Tendai monks so that they would be able to both preach to the populace and supervise construction projects which would help the common people.[102] These were the same types of activities in which Gyōgi and his followers engaged. Gyōgi was often called a bodhisattva during his lifetime; after his death people believed he was a manifestation of Mañjuśrī.[103] Since Saichō had proposed that Mañjuśrī be installed as elder (*jōza*) in the dining hall on Mount Hiei, Saichō might have regarded Gyōgi as a model of the ideal monk as manifested by Mañjuśrī. Saichō's proposal that his monks be called 'bodhisattva monks' might have reflected the influence of figures such as as Gyōgi who had been called bodhisattvas by the populace. In the *Nihon ryōiki*, Gyōgi was described in the following way: "On the outside he had the form of a monk, but within were hidden the deeds of a bodhisattva."[104] This description was derived from the *Lotus Sūtra*. Saichō cited the same passage from the *Lotus Sūtra* in his last instructions to his disciples.[105]

The *Nihon ryōiki* included a story in which Gyōgi was criticized by a monk named Chikō 智光 who claimed that Gyōgi was only a mere novice.[106] Consequently, Gyōgi was viewed as a man who had never received the proper *Ssu fen lü* ordination qualifying him to be a monk, but nevertheless dressed and acted as a monk, aiding others through practices recommended in the bodhisattva precepts.

In addition, Gyōgi was mentioned as a forerunner to Saichō in the

---

[101] Kimura, *Dengyō Daishi: daikai konryū no risō to shinnen*, pp. 125–49.

[102] Inoue Kaoru has argued that Gyōgi's projects helped the landowning classes more than they did the masses. Futaba has effectively countered his argument by maintaining that even if some of Gyōgi's projects happened to benefit the landowners, they were primarily intended to help the common people [Futaba, "Gyōgi no shōgai," pp. 37–41].

[103] Nakamura, *Miraculous Stories from the Japanese Buddhist Tradition*, p. 115.

[104] Ibid., p. 168.

[105] *Fa hua ching T* 9: 28a. *Eizan Daishiden, DZ* 5 (*Bekkan*): 40.

[106] Nakamura, *Miraculous Stories from the Japanese Buddhist Tradition*, pp. 168, 170. The story is said to have occurred at the end of Gyōgi's life, shortly after he was appointed *daisōjō*.

following discussion from the *Kenkairon:*

A Demonstration that Mahāyāna Temples Previously Existed in Japan But Were Supplanted by Temples in which Both Hīnayāna and Mahāyāna Practices Were Followed

The *sōtō* (government-appointed monastic leaders) claim: None of the types of temples (which Saichō has described) has ever existed in Japan.

I (Saichō) reply: In the two-hundred years which have passed since Shōtoku Taishi built his temple, a great many more have been built. Out of the three types of temples which I have described, at least one type must have been built (by now). The *vinaya* master (*risshi*) Yojin 影深 of Tōdaiji wrote in his treatise (attacking me): "Exclusively Mahāyāna temples already exist in Japan. The forty-nine chapels established by the chief executive (*sōjō*) Gyōgi are of this type. Moreover, when Chien-chen came to Japan, he followed Śākyamuni Buddha's teachings by conferring the precepts for *śrāvaka,* making the recipients bodhisattva monks.[107] After that time there were no exclusively Mahāyāna temples." Thus I (Saichō) know that the temples in Japan during the early period may be termed 'exclusively Mahāyāna temples,' while temples during the latter period may be called 'temples in which both Hīnayāna and Mahāyāna practices are followed.' Temples should be distinguished according to the faculties of those who practice within them. Bodhisattvas who have faculties suited to Hīnayāna or Common Teachings should receive the Hīnayāna precepts. Bodhisattvas who have faculties suited to the Unique or Perfect Teachings should receive the Mahāyāna precepts. When the *sōtō* claim that none of the (three types of) temples have existed in Japan, they contradict the treatise written by Yōjin (who was in fact defending the position espoused by the *sōtō*).[108]

Although the similarities between Gyōgi and Saichō would seem to suggest that Saichō was influenced by Gyōgi, many important differences between the two men must be noted. None of Gyōgi's activities indicate that he rejected the Hīnayāna precepts as Saichō later did. Gyōgi

---

[107] Yōjin's use of the term 'bodhisattva monk' indicates that the Risshū monks did not accept Saichō's characterization of them as Hīnayāna practitioners.

[108] *DZ* 1: 56.

did not object when the court allowed certain of his followers to receive Hīnayāna ordinations and thus become officially recognized as monks and nuns. In addition, Gyōgi did not object to being appointed to the Sōgō, the governmental organ which supervised the monks in accordance with the *Sōniryō* (Regulations for monks and nuns) and the *Ssu fen lü* precepts.

The assertion in the *Nihon ryōiki* that Gyōgi had been initiated only as a novice, and not ordained as a monk must be questioned. The *Nihon ryōiki's* record of Gyōgi's birthplace and parentage is unreliable, and thus its account of Gyōgi's status must also be doubted.[109] Moreover, according to other early sources, Gyōgi was ordained as a monk when he was twenty-four years old.[110] His receipt of government titles such as teacher (*shii*) and his appointment as great chief executive (*daisōjō*) also suggest that he was ordained, since a proper ordination was a prerequisite for such honors. Yet even if Gyōgi had been properly ordained as a monk with the full *Ssu fen lü* precepts, the legend that he was only a novice was circulating in Japan by the early Heian period when the *Nihon ryōiki* was compiled.[111] Consequently Saichō was probably aware of the legend that Gyōgi was not ordained with the full Hīnayāna precepts and might have been influenced by it.

Gyōgi's efforts to benefit others were probably inspired by the bodhisattva precepts. Since he had studied Hossō doctrines, it is likely that he was inspired by the bodhisattva precepts found in the *Yü ch'ieh shih ti ching* (*Yogācārabhūmiśāstra*).[112] In fact, many of the activities which Gyōgi carried out to assist others were specifically recommended in this work. Gyōgi may have modeled his actions on those of Dōshō, the Japanese Hossō monk who after traveling to China to study the *Yü ch'ieh shih ti lun* under Hsüan-tsang, returned to Japan and devoted his life to helping others. While Saichō relied on the *Fan wang* precepts to inspire his followers, Gyōgi was guided by the precepts of the *Yü*

---

[109] Inoue Kaoru, *Gyōgi,* Jinbutsu sōsho, vol. 24 (Tokyo: Yoshikawa kōbunkan, 1959), pp. 11–12.

[110] Futaba, "Gyōgi no shōgai," pp. 16–17.

[111] There are two theories about the date of compilation of the *Nihon ryōiki*. The first is that it was compiled around the sixth year of the Enryaku Era (789). The second is that it was compiled during the Kōnin Era (810–24). Nakamura argues that the earlier date is the correct one (Nakamura, *Miraculous Stories from the Japanese Buddhist Tradition,* p. 14).

[112] Futaba, "Gyōgi no shōgai," pp. 56–59. The major and minor precepts of the *Yü ch'ieh shih ti lun* did not include descriptions of the social welfare activities in which Gyōgi was engaged. However, the treatise's description of the three collections of precepts (*sanju jōkai*) did mention social welfare (*T* 30: 511a).

ch'ieh shih ti lun.[113]

Although Gyōgi was proclaimed a bodhisattva by others, he did not call himself a bodhisattva. In contrast, Saichō proposed that Tendai monks call themselves bodhisattva monks (*bosatsusō*). Saichō may have been inspired to do so by people who called themselves bodhisattva monks and laymen. These self-proclaimed bodhisattvas began appearing in Nara period historical sources during the Tempyō Era (722–48). About this time the *Yü ch'ieh shih ti lun* and the *Fan wang ching* also began to be listed as the texts which were studied by candidates for ordination. Their appearance indicates that texts containing the bodhisattva precepts were being widely circulated at this time. It may also imply that some men and women were inspired to call themselves bodhisattvas after learning of the bodhisattva precepts from these texts.[114]

These people often organized themselves into groups based on family or village affiliations. Some of the groups centered on the worship of Maitreya, the reputed author of the *Yü ch'ieh shih ti lun*. Maitreya worship among these groups was sometimes combined with indigenous forms of shamanism.[115] Other groups consisted of monks who, having ordained themselves 自度僧, were not recognized by the government, as well as a few officially ordained monks who were forced to wander when their temples were closed by the government. Although some of these people were married, they were not laymen since they followed certain monastic practices such as begging for their food, shaving their heads, wearing robes, and performing religious austerities. As a group, they were often called bodhisattva monks. However some people called themselves bodhisattva novices (*bosatsu shami* 菩薩沙彌) or laymen (*bosatsu ubasoku* 菩薩優婆塞).[116] Many of them travelled about Japan, preaching and begging in villages. The government attempted to suppress the bodhisattva monks since they violated laws restricting the numbers

[113] Ishida Mizumaro ["Gyōgiron," *Shūkyō kenkyū* 150 (1956): 5–6; and *Kairitsu no kenkyū*, p. 281] has maintained that Gyōgi followed the *Fan wang* precepts, but his argument is not convincing.

[114] Itō Yuishin, "Nara jidai ni okeru bosatsusō ni tsuite," *Bukkyō daigaku kenkyū kiyō* 33 (1957): 46–47, 54. Several self-proclaimed bodhisattvas appear in records concerning the copying of the *Yü ch'ieh shih ti lun*. Some of them used the character *yü* 瑜 from the *Yü ch'ieh shih ti lun* in their religious names (ibid., p. 48).

[115] The story that Asaṅga periodically ascended to Tuṣita Heaven in order to record Maitreya's teachings was probably well suited to shamanistic beliefs. Many of the people in these groups borrowed the character *ji* 慈 (compassion) from Jishi 慈氏, one of Maitreya's Japanese names, for use in their religious names (Nakai, *Nihon kodai no Bukkyō to minshū*, pp. 186–91).

[116] Ibid., p. 183.

of people who could become monks and nuns, as well as laws limiting the movements of the clergy.

Saichō may have adopted certain elements of the *bosatsusō* tradition when he proposed that his disciples follow the bodhisattva precepts, call themselves *bosatsusō,* and be freed from the supervision of the Sōgō. He differed from the *bosatsusō* tradition, however, in insisting that Tendai monks practice religious austerities on Mount Hiei for twelve years before they preached to the masses. Saichō also eliminated such elements as shamanism from the *bosatsusō's* practices and established stricter requirements to qualify candidates as *bosatsusō.* Finally, although Saichō criticized the Sōgō, he maintained a more conciliatory attitude towards the government than had some of the Nara period *bosatsusō.* Saichō was willing to place his monks under the jurisdiction of the council of State (*dajōkan*) and to accept some limitations on the number of monks allotted to the Tendai School.

Saichō's only reference to Gyōgi in the *Kenkairon* is found in the passage which was translated earlier in this section. Saichō's adversary Yōjin introduced Gyōgi into the argument and identified Gyōgi's chapels as 'exclusively Mahāyāna temples.' Saichō quoted Yōjin's treatise to prove that Yōjin held a position which contradicted that of the other monastic leaders of Nara who claimed that no such temples had ever existed in Japan. Nowhere did Saichō clearly state that he regarded Gyōgi's 'exclusively Mahāyāna temples' as forerunners to the Tendai establishment on Mount Hiei. The Perfect precepts and the educational program at Mount Hiei were radically different from those advocated by Gyōgi. As Saichō repeatedly stated, the Perfect precepts had never been conferred in Japan.[117]

In conclusion, Gyōgi's activities and the *bosatsusō* may have inspired Saichō's proposal that advanced Tendai monks devote themselves to preaching and supervising projects which would benefit the populace. However, Saichō also may have been influenced by Buddhist texts which advocated social welfare projects, by the activities of any number of Chinese monks or of Japanese monks such as Dōshō.[118] The activities of Gyōgi or the *bosatsusō* during the Nara period may have demonstrated to Saichō that a person could be a pious Buddhist monk even though he adhered to only the bodhisattva precepts and had never received a

---

[117] See footnotes 3 and 4 of this chapter.

[118] The social welfare activities of Chinese monks are described in Michihata Ryōshū, *Chūgoku Bukkyō to shakai fukushi jigyō* (Kyōto: Hozokan, 1967).

Ssu fen lü ordination. However, until better evidence is found, any theory concerning the influence of Gyōgi or the Nara period *bosatsusō* upon Saichō must remain speculative. Finally, Saichō's use of the *Fan wang* precepts and his requirement that Tendai monks practice twelve years on Mount Hiei before preaching to the general populace clearly distinguished his proposals from the activities of Gyōgi and the *bosatsusō*.

Conclusion

From among the many influences which affected Saichō's decision to ordain Tendai monks with the *Fan wang* precepts, three are especially noteworthy. First are the anti-Hīnayāna polemics and the descriptions of ordinations with bodhisattva precepts found in Mahāyāna texts. Saichō cited many of these in the *Kenkairon* to support his position. Early Mahāyāna Buddhist practitioners in India may have performed ordinations using only the bodhisattva precepts. This type of ordination and other Mahāyāna practices were not approved of by Hīnayāna Buddhists. The Mahāyāna adherents replied with scathing polemics against the Hīnayāna Buddhists.

The Chinese compilers of the *Fan wang ching* and the *Ying lo ching* included anti-Hīnayāna passages in their works. In fifth century China, the criticism of certain texts and practices as Hīnayāna (literally, inferior vehicle or teachings) served as an important means of organizing and evaluating the numerous and often contradictory Buddhist works which were being circulated. Thus if Chinese Buddhists were dissatisfied with the many, often seemingly trivial rules which were included in the full Hīnayāna *vinayas,* they could have expressed their discontent through such works as the *Fan wang ching*.[119] Saichō, too, relied on Indian and Chinese works with anti-Hīnayāna statements to support his position.

Second, the Chinese T'ien-t'ai School provided many of the doctrines which Saichō used to explain and justify his position. Chinese T'ien-t'ai masters usually relied on both the Hīnayāna and Mahāyāna precepts. However, Chih-i developed concepts such as the 'Perfect precepts' (*enkai* 圓戒) and the 'bodhisattva who performed Sudden practices' (*tongyō bosatsu* 頓行菩薩) which were to be of crucial importance to Saichō. The eighth century T'ien-t'ai scholar Ming-kuang interpreted these

---

[119] Daoxuan and other Chinese monks who lectured on the precepts complained that many of their countrymen asserted that because they were Mahāyāna Buddhist monks, they need not concern themselves with the Hīnayāna precepts [Yoshitsu Yoshihide "Chūgoku Bukkyō ni okeru Daijō to Shōjō," *Komazawa daigaku Bukkyō gakubu ronshū* 1 (1971):128–34].

concepts in such a way that he could justify adhering to the *Fan wang* rather than to the Hīnayāna *Ssu fen lü* precepts. However, Ming-kuang did not actually reject the *Ssu fen lü* ordination. Although Ming-kuang's theories were not very influential in China, they provided the doctrinal justification for Saichō's proposals.

Third, Gyōgi and the *bosatsusō* of the Nara period may have served as concrete examples of the practicality of adhering to the bodhisattva precepts, as well as demonstrated that pious Buddhist 'monks' did not necessarily have to receive Hīnayāna ordinations. Although there is no conclusive evidence in the *Kenkairon* proving that Gyōgi or the *bosatsusō* influenced Saichō, Saichō may have hesitated to refer to the *bosatsusō* because government edicts had often criticized their activities. The similarities between Saichō's proposals and the activities of the *bosatsusō* deserve additional study.

CHAPTER THIRTEEN

THE INTEGRATION OF THE TEACHINGS OF JAPANESE TENDAI

Saichō hoped to introduce much more than Tendai to Japan when he returned from his studies in China. Much of his time after his return was devoted to spreading and mastering Esoteric Buddhist teachings and rituals. Late in his life the ordination conferring the *Fan wang* precepts came to play a major role in his thought. These syncretistic elements in Saichō's teachings eventually led to new developments in Japanese Tendai doctrine and practice as Saichō's successors combined various Buddhist traditions in ways not seen in the Chinese T'ien-t'ai tradition. In this chapter Saichō's efforts to integrate the various traditions which he brought back to Japan are discussed.

Problems In Chinese T'ien-t'ai At The Time Of Chan-Jan (711–782). Chih-i (538–557) had developed a number of classification systems to organize Buddhist teachings into an understandable whole. The purpose of these systems was to prove that the *Lotus Sūtra* revealed the Buddha's ultimate doctrine. Chih-i had argued that all prior teachings pointed toward this end and thus to some extent embodied the Perfect teaching of the *Lotus Sūtra*. At the same time, Chih-i's classification systems indicated that certain teachings were farther from the ultimate teaching than others. Among the teachings criticized were those of the Ti-lun and She-lun schools, as well as Fa-yün's 法雲 (467–529) commentary on the *Lotus Sūtra*.

By Chan-jan's (711–782) time, the traditional T'ien-t'ai classifications developed by Chih-i needed to be supplemented. The She-lun and Ti-lun schools had been supplanted by other traditions. Three new and influential schools, the Fa-hsiang, Hua-yen, and Ch'an, had been established. The Fa-hsiang School had received imperial support during the early T'ang Dyanasty. At approximately the same time the T'ien-t'ai School entered a period of obscurity. In fact, practically nothing is known about the lives, teachings, and writings of the three T'ien-t'ai patriarchs between Chih-i's disciple Kuan-ting (561–632) and Chan-jan. In the middle of the eighth century, Chan-jan strove to revive the fortunes of the T'ien-t'ai School. In order to do so, he had to defend T'ien-t'ai teachings against the claims of these new rival schools. Chan-jan thus had to evaluate doctrinal systems which had not existed at Chih-i's time.

The Fa-hsiang School was one of the chief targets of Chan-jan's criticism. The de facto founder of the Fa-hsiang School, Tz'u-en 慈恩 (633–682), had written a commentary on the *Lotus Sūtra* entitled the *Fa hua hsüan tsan* 法華玄贊. The positions argued in this commentary differed substantially from many of Chih-i's interpretations. Tz'u-en argued that the *Lotus Sūtra* was not the ultimate teaching, that the three vehicles led to separate and distinct goals and that some beings could never attain Buddhahood. These themes were further developed in commentaries on the *Lotus Sūtra* written by Tz'u-en's followers. Chan-jan criticized the Fa-hsiang position in his three-fascicle work, the *Fa hua wu pai wen lun* 法華五百問論. The dispute between the T'ien-t'ai and Fa-hsiang Schools was later revived in the exchanges between Saichō and Tokuitsu.[1]

Chan-jan was a contemporary of Shen-hui 神會 (d. 760), the Ch'an monk who played a pivotal role in the establishment of the Southern School of Ch'an. Chan-jan was not very antagonistic toward the Ch'an tradition, perhaps because of the similarities between Ch'an and T'ien-t'ai practice. He did, however, criticize the Ch'an patriarch Bodhidharma and the *Leng chia ching* 楞伽經 (*Laṅkāvatārasūtra*), one of the most important *sūtras* in the Ch'an tradition. At the same time, Chan-jan may have maintained close relations with several monks from the Northern School of Ch'an.[2] Saichō's interest in Northern School and Niu-t'ou Ch'an may have had its roots in such relations between Ch'an and T'ien-t'ai monks.

Chan-jan's attitude toward the Hua-yen School was particularly complex. The fourth patriarch of the Hua-yen School, Ch'eng-kuan 澄觀 (737–838?), had studied T'ien-t'ai doctrine under Chan-jan. Probably as a result of this relationship, Chan-jan wrote a number of works

---

[1] The major differences between the T'ien-t'ai and Fa-hsiang interpretation of the *Lotus Sūtra* are discussed in Chapter 7. Chan-jan's *Fa hua wu pai wen lun* is found in *Z* 2. 5. 4. 334–401. The *Fa hua hsüan tsan* is *T* no. 1723.

[2] Chan-jan's criticisms of the Ch'an tradition are discusssed in Andō, *Tendai shōgu shisō-ron*, pp. 146–47. The evidence for Chan-jan's close relations with Northern Ch'an monks was first presented by Tajima Tokuon, "*Shikan girei* chōsakukō," *Sange gakuhō* n. s. 11 (1937). Tajima's argument has been discussed by Hibi, *Tōdai Tendaigaku kenkyū*, pp. 97–110. The relationship between T'ien-t'ai and Ch'an monks in the early T'ang has been a subject of recent scholarly debate. Sekiguchi Shindai has argued that the two traditions were very closely related (*Zenshū shisōshi*, Tokyo: Sankibō Busshorin, 1966).

criticizing the Hua-yen position on such subjects as the Buddha-nature and the classification of doctrine. However, even as Chan-jan was criticizing Hua-yen doctrines, he was also being influenced by them, adapting Hua-yen theories on the relationship between the absolute and phenomenal realms to fit T'ien-t'ai teachings. He also relied extensively on Hua-yen sources such as the *Hua yen ching* (*Avataṃsakasūtra*) and the *Ta ch'eng ch'i hsin lun* (*The Awakening of Faith*).[3] T'ien-t'ai use of Hua-yen doctrines eventually resulted in the development of *shan-chia* 山家 (mountain) and *shan-wai* 山外 (outside of the mountain) sects in the T'ien-t'ai school during the Sung Dynasty,

Saichō was influenced by Chan-jan's efforts to differentiate between T'ien-t'ai and Hua-yen teachings. As a youth, Saichō had studied Hua-yen works by Ch'eng-kuan's teacher, Fa-tsang. Chan-jan's arguments must have helped Saichō clearly distinguish the differences between T'ien-t'ai and Hua-yen doctrines. Saichō, for example, adopted Chan-jan's argument that the *Lotus Sūtra* surpassed all elements in the T'ien-t'ai classifications of four types of teaching and four methods of conversion (*Hokke chōhachi* 法華超八)[4] and was thus superior to all other *sūtras* including the *Hua Yen ching*. At the same time, Chan-jan's adoption of Hua-yen doctrines and sources also must have appealed to Saichō. In fact, Saichō had studied Hua-yen doctrine before reading T'ien-t'ai works and continued to be influenced by Hua-yen doctrines throughout his life.

Besides defending the T'ien-t'ai School against other schools, T'ien-t'ai scholars had to contend with another important problem: the growing tendency of T'ien-t'ai monks to incorporate elements of other Buddhist traditions into their teachings. As was noted earlier, Chan-jan had adopted certain Hua-yen teachings at the same time he was refuting Hua-yen criticisms of T'ien-t'ai. Monks such as I-hsing were noted for their expertise in both T'ien-t'ai and Esoteric doctrine. T'ien-t'ai monks were also interested in the *Ssu fen lü* and *Fan wang* precepts. In addition, Ch'an

---

[3] Chan-jan and Ch'eng-kuan both received their *Ssu fen lü* ordinations from the same monk, T'an-i 曇一. Chan-jan's criticisms of Hua-yen doctrine are found in the *Chih kuan i li* (*T* no. 1913), the *Chin kang pei lun* (*T* no. 1932), and his commentaries on the *Mo ho chih kuan* (*T* 46: 292b) and the *Fa hua hsüan i* (*T* 33:823b, 887b–c, 950c). Modern scholars are divided on whether Chan-jan was criticizing Ch'eng-kuan or another Hua-yen monk such as Fa-tsang. Ch'eng-kuan did not reply to Chan-jan's attacks for reasons that are not clear. These issues are discussed in Kamata Shigeo, *Chūgoku Kegon shisōshi no kenkyū* (Tokyo: Tokyo daigaku shuppankai, 1965), pp. 466–74. A summary of the complex issues discussed by Chan-jan can be found in Andō, *Tendai shōgu shisōron*, pp. 150–56.

[4] *Shugo kokkaishō, DZ* 2:214.

monks were often associated with T'ien-t'ai meditation centers. Consequently, it is not surprising that while Saichō was on Mount T'ien-t'ai, he was able to receive instruction in Tendai and Esoteric Buddhism, as well as Niu-t'ou Ch'an and the *Fan wang* precepts. In addition, Gishin's *Ssu fen lü* ordination was attended by T'ien-t'ai monks. Monks of many traditions had long gathered also at the T'ien-t'ai center at Yü-ch'üan-ssu.[5] The Northern Ch'an master P'u-chi 普寂 (651–739) and Chien-chen's teacher, the *Ssu fen lü* master Heng-ching 恒景 (634–712), were among the monks associated with Yü-ch'üan-ssu 玉泉寺.

Saichō's Syncretism

Despite their interest in other Buddhist traditions, T'ien-t'ai monks did not develop a widely accepted rationale for integrating these various teachings. Consequently when Saichō returned to Japan with his various initiations and ordinations, he probably had no clear idea of how he would integrate them. In most of his writings, Saichō wrote about the teachings of only one tradition at a time.[6] For example, in the *Kenkairon* he primarily discussed the *Fan wang* precepts and defended the proposals which he had advanced in the *Shijōshiki*. Although Tendai terms were used in the *Kenkairon,* the work cannot be considered an attempt to interpret the bodhisattva precepts with traditional Tendai, Esoteric or Ch'an teachings. In the same way, most of Saichō's writings which criticized Tokuitsu were concerned with the *Lotus Sūtra* and Tendai teachings, not with the *Fan wang* precepts, Esoteric Buddhism, or Zen. Even though Saichō's discussions of *sokushin jōbutsu* (the attainment of Buddhahood in this very existence) were influenced by Tendai, Kegon and Esoteric doctrines, in general, his writings do not indicate that Saichō attempted to develop a comprehensive system which would integrate the teachings which he brought back from China. This task fell, instead, to his successors: Kōjō, Enchō, and Tokuen, as well as to the more

---

[5] For Yü-ch'üan-ssu, see Sekiguchi, *Tendai shikan no kenkyū,* pp. 185–205. For evidence of early collaboration between Ch'an and T'ien-t'ai monks, see ibid., pp. 215–40. Hibi Nobutada lists a large number of Chinese monks of various traditions who studied T'ien-t'ai teachings in *Tōdai Tendaigaku kenkyū,* pp. 40–57. Eventually the T'ien-t'ai establishments at Yü-ch'üan-ssu and Mount T'ien-t'ai became rivals. The Yü-ch'üan-ssu monks even suggested that Hui-chen 慧眞 (633–751) rather than Chan-jan was the sixth T'ien-t'ai patriarch. However, the rivalry between the two centers was probably not pronounced until after Chan-jan's death (ibid., pp. 36–37).

[6] Of course significant exceptions to this rule can be found. For instances of Esoteric concepts applied to Tendai, see Katsumata Shunkyō, *Mikkyō no Nihonteki tenkai* (Tokyo: Shunjūsha, 1970), pp. 263–64.

famous Ennin, Enchin, and Annen.

The Authorship Of The Naishō Buppō Sōjō Kechimyakufu
內證佛法相承血脈譜 (*Also Known As The Kechimyakufu*).

Saichō's presentation of the lineages in the *Kechimyakufu*, however, suggests how he might have conceived of the relationships between the various traditions he had studied. The *Kechimyakufu* was a work primarily concerned with proving that Saichō's teachings were orthodox. The *Kenkairon engi* also included a number of documents which proved that he had studied under qualified teachers in China.

Most of the major primary sources used in this study of Saichō's biography and thought have been accepted by modern scholars as authentic works by Saicho or his immediate disciples The *Kechimyakufu*, however, has been the object of serious criticism. Since this text contained lineages demonstrating the orthodoxy of Saichō's various teachings, some scholars have argued that it may have been altered either to bolster Tendai claims that Saichō studied under eminent Chinese teachers or to prove that later Tendai teachings had their roots in China. The criticisms of the *Kechimyakufu* are investigated in this section.

The *Kechimyakufu*[7] is said to have been presented to the emperor along with the *Kenkairon* in the year 820.[8] Although its authenticity is questioned in Gishin's (781–833) bibliography,[9] it is mentioned in the *Eizan Daishiden*, the *Denjutsu isshinkaimon* and the *Jōkenkaironhyō*,[10] as well as in several of Annen's works.[11] In the bibliographies by Katō 可透 (fl. 1725) and Ryūdō 龍堂, it is listed as authentic.[12] Because most of the evidence indicates that it is authentic, most modern scholars believe that it was composed by Saichō. However, its classification as a work of doubtful authenticity in Gishin's bibliography has continued to cast a shadow on its origins.

The manuscripts used in compiling the *Dengyō Daishi zenshū* text all date from the early eighteenth century, although one manuscript does have an inscription tracing it back to a copy of the text dated 1219. Because the history of the text is unclear, and because of the bitter rivalry

---

[7] *DZ* 1:199–248.

[8] *Denjutsu isshinkaimon, DZ* 1:558.

[9] *DZ* 5 (*Bekkan*): 158. The *Kechimyakufu* is the very last work listed in the bibliography.

[10] *Eizan Daishiden, DZ* 5 (*Bekkan*): 45; *Denjutsu isshinkaimon, DZ* 1:558; and *Jōkenkaironhyō, DZ* 1:258, 261.

[11] *Kyōjisō, T* 75:355a; and *Kyōjisōron, T* 75:363c.

[12] *DZ* 5 (*Bekkan*): 165, 181.

among the Tendai, Shingon and Zen schools, some scholars have questioned the Esoteric and Zen lineages found in the *Kechimyakufu*. Since Saichō's Esoteric ordinations are discussed in his biography,[13] the following discussion will focus on his Zen initiations.

The Zen lineage was criticized by Ushiba Shingen 牛場眞玄 as an attempt by medieval Tendai scholars to prove that early Tendai teachings incorporated Zen teachings. By comparing passages from the *Kechimyakufu* with passages from it cited in Eisai's 榮西 *Kōzen gokokuron* 興禪護國論, Ushiba arrived at the dubious conclusion that the *Kechimyakufu* was written by Eisai (1141–1215) in order to prove that Zen practices had been used by Tendai monks during Saichō's time.[14]

A more serious and extensive attempt at criticism was made by Sasaki Kentoku 佐佐木憲德 in 1938. Sasaki criticized the title and the compilation of the work. In the *Jōkenkaironhyō* Saichō had stated that he had submitted the *Kenkairon* and the *Buppō kechimyaku,* a work detailing his religious lineages, to the court. Sasaki argued that since Saichō referred to the *Kenkairon* by its full name, he probably also referred to the *Buppō kechimyaku* by its full name. Consequently, the *Naishō Buppō sōjō kechimyakufu* is probably either a different work, or more likely, an expanded version of the *Buppō kechimyaku.*[15]

In addition, the *Naishō Buppō sōjō kechimyakufu* was composed in a different manner than Saichō's other works. An inscription at the end of the work notes that the work was dictated to Saichō's disciple Shinchū.[16] Yet Saichō dictated no other work to a disciple. Furthermore, the name Shinchū did not appear in any other early Heian period document. The *Eizan Daishiden,* written by One-vehicle Chū (Ichijō Chū 一乘忠), can perhaps be attributed to Shinchū 眞忠, rather than to Ninchū 仁忠, the disciple to whom it is traditionally ascribed.[17] In the Kamakura period history of the Tendai School, the *Eigaku yōki,* Shinchū is said to have occupied a number of important posts in the early Tendai School.[18] Sasaki claimed that the sudden emergence of Shinchū

---

[13] See Chapters 4 and 6.

[14] "Dengyō Daishi no zenbō sōjō ni tsuite: *Naishō Buppō kechimyakufu* wo chūshin to shite," *TG* 10 (1967): 95–100. For the text of Eisai's *Kōzen gokoku,* see Yanagita Seizan, *Chūsei zenke no shisō* (Tokyo: Iwanami shoten, 1972), pp. 19, 392. See Chapter 4 for additional comments on Saichō's Zen transmission.

[15] *Sange gakushōshiki shinshaku,* pp. 611–12, 648. Sasaki's criticisms of the *Kechimyakufu* occupy almost eighty pages of his work, pp. 46–60 and 611–74.

[16] *DZ* 1:247.

[17] For a discussion of the authorship of the *Eizan Daishiden,* see Fukui Kōjun, "*Eizan Daishiden* no saikentō," *TG* 15(1972): 8–10.

in later documents was due to the efforts of later Tendai monks to defend questionable Esoteric and Zen lineages found in the *Naishō Buppō sōjō kechimyakufu* against the attacks of monks from other schools.

Sasaki continued by arguing that the *Buppō kechimyaku* mentioned in the *Jōkenkaironhyō* had probably been only a very brief work. The *Naishō Buppō sōjō kechimyakufu* in circulation today was based on this work, but had been expanded and emended by the ninth century Tendai scholar Annen. By Annen's time, the Tendai School was competing with the Shingon School. Consequently, Sasaki asserted that Annen had altered Saichō's Esoteric lineage so that Saichō appeared to have received the dual (*ryōbu*) initiations from Shun-hsiao and Mixed Esoteric (*zōmitsu*) initiations from Chinese monks in Yüeh-chou. Sasaki claimed that originally the Esoteric lineage in the *Buppō kechimyaku* had been a lineage for the diamond precepts (*kongōhōkai*) which Saichō conferred at Esoteric initiations.[19]

Sasaki also questioned the Ch'an lineage found in the *Naishō Buppō sōjō kechimyakufu*. He maintained that Saichō had included the Northern School of Ch'an lineage in order to authenticate the ordination he had received from Gyōhyō, not to indicate that he had studied any Ch'an teachings. Moreover, Annen had later interpreted the Ch'an lineage as a reference to Ch'an teachings and expanded it by using a number of Ch'an works brought to Japan after Saichō's death. Annen thus supplemented Saichō's *Buppō kechimyaku* much as Ennin had supplemented Saichō's *Kenkairon* with the *Ken'yō daikairon* 顯揚大戒論. In addition, Sasaki argued that Saichō would not have had the time to receive the Niu-t'ou (Ox-head) Ch'an transmission in China which the *Naishō Buppō sōjō kechimyakufu* listed. This transmission had been included to supplement the Northern School of Ch'an transmission which Saichō had received from Gyōhyō.[20]

Sasaki compared the *Naishō Buppō sōjō kechimyakufu* with the *Jōshūron* 定宗論 by Renkō 蓮綱, a work which defended the Tendai School against the Nara schools. Renkō was a Tendai monk who was probably a contemporary of Enchin. He spent most of his life in Kyushu preaching Tendai doctrines. His work, the *Jōshūron*, included Tendai lineages to defend the Tendai School against Sanron claims that the

---

[18] *GR* 15:521–22.
[19] *Sange gakushōshiki shinshaku*, p. 636. For the *kongōhōkai*, see footnote 12 in Chapter 5.
[20] *Sange gakushōshiki shinshaku*, pp. 625–46. The Niu-t'ou transmission is listed in *DZ* 1:214.

Tendai School was not based on Indian Buddhist teachings. Renkō derived his lineages from Chih-i's *Mo ho chih kuan* and from some of the same works quoted in the *Naishō Buppō sōjō kechimyakufu*. However, in contrast with the lineages found in the *Naishō Buppō sōjō kechimyaku-fu*, the lineages in the *Jōshūron* were less detailed, included different numbers of patriarchs and arranged the patriarchs in different sequences.[21] Consequently, Sasaki concluded that Renkō did not have a copy of the *Naishō Buppō sōjō kechimyakufu* when he composed the *Jōshūron* even though he had access to other Tendai works. Moreover, since the *Jōshūron*'s lineages were less detailed than those in the *Naishō Buppō sōjō kechimyakufu*, Sasaki argued that the extant version of the *Kechimyakufu* was composed later than the *Jōshūron*.

Sasaki's criticism of the *Naishō Buppō sōjō kechimyakufu* was comprehensive. However, his arguments were often forced and can be easily countered. For example, the existence of the two titles *Buppō kechimya-ku* and *Naishō Buppō sōjō kechimyakufu* did not prove that two versions of Saichō's lineages had actually existed. Sasaki's arguments that the *Naishō Buppō sōjō kechimyakufu* included quotations from Ch'an works to which Saichō could not have had access was based on a similar discrepancy between the titles of several works. In fact, the quoted works could have been brought to Japan by either Saichō or by Tao-hsüan.[22] Sasaki's claim that the Esoteric and Zen lineages were originally included in Saichō's lineages because of their relevance to the precepts has little evidence to support it. The precepts were not mentioned in the Esoteric lineages and were referred to only cursorily in the Zen lineage. Sasaki supported his claims primarily with statements from Kōjō's *Denjutsu isshinkaimon* that the One-vehicle precepts (*ichijōkai*) were transmitted by Zen monks. However, Kōjō's views on this subject were different from those of Saichō.[23] Finally, the discrepancies between the *Kechi-myakufu* and Renkō's *Jōshūron* did not prove that the *Kechimyakufu* was written after the *Jōshūron*. Since Renkō lived in Kyushu, he probably did not have access to a complete collection of Tendai works. Sasaki also did not support his conclusion that Annen expanded the *Buppō kechimyaku* by analyzing works by Annen. In conclusion, although Sasaki pointed out a number of interesting problems in the *Kechimyaku-fu*, none of them conclusively proved that the work was not written by

[21] *Jōshūron*, *T* 74:314b–15a; and *Sange gakushōshiki shinshaku*, pp. 655–74.
[22] *DZ* 1:214–15.
[23] *Sange gakushōshiki shinshaku*, p. 59. For Kōjō's use of Zen, see the section on Kōjō in Chapter 15.

Saichō.[24]

Tsuji Zennosuke 辻善之助 discovered an early Heian manuscript of the *Kechimyakufu* in the National Museum in 1944[25] and thereby supported the position that the work was compiled by Saichō or his disciples soon after his death. Today most scholars recognize the work as authentic although a few believe that the work still requires more study.[26] The lineages for Tendai teachings and the *Fan wang* precepts have not been questioned.

The Lineages of the Kechimyakufu

The *Kechimyakufu* was divided into five sections which listed Saichō's religious lineages:

1. The Gozu (Ox-head) and Northern Schools of Zen
2. Tendai
3. The Tendai bodhisattva precepts
4. The Taizōkai and Kongōkai traditions of Pure Esoteric Buddhism (*junmitsu*)[27]
5. Mixed Esoteric teachings (*zōmitsu*)

An analysis of these lineages reveals how Saichō might have begun to integrate these traditions if he had lived longer.

The first section, the lineages of the Ox-head and Northern Schools of Zen, consisted of Śākyamuni Buddha as a manifestation (*Suijaku Shaka Daimunison* 垂迹釋迦大牟尼尊) followed by an unbroken lineage which continued through the Chinese patriarchs and concluded with Saichō.[28]

In contrast, the lineages of the Tendai School did not begin with Śākyamuni as the manifested Buddha who had been born into the Śākya

---

[24] Recent studies have revealed evidence which agrees with certain aspects, but not all of Sasaki's hypothesis concerning the compilation of the *Kechimyakufu*. Satō Tatsugen ["Bosatsukai no ikkōstasu," *Komazawa daigaku Bukkyō gakubu kenkyū kiyō* 34 (1976): 13–18] has noted that well over one-hundred monks of the Northern School of Ch'an were engaged in spreading the precepts. Ordination manuals were written by some of these monks. Sekiguchi Shindai ["*Jubosatsukaigi* Darumahon ni tsuite," *IBK* 9 (1961): 465–70] has discussed a reference to a Zen ordination manual in Annen's *Futsūju bosatsukai kōshaku* (*T* 74: 757b) and suggested that it might be identical to a manual by Tao-hsüan cited in Enchin's notes to the *Jubosatsukaigi* (*DZ* 1: 308). Their conclusions indicate that the Zen lineage in the *Kechimyakufu* might have originally described a transmission of the precepts and that Annen was interested in the Zen precepts.

[25] *Nihon Bukkyōshi* 1: 262–63.

[26] Tsugunaga Yoshiteru, "Daianji Gyōhyō den no kenkyū," *Bukkyō shigaku* 12, no. 3 (1966): 18–19, 31 (note 3).

[27] For a discussion of *junmitsu* and *zōmitsu*, see footnote 24 in Chapter 4 of this study.

[28] *Kechimyakufu, DZ* 1: 200–215.

clan and attained enlightenment at Buddhagāya. Rather it began with Śākyamuni as the source of such manifested Buddhas.[29] This distinction was based on the *Lotus Sūtra* passage in which the Buddha revealed that he had become enlightened myriads of eons ago.[30] The Tendai lineage began with Śākyamuni Buddha's appearance in Tahō Nyorai's (Prabhū-taratna Tathāgata) pagoda (*kuon jitsujō Tahōtatchū Daimunison* 久遠實成多寶塔中大牟尼尊), thus indicating that his ultimate teaching was the same as that of all the Buddhas of the past.[31]

In order to emphasize the orthodoxy of Tendai teachings, Saichō presented two Tendai lineages in the second section of the *Kechimyakufu*. The first combined the traditional two lineages found in the *Mo ho chih kuan*, namely the *konku* 金口 and *konshi* 今師 transmissions of the Buddha's teaching.[32] The *konku* (literally 'golden mouth') lineage began with Śākyamuni. His teaching was transmitted without any loss of content from generation to generation through a series of Indian monks. However, traditional T'ien-t'ai monks claimed that this lineage had ended when the twenty-fourth patriarch had died before he could transmit the teaching to a successor. Consequently no direct connection between the de facto founder of the T'ien-t'ai School, Chih-i, and the patriarchs of Indian Buddhism was demonstrated through the *konku* lineage. In fact, the *konku* lineage was probably included in the *Mo ho chih kuan* primarily to establish the place of Nāgārjuna in the *konshi* transmission of the Buddha's teachings.

The *konshi* 今師 (literally 'current teacher,' because it culminated with the Chinese T'ien-t'ai master Chih-i) lineage was an attempt by Chih-i's disciple Kuan-ting to explain the connection between Indian Buddhism and Chinese T'ien-t'ai. According to this lineage, the T'ien-t'ai patriarch Hui-wen had been enlightened by studying Nāgārjuna's

---

[29] Ibid., pp. 215–30.

[30] See *Lotus Sūtra*, Hurvitz trans, p. 237.

[31] In the *Lotus Sūtra*, Tahō Nyorai (Prabhūtaratna) is said to appear in a *stūpa* to testify to the truth of that *sūtra* whenever it is preached. Although Tahō Nyorai had passed into extinction, the *stūpa* (*Tahōtō*) contained his whole undecayed body, seated as if he were in a trance. After testifying to the truth of the *Lotus Sūtra*, Tahō Nyorai offered half of his seat to Śākyamuni. Because he supposedly would enter *nirvāṇa* soon after preaching the *Lotus Sūtra*, Śākyamuni entered the *stūpa* and sat next to Tahō Nyorai (Hurvitz, tr., *Lotus*, pp. 183–94). Images and paintings of the two Buddhas, who had passed into extinction but miraculously were still active, were found in China and Japan wherever belief in the *Lotus Sūtra* was popular. They appeared in the Yün-kang caves in China during the Six Dynasties Period and in Japan as early as the Asuka Period [Kabutogi Shōkō, "Tahōbutto no keifu," *Hokekyō shinkō no shokeitai*, ed. Nomura Yōshō (Kyoto: Heirakuji shoten, 1976), pp. 433–34].

[32] *Mo ho chih kuan*, fasc. 1A, *TZ* 1:30–70.

Chung lun (*Madhyamakaśāstra*) and *Ta chih tu lun* (*Mahāprajñāpāra-mitopadeśa*). Hui-wen had transmitted his teachings to Hui-ssu, who had in turn transmitted them to Chih-i.

Saichō attempted to prove that Chinese T'ien-t'ai had roots in Indian Buddhism by adopting and combining aspects of both the *konku* and *konshi* lineages into a single lineage. Saichō followed the *konku* lineage from Śākyamuni through Nāgārjuna, but discarded the ten *konku* patriarchs following Nāgārjuna, the fourteenth patriarch. He then added Kumārajīva and his teacher Sūryasoma. Kumārajīva, as the translator of the *Lotus Sūtra* and Nāgārjuna's treatises (especially the *Ta chih tu lun*), served as the link between Indian teachings and the Chinese T'ien-t'ai patriarchs of the *konshi* transmission. The link was a literary one, but since the first Chinese patriarch, Hui-wen had attained enlightenment through Nāgārjuna's writings, the connection was said to be based on a direct perception into Nāgārjuna's teachings. Saichō's Tendai lineage is diagrammed in Chart 5.

When Saichō eliminated any mention of the last ten Indian patriarchs listed in the *Mo ho chih kuan*'s *konku* lineage, he eliminated a potential source of conflict between his Tendai and Zen lineages. Although T'ien-t'ai masters had argued that the *konku* lineage ended with Siṃha's death, Ch'an masters had claimed that Siṃha did, in fact, transmit the Buddha's teaching before he died and that Śākyamuni's teaching had been brought to China by Bodhidharma. Saichō followed the Ch'an interpretation in the *Kechimyakufu*, ignoring T'ien-t'ai arguments that the Ch'an lineages were not valid.[33]

The literary connections between Kumāraījva and Hui-wen in Saichō's first Tendai lineage evidently did not completely satisfy Saichō. Consequently, he presented a second lineage in which he posited a direct link between Śākyamuni Buddha and the T'ien-t'ai patriarchs, Hui-ssu and Chih-i. The second lineage was based on a passage in the Chapter on the Lifespan of the Buddha (*Juryōbon*) of the *Lotus Sūtra* in which it was claimed that Śākyamuni was always preaching the *Lotus Sūtra* on Vulture's Peak (Ryōzen 霊山 or Gṛdhrakūta).[34] When Hui-ssu met Chih-i, early sources reported that Hui-ssu had said, "Long ago we listened together to the *Lotus Sūtra* on Vulture's Peak. Because of this karma, you have now come again."[35] Hui-ssu probably did not intend to have

---

[33] *DZ* 1:202.
[34] *Lotus* (Hurvitz trans), p. 242.
[35] *T'ien t'ai chih che ta shih pieh chuan*, *T* 50:191c; and *Hsü kao seng chuan*, *T* 50:564b.

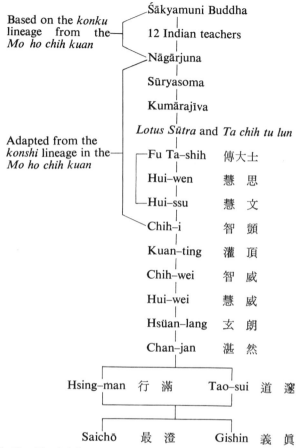

Chart 5. The Tendai lineage presented in Saichō's *Kechimyakufu*.

his words taken literally. Rather he spoke figuratively to tell Chih-i that their meeting did not take place by accident, but because they had karmic links from the past.[36] This type of idea is certainly not unusual in Buddhism. After Chih-i's death, the story was taken literally. By Chan-jan's time it was used as the basis for tracing the direct transmission of the Buddha's ultimate teaching from the *saṃbhogakāya* of Śākyamuni to Hui-ssu and Chih-i.[37] The teaching was well-known and was mentioned in the works of other schools, including Fa-tsang's *Hua*

---

[36] Ōchō, *Hokke shisō no kenkyū* (Kyoto: Heirakuji shoten, 1971), pp. 282, 286.

[37] It is not clear when monks began to take this story literally. Chan-jan referred to it in in the *Chih kuan i li* (*T* 46:454a). Taira Ryōshō ["Ryōzen dōchō ni tsuite," *TG* 14 (1971): 3–5] has argued that this interpretation probably dates back to the period immediately following Chih-i's death.

yen wu chiao chang,[38] a work studied by Saichō as a youth. Saichō was deeply impressed by the story and referred to it in many of his works.[39] This lineage is diagrammed in Chart 6.

The third section of the *Kechimyakufu* relates to the *Fan wang* precepts lineage. It presented Saichō with a new problem. Rushana Butsu (Vairocana Buddha) was the central figure in the *Fan wang ching*. Rushana manifested himself as billions of Śākyamuni Buddhas[40] who preached to sentient beings. Consequently, Saichō's *Fan wang* precepts lineage began with Rushana, who then transmitted the precepts to Śākyamuni. The precepts were subsequently transmitted through a series of Indian monks culminating in Kumārajīva, the supposed translator of the *Fan wang ching*.[41] Saichō then quoted an episode from the *(Hsü) kao seng chuan* in which the T'ien-t'ai patriarch Hui-ssu dreamt of several hundred Indian monks. The leader of the group told Hui-ssu that he needed a new ordination, presumably the *Fan wang* ordination.[42] Saichō bridged the gap between the Indian and Chinese traditions by asserting that Hui-ssu had administered the ordination vows to himself (*jisei jukai* 自誓受戒) after receiving a supernatural sign directing him to do so. In addition, Saichō adapted the Tendai Ryōzen transmission to the bodhisattva precepts, claiming that Hui-ssu and Chih-i both received the bodhisattva precepts directly from Śākyamuni on Ryōzen. Saichō was probably the first to use the Ryōzen transmission as a basic element in the lineages for both the bodhisattva precepts and Tendai.[43] Saichō's lineages for the bodhisattva precepts is diagrammed in Chart 7.

The fourth section of the *Kechimyakufu* related the Pure Esoteric (*junmitsu*) lineages. These originated with Birushana, the central figure in the two most important *sūtras* in the *junmitsu* tradition, the *Ta jih ching* (*Mahāvairocanasūtra*) and the *Chin kang ting ching* (*Sarvata-thāgatatattvasaṃgrahasūtra*).[44] The mixed Esoteric tradition (*zōmitsu*)

---

[38] *T* 40:581a; also see *T'an hsüan chi, T* 35:111b.

[39] *Fuhō engi, DZ* 5:33; *Hokke shūku, DZ* 3:279; *Shugo kokkaishō, DZ* 2:183, 236; *Ehyō Tendaishū, DZ* 3:364. Also see the *Denjutsu isshinkaimon, DZ* 1:594, 626; and *Eizan Daishi-den, DZ* 5 (*Bekkan*): 10, 33.

[40] *Fan wang ching, T* 24:1003c–4a; and *Kechimyakufu, DZ* 1:231. In Japanese Vairocana was referred to as both Birushana and Rushana among other names. Because the distinction between the two transliterations is vital to the argument in this discussion, the Japanese rather than the Sanskrit pronunciation of the Buddha's name is used.

[41] The *Fan wang ching* is generally considered to be a Chinese compilation dating from the middle of the fifth century (Ishida, *Bonmōkyō*, pp. 11–15).

[42] *Kechimyakufu, DZ* 1:232. The original passage did not refer to the *Fan wang* precepts.

[43] Taira, "Ryōzen dōchō ni tsuite," p. 10.

[44] *Kechimyakufu, DZ* 1:237–44. Saichō's Esoteric initiations are discussed in Chapter 3.

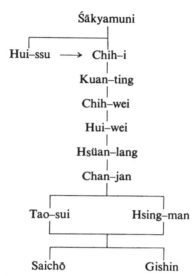

Chart 6. The Tendai Ryōzen (Vulture's Peak) lineage from Saichō's *Kechimyakufu.*

related in the fifth section of the *Kechimyakufu* originated with Śākyamuni, the central figure in most *zōmitsu* scriptures.

Integration Of The Kechimyakufu Lineages.

Saichō integrated these teachings by asserting that they all ultimately came from the same source. At the very beginning of the Tendai lineage, he quoted the *Kuan p'u hsien ching:* "Thereupon the voice in the sky will speak thus, saying, "Śākyamuni Buddha is called Birushana Who Pervades All Places, and His dwelling-place is called Eternally Tranquil Light."[45] The same passage was also quoted in the *Hokke shūku.*[46] The *Kuan p'u hsien ching* was the capping-*sūtra* for the *Lotus Sūtra* and thus was one of the ultimate authorities for the Tendai School. The placement of this quotation at the head of the Tendai lineage in the *Kechimyakufu* insured that it would be interpreted as a key doctrine for the Japanese Tendai School.

The identification of Śākyamuni with Birushana dates back at least

See Chart 3 for Saichō's *junmitsu* lineages from the *Kechimyakufu.* The difference between the central figures in *zōmitsu* and *junmitsu* texts is one of the main features differentiating these two types of Esoteric Buddhism (Matsunaga, *Mikkyō no rekishi*, p. 55).

[45] *Kuan p'u hsien ching*, T 9:392c, quoted in *DZ* 1:215. The English translation of the *Kuan p'u hsien ching* is from Kato Bunno et al., *The Threefold Lotus Sutra* (New York: Weatherhill, 1975), p. 362.

[46] *DZ* 3:266–67. Also note the opening verses to the *Kenkairon, DZ* 1:25.

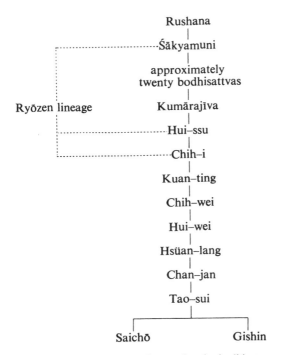

Solid line represents the traditional lineage for the bodhisattva precepts. Broken line represents the Ryōzen lineage.

Chart 7. The lineages for the bodhisattva precepts presented in Saichō's *Kechimyakufu*.

to the *Hua yen ching* (*Avataṃsakasūtra*), in which it was said that the two names were epithets of the same Buddha.[47] In the *Fan wang ching*, Rushana appeared as a *saṃbhogakāya* manifesting Śākyamuni Buddhas in thousands of worlds.[48] A number of theories were developed to further explain the relationship between Śākyamuni, Birushana, and Rushana.[49] One of the best known theories was advanced by Chih-i.[50] He argued that two of the Chinese transliterations of Vairocana's name, Birushana and Rushana, referred to two of the Buddha's bodies. Chih-i regarded Birushana as a *dharmakāya* and Rushana as a *saṃbhogakāya*. Śākyamuni was considered to be a *nirmāṇakāya*. Chih-i's theory was

[47] Ōyama Kōjun, *Mikkyōshi gaisetsu to kyōri* (Kōyasan: Kōyasan daigaku, 1961), pp. 488–89; and *BD* 5:4368c. Birushana is mentioned in the *Tsa a han ching* (*Samyuktāgama*); however, the name is used to refer to the sun rather than as an epithet of the Buddha.

[48] *T* 24:1003b–c.

[49] See Ōyama, *Mikkyōshi gaisetsu to kyōri*, pp. 488–92.

[50] *Fa hua wen chü*, *T* 24:128a; also see Andō, *Tendaigaku: konpon shisō to sono tenkai* (Kyoto: Heirakuji shoten, 1968), pp. 157–60.

influenced by Northern Chinese Ti-lun scholarship, but was also based on the *Hua yen ching* and the *Fan wang ching,* the same two sources which influenced Saichō. Lest it seem that Śākyamuni who was preacher of the *Lotus Sūtra,* was inferior to Rushana, preacher of part of the *Hua yen ching,* Chih-i emphasized that the three bodies were neither one nor of the separate. They were not to be taken as being in either a horizontal (equal) relationship or in a vertical (hierarchical) relationship. The three bodies were fundamentally the same; the seeming differences between them were due to distinctions made by the person viewing them. Among Chinese scholars of Esoteric Buddhism, I-hsing 一行 and Ennin's teacher Yüan-cheng 元政 argued that Śākyamuni and Birushana were identical.

Saichō used the teaching that the two Buddhas were identical to integrate the teachings that made up the Japanese Tendai School. On the basis of Chih-i's theory, the manifested Śākyamuni, the source of both the Zen tradition and the *zōmitsu* Esoteric Buddhist tradition, would be a *nirmāṇakāya* Buddha. Rushana in the *Fan wang ching* would be a *saṃbhogakāya* Buddha. Birushana of the Pure Esoteric (*junmitsu*) tradition would be a *dharmakāya* Buddha.

Saichō's position seemed to depart from the traditional T'ien-t'ai theory.[51] Although Chih-i had maintained that the three bodies of the Buddha were neither in a horizontal nor a vertical relationship, his identification of Śākyamuni with the *nirmāṇakāya* and Birushana with the *dharmakāya* had implied to many monks that Birushana was superior. Saichō countered this tendency by emphasizing that Śākyamuni and Vairocana were identical in all their forms. Saichō's quotation from the *Kuan p'u hsien ching* equating Śākyamuni with Birushana implied that Śākyamuni was a *dharmakāya.*[52] The quotation from the *Lotus Sūtra* stating that Śākyamuni preached eternally on Vulture's Peak indicated that Śākyamuni was also a *saṃbhogakāya.*[53] Finally the identification of Śākyamuni and Vairocana closely paralleled Saichō's insistence that the teachings of the *Lotus Sūtra* and Esoteric Buddhism were in complete agreement (*enmitsu itchi* 圓密一至).

---

[51] Saichō's remarks on the bodies of the Buddha are scattered over his works and are difficult to combine into a comprehensive, consistent position. See Asai, *Jōko Nihon Tendai,* pp. 106–28; Shioiri Ryōchū, "Dengyō Daishi no hongaku shisō," *IBK* 9 (1961): 22–27; Yūki Yoshifumi, "Saichō ni okeru Kegon shisō no eikyō," *Nanto Bukkyō* 32 (1974): 23–27. Tamaki Kōshiro's study of this subject (*Nihon Bukkyō shisōron* 1:175–87) is very useful, but overemphasizes the role of Vairocana in Saichō's thought (pp. 186–87).

[52] *Kechimyakufu, DZ* 1:215, quoted from the *Kuan p'u hsien ching, T* 9:392c.

[53] *Kechimyakufu, DZ* 1:215; quoted from the *Lotus Sūtra, T* 9:42c.

In 814 or 815 Kūkai wrote the *Benkenmitsu nikyō ron*[54] (*The Difference Between Exoteric and Esoteric Buddhism*). In this work he argued that Esoteric Buddhism was superior to exoteric teachings because Esoteric teachings were preached by Birushana, the *dharmakāya* Buddha, while exoteric teachings were preached by Śākyamuni, the *nirmāṇakāya* Buddha. Clearly this implied that the two Buddhas were unequal. Saichō died, however, before he could reply in detail to Kūkai's claims. Later, his disciples, better versed in Esoteric doctrine than Saichō, developed theories to support the position that the two Buddhas were identical.[55]

---

[54] For an English translation, see Hakeda, *Kūkai,* pp. 151–57.

[55] Asai describes early Taimitsu positions in detail, *Jōko Nihon Tendai,* pp. 227–232, 310–314, 443–456, 707–718. Many of the relevant materials have been collected in Hayashida Kōshō, *Kyōshugi gassan,* (Tokyo: 1921). Also see the discussion on Gishin in Chapter 15.

PART THREE

THE EFFECTS OF SAICHŌ'S REFORMS DURING THE EARLY HEIAN PERIOD

CHAPTER FOURTEEN

ADMINISTRATIVE REFORMS

Saichō died before the proposals in his petitions were approved. Consequently, he never wrote a detailed and systematic account of the doctrines underlying the new Tendai use of the *Fan wang* precepts, nor was he able to supervise the way in which the *Fan wang* precepts and the administrative reforms in his petitions were put into effect by the Tendai monks. In this chapter, the history of the Tendai School immediately after Saichō's death and the attempts of his followers to institute his proposals will be discussed. In addition, Saichō's motives in submitting his petitions to court will be examined further, since the actions of Saichō's followers immediately after his death and the approval of his petitions reveal much about Saichō's concerns.

This part of the study is divided into two chapters. In this chapter the manner in which Saichō's proposals for administrative reforms were instituted after his death is described. In an earlier chapter, "The Controversy over the Bodhisattva Precepts," Saichō's desire to free the Tendai School from the domination of the Sōgō (Office of Monastic Affairs) was stressed as the major motive behind his petitions. The research in this and the following chapter corroborate those results. Within a few years of Saichō's death, his disciples had faithfully instituted almost all of Saichō's proposals which had been designed to give the Tendai School more autonomy. In most cases, they carefully followed the procedures outlined in Saichō's petitions. The one significant exception was the provisional Hīnayāna ordination (*keju shōkai* 假受小戒), a proposal which was impractical and unrelated to the autonomy of the Tendai School. The significance of Saichō's reforms became evident soon after his death. They laid the foundation for the Tendai School's expansion into the provinces and its emergence as a major religious institution during the Heian period. Many of Saichō's proposals which contributed to the autonomy of the Tendai School were later adopted by the Shingon School.

The next chapter analyzes the positions which several of Saichō's disciples held on the precepts. The diversity of opinion and the disagreements that arose between Saichō's followers were at least partially due to Saichō's early death and consequent failure to author systematic treatises on the precepts and Esoteric Buddhism. Three of Saichō's disciples who were vitally concerned with the precepts are discussed.

The first, Gishin, received the ordination conferring the bodhisattva precepts in China together with Saichō, and later conducted the first *Fan wang* ordination on Mount Hiei after court approval had been obtained. Yet Gishin never wrote about either the precepts or Esoteric Buddhism even though he was asked to summarize the teachings of the Tendai School and submit them to court. Perhaps he was too unsure of his command of these two areas to write about them, especially in the absence of treatises on the subjects by Saichō or Chinese T'ien-t'ai masters. A number of other Tendai monks clearly believed that the Tendai School should incorporate Esoteric doctrines into its teachings if it were to challenge Kūkai and the Shingon School for preeminence in Japan. The resulting factionalism and preoccupation with Esoteric Buddhism among Tendai monks meant that virtually nothing concerning the Perfect precepts was written during the next few decades.

The one monk who wrote a significant work on the Perfect precepts during this period was Kōjō, Saichō's disciple and liaison with the court during the entire controversy over the bodhisattva precepts, and later, administrator of the precepts platform. Kōjō's major work, the *Denjutsu isshinkaimon,* records a number of conversations with Saichō concerning the petitions submitted to court. Kōjō was probably more knowledgable about Saichō's views on the precepts than any other man. However, Kōjō's treatment of the precepts included theories and terminology which differed from those found in Saichō's writings. The result was a position which stressed the spiritual advantages of the ordination much more than rigid adherence to the precepts. In effect, Kōjō was trying to compensate for the lack of a theoretical base for the precepts by developing doctrines which incorporated Esoteric Buddhist teachings. These were intended to enable the Tendai School to compete with the Shingon School.

The third figure to be considered is Ennin, one of Saichō's most able disciples and the Tendai School's first great Esoteric master. He is said to have served as a teacher (*kyōju ajari* 教授阿闍梨) at the first *Fan wang* ordination on Mount Hiei after Saichō's death. His major work on the precepts, the *Ken'yō daikairon* 顯揚大戒論 (Treatise on Revealing and Praising the Mahāyāna Precepts), was written almost forty years after Saichō's death. Ennin adopted a more conservative position than Kōjō, using many of the same sources as Saichō and refusing to interpret the precepts in terms of Esoteric Buddhist doctrines. He was also more concerned with close adherence to the precepts than was Kōjō. At times Ennin almost seemed to be trying to reconstruct Saichō's view of the precepts.

The variety of views on the precepts found among Saichō's disciples suggests that Saichō died before he could define his position on the more theoretical aspects of the precepts. These differences of opinion clearly contrast with his disciples' virtual unanimity of opinion on the administrative reforms which Saichō had proposed. Other than a few objections by Ninchū, Saichō's disciples were in close agreement on the objectives of their teacher's administrative reforms and how those reforms were to be put into effect. Their unanimity suggests that these reforms were the motivating force behind Saichō's petitions.

The Recognition Of Enryakuji And The Installation Of The Zoku Bettō

On the twenty-sixth day of the second month of 823, the Emperor decreed that the Tendai temple Hieizanji was to be given the new name Enryakuji 延暦寺.[1] While the court had long recognized the Tendai School, it had not officially recognized its main temple as an independent entity. Thus Tendai monks had been registered as being affiliated with the Nara temples.[2] Official recognition of the Tendai temple prepared the way for the various administrative changes which Saichō had requested. The temple's new name Enryakuji referred back to Emperor Kanmu's era name.

The following day, the Council of State (*dajōkan*) ordered that Saichō's proposal be put into effect. The lay administrators (*zoku bettō*) were to test the Tendai yearly ordinand (*nenbundosha*) candidates and report the results first to the Council of State, and later to the Ministry of Civil Administration (*jibushō*). The Council of State would issue the initiation certificate.[3] The test questions were to follow the guidelines laid down in 806.[4]

On the third day of the third month, the Provisional Vice-councillor (*gonchūnagon*) Fujiwara no Mimori and the Vice Controller of the Right (*uchūben*) Ōtomo no Kunimichi were appointed lay administrators

---

[1] *Eizan Daishiden, DZ* 5 (*Bekkan*): 43.
[2] According to the *Gakushō meichō* (*DZ* 1:250–53), most of the Tendai *nenbundosha* were registered with other temples.
[3] *Eizan Daishiden, DZ* 5 (*Bekkan*): 43–44.
[4] *Kenkairon engi, DZ* 1:295.

of Mount Hiei by the court.[5] These two men had been among Saichō's staunchest lay supporters during his lifetime. The lay administrators were to be in charge of the Tendai School's relations with the government. Thus they oversaw the testing of yearly ordinand candidates and the issuance of ordination certificates. They also shepherded the Tendai School's proposals through court channels, assisted the school financially, and occasionally intervened to help settle disputes. Their high positions at court made them invaluable allies for the struggling Tendai School, since they served as influential advocates of the Tendai position in governmental proceedings.[6]

Saichō was the first person in Japan to propose that the position of lay administrator be established. He seems to have modeled the post on the T'ang Dynasty office of *kung te shih* 功德使 (Commissioner of Good Works).[7] *Kung te shih* first became prominent during Tai-tsung's reign (762–779). The office was usually held by the generals of the *Shen ts'e* 神策 armies. At first they were only to aid the temple in meritorious activities, but by 788 they had been officially placed in charge of all Buddhist monastic activities.[8]

Like so many of his other administrative reforms, Saichō's recommendation that *zoku bettō* be appointed may have been based on passages in the *Pu k'ung piao chi* 不空表記, a compilation of documents concerning Amoghavajra's life.[9] Two of Amoghavajra's chief lay disciples held the positions of *kung te shih*. Saichō probably expected the same type of aid from the *zoku bettō* that Amoghavajra had received from the *kung te shih*.

The two Tendai *zoku bettō* posts were usually held by the Grand Minister of the Left (*sadaijin*) and by either the Controller of the Left

---

[5] *Eizan Daishiden, DZ* 5 (*Bekkan*): 44.

[6] Note Kōjō's lavish praise of the first two *zoku bettō* in *Denjutsu isshinkaimon, DZ* 1: 569–70.

[7] *DZ* 1:180, 559. Some modern scholars have maintained that the Japanese offices of *hōzu* 法主 and *zō-Tōdaiji-shi* 造東大寺司 were models for the office of *zoku bettō*. However, Saichō was primarily influenced by the office of *kung te shih*. See Kikuchi Kyōko's informative study, "Zoku bettō no seiritsu," *Shirin* 51 (1968): 103–33.

[8] The office of *kung te shih* during the mid-T'ang Dynasty is described in Tsukamoto Zenryū, "Tōchūki irai no Chōan no kudokushi," *Tsukamoto Zenryū chōsakushū* 3:251–84; Chou Yi-liang "Tantrism in China," *Harvard Journal of Asian Studies* 8(1945): 325–26; and Stanley Weinstein, "Buddhism under the T'ang," *Cambridge History of China*, T'ang volume, no. 2, forthcoming.

[9] For an example see *Kenkairon, DZ* 1:151–53, where Saichō quoted the *Pu k'ung piao chi, T* 52:835b. The office of *kung te shih* was an extra-legal institution in the sense that it was not mentioned in the official codes of the empire. Thus Saichō could not have learned of it from either the Chinese or Japanese legal codes.

(*sadaiben*) or the Recorder of the Left (*sadaishi*). The senior man was also called *kengyō* (examiner).[10] In addition, these men often held positions in the Palace Secretariat (*kurō dokoro* 藏人所).[11] Their close access to the emperor gave them additional power to aid the Tendai School.

The post of *zoku betto* proved to be extremely useful to the early Tendai School. It was soon adopted by Shingon temples, beginning with Kongōbuji in 836 and Tōji in 838.[12] Later the temples of other schools also appointed *zoku bettō*. The system contributed much to the growing influence of the nobility in the Tendai School during the Heian Period.

Installation Of The Zasu

Gishin was appointed monastic head (*zasu* 座主) of the Tendai School on the twenty-second day of the sixth month of 824. On the thirteenth day of the seventh month, three subordinate monastic officials (*sangō* 三綱) were appointed. Ninchū 仁忠 served as *jōza* 上座 (presiding officer), Dōei 道叡 as *jishu* 寺主 (director) and Kōzen 興善 as *tsuina* 都維那 (provost).[13] Because the *zasu* was free from the supervision of the Sōgō (Office of Monastic Affairs) and Genbaryō (Bureau of Buddhism and Aliens), he had much more automony than did the leaders of the Nara schools. For example, when alterations in the monastic registers were made because of the death of a monk, the Tendai *zasu* was responsible for destroying the monk's certificates and entering the necessary changes in the registers. In contrast, the Nara schools were required to submit any alterations to the Sōgō and Genbaryō.[14] The autonomy of the Tendai *zasu* was sufficiently attractive that in 876 the Shingon monk Shinga 眞雅 (801–879) asked that the Tendai plan be used at Jōkanji 貞觀寺. If the *zasu* of Jōkanji or an officially-supported monk from Jōkanji were appointed to the Sōgō, Shinga further requested that he be prohibited from staying at Jōkanji in order to prevent any conflicts of interest between Jōkanji and the Sōgō.[15] His petition was approved.

As part of the general administrative reform at Enryakuji, rules for governing the Tendai monks were formulated shortly before

---

[10] *Tendai zasuki*, p. 6.

[11] Kikuchi, "Zoku bettō no seiritsu," p. 105.

[12] Ibid., pp. 117, 130. For documents concerning the Shingon School's adoption of the *zoku bettō* system, see Ogami Kanchū, "Dengyō Daishi nyūmetsugo no Tendaishū kyōdan," *DDK*, pp. 219–20.

[13] *Tendai zasuki*, p. 6. The *Shoreishō* gives a date of 822 for Gishin's installation.

[14] Ogami Kanchū, "Dengyō Daishi nyūmestugo," *DDK*, p. 214; and Sansom, "Early Japanese Law and Administration: Part 2," p. 132.

[15] Takagi, *Heian jidai Hokke Bukkyōshi kenkyū*, p. 23.

Gishin's installation. A list of twenty-two rules was approved by Gishin, Enchō and Ninchū on the twenty-third day of the fifth month of 824.[16] The *zoku bettō* endorsed the rules on the fifth day of the seventh month. The rules concerned problems not adequately covered in the *Fan wang* precepts, such as the correct procedure for using the latrine, the use of another's footwear or mat for sitting, the monastic seating order, the demeanor of monks in monastery buildings, the disposal of a deceased monk's possessions, the compilation of monastic registers, the length of time a monk might live in the same building, and the responsibility of monks to properly educate temple boys. The rules often referred back to instructions given by Saichō.

In subsequent years Tendai monks composed many similar sets of rules[17] which often referred to the earlier sets written by Saichō and his disciples. Sometimes these were regulations issued by the *zasu* on Mount Hiei for the entire Tendai School. At other times, prominent monks issued a code of behavior for their followers. Regulations were occasionally composed by Tendai monks, but issued by the court. The content of these rules varied from general statements on the principles of proper behavior to very specific regulations written to resolve certain problems.

The First Fan Wang Ordinations On Hieizan

The Tendai monks naturally wanted to perform bodhisattva initiations and ordination ceremonies as soon as possible after the court granted permission. On the eleventh day of the third month of 823, the newly appointed *zoku bettō*, Ōtomo no Kunimichi went to Mount Hiei to administer qualifying examinations to candidates for the position of yearly ordinand.[18] As Saichō had requested, the Tendai yearly ordinands were initiated as novices on the anniversary of Emperor Kanmu's death, the seventeenth day of the third month.[19] Three and one-half

---

[16] *Enryakuji kinseishiki, Tendai kahyō,* fasc. 5A, *BZ* 42:4–5. Only fifteen of the rules are extant. Some versions edit the rules in a slightly different way and list seventeen rules, but the contents are the same as in the fifteen-rule versions (*BKD* 1:273–74).

[17] Thirty-six sets of rules by Tendai monks dating from Saichō's *Yuigō* (*Final Admonitions*) to the nineteenth century are listed in Ogami Kanchū, "Tendaishū ni okeru kyōdan goji no shomondai," *Nihon Bukkyō gakkai nenpō* 39 (1973): 152–55. Chih-i also wrote a list of rules to supplement the *vinaya* which are included in the *Kuo ch'ing pai lu, T* 48: 793; for an annotated version of Chih-i's rules see Ikeda Rosan, "Tendai Chigi no ryūseihō," *Komazawa daigaku Bukkyō gakubu ronshū* 29 (1971): 88–103.

[18] *Denjutsu isshinkaimon, DZ* 1:571; *Eizan Daishiden, DZ* 5 (*Bekkan*): 44.

[19] *Denjutsu isshinkaimon, DZ* 1:568.

weeks later, on the fourteenth day of the fourth month, fourteen monks were ordained with the full set of the *Fan wang* precepts in the One-vehicle Meditation Hall (Ichijō shikan'in) on Mount Hiei.[20] Since Gishin had been chosen as Saichō's successor and had already received the *Fan wang* precepts in China with Saichō, he presided over the ceremony.[21] Ninchū unsuccessfully objected to the choice of Gishin.[22]

After the ceremonies, initiation (*dochō*) and ordination certificates (*kaichō*) had to be issued. These certificates were a matter of grave importance since they stated that a monk was legally ordained and exempted him from tax and corvée labor obligations. Traditionally, an official of the Ministry of Civil Administration (Jibushō) who was in charge of monastic registers, and an official of the Ministry of Popular Affairs (Minbushō) would meet and verify the identity of the monk and the validity of his ordination. The monk's registration would then be transferred from the Ministry of Popular Affairs to the Ministry of Civil Administration. The monks in the Tendai order, however, disagreed over the way in which this procedure would be performed under the new system of ordinations. Ninchū suggested that the Bureau of Buddhism and Aliens (Genbaryō), a division of the Ministry of Civil Administration, should handle the investigation.[23] Such a solution was essentially the same as the previous procedure and would have effectively undermined Saichō's proposal that Tendai monks remain registered with the Ministry of Popular Affairs. Kōjō asked the two *zoku bettō* to intercede at court and to request that the Ministry of Popular Affairs check the records without any assistance from the Ministry of Civil Administration. Thus the newly ordained monk's name would remain on the lay registers, but he would not be subject to taxes. Following the negotiations, the Council of State (Dajōkan) issued the desired order to the Ministry of Popular Affairs. Verification of the records was to be carried out on Mount Hiei. In this way, the recently ordained monks would

---

[20] *Eizan Daishiden* 5 (*Bekkan*): 44. The account of the ordination in Ennin's biography (*Jikaku Daishiden, ZGR* 8:686) emphasizes Ennin's role in the ceremony. According to this account, Ennin served as an instructor (*kyōjushi* 教授師) at the ceremony while Gishin served as the teacher who transmitted the precepts (*denkaishi* 傳戒師). Since Ennin is not mentioned in earlier accounts of the ceremony, his role in it remains unclear. In the account in the *Jikaku Daishiden*, the ordination was held in front of an image of Yakushi Nyorai (*Bhaiṣajyaguru Tathāgata*). The fourteen monks who were ordained were not named; however, the *Eizan Daishiden* [*DZ* 5 (*Bekkan*): 47] listed fifteen key monks including Gishin from the Tendai School. The first ordination probably included many of them.

[21] *Denjutsu isshinkaimon, DZ* 1:531.

[22] Ibid., p. 577.

[23] Ibid., pp. 568–69.

not be required to travel to Kyoto and could begin their twelve-year period of training on Mount Hiei immediately after their ordinations.

The question of which office should issue the certificates remained. At the time Saichō submitted his positions to the court, initiation certificates were issued by the Council of State, and ordination certificates were issued by the Ministry of Popular Affairs. After conferring with Kōjō, the *zoku bettō* Ōtomo no Kunimichi asked the court to allow the Council of State to issue both.[24]

The examination, ordination, and administrative system used at Enryakuji thus agreed closely with Saichō's proposals. The differences between the old and new systems of governmental control are shown schematically in Chart 8.[25]

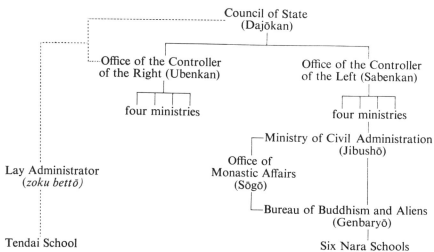

Solid lines represent the traditional system. Broken lines represent Saichō's new system.
Chart **8.** Comparison of the traditional system for overseeing monks and nuns with Saichō's new system for the Tendai School.

The Appointment Of Lecturers And Readers.

In the *Rokujōshiki* Saichō requested that some of the Tendai monks who completed the twelve-year training course on Mount Hiei be

---

[24] Ibid., pp. 570–71. Extant initiation and ordination certificates for Kōjō and Enchin indicate that these procedures were followed (*Tendai kahyō,* fasc. 2B, *BZ* 41:259; ibid., fasc. 4B, *BZ* 41:376).

[25] Adapted from Furukawa Yoshihide, "*Gakushōshiki* ni okeru Tendai shūdan," *TG* 3 (1959): 14. The translations of the government organs are based on Sansom, "Early Japanese Law and Administration."

appointed as lecturers (*kōji*) and readers (*dokushi*) in the provinces.[26] In an attempt to put Saichō's plan into effect, Gishin submitted a petition to the emperor through Fujiwara no Yoshifusa 藤原良房 (804–871), who was at that time rising rapidly through the imperial guards to become vice-councillor (*chūnagon*).[27] The petition was submitted on the seventh day of the sixth month of 833, probably in anticipation of giving appointments to some of the first graduates of the Tendai training system. With Yoshifusa's aid the request was approved on the second day of the seventh month. However, Gishin died two days later, and the appointments were not made due to the bitter fight for succession to *zasu* that ensued. After Enchō had been appointed *zasu*, representations were again made to the court through Fujiwara no Mimori and Yoshifusa.[28] A proclamation approving the plan was issued by the Council of State on the fifteenth day of the tenth month of 835.

Until this time, appointments as lecturers and readers had been proposed by the Sōgō and Genbaryō. The lecturers and readers were, in effect, the Sōgō's representatives in the provinces. The Tendai appointees would need a new appointment procedure. Thus nominations of Tendai monks were sent directly to the Council of State, bypassing the Sōgō and Genbaryō. Tendai lecturers and readers reported to the Council of State, not to the Sōgō. The Sōgō was informed of Tendai appointments only after they had been made.[29]

These changes brought about a fundamental transformation in the office and function of the lecturers. Until 835 they had been responsible primarily for preaching and overseeing provincial monastic communities. They had usually resided at the Kokubunji. The Tendai lecturers, however, seem to have been more sectarian than their predecessors, and to have acted as important agents for the early Tendai School's expansion into the provinces. Unfortunately, almost nothing is known of the activities of the first Tendai appointees. The edict from the Council of

---

[26] See footnotes 51 and 52 of Chapter 8 for more information on lecturers. Saichō had also asked that certain ranks be given to Tendai monks who had completed a twelve-year training period on Mount Hiei. The *Engishiki* included a set form (*iki* 位記) for documents conferring these ranks on Tendai monks which clearly acknowledged the value of their twelve years on Mount Hiei. Thus the court recognized the merit of Saichō's plan and rewarded those monks who had completed their training. The earliest surviving example of an *iki* is one which granted Enchin the rank of *Dentō hosshi*, issued in the year 846 (Ogami Kanchū, "Dengyō Daishi nyūmetsugo no Tendaishū kyōdan," *DDK*, pp. 212–13).

[27] *Denjutsu isshinkaimon*, *DZ* 1:606–7.

[28] *Ruijū sandaikyaku*, *KT* 25:128–29.

[29] *Engishiki*, *Genbaryō*, *KT* 26:539–40.

State had called for annual appointments of Tendai monks as lecturers and readers, but it is not known whether this was carried out or not. The only surviving information on a Tendai lecturer before 855 concerns Anne 安慧 (d.868), later the fourth *zasu* of Enryakuji. He was appointed lecturer in Dewa in 844. Although the region was a stronghold of Hossō believers, Anne is said to have converted them all to Tendai.[30] Since Tendai *Fan wang* ordinations could only be performed on Mount Hiei, prospective Tendai monks would have been required to travel to the Tendai headquarters for their ordination, thus strengthening their new ties with the Tendai School.

In accordance with the *Rokujōshiki's* instructions, the Tendai lecturers were to devote themselves to the people's welfare by assisting with various projects. Money allocated by the government to help pay for robes for the summer retreat was to be spent on these projects. However, these funds probably did not amount to very much.[31]

Two years after the Tendai School was allowed to submit the names of candidates for lecturer directly to the Council of State, the Shingon School was also permitted to nominate lecturers in this same way.[32] The two schools began competing to extend their influence to the provinces. By 881 the competition was so intense that the court established a system of alternating appointments between the Tendai and Shigon Schools.[33] As appointments to the posts became increasingly important, monks were required to qualify for a lectureship by participating in certain monastic assemblies.[34] Monks from the Nara schools also participated in this system.

Tendai and Shingon expansion into the provinces during the last half of the ninth century also depended on another institution: branch temples (*betsuin* 別院) affiliated with the schools' main temples. Lecturers served six-year terms. Consequently, the Tendai School needed more permanent bases for its operations in the provinces. The *betsuin* served this purpose. The Tendai-affiliated Tado Jingūji 多度神宮寺 in Ise, the first instance of the institution, dates from 839.[35] While *betsuin* were not mentioned in Saichō's petitions, their establishment was a

---

[30] *Shūi ōjōden, BZ* 68: 204a.

[31] Takagi (*Heian jidai Hokke Bukkyōshi kenkyū*, pp. 34–35) notes that in the case of Dewa the amount allocated for monastic robes was probably substantially less than 2680 bundles (*soku*) of grain. Thirty thousand bundles were allocated to irrigation projects in Dewa.

[32] *Ruijū sandaikyaku, KT* 25:129.

[33] Ogami Kanchū, "Dengyō Daishi nyūmetsugo no Tendaishū kyōdan," *DDK*, p. 221.

[34] Takagi, *Heian jidai Hokke Bukkyōshi kenkyū*, p. 31.

[35] Ibid., p. 46.

direct consequence of his desire to have Tendai monks propagate the Tendai School in the provinces.

The Precepts Platform (kaidan 戒壇)

Saichō's struggle to ordain monks with the bodhisattva precepts has been frequently described by later scholars as a struggle to attain approval for the construction of a precepts platform on Mount Hiei.[36] Yet Saichō never mentioned the precepts platform in his petitions. In order to understand how this change in the interpretation of Saichō's petitions occurred, the function of the precepts platform must first be considered.[37]

When a Buddhist order conducted any official business such as the fortnightly recitation of the precepts, the ordination of new monks, or the disciplining of monks for transgressions of monastic discipline, everyone in the order was required to be present or accounted for and to agree on the action taken. Such a system was, of course, time consuming. To relieve some of the demands on time created by these meetings, all of the members of the order could agree to designate a special area which would technically constitute a separate order of monks. This area was usually small, often about the size of a building.[38] In it the minimum

[36] Fukuda Gyōei (*Tendaigaku gairon*, pp. 541–43) was the first modern scholar to argue that Saichō was not concerned with a precepts platform. Since then Ishida Mizumaro has taken a similar position (*Kairitsu no kenkyū*, p. 147). Michihata Ryōshū disagreed, arguing that even though the precepts platform was not mentioned in the government proclamation issued a week after Saichō's death, it is reasonable to assume that the permission to build the platform was implied in the proclamation ("Daijō kaidan to bosatsusō," *DDK*, pp. 1406–17). However, Michihata's argument seems forced.

[37] Remarks on the function of the *kaidan* are based on Tokuda Myōhon, "Tōshōdaiji kaidan kō," *Nanto Bukkyō* 10 (1962): 30–45, and Hirakawa Akira, *Genshi Bukkyō no kenkyū*, pp. 372–96.

[38] The Indian term for *kaidan* was *sīmāmaṇḍala*, a word which indicated that boundaries were established for the separate order, but not that the designated area was higher than the surrounding land. The term which appeared in most Chinese translations of the *vinaya* was *chieh ch'ang* 戒場 (Jap. *kaijō*) 'precepts place.' Only in the *Wu fen lü* (*T* 1421, *Mahīśāsakavinaya*?) was the translation *chieh t'an* 戒壇 (Jap. *kaidan*) found. Although raised platforms were sometimes used as *sīmāmaṇḍala* in India, the practice of constructing a special raised area as a *kaidan* became especially popular in China. A platform had two major advantages over an open, flat piece of land: (1) the boundaries were clearly marked by the platform, (2) a specially constructed platform could symbolize important concepts and enhance a ceremony by instilling a sense of its importance in the participants. See Miyabayashi Akihiko, "Chūgoku Bukkyō ni okeru kaidan ni tsuite," *Taishō daigaku kenkyū kiyō* 56 (1971): 1–17.

The grandeur of some precepts platforms in China is illustrated by Ennin's description of the Wan-sheng platform. It was a three-foot high octagon made of white jade with a base made of plaster mixed with powdered incense. The top of the platform was covered with a silk rug of five colors (E. O. Reischauer, trans., *Ennin's Diary: The Record of a Pilgrimage to China*, p. 228).

number of monks necessary to perform a specific ceremony could assemble, and thus allow the rest of the order to go about their business. For example, in a monastery of one-hundred monks, ten monks might assemble at the precepts platform to ordain a monk after obtaining permission from the whole order at a general meeting. Since the monks on the platform constituted a separate order, the requirements of full attendance and agreement would be met even though most of the monks from the 'larger order' were not present. A precepts platform would not be used for the biweekly recitation of the precepts, however, since every monk was required to attend those meetings if he could possibly do so.

For Saichō the precepts platform was not a necessary part of his petition. Ordinations could be performed anywhere on Mount Hiei by the whole order, or a certain area could be designated as a special place for the performance of monastic business (*kaijō*). In fact, the first ordination on Hieizan was performed in the meditation hall (*ichijō shikan'in*). The events behind the construction of the precepts platform on Mount Hiei indicates that it was actually more of an important convenience than an absolute necessity for the Tendai monks.

Sometime around the year 825[39] Vice Councillor (*Chūnagon*) Yoshimine no Yasuyo, an early supporter of the Tendai School, climbed Mount Hiei and spent the night. In conversations with Gishin and Kōjō, the subject of building a precepts platform was raised. Saichō's disciples argued that a precepts platform was necessary to inspire awe and respect when candidates were ordained. In the discussions that followed, they decided to build a precepts platform, a lecture hall (*kōdō*) and several smaller buildings. In 825 the court authorized payment of ninety-thousand sheaves of rice to pay for the buildings. The rice was to come from the taxes of Ōmi Province. The platform was built shortly thereafter.

The precepts platform probably had three images on it: Śākyamuni, flanked by Mañjuśrī and Maitreya. The choice of images was based on the ordination ceremony described in the *Kuan p'u hsien ching* which was then adapted for use in Tendai ordination ceremonies. The roles of the three figures are described in Chan-jan's ordination manual and Saichō's *Shijōshiki*. A Tahō (Prabhūtaratna) pagoda 多寶塔 may also have been installed on the platform to indicate a connection with the *Lotus Sūtra*.[40] A work compiled several centuries after Saichō's death

---

[39] This date is based on *Enryakuji konryū engi* (*BZ* 41:303a). Other sources date the event in 827 or 828. The *Tendai zasuki* gives dates of both 827 and 828 (pp. 7, 9). However, the *Enryakuji konryū engi* is the earliest and most reliable source. This account is based mainly on the *Denjutsu isshinkaimon, DZ* 1:588–90.

stated that four precious vases (*hōbyō*) were placed at its corners to represent Samantabhadra, Maitreya, Mañjuśrī, and Avalokiteśvara, with a fifth vase in the center.[41] Many questions concerning the arrangement of the first precepts platform on Mount Hiei remain unanswered.[42]

When Ennin traveled through China he saw the precepts platforms on Mount Wu-t'ai and at the K'ai-yüan Temple 開元寺 in Pei-chou 貝州 (in Hupeh Province), and took extensive notes on their measurements and color schemes.[43] He mentioned nothing about the platform on Mount Hiei, however, in his travel diary. Perhaps at that time the Japanese Tendai monks, including Ennin, were still considering the arrangement of the platform on Mount Hiei.

Ennin also saw a precepts platform for nuns at Shan-kuang-ssu in Pei-chou.[44] After his return to Japan, he apparently told the empress dowager about this platform and plans were made by her to build a precepts platform for nuns. However, Ennin died before that plan could be realized.[45]

In later years, the precepts platform on Mount Hiei became the symbol of the autonomy of the Tendai School. Consequently, Saichō's dispute with the monks of Nara was interpreted as a dispute over the establishment of a precepts platform on Mount Hiei. The earliest source in which the dispute was viewed in this way was probably the *Eigaku yōki*,[46] a Tendai work describing the various structures on Mount Hiei, compiled in the late Heian or early Kamakura period. At least two reasons can be suggested for this shift in the interpretation of Saichō's proposals.

First, few temples in Japan were permitted by the court to build a precepts platform. Ever since Chien-chen (Ganjin) had arrived in Japan,

---

[40] The original platform and the building surrounding it burned down in the middle ages. Etani Ryūkai has attempted to determine its plan on the basis of surviving documents (*Endonkai gaisetsu*, p.117; also note the diagram on p.119). See the translation of the *Shijōshiki* in Chapter 8. The roles of Śākyamuni, Mañjuśrī, and Maitreya are also mentioned in Chan-jan's *Shou p'u sa chieh i* (*JZ* 15:873) and in the *Jubosatsukaigi*, attributed to Saichō (*DZ* 1:306–307).

[41] *Ichijōkai konganki*, *DZ* 1:429–32. This work is attributed to Saichō, but most modern scholars believe that it was compiled no earlier than the late Heian period (Ōno Hōdō, *BKD* 1:142; Asai, *Jōko Nihon Tendai*, p. 50).

[42] Ōchō Enichi, "*Ken'yō daikairon* zatsukan," in *Jikaku Daishi kenkyū*, ed. Fukui Kōjun, (Tokyo: Taishō daigaku Tendai gakkai, 1964). p. 418.

[43] Ono, *Nittō guho junrei kōki no kenkyū* 2:379–80, 433–35.

[44] Ibid., 2:381.

[45] *Jikaku Daishiden*, *ZGR* 8:696a. Apparently the platform was never built since no mention of it is made in later literature.

[46] *ZGR* 46:554. The passage in question is said to be from a government order dated 939.

the court had attempted to control the number of monks ordained by requiring that ordinations be performed on the precepts platforms at certain temples. Thus obtaining government recognition of the Tendai School's right to ordain monks was equated with the right to build a precepts platform on Mount Hiei.[47]

Second, during the late Heian period the precepts platform was the center of a number of disputes which concerned the autonomy of either Enryakuji or of certain elements within the Tendai School. Thus the split of the Tendai School into the *jimon* 寺門 and *sanmon* 山門 branches in the eleventh century focussed partly on the Onjōji 園城寺 monastery's right to establish a precepts platform which would be independent of the one on Mount Hiei.

According to medieval Risshū sources, when the Tendai precepts platform was constructed, the monks on Mount Hiei asked for some earth from the precepts platform at Tōdaiji which had been established by Chien-chen. This request was described as both an attempt by the Tendai monks on Mount Hiei to placate the Nara schools and as an attempt to give the new Tendai precepts platform more authority. However, the story is almost certainly a Risshū fabrication designed to prove that the Mount Hiei precepts platform ultimately derived its authority from Tōdaiji. The earliest account of this episode is found in a memorial dated 1163,[48] in which the Hossō temple Kōfukuji asked that ordinations on Mount Hiei be ended and that Enryakuji be recognized as a branch temple of Kōfukuji.

Disputes such as those between the *sanmon* and *jimon* branches of the Tendai School or between Kōfukuji and Enryakuji gradually caused monks to equate Saichō's concern with the bodhisattva precepts with the establishment of a precepts platform on Mount Hiei.

No example of a purely Mahāyāna precepts platform prior to the one on Mount Hiei has been identified. However, the Mount Hiei platform may have inspired a Mahāyāna platform in Sung Dynasty China. In an entry dated 1010 in the *Fo tsu t'ung chi* 佛祖統記, the Tz'u-hsiao-ssu 慈孝寺 temple in the capital was reported to have a Mahāyāna precepts platform 大乘戒壇. This platform may have been inspired by the Mount Hiei example; however, the Chinese platform was undoubtedly

---

[47] The precepts platform at Tōshōdaiji is an important exception to this statement since little evidence indicates that it was founded as an ordination platform. Chien-chen probably used it to train monks to perform other types of *karman* (ceremonies). See Tokuda Myōhon, "Tōshōdaiji kaidankō," *Nanto Bukkyō* 10 (1962): 30–45.

[48] *Kōfukuji sōgō daihosshitō sōjō*, *BZ* 61:5–7; Tokuda, *Risshū gairon*, p. 569.

used to confer the bodhisattva precepts on monks who had already received the full Hīnayāna precepts and not to ordain monks with the bodhisattva precepts.[49]

Conflicts With The Nara Schools And The Appointment Of Tendai Monks To The Sōgō

The Tendai School had freed itself from the domination of the Sōgō and the Nara schools. But in doing so, it had further increased the enmity between itself and the Nara schools. Besides supervising monks, the Sōgō served as a conduit for government funds and special appointments. Thus such support was not readily given to Enryakuji. Kōjō wrote of dire poverty on Mount Hiei after Saichō's death. The Tendai lay administrators helped to alleviate the problem by securing lectureships for the rainy season at Shitennōji 四天王寺 and Hōryūji 法隆寺 for some of the Tendai monks.[50] These two temples were probably chosen because of their association with Shōtoku Taishi, the supposed reincarnation of the T'ien-t'ai patriarch Hui-ssu 慧思. Enryakuji's financial problems were further alleviated in 831 when the court made provisions for the support of twenty-four yearly ordinands from the taxes allocated for the Kokubunji (Provincial temple) in Ōmi Province.[51]

Opposition by the Nara schools continued to affect the Tendai School long after Saichō's death. The most obvious evidence of friction between the monastic establishments at Nara and Mount Hiei is found in the early Tendai School's finances, especially in the slow rate at which the headquarters of the Tendai School on Mount Hiei was built. Saichō had planned a large complex of buildings, as was shown by his proposals for nine halls, and later for sixteen halls. During his lifetime he was able to construct only one or two of these buildings. The year after his death, the court gave Mount Hiei funds to assist in the construction of several pagodas and to purchase lamps.[52] Several years later, the court helped the Tendai School build a precepts platform. Subsequent funds came slowly, largely from imperial sources.[53] The Tendai School was growing,

---

[49] See Michihata Ryōshū, "Daijō kaidan to bosatsusō," *DDK*, pp. 1417–21.

[50] *Denjutsu isshinkaimon, DZ* 1:593. These events are corroborated by records which indicate that Ennin lectured on the *Lotus Sūtra* at Hōryūji in 828, and on the *Lotus Sūtra* and the *Jen wang ching* in 829 (*Jikaku Daishiden, ZGR* 8:686; also see Kōjō's biography, the *Enryakuji konaigubu wajō gyōjō,* ibid., p. 683).

[51] *Nihon kiryaku:* zenpen, *KT* 10:331.

[52] *Eizan Daishiden, DZ* 5 (*Bekkan*): 45.

[53] A summary of the buildings constructed on Mount Hiei during the years after Saichō's death is found in Ishida Mizumaro, "Tendaishū kyōdan hatten katei ni okeru teikyō to

but at a slow rate because of the obstructionist tactics of the Sōgō and the Nara schools. Consequently, in 863 Enryakuji received only one-third as many funds as the main Nara temples had been allocated to repair and maintain their buildings.[54] The Tendai School's request that its graduates serve as lecturers in the provinces was delayed a year. When the Tendai School finally expanded into the provinces, certain temples would be designated Tendai establishments, only later to be returned to their former status when the Nara schools objected.[55]

Tendai growth was also inhibited by Shingon popularity. Kūkai's influence was at its peak during the period immediately after Saichō death. Although Kūkai had been critical of the Nara schools in his writings, he had also cooperated with them in many ways. He thus had not drawn their enmity. The result was that Shingon monks had captured the imaginations and the financial support of the nobility with little opposition from the Nara schools. Consequently, they took much of the support and many of the positions which might otherwise have been allocated to the Tendai School. Shingon relations with the influential Fujiwara clan were especially strong.[56]

Nara opposition to the Tendai School also manifested itself in appointments to the three major annual monastic meetings of the early Heian period: the Yuimae 維摩會 (lectures on the *Vimalakīrtinirdeśasū-tra*) at Kōfukuji, the Saishōe 最勝會 (lectures on the *Suvarṇaprabhāsasū-tra*) at Yakushiji, and the Gosaie 御齋會 (also lectures on the *Suvarṇa-prabhāsasūtra*) in the palace. Appointments as lecturers at these assemblies were important steps in a monk's career and served to qualify him for government ranks and appoinments. Although Gishin served as lecturer at the Yuimae in 832, subsequent appointments of Tendai monks to the assemblies were not readily made. At times Nara monks in the Sōgō even ignored court edicts which established the procedures for appointments to the assemblies in order to block the Tendai monks.[57]

The Tendai monks were not even secure in their own field of expertise, the *Lotus Sūtra*. In 826 the court sponsored an assembly at Saiji 西寺 in honor of Saichō's patron, the late Emperor Kanmu. The meeting, held on the anniversary of the emperor's death, was to consist of seven days of lectures on the *Lotus Sūtra*. Although a Tendai School monk would

dakyō," *Nihon Bukkyō* 9 (1960): 9.
[54] Ishida, *Kairitsu no kenkyū*, p. 316.
[55] Ibid., pp. 313, 315.
[56] Tsuji, *Nihon Bukkyōshi* 1:385.
[57] Ishida, *Kairitsu no kenkyū*, pp. 311–18.

have been the logical choice to conduct the meeting, Saichō's former adversary Gomyō was chosen. Gomyō had resigned his office at the Sōgō in 823, following court approval of Saichō's petitions, but was later reappointed and raised to the highest rank ·of chief executive (sōjō) in 827.[58]

Tendai monks responded to these attacks in several ways. First, they tried to develop a form of Esoteric Buddhism which could compete with that of the Shingon School. These efforts resulted in voyages to China by Ennin, Enchin and others. Second, they began making efforts to have Tendai monks appointed to positions of importance within the monastic hierarchy. Since Saichō had severely criticized the Sōgō, Tendai monks were probably reluctant to participate in it, but the passage of time dulled their antipathy to the institution. Moreover, practical and economic considerations made participation a necessity. The Sōgō too had begun to change during the last half of the ninth century. Originally it had consisted of a limited number of monks appointed to govern the clergy; but by the late ninth century, the number of appointments was increasing. Moreover, appointments were often made primarily to honor a particular monk. At the same time, the bureaucratic duties of the appointees were lessening. By 869 seventeen monks held positions in the Sōgō even though the legal codes had made provision for only eight monks.[59]

The exact time when Tendai monks first began making efforts to obtain positions in the Sōgō is unclear. The first example of such an appointment is Anne 安慧 who was named provisional vinaya master (gon-risshi) in 864, the same year he assumed the post of head (zasu) of the Tendai School. Anne died in 868. The next year, Henjō 遍照 (817–890) was appointed to the Sōgō and by 879 he had risen to the position of provisional chief executive (gon-sōjō). In Henjō's case, some of the reasons for his appointment and rapid rise in the Sōgō are clear. He was the grandson of Emperor Kanmu and the son of Yoshimine no Yasuyo, both very powerful men and great patrons of the Tendai School. Henjō and, later, Enchin (who was named to the Sōgō in 883) were appointed partly as a reward for their roles in praying for the protection of Emperor Yōzei (868–949, r. 876–884) while he was still crown prince. Only fifty years after Saichō's death, Tendai monks were active in the institution he had so vehemently fought.

---

[58] Ibid., p. 316.
[59] Ibid., pp. 331–32.

In order to further Tendai aims, Henjō and his colleagues tried to ameliorate the antagonism between the Tendai and Nara schools. One of their more interesting attempts is revealed in an order from the Council of State which was dated 887 and based on a petition by the Tendai monk Kansei 觀栯. The edict concerned a dispute over who should supervise the two Tendai yearly ordinands assigned to the Kamo 賀茂 and Kasuga 春日 shrines. In discussing the procedure for ordaining the yearly ordinands, the order noted that they were to be ordained with the Hīnayāna precepts. Unfortunately, little is known about the circumstances surrounding the edict or whether it was ever put into effect. An investigation of contemporary events, however, shows that at this time, Henjō, the first Tendai monk to gain an important position in the Sōgō, was working to establish the temple Gangyōji 元慶寺 in honor of Emperor Yōzei. Henjō succeeded in obtaining a guarantee that Gangyōji monks would be awarded a place at the annual assembly on the *Vimalakīrtinirdeśasūtra* at Kōfukuji, and in having Gangyōji monks appointed lecturers or readers when a vacancy in these positions occurred.

Henjō's achievements were important ones for the Tendai School; but they were probably not accomplished without some conciliatory move from the Tendai School which would have helped Henjō shepherd them through bureaucratic channels. One such action was a proposal by Henjō that Gangyōji monks be allowed to study both Tendai and Nara teachings. Another conciliatory move might well have been Kansei's proposal to allow the Tendai yearly ordinands for the Kamo and Kasuga Shrines to be ordained with the Hīnayāna precepts. Kansei's proposal, however, was a one-time strategy and was never repeated.[60]

Even after Anne and Henjō had been appointed to the Sōgō, such Tendai appointments continued to be opposed by the Nara monks for many years. A comparison of Tendai and Shingon appointments reveals the effect that Nara opposition had on the numbers of Tendai monks appointed to the Sōgō. Kūkai was the first Shingon monk to hold a position in the Sōgō, being named lesser supervisor (*shōsōzu*) in 824 and greater superviser (*daisōzu*) in 827. Tendai monks did not hold such positions until forty years later. Even after Tendai monks began receiving appointments to the Sōgō, Nara monks continued to oppose them. As a result, Tendai monks were generally limited to the lower ranks of

---

[60] No biography for Kansei survives, and nothing is known about his relations with Henjō. However this explanation of Kansei's proposal seems to be the only satisfactory one. See Ishida, *Kairitsu no kenkyū*, pp. 310–33, and Ishida, "Tendaishū kyōdan," pp. 1–22.

the Sōgō.[61] Of twelve Tendai monks who participated in all three of the annual important monastic meetings (san'e 三會), only eight were awarded positions in the Sōgō, even though participation in the meetings was an accepted road to an appointment in the Sōgō.[62] Not until Ryōgen's (912–985) time did Tendai monks succeed in completely eliminating the barriers set up by the Nara monks.

The Tendai School's eventual triumph is revealed by monastic records indicating the population of the Tendai establishment on Mount Hiei. During the ninth and tenth centuries, the Tendai School received more yearly ordinands (nenbundosha) than the Shingon School, and more than all of the Nara schools combined.[63] By the early eleventh century, about three thousand monks were living on Mount Hiei.[64] Later, Mount Hiei was to play a crucial role in the development of the Kamakura schools. Saichō's administrative reforms proved to be such a resounding success during the Heian period that even the Shingon School adopted such features as appointing a head monk (zasu) and lay administrators (zoku bettō).

---

[61] Tagaki, *Heian jidai Hokke Bukkyōshi kenkyū,* pp. 23–30.
[62] Ibid., pp. 28–29.
[63] Ibid., p. 22.
[64] Ibid.. p. 67.

CHAPTER FIFTEEN
SAICHŌ'S DISCIPLES AND THE PRECEPTS

Gishin, Enchō and Factionalism in the Early Tendai School

As a youth, Gishin studied Hossō doctrines under Jiun of Kōfukuji, and spoken Chinese with Jikan of Tōdaiji. Because of his linguistic ability, Gishin was asked to accompany Saichō to China and serve as Saichō's translator. During his stay in China, Gishin was ordained as a monk, studied T'ien-t'ai doctrine, and received the bodhisattva precepts and Esoteric initiations along with Saichō. His relationship to Saichō was somewhat ambiguous. Since he was younger than Saichō, he was called a disciple and was usually regarded as Saichō's disciple by traditional Tendai scholars; however, he received his Esoteric initiations and his ordination with the bodhisattva precepts at the same time as Saichō. Consequently, he could also be regarded as Saichō's contemporary and fellow student.[1]

In 822 Saichō appointed Gishin as his successor. Although the other disciples accepted the appointment, they seem to have been uneasy about it. Saichō had appointed Enchō successor ten years earlier, but in 822 he had supplanted Enchō with Gishin on the grounds that Gishin was the senior monk. The monks on Mount Hiei probably felt that Gishin was a comparative latecomer to Mount Hiei. Although Gishin had accompanied Saichō to China, the *Denjutsu isshinkaimon* indicates that he had spent much of his subsequent time away from Mount Hiei.[2] When Saichō wrote his will of 812, for example, Gishin was in Sagami. Gishin also did not accompany Saichō to Takaosan to study Esoteric Buddhism, a lapse which could have led some Tendai monks to raise questions about his ability to lead the *shanagō* (Esoteric) students. Consequently, the monks on Mount Hiei were potentially divided into at least two major groups at Saichō's death: those who supported Gishin and those who supported Enchō. It was only Kōjō's careful questioning of Saichō in 822 that established a clear hierarchy between Saichō's two preeminent disciples and thus staved off arguments between the two factions.

---

[1] Note, for example, Saichō's treatment of Gishin in the *Kechimyakufu* (*DZ* 1:230, 236, 244, 247) and his inclusion of documents concerning Gishin in the *Kenkairon engi*.

[2] *Denjutsu isshinkaimon*, *DZ* 1:628, 640; also see Nakao Shunpaku's analysis in *Nihon shoki Tendai no kenkyū* (Kyoto: Nagata Bunshōdō, 1973), p. 250.

In the *Denjutsu isshinkaimon,* the existence of a third group surrounding Ninchū 仁忠 is also indicated. Ninchū objected to the appointments of both Gishin and Enchō to various posts, but was always overruled.[3] Unfortunately Kōjō's work does not include enough detail to determine the reasons behind Ninchū's objections.

Gishin's tenure as head of the Tendai School (*zasu*) was not an easy one. Although he had some successes, such as presiding over the first *Fan wang* ordination on Mount Hiei and constructing the precepts platform (*kaidan*), he failed to meet a number of challenges from outside Mount Hiei. His problems are best illustrated by the Tendai response to an imperial request that each Buddhist school submit a work describing its doctrines.[4] A number of the works submitted were either implicitly or explicitly critical of the Tendai School. Kūkai's *Jūjūshinron* 十住心論 (The Ten stages of the Development of Mind) ranked the Tendai School below both the Shingon and the Kegon Schools.[5] Gen'ei's 玄叡 *Daijō sanron daigishō* 大乘三論大義鈔 (Essentials of the Great Doctrines of the Mahāyāna Three Treatises) attacked the Tendai School's assertion that Hui-ssu, the second patriarch of the T'ien-t'ai School, was reborn as Shōtoku Taishi. The commentary on the *Lotus Sūtra* attributed to Shōtoku Taishi (547–622) had been based on a work written earlier by Fa-yün 法雲 (467–529); however, Chih-i, the de facto founder of the T'ien-t'ai School had attacked Fa-yün's work in his commentaries. If Hui-ssu had been reborn as Shōtoku Taishi, then Chih-i had actually criticized positions advocated by a later incarnation of his own teacher.[6]

The Risshū monk Buan 豊安 assailed the Tendai School's assertion that it alone possessed a truly Mahāyāna set of precepts.[7] Buan used

---

[3] *Denjutsu isshinkaimon, DZ* 1:560, 577. Perhaps Ninchū objected because he believed that Gishin and Enchō were not able administrators. Ninchū's position as presiding officer (*jōza*) on Mount Hiei and his authorship of a set of rules for monks in 824 indicate his concern with administering the order (*Enryakuji kinsei shiki, Nihon daizōkyō* 46: 281–83).

[4] The date of submission of the works presented by the heads of the various schools is problematic. Although some later sources state that they were written in 822 or 823 (*BD* 6:185), internal evidence in the texts suggests that a date of 829 or 830 is more likely (Nakao, *Nihon shoki Tendai no kenkyū,* p. 217). The *Tendai hokkeshū gishū* did not have a specific date in it, but did include a passage indicating that it was compiled during the Tenchō Era (824–834) (*BZ* 38:86a). It was probably submitted in 830 at the same time as the other works for which specific dates exist.

[5] *Kōbō Daishi chōsaku zenshū* 1:506ff.

[6] *T* 70: 168a. The commentaries by Fa-yün and Shōtoku Taishi correspond to *T* nos. 1715 and 2187.

[7] Quoted in Gyōnen's *Risshū kōyō.* See Tokuda, *Risshū gairon,* pp. 128–30. The quotation is not found in the one surviving fascicle of Buan's work, the *Kairitsu denraiki* 戒律傳來記 (Record of the Transmission of the Precepts; *BZ* 64:146–149).

the term 'bodhisattva vinaya master' (*bosatsu risshi*) to refer to Risshū scholars and challenged Saichō's assertion that Risshū monks were Hīnayānists.[8] Finally, all of these works, as well as the Hossō scholar Gomyō's *Daijō hossō kenjinshō* 大乘法相研神章, completely ignored the Tendai School's claims that it included Esoteric Buddhist doctrines and rituals.

How did the Tendai School respond to the criticisms advanced by the other Buddhist schools? As head of the Tendai School, Gishin wrote the one-fascicle *Tendai Hokkeshū gishū* 天台法華宗義集 (*Collected Doctrines of the Tendai Hokke School*) to defend the Tendai School.[9] This work was a systematic explication of Tendai doctrine culled from Chih-i's three major works and Chan-jan's commentaries on them. Although the work fulfilled an important need for an introductory text on Tendai doctrine, it did not even mention the bodhisattva precepts or Esoteric Buddhism. It thus did little to defend the Tendai School against its detractors. Moreover, it was by far the shortest work submitted to the throne. The other texts ranged from Kūkai's ten-fascicle work to Buan's three-fascicle piece; Gishin wrote only one fascicle.

The Tendai monks must have particularly wanted to be able to answer Kūkai's criticisms. Saichō had attempted to master Esoteric Buddhism, but had died without succeeding and entrusted the task to his disciples. In the years since Saichō's death, Kūkai and the Shingon School had attracted the interest of court nobles and the monks of Nara. Mount Hiei, however, remained without a competent master of Esoteric Buddhism. Consequently in 831, Enchō and thirty-five other monks, as well as the lay administrators wrote to Kūkai requesting permission to study with him.[10] Kūkai apparently responded favorably, since Kōjō's *Denjutsu isshinkaimon* mentioned that Enchō had studied with Kūkai at this time.[11] His stay with Kūkai must have been cut short, however, by Kūkai's illness and Gishin's death in 833. Thus Mount Hiei remained without a competent master of Esoteric Buddhism.

In writing this letter to Kūkai, Enchō was pursuing an interest in Esoteric Buddhism which had begun even before Saichō went to China.[12] His concern with Esoteric Buddhism was in striking contrast to Gishin's

---

[8] See the translation of the *Shijōshiki* included in Chapter 8.

[9] *T* no. 2309.

[10] See footnote 25 of Chapter 6 of this study for an evaluation of the authenticity of the letter.

[11] *DZ* 1:639.

[12] See footnote 43 of Chapter 4 of this study.

lack of competence in that field. Gishin's failure to sign Enchō's letter was probably indicative of a deepening rift between the two men over how Tendai monks were to pursue the study of Esoteric Buddhism. The difference in attitude is also reflected in the questions which the two men sent to China. After Saichō's death, some of the leading monks of the Tendai School had compiled lists of questions which were to be carried to China by Japanese Tendai monks and answered by Chinese T'ien-t'ai masters. The questions, called *Tōketsu* 唐決 (Decisions on Doctrine from China), provide many insights into the concerns of early Japanese Tendai masters. The questions attributed to Gishin concerned lineages, Tendai doctrines, and Hsüan-tsang's travel diary; they included nothing about either the bodhisattva precepts or Esoteric Buddhism.[13] Perhaps Gishin was hesitant to ask Chinese monks about issues which he felt were vital concerns only of the Japanese Tendai School. Or perhaps Gishin was simply not interested in these issues.

Enchō's questions were mainly concerned with Tendai doctrine; however, he did ask a question about Esoteric Buddhism which indicated that he was still vitally interested in Saichō's view that Tendai and Esoteric doctrines were the Buddha's ultimate teaching (*enmitsu itchi* 圓密一至). Enchō asked the Chinese T'ien-t'ai monks to determine the place of the *Ta jih ching* 大日經 (*Mahāvairocanasūtra*), one of the most important texts in East Asian Esoteric Buddhism in the traditional Tendai classification of Buddhist teachings. Two eminent monks on Mount T'ien-t'ai, Kuang-hsiu 廣修 (770–844?) and his disciple Wei-chüan 維蠲, answered that the *Ta jih ching* was to be classified in the third period of the Buddha's life with miscellaneous Mahāyāna sūtras.[14] This answer did not satisfy the Japanese Tendai monks who clearly wanted a response which would have awarded the *Ta jih ching* status equal to that of the *Lotus Sūtra*.[15] They were to receive the answer they wanted five years later when Ennin presented questions by the Japanese Tendai

---

[13] *Tōketsushū, Nihon daizōkyō* 46:286–87. Because the work does not give the name of the questioner, the name of the person who replied, or the date of its composition, the identification of the author of the questions as Gishin is problematic. However, the statement at the beginning of the work that it is "in answer to questions by resident(s) of the Shuzen'in 修禪院," as well as its contents, seem sufficient to identify it with either Gishin or a small group of followers surrounding him (Asai, *Jōko Nihon Tendai*, p. 216; Ono, *Nittō guhō junrei kōki no kenkyū* 1:443–44; and Nakao, *Nihon shoki Tendai no kenkyū*, pp. 298–303).

[14] *Tōketsushū, Nihon daizōkyō* 46:384–85, 393–94. This work is generally accepted as authentic. Kuang-hsiu was Tao-sui's disciple and is considered to be the eighth patriarch of the T'ien-t'ai School. Wei-chüan was one of his leading disciples.

[15] For example, see Enchin's comments in the beginning of the *Daibirushanakyō shiki* in which he criticized the answers of the two Chinese T'ien-t'ai masters (*BZ* 41:35).

monk Tokuen 德圓 to a more progressive Chinese T'ien-t'ai monk Tsung-ying 宗穎, who was residing in Ch'ang-an, the capital of China and the center of Esoteric Buddhist scholarship.[16]

Much of the energy and time of the early Tendai School must have been occupied by such efforts to organize Tendai doctrines and defend them against the attacks of the Shingon and Nara schools. In addition, political maneuvering among the factions on Mount Hiei must have been steadily increasing since it eventually reached serious proportions upon Gishin's death.

Gishin died on the fourth day of the seventh month of 833, after designating his disciple Enshū 圓修 to succeed him.[17] The choice proved to be unsatisfactory to many monks, especially to those supporting Enchō, who had been designated as Saichō's successor in 812. Although Kōjō asked Enshū to step aside in favor of Enchō, Enshū refused.[18] The dispute continued for eight months and completely paralyzed the order. During this time, Kōjō attempted to obtain outside intervention to settle the dispute. On the twenty-fourth day of the tenth month, he wrote to the lay administrator Fujiwara no Mimori. Four days later, he petitioned the court. Kōjō also wrote the *Denjutsu isshinkaimon* at this time. Finally, the court appointed the Controller of the Right (*udaiben*) Wake no Matsuna as imperial messenger and dispatched him to resolve the dispute. On the sixteenth day of the third month of 834, the Council of State ordered that Enchō be installed as *zasu*. Enshū and more than fifty Tendai monks who had supported him were expelled from Mount Hiei. The seriousness of the split on Mount Hiei is indicated by the fact that the six Tendai monks who were promoted to the rank of *Dentō man'i* in 832 were evenly divided between the two sides.[19]

After his expulsion Enshū went to Murōji 室生寺 in Yamato. Murōji was a branch temple of Kōfukuji, the temple at which both Gishin and Enshū were registered. It was probably founded by Shūen 修圓 (d. 835), a former ally of Saichō.[20] Although Shūen was a Hossō monk,

---

[16] *Tōketsushū, Nihon Daizōkyō* 41:415. Tokuen's questions are the most penetrating of all the *Tōketsu* questions. The work is probably authentic (Asai, *Jōko Nihon Tendai*, pp. 219–20, 840), although Tajima Tokuon has cast some doubt on it (*BKD* 8:223–24).

[17] This account is based primarily on the *Denjutsu isshinkaimon, DZ* 1:640–48 and the *Tendai zasuki*, p. 8.

[18] The close association between Enchō and Kōjō is amply documented by the *Denjutsu isshinkaimon*. In his *Tōketsu*, Enchō asked a question concerning whether the precepts must be literally observed. His inquiry points towards some of the doctrines found in Kōjō's writings (*Nihon daizōkyō*. 46:378, 402–3).

[19] *Ruijū kokushi* 6:291; *Denjutsu isshinkaimon, DZ* 1:643.

[20] The early history of Murōji is discussed by Sonoda Kōyū in "Sōsōki Murōji wo me-

he was also interested in Esoteric Buddhism and welcomed both Tendai and Shingon monks to the temple. In addition, Shūen belonged to a different faction of the Hossō School, the Kōfukuji tradition, than Saichō's old antagonist Gomyō, who belonged to the Gankōji tradition. The Murōji was a center for the practice of religious austerities at which adherents of various schools congregated. At the time Enshū and his followers went there, one of Kūkai's leading disciples, Shintai 眞泰, also registered at Kōfukuji, may have been at Murōji, Thus Enshū may have hoped to learn about Esoteric Buddhism and then renew his claim to be head of the Tendai School.[21]

In 843 Enshū and another Japanese Tendai monk Kenne 堅慧 went to China and journeyed to the Ch'an-lin Temple on Mount T'ien-t'ai.[22] The eighth T'ien-t'ai patriarch, Kuang-hsiu (772–844?) managed to transmit the precepts and T'ien-t'ai teachings to Enshū just before the Chinese patriarch died.[23] The following year a lineage testifying to the transmission was composed and signed by some thirty Chinese T'ien-t'ai monks.[24] Armed with this document, Enshū was ready to return to Japan and press his case. While on Mount T'ien-t'ai, however, Enshū met Ensai 圓載, a Japanese monk who had been sent to China by Enryakuji. Resentments stemming from the dispute over the succession must still have been strong since Ensai is said to have hired a Korean monk to poision Enshū. The attempt failed and Enshū returned to Japan in 844.[25] Ensai apparently died at sea while returning to Japan after a

---

guru sōryo no dōkō," *Kokushi ronshū*, ed. Kokushikai (Kyoto: Kyoto daigaku bungakubu, 1959), pp. 411–26. Enshū and Shūen have been confused with each other by both traditional and modern scholars because they were both connected to Murōji and because the two monks wrote their names with the same characters although in different orders. The scarcity of material on Enshū, the loser in the dispute with Enchō, contributed to the confusion.

[21] Very few documents concerning Enshū exist, probably because he was vilified by most later Tendai monks. The above interpretation of events is based on a brief and rather vague letter from Shintai to Gishin (*Kōya zappitsushū, Kōbō Daishi chōsaku zenshū*, 3:540). See Nakao Shunpaku, "Murō Tendai to Jakkō Daishi Enchō," in *Bukkyō shisō ronshū* (Okuda Jiō festschrift), Kyoto Heirakuji shoten, 1976, pp. 294–295.

[22] The date of Kenne's voyage to China is not known, but he probably accompanied Enshū.

[23] Chinese monks seem to have been very willing to transmit their teachings to Japanese monks. The account of Hui-kuo and Kūkai is another good example. Chinese interest in the Japanese monks may have been partly due to predictions of monks coming from the east and stories linking Hui-ssu and Shōtoku Taishi. See Ono Katsutoshi, "Nittōso Enshū Kenne to sono *Kechimyaku zuki*," *Ishihama,Sensei koki kinen: Tōyō ronshū* (Kyoto: Ishihama Sensei koki kinenkai, 1958), p. 108.

[24] *BZ* 65:207–8. The text with a detailed analysis is also found in Ono's article cited in the previous footnote.

[25] Enchin, *Gyōryakushō BZ* 52:189a-b. Enchin recorded a number of unflattering episo-

long period of study in China

After his return to Japan, Enshū settled at Izumodera 出雲寺 in Kyoto.[26] In 850 he participated as the Tendai representative in a lecture series on the *Chin kuang ming ching* (*Suvarṇaprabhāsasūtra*) held at court. Other monks represented the Kegon, Sanron, and Hossō schools.[27] Enshū apparently never did succeed in pressing his claim to become the Tendai *zasu*. The date of his death is not known.

Enchō was appointed as *zasu* in 834 and presided over an ordination ceremony the following month. He probably lived until sometime in 837.[28] Following his death, no *zasu* was appointed. Instead, Kōjō (779–858) administered affairs on Mount Hiei in the capacity of administrator (*bettō*). The Tendai monks may have feared that selecting a new *zasu* would have provoked another succession dispute, Or the court may have insisted that no appointment be made until the results of the studies in China by Enshū, Ennin and others could be ascertained. Finally, in 854 Ennin (794–864) was appointed *zasu*. No dispute occurred with his selection since he had studied under Saichō and had also studied Esoteric Buddhism in China. However, the factional disputes in the early Tendai School had planted the seeds which eventually led to its split into *sanmon* and *jimon* factions.

Kōjō

Kōjō was one of Saichō's most trusted disciples. During the controversy over the bodhisattva precepts, he served as Saichō's liaison with the court, conveying Saichō's petitions to the authorities and lobbying for the support of various officials. He was thus in an excellent position to know Saichō's thoughts concerning the precepts. After Saichō's death, Kōjō continued to be actively concerned with the precepts, eventually serving as administrator of the precepts platform hall (*kaidan'in*). His major work, the *Denjutsu isshinkaimon*, was a spirited defense of

des concerning Ensai. See Katō Shigekimi, "Nittō ryūgakusō Ensai ni tsuite," *Shigaku zasshi* 41, no. 7 (1930):114–16. Enchin's criticisms of Ensai may indicate that Enchin was somewhat sympathetic to Enshū's plight. Both men had studied under Gishin. Ono has suggested that Enchin may have exaggerated his criticisms against Ensai ("Nittōsō Enshū," pp. 111–112). Elsewhere Ensai is mentioned in favorable terms and sorrow is expressed that he did not return to Japan to transmit T'ien-t'ai and Esoteric teachings (Uesugi, *Nihon Tendaishi*, p. 227).

[26] *Genkō shakusho, BZ* 62:226b. Ono ("Nittōsō Enshū," p. 120) alters the name of the temple from 山雲寺 to 出雲寺.

[27] *Nihon kōsōden yōmonshō, BZ* 62:50a-b.

[28] A number of dates for Enchō's death exist. They are discussed by Ono, "Nittōsō Enshū," p. 118.

Enchō's right to succeed Gishin as *zasu*. In addition, it is an invaluable source for the history of the Tendai precepts.

Despite his extensive contacts with Saichō, Kōjō's position on the precepts differed substantially from that of his teacher. He abandoned Saichō's plan which called for provisional Hīnayāna ordinations (*keju shōkai* 假受小戒) for Tendai monks.[29] Kōjō's theory of the precepts was based on certain elements in Saichō's writings, with a number of innovations added to meet the changing circumstances after Saichō's death. The most important term in Kōjō's writings on the precepts, 'the One-mind precepts' (*isshinkai* 一心戒), did not even appear in Saichō's writings. The concept of *isshinkai* was developed primarily through Kōjō's efforts to formulate a theory of the precepts which would enable the Tendai School to compete with the Shingon School. The *isshinkai* also reflected Kōjō's attempt to integrate the various teachings which Saichō had brought back from China into a comprehensive whole.

The result of Kōjō's efforts was a short but difficult passage of about 2100 characters at the end of the *Denjutsu isshinkaimon* concerning the precepts.[30] Recent scholarship by Ishida Mizumaro has revealed that the passage was composed largely of quotations and paraphrases from Ming-kuang's *T'ien t'ai p'u sa chieh su*, the *Kuan p'u hsien ching*, I-hsing's *Ta p'i lu che na ch'eng fo ching su*, Kuan-ting's *Kuo ch'ing pai lu*, the *Fan wang ching*, and Tao-hsüan's commentary on the *Fan wang ching*.[31] A summary of the main ideas in this passage and an analysis of how they differ from Saichō's position follows.

Kōjō treated the mind (*shin* 心) as the origin of the myriad *dharmas* (*manbō* 萬法). In doing so, he departed from the traditional view of Chinese T'ien-t'ai scholars who refused to impose any hierarchical relationship on mind and *dharmas*.[32] Kōjō gave the mind the paramount

---

[29] Additional information on Kōjō is presented in a number of other sections of this study. His relationship with Saichō is discussed in Chapters 6 and 8. His career after Saichō's death is treated in this chapter in the section on "Gishin and Factionalism in the Early Tendai School." Finally, Kōjō's rejection of the provisional Hīnayāna ordination is analyzed in Chapter 10.

[30] *DZ* 1:629–36. Most modern scholars believe this extremely difficult passage represents Kōjō's basic position on the precepts. The following studies are helpful in interpreting the text: Ishida, *Kairitsu no kenkyū*, pp. 361–71; Asai, *Jōko Nihon Tendai*, pp. 255–61; and Tamaki, *Nihon Bukkyō shisō ron* 1:204–30.

[31] In *Kairitsu no kenkyū*, pp. 371–82, Ishida included the full text of this passage from the *Denjutsu isshinkaimon* along with the original passages from the works which Kōjō quoted for easy comparison. The works cited correspond to T nos. 1812, 277, 1726, 1934, and 1484. The commentary by Tao-hsüan is not extant.

[32] *DZ* 1:565–66. For the Chinese T'ien-t'ai position, see Hurvitz, *Chih-i*, pp. 290–301.

position and then proceeded to identify the essence of the mind (*shinshō* 心性) with Birushana Nyorai.[33]

Kōjō identified both the precepts (*kaihō* 戒法) and their uncondi-tioned karmic essence (*musa kaitai* 無作戒體) with the mind which per-ceives things as they really are (*jissōshin* 實相心). Kōjō borrowed this position from Ming-kuang's writings, but did not identify the source of his ideas.[34]

Kōjō described the precepts themselves by citing passages from two sources. First, he quoted from I-hsing's commentary on the *Ta jih ching*, again without identifying the source. The passage discussed the precepts in Esoteric terms.[35] Although it originally had referred to the Esoteric precepts (*sanmayakai* 三昧耶戒), Kōjō used it to describe the *Fan wang* precepts. The term *isshin* 一心 (one-mind) appeared in this passage and was used to describe how the precepts encompassed physical, verbal, and mental activities.

Secondly, Kōjō quoted from Ming-kuang's commentary on the *Fan wang ching* without identifying his source.[36] In the passage, a hierar-chical list of ten aspects of the precepts was described.[37] The first four aspects were associated with precepts which were formulated as rules (*jikai* 事戒). The ten major and forty-eight minor precepts of the *Fan wang ching* were mentioned in this section. This was one of only two references to the precepts as rules to be found in this section of the *Den-jutsu isshinkaimon*. The last six aspects were associated with the precepts in a more abstract sense, and referred to the principles underlying the precepts (*rikai* 理戒). A correct understanding of these principles, especi-ally of nonsubstantiality, was conducive to, if not identical with, holding the precepts. These last six aspects of the precepts corresponded to the three truths (non-substantial, provisional, and middle). By comprehend-ing the three truths simultaneously (*isshin sankan* 一心三觀), all ten aspects of the precepts were encompassed. A person with such compre-hension was a bodhisattva.

When the practitioner attained mastery of the precepts, he became aware that he was inherently pure (*jishō jōshō* 自性清淨) and could no longer break the precepts. His practice was unhindered and immovable

---

[33] *DZ* 1:605.

[34] *T* 40:584a.

[35] *T* 39:629c.

[36] *T* 40:580c–81a.

[37] The ten aspects are discussed in the section on the T'ien-t'ai view of the precepts in Chapter 12.

(*kokū fudō* 虚空不動).[38] Meditation and wisdom were encompassed in such precepts. Thus the practitioner completed and embodied the three studies (*sangaku*). Mastery of the precepts enabled him to enter the ranks of the Buddhas.[39] Kōjō identified this state with understanding the Esoteric teachings on the syllable 'A' (*ajimon* 阿字門), one of the fundamental teachings of Esoteric Buddhism, a conclusion which was based on a quotation from I-hsing's commentary on the *Ta jih ching*. Again, the source of the quotation was not identified.[40]

Kōjō stressed that a correct understanding of the essence of the precepts was of fundamental importance to the practitioner. Strict adherence to the rules was not a major concern in the *Denjutsu isshin-kaimon*. In this respect he differed from Saichō who was more concerned with adherence to the rules than with theoretical explanations of how the precepts affected the recipient.

Saichō's position on the *Fan wang* precepts was greatly influenced by Ming-kuang. He was also familiar with I-hsing's commentary on the the *Ta jih ching*, and awarded I-hsing an honored place in his work on lineages, the *Kechimyakufu*.[41] Kōjō was clearly influenced by Saichō's ideas, as well as by the same texts as Saichō. However the two men differed markedly in their use of these works. In general, Saichō did not integrate Tendai teachings, Esoteric Buddhism, and the precepts into one system. These teachings were transmitted separately as was indicated by the lineages in the *Kechimyakufu*. In contrast, Kōjō attempted to combine the various teachings into a single system. He put together his exposition of the precepts using a series of quotations from various works. By not identifying the sources of his quotations, he treated the ideas which they presented as his own. Kōjō's 'scissors and paste' exposition of the One-mind precepts (*isshinkai*) was thus an attempt to discuss the *Fan wang* precepts in terms of the various traditions which Saichō brought back from China.

---

[38] The terms *kokū fudō* and *jishō shōjō* are included in a quotation from Tao-hsüan's commentary on the *Fan wang ching* which in turn cited Kuan-ting's *Kuo ch'ing pai lu* (*Denjutsu isshinkaimon, DZ* 1:633). Kōjō did identify the source of this quotation.

[39] This was quoted from Ming-kuang's commentary (*T* 40:585b), but Kōjō did not identify the source of the quotation. Elsewhere, Kōjō called *sokushin jōbutsu* (the attainment of Buddhahood in this existence) a basic Tendai teaching (*DZ* 1:605). The statement that the conferral of the *Fan wang* precepts allows the recipient to enter the ranks of the Buddhas is based on the *Fan wang ching* (*T* 24:1003c).

[40] *T* 39:589a, c.

[41] Ming-kuang is discussed in Chapter 12 of this study. For information on I-hsing, see footnote 58 of Chapter 4; *Ehyō Tendaishū, DZ* 3:358–60; and *Kechimyakufu, DZ* 1:239–42.

Kōjō's attempt to integrate Esoteric and Tendai elements with the *Fan wang* precepts may have had its origin in an Esoteric initiation which he received from Kūkai in 813. The initiation was called the *Hokke giki isson no hō* 法華儀軌一尊之法[42] and was probably based on a work which is traditionally said to have been translated by Amoghavajra, but in fact may actually have been composed by Amoghavajra. If the work was written by Amoghavajra, it represented his attempt to integrate two Pure Esoteric traditions, the Womb-realm (Taizōkai) and Diamond-realm (Kongōkai) *maṇḍalas,* with Tendai and *Lotus* doctrines.[43] It thus provided Kōjō with a precedent for his attempts to combine Esoteric and Tendai teachings. In contrast, Saichō never received an initiation which combined teachings from the *Lotus Sūtra* and Esoteric Buddhism, nor did he mix the two traditions in his writings.

A key element in Kōjō's efforts to synthesize Esoteric Buddhist teachings with the precepts was his treatment of Birushana. Saichō had been content to designate Rushana, the *saṃbhogakāya* of Birushana, as the source of the *Fan wang* precepts. He then claimed that Rushana had transmitted the precepts to Śākyamuni, the *nirmāṇakāya* of Birushana and the Buddha who served as preceptor in the ordination.

Saichō's explanation eventually proved to be a liability for the Tendai School, especially when it was juxtaposed with doctrines advocated by Kūkai in his later years. Kūkai had argued that Esoteric doctrines were preached by the *dharmakāya* while exoteric doctrines such as the *Lotus Sūtra* were preached by the *nirmāṇakāya,* and were thus inferior to Esoteric doctrines.[44] Tendai scholars, including Kōjō, replied to these claims by stressing the identity of Birushana and Śākyamuni. They based much of their argument on the passage from the *Kuan p'u hsien ching* which Saichō had quoted at the beginning of the Tendai lineage in the *Kechimyakufu.*[45]

Kōjō argued that the *Fan wang* precepts were not the precepts of

---

[42] *Denjutsu isshinkaimon, DZ* 1:530.

[43] The work is entitled the *Ch'eng chiu miao fa lien hua ching wang yü ch'ieh kuan chih i kuei* and corresponds to *T* no. 1000. It is listed in Kūkai's *Goshōrai mokuroku, Kōbō Daishi chōsaku zenshū* 2:10. The work is discussed by Osabe Kazuo in "Hokke no mikkyōka ni kansuru shiken," *Mikkyō bunka* 26 (1954): 38–47.

[44] See Hakeda, *Kūkai,* pp. 81–93, 151–57.

[45] *DZ* 1:215. Kōjō also raised this issue in his *Tōketsu (Nihon daizōkyō* 46:421–22). The relationship between Śākyamuni and Birushana was a vital concern of Saichō's disciples (Asai, *Jōko Nihon Tendai,* pp. 227–32). Tokuen raised a similar problem in his *Tōketsu (Nihon Daizōkyō* 46:414–15). The identification of Śākyamuni and Birushana is discussed further in Chapter 13.

a *saṃbhogakāya,* but the precepts of the *dharmakāya.* The Buddhas and bodhisattvas who played roles in the *Fan wang* ordination were treated as manifestations of Birushana. The precepts themselves originated with Birushana and were the precepts of the *dharmakāya.*

Kōjō elaborated on this position by dividing the precepts into two types or aspects. First were the precepts of *Dainichi Nyorai* (Birushana). They were called the basic precepts (*honkai* 本戒) or self-realized precepts (*jishō kaihō* 自證戒法). They were the precepts of the *dharmakāya* in bliss, in its self-oriented aspect (*jijuyō hosshin* 自受用法身). The second aspect of the precepts arose when the Buddha turned outward to grant the precepts to others. These were the precepts granted by Rushana, but by Rushana as the *dharmakāya* in bliss, oriented towards others (*tajuyō hosshin* 他受用法身). Kōjō called them the One-mind precepts (*isshinkai*) or the branch precepts (*makkai* 末戒), as opposed to the basic or root precepts (*honkai* 本戒). These two aspects of the precepts were neither identical nor different.[46]

In this way Kōjō attempted to integrate the *Fan wang* precepts with Tendai and Esoteric concepts. In addition, he assigned Bodhidharma an important role in the *Denjutsu isshinkaimon,* thereby introducing Zen elements into his interpretation of the precepts. However, Kōjō used many more Esoteric elements than Zen elements in his system. Kōjō distinguished between Bodhidharma's precepts and the Tendai precepts in his terminology. The term *isshinkai* was used only in reference to the *Fan wang* precepts. Bodhidharma's precepts were usually called the One-vehicle precepts (*ichijōkai* 一乘戒), a more ambiguous term which could refer to several interpretations of the precepts, including the *Fan wang* precepts.[47]

Kōjō's attempt to combine Tendai, Esoteric, and Zen elements with the precepts met with little success, perhaps because he never succeeded

---

[46] *DZ* 1:634.

[47] *DZ* 1:559, 616. Bodhidharma is said to have transmitted One-mind precepts which were a reflection of the originally pure nature of the mind. The authenticity of this tradition is questionable (Komazawa daigakunai Zengaku daijiten hensansho, *Zengaku daijiten,* Tokyo: Daishūkan shoten, 1978, 1:44a). However, Ch'an monks from the time of Tao-hsin (the fourth patriarch) onwards, were interested in the Mahāyāna precepts and were writing ordination manuals (Sekiguchi Shindai, "Jubosatsukaigi 'Darumahon' ni tsuite," *IBK* 9.2 [1961]: 55–60). Tao-hsüan, the Chinese monk who transmitted Northern School Zen, Kegon, and the precepts to Saichō's teacher Gyōhyō, might also have transmitted Zen teachings concerning the precepts; but the evidence concerning such a transmission remains extremely scanty (see Tokiwa Daijō, *Nihon Bukkyō no kenkyū,* pp. 410–420, 452–465, 471–75; Ishida Mizumaro, *Kairitsu no kenkyū,* pp. 44–46, 225–265).

in expressing his ideas on the subject with much clarity. Later Tendai scholars who wrote on the precepts such as Ennin, Enchin, and Annen never mentioned the One mind precepts (*isshinkai*). In fact, one of the few places where the term 'One-mind precepts' appears in later times is in a short work by Eisai 榮西 (1141–1215) entitled the *Endon sanju isshinkai* (The Perfect-Sudden One-Mind Precepts in Three Groups).[48] Kōjō's efforts to interpret the precepts in terms of Esoteric Buddhist doctrines were ignored by Tendai scholars of Esoteric Buddhism such as Ennin 圓仁 (794–864) and Enchin 圓珍 (814–891). However, in the late ninth century, the Tendai scholar Annen 安然 (841–889?) wrote a commentary on the ordination manual by Chan-jan which interpreted the precepts in terms of Esoteric Buddhist teachings. In particular, Annen elevated the Esoteric *sanmayakai*[49] to a position over the *Fan wang* precepts. The tendency to integrate the precepts with the other doctrinal components of Saichō's Tendai School and to emphasize the role of a proper state of mind over literal adherence to rules progressed with the appearance of Annen's commentary on the ordination ceremony, the *Futsūju bosatsukai kōshaku*.[50] However, Zen teachings did not play a large role in Annen's interpretation.

Ennin

At the time of Saichō's death in 822, Ennin was only twenty-nine years old. Even as a young man, he had already established himself as one of Saichō's leading disciples. Having received the bodhisattva precepts from Saichō in 817, he served as a teacher at the first ordination conferring the bodhisattva precepts after Saichō's death in 823.

Near the end of his life, Ennin began writing a work on the precepts, the *Ken'yō daikairon* 顯揚大戒論 (Treatise on Revealing and Praising the Mahāyāna Precepts) in eight fascicles; he died in 864, however, without finishing it. Several years later, Anne 安慧 (795–868), who had studied under both Saichō and Ennin, completed it.[51] Although the

---

[48] Taga Munehaya, "Eizan bunkozō *Endon sanju isshinkai*," *Bukkyō shigaku*, 9(1961): 53–57.

[49] For a discussion of the *sanmayakai*, see footnote 12 of Chapter 5.

[50] *T* no. 2381, also see Ishida Mizumaro's analysis of the relationship between Esoteric teachings and the precepts in the Tendai tradition, "Enkai to mikkyō no kōshō," *IBK* 9.1 (1961): 277–280.

[51] Evidence for the authorship comes from two documents in the *Tendai kahyō*. The first is an introduction to the *Ken'yō daikairon* which was probably written by Sugawara no Michizane (845–903) when he was twenty-two years old (*BZ* 41:202). This introduction is also found in *T* 74:661, but without the comments of Jihon, compiler of the *Tendai kahyō*.

authorship of the various sections of the work can not be definitely determined, differences are apparent. The first two fascicles, more theoretical than the other fascicles, are concerned with refuting the criticisms which were still being made by monks from Nara. The author quoted sources proving that distinct sets of Hīnayāna and Mahāyāna precepts existed, that the Mahāyāna set was superior to the Hīnayāna set, and that the Mahāyāna precepts were sufficient by themselves to ordain Mahāyāna monks. He also argued for the existence of separate categories of lay and monastic bodhisattvas. In defending the Tendai position, the *Ken'yō daikairon* was not nearly as antagonistic toward the Nara schools as Saichō's *Kenkairon*. Since Saichō's petitions had been approved almost forty years earlier, the author apparently saw little advantage in continuing to antagonize the Nara monks. These two fascicles were composed largely of quotations from *sūtras* and their commentaries, but also contained some long passages by the author. This part of the work probably corresponds to the section which Ennin completed.

The problems discussed in the first two fascicles were similar to those in the *Kenkairon*. Ennin often quoted the same works which Saichō had used. Even though the *Ken'yō daikairon* was composed at least thirteen years after his return from China, Ennin did not use the works which he had brought back with him. Perhaps he did not have a chance to read them thoroughly for their relevance to the bodhisattva precepts, or he may not have wanted to open the way to new interpretations which he might not live to oversee.

Ennin's conservative attitude toward the precepts was also evident in his use of Esoteric teachings in the *Ken'yō daikairon*. He extensively discussed the Esoteric *sanmayakai* in the *Kanjō sanmayakaiki* 灌頂三昧耶戒記[52] and analyzed Esoteric teachings and practices in many of his other works. Yet in the *Ken'yō daikairon,* he ignored the *sanmayakai* and Esoteric doctrines, and mentioned Esoteric practices only twice. Both times he suggested that recitation of a *dhāraṇī* would help the candidate for ordination to purge himself of wrongdoings when he confessed before receiving the precepts.[53] The recitation of *dhāraṇī* did not indicate any laxness in the performance of the confession; Ennin devoted ample space in his work to inculcating a serious attitude in confession.

The second piece of evidence is a letter from Anne to Sugawara no Koreyoshi, Michizane's father (*BZ* 41:264–65).

[52] *Nihon daizōkyō: Taimitsu shōsho* 1:175–80.

[53] *T* 74:705a, 735b.

Ennin's reluctance to include Esoteric elements with the precepts was very different from Kōjō's free use of them in the *Denjutsu isshinkaimon*. Ennin probably feared that interpreting the precepts with Esoteric doctrines might lead monks to be lax in their observance of the precepts. His criticisms of the negligence of some Tendai monks toward monastic discipline may have been directed toward Kōjō's followers.[54]

The last six fascicles of the *Ken'yō daikairon* were composed primarily of quotations from the Buddhist canon with very few comments by the authors. This difference in style has led some scholars to conclude that Ennin died before he could complete this part of the work and that Anne finished it for him. Perhaps, however, comments were unnecessary since these fascicles differ in content from the first two fascicles and are largely self-explanatory.[55] While the first two fascicles of the work consisted of a defense of the Tendai system against its outside detractors, the last six fascicles defined and tightened the application of the precepts and the ordination procedure. The latter sections were thus directed towards the Tendai monks, not against outside critics.

The precepts in the *Fan wang ching* are brief and do not include much detail. Consequently they do not discuss the administration of the precepts or problems of interpretation. Usually these subjects were left to commentators. Saichō was primarily concerned with obtaining official approval for his proposals, and died before he was able to confront the practical problem of administering the precepts. As a result, his disciples had to decide how the precepts would be administered and defined. The *Ken'yō daikairon* was one of the first attempts to discuss these practical problems extensively.

For example, a large section of the text was devoted to distinguishing between the severity of various offenses which a monk might commit.[56] Elsewhere Mahāyāna precepts were quoted which concerned such subjects as begging for food, the rainy season retreat, the fortnightly assembly, seating order in monastic assemblies, ordinations, shaving the head, robes, begging bowls, and beds.[57] Ennin and Anne wanted to be sure that Tendai monks generally followed traditional Buddhist monastic practices, even if those practices were not fully spelled out in

---

[54] Ibid., pp. 661a-b. Similar warnings are found in Enchin's works (Asai, *Jōko Nihon Tendai*, p. 261).

[55] Ishida, *Kairitsu no kenkyū*, p. 396. Also see Ōchō Enichi, "*Ken'yō daikairon* zatsukan," *Jikaku Daishi kenkyū*, p. 411.

[56] *Ken'yō daikairon*, *T* 74: 713–746.

[57] Ibid., pp. 708–714.

the *Fan wang ching*.

In interpreting the precepts, Ennin quoted a variety of works which were concerned with the Mahāyāna precepts, including the *Ta chih tu lun* (*Mahāprajñāpāramitopadeśa*) and Yogācāra works such as the *P'u sa ti ch'ih ching* and the *P'u sa shan chieh ching* (two translations of the *Bodhisattvabhūmi*), as well as commentaries by Chinese monks.[58] In addition to considering the *Fan wang* precepts, other Mahāyāna formulations such as the ten good precepts (*jūzenkai*) were discussed in the *Ken'yō daikairon*.

Ennin departed from Saichō's position in one significant way. The *Fan wang* precepts were traditionally conferred on both laymen and monks. Saichō emphasized their universality, noting that they could be received and conferred by almost anyone. The main distinction between laymen and monks was to be the number of precepts taken. In contrast, Ennin emphasized the distinctions between laymen and monks, arguing that monks were superior to laymen.

The same attitude can also be seen in Enchin's writings. His notes to the *Jubosatsukaigi*, an ordination manual for the bodhisattva precepts which was written by Saichō or one of his disciples, brought the bodhisattva precepts ordination closer to the Hīnayāna ceremony than it had been before. Enchin adopted elements from the full (*upasampadā*) *Ssu fen lü* ordination and applied them to the bodhisattva precepts ordination. He asserted that the candidate for monastic ordination had to be at least twenty years of age, have his begging bowl and monastic robes, as well as permission from his parents and ruler.[59] These requirements were virtually identical to those asked of candidates for the full Hīnayāna ordination. In addition, by this time all ordinations were presided over by the *zasu*.[60] Saichō's assertion that anyone who had previously received the *Fan wang* precepts could confer them was too idealistic to be put into practice.

Enchin seems to have been purposefully trying to adopt certain elements from the *Ssu fen lü* for use in Japanese Tendai monastic practice. During his studies in China, he studied the *Ssu fen lü* under Ts'un-shih 存式.[61] Among the texts he brought back from China were a large

---

58 *T* nos 1509, 1581 and 1582.
59 *DZ* 1:319–21.
60 *BKD* 5:112–13.
61 Kotera Bun'ei, "Annen oshō to enkai," *Annen oshō no kenkyū* (Kyoto: Dōhōsha, 1974), part 1, p. 87.

number concerning the *Ssu fen lü* precepts.[62] Studying the *Ssu fen lü* precepts under a Risshū monk in Nara would have been very embarrassing for the Tendai monks after the bitter fights between Saichō and the Nara monastic establishment over the ordination ceremony. However, Enchin could freely study the *Ssu fen lü* in China and then use only those elements of the Hīnayāna precepts suitable for Japanese Tendai practice once he was back in Japan. Enchin never attempted to reinstate Saichō's plan for 'provisional Hīnayāna ordinations.' Clarifying the practical application of the Perfect precepts by using selected elements from the *Ssu fen lü* obviated any need for actual *Ssu fen lü* ordinations.[63]

These changes did not indicate that laymen were no longer to participate in Tendai ceremonies. Ennin conferred the *Fan wang* precepts on laymen, including the emperor, and laymen often participated in Esoteric initiations with monks.[64] However leaders like Ennin and Enchin did insist on firm distinctions between laymen and monks.

Ennin's treatment of the precepts differed from that of Saichō in at least one other significant way. Ennin did not equate the transmission of the precepts with the protection of the state. By Ennin's time, Esoteric Buddhism was thoroughly established, and its rituals were used to protect the state. Consequently, Ennin felt no need to equate ordinations with ceremonies to protect the state as Saichō had done.[65] Despite these differences, Ennin's attitude towards the precepts was not significantly different from that of Saichō. Both men stressed the importance of strict adherence to the precepts. Ennin relied on many of the same sources as Saichō. Like Saichō, he did not speculate on the nature of the absolute precepts (*rikai*). In this last respect, Ennin clearly differed from Kōjō who was vitally concerned with the *rikai*.

Conclusion

The events which occurred during the decades following Saichō's death illustrate both the strengths and weaknesses of Saichō's petitions, as well as the significance of his proposals for the history of Japanese Buddhism. The training program which Saichō proposed for Mount Hiei provided the structure for an educational system which flourished for centuries after his death. During the Heian and Kamakura periods,

---

[62] Seita Yoshihide, "Eizan no gōgisei," *DDK* (*Bekkan*), pp. 226–230.

[63] Kotera Bun'ei, "Chishō Daishi to enkai," *TG* 15 (1973): 76–77.

[64] Ogami, "Dengyō Daishi no nyūmetsugo," *DDK*, pp. 232–33.

[65] For a discussion of Saichō's use of Buddhism to protect the state, see the section on "Saichō's View of Japan" in Chapter 9 of this study.

Tendai temples produced many of the most eminent monks of Japan. In addition, the founders of the Kamakura schools of Buddhism studied on Mount Hiei.

Saichō's administrative proposals were faithfully instituted by his disciples and soon provided the foundation for a strong autonomous order of monks. Saichō's plan also enabled the Tendai School to expand its influence into the provinces. Many of Saichō's administrative reforms were adopted by the Shingon School, the chief rival of the Tendai School during the Heian period.

Saichō's proposals created a number of new problems for the Tendai School. By abandoning the *Ssu fen lü* precepts traditionally followed by Chinese and Japanese Buddhist monks, Saichō opened the way for various new interpretations of the precepts. Since Saichō did not live long enough to discuss the practical problems of implementing the *Fan wang* precepts or to elaborate his theoretical position on the precepts, these tasks were left to his disciples. However, disagreements over the precepts quickly arose. Kōjō and Ennin adopted divergent positions on such issues as whether Esoteric Buddhist teachings were to be used to interpret the precepts. The abandonment of Saichō's plan for advanced Tendai monks to provisionally receive the *Ssu fen lü* precepts meant that all Tendai monks were to follow the *Fan wang* precepts, a set of regulations which had never been intended to serve as an authoritative guide for monastic discipline.

During the centuries after Saichō's death, Tendai monks debated the importance of rigid adherence to the *Fan wang* precepts. Eventually, monastic discipline among Tendai monks, as well as among the adherents of other schools, precipitously declined. The role of the precepts in Buddhist practice was a major concern for many of the founders of the Kamakura schools of Buddhism. Figures such as Shinran went to the extreme of completely rejecting the precepts.

Despite periodic attempts to revive and encourage monastic discipline throughout Japanese history, Japanese Buddhism has exhibited a more tolerant attitude towards transgressions of the precepts than perhaps any other Buddhist tradition. At the same time, Japanese monks devised a rich variety of innovative interpretations of the precepts, most of which Saichō could never have envisioned. Saichō's proposals opened the way for these changes by freeing Japanese monks from the burden of observing precepts which had been compiled over one-thousand years earlier in India.

CHAPTER SIXTEEN

CONCLUSION

Japanese Buddhism was transformed in a number of fundamental ways during Saichō's lifetime. Many of these changes were due to the activities of Saichō and Kūkai, even though the results of their efforts were not always what they had envisioned. Frequently the reforms advocated by the two men were similar although their methods for achieving their goals were very different. Saichō was often uncompromising and intractable in his demands while Kūkai was more conciliatory, particularly towards the Nara schools.

Saichō and Kūkai both placed more emphasis on meditation and other religious practices than had been common in Nara Buddhism. Although prolonged retreats to mountain temples for the practice of religious austerities had not been unknown during the Nara period, such retreats were not encouraged by the court and did not play a significant role in the lives of most Nara monks. Both Saichō and Kūkai established monastic centers in the mountains in order to provide quiet retreats where their monks could meditate free from the distractions of life in the city. It was the detailed instructions concerning meditation found in Chih-i's writings which first attracted Saichō to Tendai teachings. Saichō's requirement that Tendai monks spend twelve years on Mount Hiei without any breaks indicates the earnestness of his attitudes towards intense and sustained religious austerities.

The ultimate goal of religious practice for both Saichō and Kūkai was conceived of as being much more immediate than it had generally been for Nara monks. Buddhahood and enlightenment in this very existence was a real possibility. The Hossō view that Buddhahood required three incalculable eons was rejected. Moreover, according to both Tendai and Shingon teachings, everyone had the potential to realize Buddhahood. Buddhism was not a teaching solely for the elite, but had relevance for all people. Saichō argued vigorously against the Hossō belief that some people could never realize Buddhahood. Saichō and Kūkai thus helped lay the doctrinal groundwork for the propagation of Buddhism among the masses in Japan. Saichō established the institutional basis for the further spread of Buddhism to the provinces with his proposal that graduates of the Tendai educational system be dispatched to the provinces to preach and help the populace with construction projects.

During the early Heian period Esoteric Buddhist doctrine and ritual became influential forces in Japanese religious life. Although Esoteric Buddhism had been present in Japan during the Nara period, it had been used primarily for worldly goals such as protecting the state and curing illnesses. Under the leadership of Kūkai and, to a lesser extent Saichō, Esoteric Buddhist practices and doctrines were used to realize enlightenment. The influence of Esoteric Buddhism was so pervasive, in fact, that it eventually was adopted by monks of the Nara schools. In the Tendai School, several decades after Saichō's death, Esoteric Buddhism overshadowed the exoteric doctrines of Chih-i's T'ien-t'ai system.

Saichō's most significant contribution to Japanese Buddhism was his reform of the ordination system, particularly his substitution of the *Fan wang* precepts for the *Ssu fen lü* precepts. If the Tendai School had not gained substantial control over the initiation and ordination of its novices and monks, the school would have developed much more slowly and possibly might not have survived. In addition, Saichō's advocacy of the *Fan wang* precepts opened the door for many innovations in religious practice by his successors. Although Saichō never intended his changes in the precepts to lead to negligence in the observance of monastic discipline, the first signs of a decline in compliance with the precepts appeared shortly after Saichō's death. Yet, at the same time, Saichō's unprecedented reform of the precepts opened the way to uniquely Japanese interpretations of Buddhist practice.

The Tendai School eventually became the dominant force in Japanese Buddhism during the middle and late Heian period. Its success was due in no small part to Saichō's activities. Saichō's proposals for a reform of the ordination system gave the Tendai School more independence from government control than the other schools. The Tendai School was still subject to certain regulations, but compliance to the regulations was supervised by lay administrators sympathetic to the Tendai School, rather than by monastic officials of the Sōgō hostile to it. The lay administrators were usually high officials at court who served as effective lobbyists for Tendai concerns. The petitions also provided guidelines for an aggressive expansion into the provinces. These activities often were conducted by monks who had spent twelve years in training on Mount Hiei and who were among the better educated men in the country.

Saichō died without mastering Esoteric Buddhism and without integrating the various elements of his syncretistic form of Tendai into a unified system. Yet, even these shortcomings eventually worked to the advantage of the Tendai School. Saichō's successors were forced to strive to integrate and interpret the various traditions which Saichō had introduced. Saichō's syncretism and incomplete mastery of Esoteric Buddhist doctrines thus proved to be a major impetus to the development of Tendai doctrine. In contrast, the Shingon School with its more complete doctrinal system often seemed to languish after Kūkai's time.

BIBLIOGRAPHY

Akamatsu Toshihide. *Kyōto jishikō.* Kyoto: Hōzōkan, 1972.

_____. "Saichō to Kūkaī." *Ōtani gakuhō* 53, no. 2 (1973): 1–13.

Andō Kōsei. *Ganjin.* Tokyo: Yoshikawa kōbunkan, 1967.

Andō Toshio. *Tendaigaku: konpon shisō to sono tenkai.* Kyoto: Heirakuji shoten, 1968.

_____. *Tendaigaku ronshū.* Kyoto: Heirakuji shoten, 1975.

_____. *Tendai shōgu shisōron.* Kyoto: Hōzōkan. 1953.

Aoki Kōshō. "Chūgoku Bukkyō ni okeru kaitaikan ni tsuite no ikkōsatsu." *Indogaku Bukkyōgaku kenkyū* 20 (1972): 776–80.

Asada Masahiro. *"Shugo kokkaishō* ni okeru shikan." In *Bukkyō ni okeru jissen genri,* pp. 515–38. Edited by Sekiguchi Shindai. Tokyo: Sankibō Busshorin, 1977.

_____. "Tokuitsu no *Chuhengikyō* senjutsu izu." *Bukkyōgaku kenkyū* 31 (1975): 74–99.

Asaeda Zenshō. *Heian Bukkyōshi kenkyū.* Kyoto: Nagata bunshōdō, 1980.

Asai Endō. *Jōko Nihon Tendai hōmon shisōshi.* Kyoto: Heirakuji shoten, 1973.

Bender, Ross. "The Hachiman Cult and the Dōkyō Incident." *Monumenta Nipponica* 34 (1979): 125–153.

Buddhaghosa. *The Path of Purity.* Translated by Bhikkhu Ñyāṇamoli. 2 vols. Berkeley: Shambala, 1976.

Chae In-hwan. *Shiragi Bukkyō ni okeru kairitsu shisō no kenkyū.* Tokyo: Kokusho kankōkai, 1977.

_____. "Shiragi ni okeru *Senzatsu* sange kaihō ni tsuite." In *Bukkyō no jissen genri,* pp. 379–99. Edited by Sekiguchi Shindai. Tokyo: Sankibō Bussborin, 1977.

Chappell, David. "Early Forebodings of the Death of Buddhism." *Numen* 27 (1980): 122–154.

Ch'en Kenneth. *The Chinese Transformation of Buddhism.* Princeton: Princeton University Press, 1973.

Conze, Edward, tr. *The Perfection of Wisdom in Eight Thousand Lines.* Bolinas, California: Four Seasons Foundation, 1973.

DeBary, William, ed. *The Buddhist Tradition.* New York: Modern Library, 1969.

DeGroot, J. J. M. *Le Code du Mahayana en Chine: son influence sur le vie moncal et sur le monde laique.* Amsterdam: Verhider Kon. Ak. van Wetensch, 1893.

Etani Ryūkai. *Endonkai gairon.* Tokyo: Daitō shuppansha, 1937.

_____. "Endonkai no kaitai ni tsuite." In *Fukui hakushi shōju kinen: Tōyō bunka ronshū,* pp. 137–50. Tokyo: Waseda Daigaku shuppanbu, 1969.

Fukaura Seibun. *Yuishikigaku kenkyū.* 2 vols. Kyoto: Nagata bunshōdō, 1954.

Fukuda Gyōei. *Tendaigaku gairon.* 2 vols. Tokyo: Bun'ichi shuppansha, 1954–59.

Fukui Kōjun. *"Eizan Daishiden* no saikentō." *Tendai gakuhō* 15 (1972): 1–10.

_____. *Tōyō shisō no kenkyū.* Tokyo: Risōsha, 1955.

Furue Ryōnin. "Nara jidai ni okeru yamadera no kenkyū." *Taishō daigaku kenkyū kiyō* 39 (1954): 1–47.

308

Furukawa Yoshihide. *"Gakushōshiki* ni okeru Tendai shūdan." *Tendai gakuhō* 3 (1959): 12–18.

Futaba Kenkō. "Bukkyō ni taisuru kokka tōsei seido no seiritsu to sono seikaku: jūji to jūdaitoku." *Ryūkoku daigaku ronshū*, no. 396 (June 1971), pp. 1–29.

_____. "Gyōgi no shōgai to hanritsuryō Bukkyō no seiritsu." *Nanto Bukkyō* 5 (1961): 1–76.

_____. "Nara jidai ni okeru risshū to kairitsu." *Indogaku Bukkyōgaku kenkyū* 13 (1965): 292–96.

_____. "Nenbundosha no gengi to sono henka." In *Kimura Takeo sensei no kanreki kinen: Nihonshi no kenkyū*, pp. 83–104. Kyoto: Mineruva shobō, 1970.

Greenblatt, Kristin Yü. "Chu–hung and Lay Buddhism in the Late Ming." In *The Unfolding of Neo–Confucianism*, pp. 93–140. Edited by Wm. Theodore de Bary. New York: Columbia University Press, 1975.

Hakeda Yoshito. *Kūkai: Major Works.* New York: Columbia University Press, 1972.

Hanawa Hokinoichi, ed. *Gunsho ruijū.* 19 vols. Tokyo: Keizai zasshisha, 1893–1902.

_____. *Zoku gunsho ruijū.* 70 vols. Tokyo: Zoku gunsho ruijū kankōkai, 1923–30.

Hayashi Mikiya. *Taishi shinkō: sono hassei to tenkai.* Nihonjin no kōdō to shisō, vol. 13. Tokyo: Hyōronsha, 1972.

Hayashida Kōshō. *Kyōshugi gassan.* Tokyo: Kokugaku mikkyō kankōkai, 1921.

Hazama Jikō. *"Kenkairon* no Hiso jinenchi shikō." *Sange gakuhō* vol. 1, no. 4 (1931): 164–79.

_____. *Nihon Bukkyō no kaiten to sono kichō.* 2 vols. Tokyo: Sanseidō, 1948.

Hibi Nobutada. *Tōdai Tendaigaku kenkyū.* Tokyo: Sankibō Busshorin, 1975.

Hieizan senshuin, ed. *Dengyō Daishi zenshū.* 5 vols. 2nd ed. Hieizan: Tosho kankōkai, 192–27; reprint ed., Tokyo: Nihon Bussho kankōkai, 1975.

Hirai Shun'ei. "Heian shoki ni okeru Sanron Hossō kakuchiku wo meguru shomondai." *Komazawa daigaku Bukkyō gakubu kenkyū kiyō* 37 (1979): 72–91.

Hirakawa Akira. "Chigi no kaitai ni tsuite." In *Okuda Jiō sensei kiju kinen: Bukkyō shisō ronshū*, pp. 755–768. Kyoto: Heirakuji shoten, 1976.

_____. "Daijō Bukkyō kyodan no seiritsuteki kenkyū." In *Daijō Bukkyō no seiritsuteki kenkyū*, pp. 447–82. Edited by Miyamoto Shōson. Tokyo: Sanseidō, 1954.

_____. "Daijōkai to Bosatsukaikyō." In *Fukui Hakushi shōiu kinen: Tōyō shisō ronshū*, pp. 522–44. Tokyo: Waseda daigaku shuōpanbu, 1960.

_____. *"Dōsen no Hokekyō* kan." In *Hokekyō no Chūgokuteki tenkai*, pp. 319–42. Edited by Sakamoto Yukio. Kyoto: Heirakuji shoten, 1972.

_____. *Genshi Bukkyō no kenkyū.* Tokyo: Shunjūsha, 1964.

_____. "Gyōnen no kairitsu shisō." *Nanto Bukkyō* 28 (1972): 1–17.

_____. *"Kegonkyō* ni mirareru shoki daijōkyōto no shūkyō seikatsu." In *Kegon shisō*, pp. 147–98. Edited by Nakamura Hajime. Kyoto: Hōzōkan, 1960.

_____. "The Rise of Mahāyāna Buddhism and Its Relationship to the Worship of Stūpas." *Memoirs of the Tōyō Bunko*, no. 22 (1963), pp. 58–106.

_____. "Shoki Daijō Bukkyō no kaigaku to shite no juzendō." In *Bukkyō kyōdan no kenkyū*, pp. 167–203. Edited by Yoshimura Shūki. Tokyo: Hyakkaen, 1968.

_____. *Shoki Daijō Bukkyō no kenkyū.* Tokyo: Shunjūsha, 1969.

Horner, I. B., tr. *The Book of the Discipline: Part 4*. London: Luzac and Company Ltd., 1962.

Hosokawa Kōshō. "Ganjin no ikkōsatsu." *Rekishi chiri* 76 (1940): 235–61.

Hurvitz, Leon. *Chih-i. Mélanges Chinois et Bouddhiques* no. 12 (1960–62).

_____, tr. *Scripture of the Lotus Blossom of the Fine Dharma*. New York: Columbia University Press, 1976.

Ienaga Saburō. *Jōdai Bukkyō shisōshi kenkyū*. Revised ed. Kyoto: Hōzōkan, 1966.

Ikeda Genta. "Iwabuchidera Gonsō to Heian Bukkyō." *Nanto Bukkyō* 5 (1958): 26–40.

Ikeda Rosan. "Bosatsukai shisō no keisei to tenkai." *Komazawa daigaku Bukkyō gakubu kenkyū kiyō* 28 (1970): 106–125.

_____. "Keikei no *Junimon kaigi* ron." *Indogaku Bukkyōgaku kenkyū* 18 (1969): 220–22.

_____. "Tendai Chigi no ryūseihō." *Komazawa daigaku Bukkyō gakubu ronshū* 2 (1971): 88–103.

Inoue Kaoru. *Gyōgi*. Jinbutsu sōsho, vol. 24. Tokyo: Yoshikawa kōbunkan, 1959.

_____. *Narachō Bukkyō no kenkyū*. Tokyo: Yoshikawa kōbunkan, 1966.

_____. "Sayama ikesho to Gonsō." *Bukkyō shigaku* 12, no. 3 (1966): 33–38.

Inoue Mitsusada. *Nihon kodai kokka to Bukkyō*. Tokyo: Iwanami shoten, 1971.

_____. "*Tōiki dentō mokuroku* yori mitaru Nara jidai sōryo no gakumon." *Shigaku zasshi* 57 (1946): 155–76, 215–37.

Ishida Mizumaro. *Bonmōkyō*. Butten kōza, vol. 14. Tokyo: Daizō shuppan kabushiki kaisha, 1971.

_____. "*Gakushōshiki mondō* no gisen ni tsuite." *Indogaku Bukkyōgaku kenkyū* 8 (1960): 495–99.

_____. "Ganjin ni okeru fusatsu no mondai." *Nanto Bukkyō* 21 (1968): 1–8.

_____. *Ganjin: sono kairitsu shisō*. Tokyo: Daizō shuppansha, 1973.

_____. "Enkai to mikkyō no kōshō." *Indogaku Bukkyōgaku kenkyū* 19 (1961): 277–280.

_____. "Gyōgi ron." *Shūkyō kenkyū* 150 (1956): 5–6.

_____. *Nihon Bukkyō ni okeru kairitsu no kenkyū*. Tokyo: Zaike Bukkyō kyōkai, 1963.

_____. "Saichō to deshi Kōjō." *Indogaku Bukkyōgaku kenkyū* 7 (1959): 590–93.

_____. "Tendaishū kyōdan hatten katei ni okeru teikyō to dakyo." *Nihon Bukkyō* 9 (1960): 1–22.

Ishizu Teruji. *Tendai jissōron no kenkyū*. Tokyo: Kōbundō, 1947.

Itō Yuishin. "Nara jidai ni okeru bosatsusō ni tsuite." *Bukkyō daigaku kenkyū kiyō* (1957): 45–65.

Jōdoshūten kankōkai, ed. *Jōdoshū zensho*. 23 vols. 2nd ed., 1928; reprint ed., Tokyo: Sankibō Busshorin, 1971.

Kabutogi Shōkō. "Tahōbuttō no keifu." In *Hokekyō shinkō no shokeitai*, pp. 429–49. Edited by Nomura Yōshō. Kyoto: Heirakuji shoten, 1976.

Kamata Shigeo. *Chūgoku Kegon shisōshi no kenkyū*. Tokyo: Tokyo daigaku shuppankai, 1965.

Kamata Shigeo and Tanaka Hisao. *Kamakura kyūbukkyō*. Nihon shisō taikei vol. 15. Tokyo: Iwanami shoten, 1971.

Kamimura Shinjō. "Shugoshō no ronri." Indogaku Bukkyōgaku kenkyū 8 (1960): 192–97.

Kanja Entatsu. "Dōsen no Shina kairitsushijō ni okeru chii." Shina Bukkyō shigaku 3, no. 2 (1939): 1–21.

Katō Bunnō, et al., tr. The Threefold Lotus Sūtra. New York: Weatherhill, 1975.

Katō Shigekimi. "Nittō ryūgakusō Ensai ni tsuite." Shigaku zasshi 41 (1930): 876–78.

Katsumata Shunkyō. "Bosatsugyō to shite no sanju jōkai ni tsuite." In Bukkyō ni okeru gyō no mondai, pp. 163–79. Edited by Nihon Bukkyō gakkai. Kyoto: Heirakuji shoten, 1965.

_____. Mikkyō ni okeru Nihonteki tenkai. Tokyo: Shunjūsha, 1970.

Katsuno Ryūshin. "Dengyō Daishi tanjō nengi no mondai." Bukkyōshi kenkyū 12 (1969): 4–36.

_____. Hieizan to Kōyasan. Tokyo: Shibundō, 1963.

_____. "Kanmuchō ni okeru shūkyō seisaku." In Kanmuchō no shomondai, pp. 216–28. Edited by Kodaigaku kyōkai.

_____. "Shūso Goyuikai ni okeru fuku no mondai." Tendai gakuhō 3 (1961): 2–11.

Kawasaki Kōshi. "Dengyō Daishi shōsoku ni tsuite." In Tayama Hōnan sensei kakō kinen ronbunshū, pp. 36–46. Tokyo: Tayama Hōnan sensei kakō kinenkai, 1963.

Kawasaki Tsuneyuki. "Saga Tennō to Saichō Kūkai." In Nihon jinbutsushi taikei. 7 vols. Vol. 1: Kodai, pp. 136–69. Tokyo: Asakura shoten, 1961.

Kikuchi Kyōko. "Zoku bettō ni tsuite." Shirin 51 (1968): 103–33.

Kimura Shūshō. Dengyō Daishi: daikai konryū no risō to shinnen. Tokyo: Nakayama shobō, 1961.

_____. "Shōu ichigū setsu ni kansuru gimon." Tendai gakuhō 15 (1973): 52–60.

Kiuchi Hiroshi. "Dengyō Daishi ni okeru boastsu kyōdan no kōsō." Taishō daigaku kenkyū kiyō 61 (1975): 115–30.

_____. "Dengyō Daishi no mikkyō sōjō to Fukū sanzō." Indogaku Bukkyōgaku kenkyū 17 (1968): 247–49.

_____. "Dengyō Daishi no montei to Mikkyō." Tendai gakuhō 8 (1967): 59–62.

_____. Dengyō Daishi no shōgai to shisō. Tokyo: Daisan bunmeisha, 1976.

_____. "Dengyō Daishi no taikon ryōbu ni tsuite." Indogaku Bukkyōgaku kenkyū 13 (1964): 164–65.

_____. "Kenkairon engi ni okeru ichi mondai." Tendai gakuhō 14 (1972): 157–64.

_____. Saichō to Tendai kyōdan. Tokyo: Kyōikusha, 1978.

Komazawa daigakunai Zengaku daijiten hensansho, ed. Zengaku daijiten. 3 vols. Daishukan shoten, 1978.

Kotera Bun'ei. "Annen oshō no enkai." In Annen osho no kenkyū, part I, pp. 82–93. Kyoto: Dōhōsha, 1974.

_____. "Chishō Daishi to enkai." Tendai gakuhō 15 (1973): 72–77.

_____. "Dengyō Daishi ni oyoboshita Myōkōsho no eikyō." Indogaku Bukkyōgaku kenkyū 15 (1966): 312–14.

_____. "Enkai ni okeru sanjusetsu no tenkai." Tendai gakuhō 9 (1967): 16–24.

_____. "Enkai to Shianrakugyō." In Bukkyō no jissen genri, pp. 605–18. Edited by Sekiguchi Shindai. Tokyo: Sankibō Busshorin, 1977.

_____. "Hochibō Shōshin no *Jike bosatsukaihō ryakusahō* ni tsuite." *Indogaku Bukkyōgaku kenkyū* 18 (1970): 755–60.

_____. "*Kenkairon* kikyōge kō." *Ryūkoku daigaku Bukkyō bunka* 7 (1968): 105–8.

Kuge Noburu. "*Shugo kokkaishō* ni okeru Tōshamon Hōbō no Busshōron." *Bukkyō daigakū kenkyū kiyō* 59 (1975): 15–38.

Kūkai. *Kōbō Daishi chōsaku zenshū.* Edited by Katsumata Shunkyō. 3 vols. Tokyo: Sankibō Busshorin, 1968–73.

_____. *Kōbō Daishi zenshū.* Edited by Sofu sen'yōe. 15 vols. Tokyo: Yoshikawa kōbunkan, 1910.

Kuno Hōryū. "Saichō wo shūten to suru *Jubosatsukaigi* no seiritsu katei." In *Tokiwa hakushi ranreki kinen: Bukkyō ronshō,* pp. 95–121. Edited by Tokiwa hakushi kanreki kinenkai. Tokyo: Kōbundō shobō: 1933.

Kuroita Katsumi, ed. *Shintei zōhō Kokushi taikei.* 66 vols. Tokyo: Yoshikawa kōbunkan, 1929–66.

Kyōkai. *Miraculous Stories from the Japanese Buddhist Tradition.* Translated by Nakamura Kyoko. Harvard–Yenching Institute Series, vol. 20. Cambridge. Mass.: Harvard University Press, 1973.

Lamotte Étienne, tr. *Le Traité de la Grande Vertu de Sagesse de Nāgārjuna.* 4 vols. Louvain: Institut Orientaliste, 1949–76.

_____. "Mañjuśrī." *T'oung pao* 48 (1960): 1–96.

Masaka Tadao. "Saichō no Tendai ryūkyō to sono shūhen." In *Nishida sensei kinen: Nihon kodaishi ronsō,* pp. 657–70. Edited by Kodaigaku kyōkai. Tokyo: Yoshikawa kōbunkan, 1960.

Matsunaga Yūkei. *Mikkyō no rekishi.* Sāra sōsho, no. 19. Kyoto: Heirakuji shoten, 1969.

_____. *Mikkyō no sōjōsha.* Tōyōjin no kōdō to shisō, vol. 3. Kyoto: Hyōronsha, 1973.

Michihata Ryōshū. *Chūgoku Bukkyō no kenkyū.* Kyoto: Hōzōkan, 1970.

_____. *Chūgoku Bukkyō to shakai fukushi jigyō.* Kyoto: Hōzōkan, 1967.

Misaki Ryōshū. "Butsuchōkei no mikkyō." In *Yoshioka hakushi kanreki kinen: Dōkyō kenkyū ronbunshū,* pp. 477–499. Tokyo: Kokusho kankōkai, 1977.

_____. "Dengyō Daishi no mikkyō shisō." *Firosofia* 56 (1969): 41–66.

_____. "Junmitsu to zōmitsu ni tsuite." *Indogaku Bukkyōgaku kenkyū* 15 (1966): 525–40.

_____. "Nara jidai no mikkyō ni okeru shomondai." *Nanto Bukkyō* 22 (1968): 55–73.

_____. "Shishu sanmai to mikkyō" In *Shikan no kenkyū,* pp. 350–372. Edited by Sekiguchi Shindai. Tokyo: Iwanami shoten, 1976.

Miura Shūkō. *Dengyō Daishi den.* Hieizan: Tendai shūmuchō, 1921.

Miyabayashi Akihiko. "Chūgoku Bukkyō ni okeru kaidan ni tsuite." *Taishō daigaku kenkyū kiyō* 56 (1971): 1–17.

_____. "Dōsen no mappōkan to kaigaku." *Taishō daigaku kenkyū kiyō* 61 (1975): 17–26.

_____. "Dōsen no sangakukan." In *Bukkyō no jissen genri,* pp. 189–200. Edited by Sekiguchi Shindai. Tokyo: Sankibō Busshorin, 1977.

Mizukami Bungi. "Dengyō Daishi no mikkyō shiryō ni kansuru ichi ni no kōsatsu." *Tendai gakuhō* 18 (1976): 151–156.

Mochizuki Shinkō. *Jōdokyō no kigen oyobi hattatsu.* Originally published in 1930; reprint ed. Tokyo: Sankibō Busshorin, 1972.

_____, ed. *Bukkyō Daijiten.* Second ed. 10 vols. Tokyo: Sekai seiten kankō kyōkai, 1958–63.

Murao Jirō. *Kanmu Tennō.* Jinbutsu sōsho, vol. 112. Tokyo: Yoshikawa kōbunkan, 1963.

Nakai Shinkō. *Nihon no Bukkyō to minshū.* Tokyo: Hyōronsha, 1973.

Nakano Tatsue et al., eds. *Dainihon zokuzōkyō.* 750 books. Tokyo: Zōkyō shoin, 1905–12.

Nakano Tatsue et al., eds. *Nihon daizōkyō.* 51 vols. Tokyo: Zōkyō shoin, 1914–21.

Nakao Shunpaku. "Dengyō Daishi Saichō no *Hokekyō*kan." *Tōyō gakujutsu kenkyū* 14, no. 3 (1975): 95–118; and no. 4: 79–104.

_____. "Dengyō Daishi Saichō no kyōhanron." *Indogaku Bukkyōgaku kenkyū* 24 (1975): 276–79.

_____. "Murō Tendai to Jakkō Daishi Enchō." In *Okuda Jiō sensei kiju kinen: Bukkyō shisō ronshū.* Kyoto: Heirakuji shoten, 1976.

_____. *Nihon shoki Tendai no kenkyū.* Kyoto: Nagata bunshōdō, 1973.

_____. *Sange gakushōshiki josetsu.* Kyoto: Nagata bunshōdō, 1980.

Nanba Toshinari. "Kodai chihō no sōkan ni tsuite." *Nanto Bukkyō* 28 (1972): 30–50.

Nihon Bussho kankōkai, ed. *Chūge gohen Tendai Daishi zenshū.* 11 vols. Tokyo: Nihon Bussho kankōkai, 1969.

Ninchū. *Yakuchū Eizan Daishiden.* Translated and annotated by Honda Kōyū. Hieizan: Goonki jimukyoku, 1917.

Nishiguchi Junko. "Kyūjū seiki ni okeru chihō gōzoku no shiji." *Bukkyō shigaku* 11 (1965): 20–43.

Ōchō Enichi. *Chūgoku Bukkyō no kenkyū.* 2 vols. Kyoto: Hōzōkan, 1958.

_____. *Hokke shisō no kenkyū.* Kyoto: Heirakuji shoten, 1971.

_____. "Ken'yō daikairon no zatsukan." In *Jikaku Daishi kenkyū.* Edited by Fukui Kōjun. Tokyo: Taishō daigaku Tendai gakkai, 1964.

_____. "Tendai Chigi no shōgo no haikei ni tsuite." *Tōyō gakujustsu kenkyū* 14 (1967): 17–38.

Ogami Kanchū. "Tendaishū ni okeru kyōdan goji no shomondai." *Nihon Bukkyō gakkai nenpō* 39 (1973): 151–71.

Ōkubo Ryōjun, Tada Kōryū, Tamura Yoshirō. *Tendai hongakuron.* Nihon shisō taikei, vol. 9. Tokyo: Iwanami shoten, 1973.

Ono Genmyō, ed. *Bussho kaisetsu daijiten.* 14 vols. Tokyo: Daitō shuppansha, 1964–78.

Ōno Hōdō. *Daijō kaikyō no kenkyū.* Tokyo: Risōsha, 1954.

_____. "Kaitai ni tsuite." *Nanto Bukkyō* 5 (1958): 1–13.

Ono Katsutoshi. "Nittōsō Enshū Kenne to sono *Kechimyaku zuki.*" In *Ishihama Sensei koki kinen: Tōyōgoku ronshō,* pp. 100–120. Osaka: Ishihama Sensei koki kinenkai, 1958.

_____. *Nittō guhō junrei kōki no kenkyū.* 4 vols. Tokyo: Suzuki gakujutsu zaidan, 1964–69.

_____. "Saichō Kūkai kōyūkō." *Ryūkoku daigaku ronshū,* no. 394 (1970): 1–29.

Osabe Kazuo. "Hokke no mikkyōka ni kansuru shiken." *Mikkyō bunka* 26 (1954): 38–47.

_____. *Ichigyō Zenji no kenkyū*. Kobe: Kobe shōka daigaku gakujutsu kenkyūkai, 1963.

_____. "Kuden hōmon ni okeru hitsuden no kigen to *Tōketsu* to no kankei." *Mikkyō bunka* 35 (1956): 19–43.

_____. *Tōdai Mikkyōshi zatsukō*. Kobe shōka daigaku gakujutsu kenkyūkai, 1971.

Ōsawa Nobuo. "Shoki daijō ni okeru jukai shisō no ikkōsatsu." *Indogaku Bukkyōgaku kenkyū* 23 (1975): 768–71.

_____. "Zaikekai no juju ni tsuite." *Bukkyō daigaku seminā* 24 (1976): 53–66.

Ōyama Kōjun. *Mikkyōshi gaisetsu to kyōri*. Kōyasan: Kōyasan daigaku, 1961.

Ōyama Ninkai. "Nanatsudera issaikyō." *Nihon Bukkyō* 30 (1969): 47–54.

Rhodes, Robert. "Saichō's *Mappō Tōmyōki*: The Candle of the Latter Dharma." *Eastern Buddhist* 13 (1980): 79–103.

Sakaino Kōyō. *Shina Bukkyō seishi*. Tokyo: Sakaino Kōyō haukshi ikō kankōkai. 1935.

_____. *Shina Bukkyōshi kōwa*. 2 vols. Tokyo: Kyōritsusha, 1927.

Sakuma Ryū. "Kaishi shōsei ni tsuite." *Nanto Bukkyō* 8 (1960): 62–74.

_____. "Kodai sōkan kō." *Bukkyō shigaku* 13 (1967): 1–13.

Sansom, George. "Early Japanese Law and Administration." *Transactions of the Asiatic Society of Japan*, second series 9 (1932): 66–109; and 11 (1934): 117–49.

_____. *A History of Japan to* 1334. Stanford, CA: Stanford University Press, 1958.

Sasaki Kentoku. "Kōbō Daishi no *Goyuigō* wo utagaute Jungyō Ajari no koto ni oyobu." *Nihon Bukkyōgaku kyōkai nenpō* 12 (1939): 91–140.

_____. *Sange gakushōshiki shinshaku*. Yamazaki: Hōbundō, 1938.

Satō Tatsugen. "Bosatukai no ikkōsatsu." *Komazawa daigaku Bukkyō gakubu kenkyū kiyō* 34 (1975): 1–25.

_____. "Chūgoku Nanbokuchō jidai ni okeru kairitsu no kyōsen tenkai." *Komazawa daigaku Bukkyō gakubu kenkyū kiyō* 29 (1971): 74–92.

Satō Tetsuei. "Sankan shisō no kigen oyobi hattatsu." In *Shikan no kenkyū*, pp. 217–51. Edited by Sekiguchi Shindai. Tokyo: Iwanami shoten, 1975.

_____. *Tendai Daishi no kenkyū*. Kyoto: Hyakkaen, 1960.

Sekiguchi Shindai. "*Jubosatsukaigi* Darumahon ni tsuite." *Indogaku Bukkyōgaku kenkyū* 9 (1961); 465–70.

_____. *Tendai shikan no kenkyū*. Tokyo: Iwanami shoten, 1969.

Shibuya Jikai, ed. *Kōtei sobu Tendai zasuki*. Tokyo: Daiichi shobō, 1973.

_____. ed. *Teisei Nihon Tendaishū nenpyō*. Tokyo: Daiichi shobō. 1973.

Shimaji Daitō. *Tendai kyōgakushi*. Tokyo: Meiji shoin, 1929; reprint ed. Gendai Bukkyō meichō zenshū, vol. 9. Tokyo: Ryūbunkan. 1964.

Shimizutani Kyōjun. *Tendai Mikkyō no seiritsu ni kansuru kenkyū*. Tokyo: Bun'ichi shuppansha, 1972.

Shioiri Ryōchū. *Dengyō Daishi*. Tokyo: Nihon hyōronsha, 1937.

_____. "Dengyō Daishi no hongaku shisō: Busshinron wo chūshin to shite." *Indogaku Bukkyōgaku kenkyū* 9 (1961): 22–27.

_____. *Shin jidai no Dengyō Daishi no kyōgaku*. Tokyo: Daitō shuppansha, 1939.

314

Shiori Ryōdō. "Chūgoku Bukkyō ni okeru raisan to Butsumyō kyōten." In *Yūki kyōju shōju kinen: Bukkyō shisōshi ronshū*, pp. 569–90. Osaka: Meikyōsha, 1964.

_____. "Chūgoku Bukkyō ni okeru sange no juyō katei." *Indogaku Bukkyōgaku kenkyū* 11 (1963): 731–36.

_____. "Dengyō Daishi ni atsukawareta sange." *Tendai gakuhō* 14 (1971): 91–100.

_____. "Senbō no seiritsu to Chigi no tachiba." *Indogaku Bukkyōgaku kenkyū* 7 (1959): 440–50.

_____. "Shishu sanmai ni atsukawareta Chigi no senbō." *Indogaku Bukkyōgaku kenkyū* 8 (1960): 677–82.

_____. "Shoki Tendaisan no kyōdanteki seikaku." *Nihon Bukkyō gakkai nenpō* 39 (1973): 133–49.

Shioiri Ryōdō and Tōdō Kyōshun. *Ajia Bukkyōshi, Chūgokuhen* 1, *Kanminzoku no Bukkyō*. Tokyo: Kōsei shuppansha, 1975.

Shioiri Ryōtatsu. *"Denjutsu isshinkaimon* ni okeru ni san no mondai." *Taishō daigaku kenkyū kiyō* 61 (1975): 553–66.

Shioiri Ryōtatsu and Nakano Yoshiteru, eds. *Dengyō Daishi Kōbō Daishi shū*. Vol. 3 of Bukkyō kyōiku hōten. Tokyo: Tamagawa daigaku shuppanbu, 1972.

Shirato Waka. "Eikyūnenchū shosha *Shukke sahō* ni tsuite." *Bukkyōgaku seminā* 21 (1975): 9–29.

Shizutani Masao. "Daijō kyōdan no seiritsu ni tsuite." *Bukkyō shigaku* 13 (1969): 146–74, 200–18; and 14 (1970): 32–49.

Shōwa shinsan kokuyaku daizōkyō. 48 vols. Tokyo: Tōhō shoin, 1928–32.

Sonoda Kōyū. *"Eizan Daishiden* no sakkan oyobi ryūden." In *Umehara Shinryū kangaku kanreki kinen ronshū*, pp. 302–7. Edited by Kenshin gakkai. Kyoto: Kenshin gakkai, 1956.

_____. "Heian Bukkyō no seiritsu." In Ajia Bukkyōshi, Nihonhen 2: Heian Bukkyō, pp. 87–164. Edited by Nakamura Hajime et al. Tokyo: Kōsei shuppansha, 1974.

_____. "Kodai Bukkyō ni okeru sanrin shugyō to sono igi." Nanto Bukkyō 4 (1957): 45–60.

_____. "Saichō no ronshō wo tsūjite mita Nanto kyōgaku no keikō." *Shirin* 42 (1959): 165–93, 569–91.

_____. "Saichō no Tōgoku dendō ni tsuite." *Bukkyō shigaku* 3 (1952): 49–63.

_____. "Sōsōki Murōji wo meguru sōryo no dōkō." In *Kokushi ronbun*, pp. 411–26. Edited by Kokushikai. Kyoto: Kyoto daigaku bungakubu, 1959.

Sonoda Kōyū and Andō Toshio. *Saichō*. Nihon shisō taikei, vol. 4. Tokyo: Iwanami shoten, 1974.

Strong, John. "The Legend of the Lion-roarer: a Study of the Buddhist Arhat Piṇḍola Bhāradvāja." *Numen* 26 (1979): 50–88.

Suzuki gakujutsu zaidan, ed. *Dainihon Bukkyō zensho*. 2nd ed 100 vols. Tokyo: Suzuki gakujutsu zaidan, 1972–75.

Taga Munehaya. "Eizan bunkozō *Endon sanju isshinkai*." *Bukkyō shigaku* 9 (1961): 53–57.

Taira Ryōshō. "Den-Eshi-hon *Jubosatsukaigi* ni tsuite." *Taishō daigaku kenkyū kiyō* 40 (1955): 1–36.

315

_____. "Dengyō Daishi Saichō no enki ijukusetsu." *Indogaku Bukkyōgaku kenkyū* 14 (1965): 122–23.

_____. "Dengyō Daishi-sen *Jubosatsukaigi* ni tsuite." *Indogaku Bukkyōgaku kenkyū* 3 (1956): 422–25.

_____. "Enkai no en ni tsuite." *Tendai gakuhō* 8 (1966): 3–11.

_____. "Enkai seiritsu kō." In *Fuyō hakushi koki kinen: Mikkyō bunka ronshū.* Special issue of *Chizan gakuhō* 19 (1970): 183–98.

_____. "Myōkō-sen *Tendai bosatsukaisho* ni tsuite." *Tendai gakuhō* 10 (1968): 108–14.

_____. "Ryōzen dōchō ni tsuite." *Tendai gakuhō* 14 (1971): 1–11.

Tajima Tokuon. "*Shikan girei* chosakukō." *Sange gakuhō* new series 11 (1937).

Takagi Yutaka. *Heian jidai Hokke Bukkyōshi kenkyū.* Kyoto: Heirakuji shoten, 1973.

Takakusu Junjirō. *A Record of the Buddhist Religion as Practiced in India and the Malay Archipelago.* London: Clarendon Press, 1896; reprint ed., Delhi: Munshiram Manoharlal, 1966.

Takakusu Junjirō and Watanabe Kaigyoku, eds. *Taishō shinshū daizōkyō.* 100 vols. Tokyo: Taishō issaikyō, 1922–32.

Takeda Chōten. "Dengyō Daishi ni okeru ichijō shisō no jissenteki igi." *Taishō daigaku kenkyū kiyō* 62 (1976): 23–38.

_____. "Dengyō Daishi no kiruikan." *Indogaku Bukkyōgaku kenkyū* 13 (1960): 681–86.

_____. "Dengyō Daishi ni okeru risōteki ningenzō." *Taishō Daigaku kenkyū kiyō* 61 (1975): 27–38.

_____. "Heian Bukkyō to *Fukūhyō seishū*." *Taishō daigaku kenkyū kiyō* 57 (1972): 17–33.

_____. "Juyō kyōten ni mirareru Nara Bukkyō no seikaku." *Nanto Bukkyō* 25 (1970: 17–33.

_____. "Kōso yori shūso ni itaru kaikan no tenkai." *Tendai gakuhō* 7 (1964): 34–45.

_____. "Shomusakeshiki no kaitairon." *Tendai gakuhō* 4 (1962): 4–16.

Takeuchi Rizō. *Ritsuryōsei to kizoku seiken,* 2 vols. Tokyo: Ochanomizu shobō. 1957–58.

_____. ed. *Heian ibun.* Revised ed. 8 vols. Tokyo: Yoshikawa kōbunkan, 1963–70.

Tamaki Kōshirō. *Nihon Bukkyō shisōron: jō.* Tokyo: Heirakuji shoten, 1974.

Tamura Enchō. *Asuka Bukkyōshi kenkyū.* Tokyo: Hanawa shobō, 1969.

Tamura Kōyū. "Daijō kaidan dokuritsu ni tsuite." *Indogaku Bukkyōgaku kenkyū* 5 (1957): 217–20.

_____. "Saichō *Ehyōshū* ni tsuite." *Indogaku Bukkyōgaku kenkyū* 21 (1973): 60–65.

_____. "*Shaikenshō* ni tsuite.*" *Indogaku Bukkyōgaku kenkyū* 18 (1971): 688–93.

Tamura Yoshirō. *Kamakura shinbukkyō shisō no kenkyū.* Kyoto: Heirakuji shoten, 1965.

Tendai gakkai, ed. *Dengyō Daishi kenkyū.* Tokyo: Waseda daigaku shuppanbu, 1973.

Tendai shūten kankōkai, ed. *Tendaishū zensho.* 26 vols. Hieizan: Tendai shūten kankōkai, 1935–37; reprint ed., Tokyo: Daiichi shobō. 1973–74.

Tokiwa Daijō. *Busshō no kenkyū*. Tokyo: Meiji shoin 1944; reprint ed., Tokyo: Kokusho kankōkai, 1972.

————. *Nihon Bukkyō no kenkyū*. Tokyo: Shunjūsha, 1943.

————. *Zoku Shina Bukkyō no kenkyū*. Tokyo: Shunjūsha, 1941.

Tokuda Myōhon. "Ganjin Wajō no Risshū." *Nanto Bukkyō* 24 (1970): 39–49.

————. "Nanzan Risshū to shite no Saidaijiha ni tsuite." *Nanto Bukkyō* 18 (1966): 13–35.

————. *Risshū bunken mokuroku*. Kyoto: Hyakkaen, 1974.

————. "Risshū bunken mokuroku." In *Bukkyō kyōdan no kenkyū: furoku*, pp. 3–151. Edited by Yoshimura Shūki. Kyoto: Hyakkaen, 1968.

————. *Risshū gairon*. Kyoto: Hyakkaen, 1969.

————. "Tōshōdaiji kaidan kō." *Nanto Bukkyō* 24 (1959): 30–45.

Tonegawa Kōgyō. "Tendai kaisho no jikkai." *Indogaku Bukkyōgaku kenkyū* 23 (1974): 170–71.

Tsuchihashi Shūkō. "Chūgoku ni okeru kairitsu no kussetsu: sōsei shingi wo chūshin ni." *Ryūkoku daigaku ronshū* 393 (1970):27–60.

————. "Daijōkai to shōjōkai." In *Bukkyō ni okeru kai no mondai*, pp. 112–28. Edited by Nihon Bukkyō gakkai. Kyoto: Heirakuji shoten, 1967.

————. "Dōsen no bosatsukai." *Indogaku Bukkyōgaku kenkyū* 15 (1966): 131–35.

————. "Juhachisaikaigi no hensen: Stainhon wo chūshin ni." In *Iwai Hakushi koki kinen: Tenseki ronshū*, pp. 379–400. Shizuoka-ken, Hamamatsu-shi: Kaimeidō, 1963.

————. "Jukai reigi no hensen." In *Bukkyō kyōdan no kenkyū*, pp. 205–82. Edited by Yoshimura Shūki. Kyoto: Hyakkaen, 1968.

————. "Kairitsu no zaizokusei." *Indogaku Bukkyōgaku kenkyū* 23(1975):528–33.

————. "Kairitsu to Ōron." *Ryūkoku daigaku ronshū*, no. 404 (1974), pp. 20–54.

————. "Kaitai ni tsuite." *Indogaku Bukkyōgaku kenkyū* 20 (1971): 62–66.

————. "Periohon *Shukkenin jubosatsukaihō* ni tsuite," In *Bukkyō bunken no kenkyū*, pp. 93–148. Edited by Ryūkoku daigaku Bukkyō gakkai. Kyoto: Hyakkaen, 1968.

————. "Ritsukyō no kaishū." *Bukkyōgaku kenkyū* 30 (1973): 54–70.

————. "Shunjō Risshi no teiki seru bosatsukai jūju ni tsuite." In *Shunjō Risshi no kenkyū*, pp. 83–101. Edited by Ishida Mitsuyuki. Kyoto: Hōzōkan, 1972.

————. "Tonkōhon *Jubosatsukaigi* kō." *Indogaku Bukkyōgaku kenkyū* 8 (1959): 33–42.

————. "Tonkōhon ni mirareru shuju no bosatsukaigi." In *Rekishi to bijutsu no shomondai*, pp. 95–175. Saiiki bunka kenkyū, vol, 6. Kyoto: Hōzōkan, 1963.

————. "Sange to chibatsu: kairitsu shisō no ichi shiten." *Bukkyō bunka kenkyūjo kiyō* 11 (1972): 14–30.

Tsuda Sōkichi. "Chigi no Hokke senbō." *Tōyō gakuhō* 31 (1947): 1–52.

Tsugunaga Yoshiteru. "Daianji Gyōhyō den no kenkyū." *Bukkyō shigaku* 12; no. 3 (1966): 16–31.

————. "Dengyō Daishi den ni kansuru ichi ni no kōsatsu." *Rekishi kyōiku* 13, no. 5 (1965): 69–75.

Tsuji Zennosuke. "*Kenkairon* senjutsu no yūrai ni tsuite." In *Nihon Bukkyōshi no kenkyū*, pp. 195–209. Tokyo: Kinkōdō, 1919.

_____. *Nihon Bukkyōshi.* 10 vols. Tokyo: Iwanami shoten, 1944–55.

Tsukamoto Zenryū. "Tōchūki irai no Chōan no kudokushi." In *Tsukamoto Zenryū chōsakushū.* 7 vols. Vol 3: *Chūgoku chūsei Bukkyōshi ronkō,* pp. 251–84. Tokyo: Daitō shuppansha, 1974.

Tsuruoka Shizuo. *Nihon kodai Bukkyōshi no kenkyū.* Tokyo: Bungadō shoten, 1962.

_____. *Kodai Bukkyōshi kenkyū.* Tokyo: Bungadō shoten, 1967.

Tsutsui Eishun, ed. *Tōdaiji yōroku.* Osaka: Zenkoku shobō. 1934.

Ueda Tenzui. *Kairitsu no shisō to kenkyū.* Wakayama-ken, Kōyasan: Mikkyō bunka kenkyūjo, 1967.

Uesugi Bunshū. *Nihon Tendaishi.* 2 vols. Nagoya: Hajinkaku shobō, 1935.

Ui Hakuju. *Bukkyō hanron.* Single vol. ed. Tokyo: Iwanami shoten, 1963.

_____. *Nihon Bukkyō gaishi.* Tokyo: Iwanami shoten, 1951.

_____. *Shaku Dōan no kenkyū.* Tokyo: Iwanami shoten, 1956.

Umeda Yoshihiko. *Kaitei sōbu Nihon shūkyō seidoshi.* 4 vols. Tokyo: Tokyo shuppansha, 1971.

Ushiba Shingen. "Dengyō Daishi no zenbō sojō ni tsuite: *Naishō Buppō kechimyakufu* wo chūshin to shite." *Tendai gakuhō* 10 (1967): 95–100.

_____. "*Denjutsu isshinkaimon* ni tsuite no utagai" *Nanto Bukkyō* 30 (1972): 54–75.

_____. "*Eizan Daishiden* ni okeru ni san no mondai." *Nanto Bukkyō* 26 (1971): 59–77.

_____. "*Jōdoinhan Dengyō Daishi shōrai mokuroku* ni tsuite." *Tendai gakuhō* 12 (1970): 84–92; 14 (1972): 60–67.

Waley, Arthur, tr. *The Analects of Confucius.* New York: Vintage Books, 1938.

Watanabe Shōkō. *Saichō Kūkai shū.* Nihon no shisō, vol. 1. Tokyo: Chikuma shobō, 1969.

Watanabe Shōkō and Miyasaka Yūshō. *Sangō shiki: Shōryōshū.* Nihon koten bungaku taikei, vol. 71. Tokyo: Iwanami shoten, 1965.

Watanabe Shujun. *Dengyō Daishi Saichō no kokoro to shōgai.* Tokyo: Yuzankaku, 1977.

Weinstein, Stanley. "The Ālaya-vijñāna in Early Yogācāra Buddhism: A Comparison of Its Meaning in the *Saṃdhinirmocana-sūtra* and the *Vijñaptimātratā-siddhi* of Dharmapāla." *Transactions of the International Conference of Orientalists in Japan* 3 (1958): 46–58.

_____. "The Beginnings of Esoteric Buddhism in Japan." *Journal of Asian Studies* 34 (1974): 177–91.

_____. "A Biographical Study of Tz'u-en." *Monumenta Nipponica* 15 (1959): 119–49.

_____. "Buddhism under the T'ang." In *The Cambridge History of China.* Edited. by Dennis Twitchett. Cambridge: Cambridge University Press, forthcoming.

_____. "The Concept of Ālaya-vijñāna in Pre-T'ang Chinese Buddhism." In *Yūki kyōju shōju kinen: Bukkyō shisōshi ronshū,* pp. 33–50. Tokyo: Daizō shuppansha, 1964.

_____. "Imperial Patronage in the Formation of T'ang Buddhism." In *Perspectives on the T'ang,* pp. 265–306. Edited by Arthur Wright and Dennis Twitchett. New Haven: Yale University, 1973.

Welch, Holmes. *The Practice of Chinese Buddhism.* Cambridge: Harvard University

318

Press, 1967.

Yamaguchi Kōen. *Tendaishūten mokuroku.* Sakamoto: Hieizan senshuin shuppanbu, 1941.

Yanagita Seizan. *Chūsei zenke no shisō.* Nihon shisō taikei, vol. 16. Tokyo: Iwanami shoten, 1972.

Yokota Ken'ichi. "Wakeshi to Saichō to Daianji to Hachimanjin." In *Nihon kobunka ronkō,* pp. 415–30. Edited by Kashihara kōko kenkyūjo. Tokyo: Yoshikawa kōbunkan, 1970.

Yoshitsu Yoshihide. "Chūgoku Bukkyō ni okeru daijō to shojō." *Komazawa daigaku Bukkyō gakubu ronshū* 1 (1971): 128–38.

Yoshizawa Dōnin. "*Ehyō Tendai shū* ni tsuite." *Tendai gakuhō* 14 (1972): 97–201.

Yūki Reimon. "Nangaku Tendai to Shianrakugyō." *Tōhō shūkyō* 1, no. 6 (1954): 16–27.

Yūki Yoshifumi. "Saichō ni okeru Kegon shisō no eikyō." *Nanto Bukkyō* 32 (1974): 13–28.

INDEX